10^{00}
FVPL

Drought & Depression

Drought & Depression

HISTORY OF THE PRAIRIE WEST SERIES, VOL. 6

Edited by Gregory P. Marchildon

 University of Regina Press

Printed and bound in Canada at Marquis. The text of this book is printed on 100% post-consumer recycled paper with earth-friendly vegetable-based inks.

COVER AND TEXT DESIGN: Duncan Campbell, University of Regina Press
TYPESET BY: John van der Woude, JVDW Designs
PROOFREADER: Kristine Douaud
INDEXER: Patricia Furdek
COVER ART: Dust Storm on Farm (Courtesy of the Provincial Archives of Saskatchewan / R-A3524)

Library and Archives Canada Cataloguing in Publication

Drought and depression / edited by Gregory P. Marchildon.

(History of the Prairie West series ; vol. 6) Includes bibliographical references and index. Issued in print and electronic formats. ISBN 978-0-88977-539-8 (softcover).—ISBN 978-0-88977-540-4 (PDF).—ISBN 978-0-88977-541-1 (HTML)

1. Depressions—1929—Prairie Provinces. 2. Droughts-Prairie Provinces—History—20th century. 3. Prairie Provinces—Social conditions—1905-1945. 4. Prairie Provinces—Economic conditions—1905-1945. 5. Prairie Provinces—Politics and government—1905-1945. I. Marchildon, Gregory P., 1956-, editor II. Series: History of the Prairie West series ; v. 6

FC3242.9.D35D76 2018   971.2'02   C2017-907466-0   C2017-907467-9

10   9   8   7   6   5   4   3   2   1

University of Regina Press, University of Regina
Regina, Saskatchewan, Canada, S4S 0A2
tel: (306) 585-4758   fax: (306) 585-4699
web: www.uofrpress.ca

We acknowledge the support of the Canada Council for the Arts for our publishing program. We acknowledge the financial support of the Government of Canada. / Nous reconnaissons l'appui financier du gouvernement du Canada. This publication was made possible with support from Creative Saskatchewan's Creative Industries Production Grant Program.

CONTENTS

Preface

Since its inception in 1975, *Prairie Forum* has been a major repository of articles on the history of the northern Great Plains, in particular the region encompassed within the current political boundaries of the three Prairie Provinces of Manitoba, Saskatchewan, and Alberta. The purpose of the History of the Prairie West Series is to make available the very best of *Prairie Forum* to as broad an audience as possible. Each volume in this series is devoted to a single, focused theme. Accompanied by dozens of new illustrations and maps as well as a searchable index, these volumes are intended to be of interest to the general reader as well as the professional historian.

The general editor of the History of the Prairie West Series is Gregory P. Marchildon. From 2003 until 2015, he was a Canada Research Chair in Public Policy and Economic History at the University of Regina. Although he now holds a research chair at the University of Toronto, Marchildon lives in northern Saskatchewan during the summer months. In addition to selecting and organizing the articles based upon their quality and thematic connections to the subject of each volume, he has chosen a cover painting or image for each volume which reflects, for him, the essence of each period and theme.

Acknowledgements

As the volume editor, I would like to thank the University of Regina Press for its support in making this publication possible. I am grateful to the kinetic Director of the Press, Bruce Walsh, and his talented staff, including David McLennan for overseeing the volume, Duncan Campbell for designing the exquisite cover, and especially Donna Grant, with assistance from interns Jeanelle Mandes and Mazin Saffou, for ensuring quality control in the final production. I would like to dedicate this particular volume to my mother, a child of the Great Depression. She continues to live with the memories of those years.

Introduction to *Drought & Depression*

Gregory P. Marchildon

The Great Depression of the 1930s in North America has become synonymous with images of the drought-stricken Great Plains. Popular historians of the Great Depression in Canada used evocative titles such as the "Ten Lost Years" (Barry Broadfoot) and the "Winter Years,"[1] even though the decade-long economic slump was a national, even a global, phenomenon.[2] There is one good reason for this close identification between drought and depression. Prolonged drought exacerbated the economic effects of the Great Depression to such a degree that the Prairie West became the epicentre of the disaster in Canada. Between 1929 and 1932, per capita incomes fell by 49 percent in Manitoba, 61 percent in Alberta and an astounding 72 percent in Saskatchewan. By 1931, net farm income in Saskatchewan was *negative* $31 million as farm families were forced to live off their capital or abandon their farms.[3]

It is even possible to trace the origins of the Great Depression to the Prairie Provinces. Known as the breadbasket of the world, the Canadian Prairies exported more wheat to the rest of the world than similar regions in the United States, Australia, and Argentina. In the five crop years starting in 1927 and ending in 1932, Canadian wheat constituted almost 35 percent of all wheat exports in the world. In 1928, a bumper crop of Prairie wheat led to a sudden drop in the global price of wheat. In the weeks and months that followed, farmers throughout the Great Plains quit buying trucks, cars, and farm machinery, and began to miss payments on loans and mortgages, a major factor in the ensuing stock market collapse in New York in October 1929 and the trigger for a chain reaction in capital markets in the rest of the world.[4]

Drought became a regular feature of the vast area known as the Palliser Triangle from 1929 until 1939.[5] Straddling the Alberta-Saskatchewan border, the Dry Belt constitutes the dry inner core of the Palliser Triangle.[6] The result was enormous social and political upheaval throughout the region that sent shockwaves through the rest of the country. Drought and depression led to a major political realignment. Two vigorous protest parties—Social Credit and the Co-operative Commonwealth Federation (CCF)—were born out of the chaos and challenged the hegemony of the established parties.[7]

Although government relief efforts prevented a large-scale famine, most other policy responses to deal with the crisis were too little, too late. The resulting poverty and out-migration would mark the people and the culture of the region for generations.[8] Given the extent to which the Great Depression scarred the Prairie West, it should not be surprising that *Prairie Forum*, the only journal dedicated to the region, would attract more than its share of original scholarly contributions to our understanding of this era. This book brings together a select number of these articles in order to paint the picture of this tumultuous time.

The chapters in this volume have been divided into three sections. Part I focuses on the phenomenon of agricultural drought in the southern Prairies before and during the Great Depression. Part II deals with dislocation caused by drought and depression acting in tandem, including the migration of southern wheat farmers to the forest fringes of northern Alberta and Saskatchewan, and the hardships and conflicts endured by workers and the unemployed. The final section addresses the political upheaval caused by the crisis, with particular attention paid to some of the policy responses by governments in response to the dual crisis of drought and depression in the Prairie West.

DROUGHT AND THE DRY BELT

The first chapter describes the climate history of the Dry Belt. Although the Dry Belt was given a notional boundary by geographers and government organizations, this study illustrates the extent to which climate can redefine the size of the Dry Belt depending on the era. Because of the prolonged drought covering most of the Palliser Triangle from the late 1920s until the late 1930s, the region became, in effect, one enormous semi-arid desert, reflecting the conditions that were once restricted to a smaller core located in southeastern Alberta and southwestern Saskatchewan.

The Dry Belt was one of the last regions in the Canadian Plains to be settled. After the Killer Winter of 1906–07 almost wiped out cattle ranching in the region, wheat farms were established. For the next decade, farmers enjoyed bumper wheat crops. However, beginning in 1917, Dry Belt farmers suffered a succession of droughts, and the exodus out of the area began.

Before the 1930s, multi-year droughts were largely restricted to the Dry Belt. Although they covered an area considerably smaller than the Palliser Triangle, these droughts nonetheless caused significant dislocation on both sides of the Alberta-Saskatchewan border.

David Jones is the author of *Empire of Dust*, the classic account of the initial settlement and subsequent abandonment of vulnerable wheat farms on the Alberta side of the Dry Belt.[9] As narrated in Jones's chapter, dwindling tax bases competed with the desire of farm families to keep their children in school. Jones shows us how, quite paradoxically, the stubborn survival of Dry Belt schools ended up dividing neighbours and further fracturing the already vulnerable communities.

This Alberta portion of the Dry Belt became known as the Special Areas. The formation of this administrative district formed a unique response to

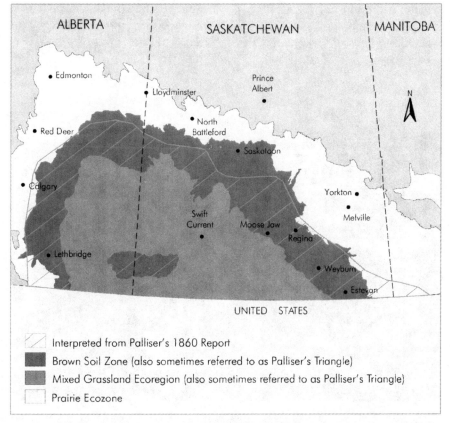

Figure I.1. The Palliser Triangle extends over most of southern Saskatchewan and southwestern Alberta.

drought, the history of which is recounted in Chapter 3. Replacing the bankrupt local governments, the Special Areas were established in the early- to mid-1930s by the Alberta government, and then consolidated under a single appointed body with a head office in Hanna in 1938. Strangely enough, this temporary expedient turned into a permanent arrangement, and to this day, the Special Areas continue to administer 5.2 million acres (2.1 million hectares) of land in this southeastern part of Alberta, a continuing legacy of the Great Depression.[10]

Although there is evidence that the droughts of the 1920s were more concentrated on the Alberta side of the Dry Belt, the Saskatchewan Dry Belt also suffered from periodic drought before the 1930s. Perhaps because of the lack of any dramatic response by the Saskatchewan government to land abandonment in the area, there was less scholarly attention devoted to the Saskatchewan Dry Belt. That is, until Curtis McManus's recent history of this drought-prone region.[11] McManus's chapter focuses on the impact of drought and depopulation in southwestern Saskatchewan in the 1920s as a precursor to the Great Depression when drought would cover a much larger area. Although his assumption that

Wheat grown in the Palliser Triangle made Canada the breadbasket of the world in the first half of the twentieth century (Courtesy of the Provincial Archives of Saskatchewan / R-B1337).

the drought was as severe in Saskatchewan as in Alberta does not match with the scientific evidence (which, it should be said, he did not have access to at the time the article was written), McManus is entirely accurate in his portrayal of the dislocation caused in this region by these earlier droughts.[12]

DISLOCATION AND CONFLICT

Drought and plummeting grain prices caused enormous dislocation throughout the Palliser Triangle and beyond. Farm hands were let go and became part of a transient population riding the rails to look for jobs. With the collapse of the farm economy came unemployment in Prairie villages, towns, and cities. Businesses went bust in the absence of buyers and customers. The businesses that continued operating could exact concessions from workers in terms of lower wages and more repressive working conditions. This accelerated a growing political polarization, and workers in some industries were attracted to unions associated with more radical labour organizations and the Communist Party.

One example of the latter were the coal miners near Estevan, Saskatchewan. The author of the major work on the thirty-day Estevan strike of 1931, Stephen Endicott, describes the struggle between the coal miners and the mine owners.[13] The owners were able to break the strike and insert a company union with the considerable support of the provincial government and the armed intimidation of the Royal Canadian Mounted Police. The strike radicalized a young Tommy Douglas, then a new Baptist minister in nearby Weyburn, Saskatchewan. He supported the strikers by speaking at a mass rally. Although he was uncomfortable with the communist influences within the Workers' Unity League that organized the strike, he nonetheless "considered it a mistake to 'give up on a good cause because there are a few communists in it.'"[14]

As shown by Lorne Brown, rising unemployment precipitated demonstrations and hunger marches, with governments cracking down on the unemployed protesters. Fearing widespread civil disorder, the federal government created a series of relief camps throughout the country, generally located well outside of the urban centres.[15] Offered a bunk and three meals a day, unemployed men were paid twenty cents a day to build roads, construct buildings, plant trees, or clear bush. While families were given the option of relief where they lived, single men had to go to the work camps.[16]

Understandably, many of the men grew to resent the isolation and low wages of the camps. In 1935, 1,500 men in the British Columbia camps went on strike. After protesting for two months in Vancouver, the strikers set out on the On-to-Ottawa Trek to bring their demands to the federal government.

The federal government confronted the strikers in Regina, and the protest turned into a riot, leaving one policeman dead and one hundred protestors seriously injured.[17]

As Cecilia Danysk reveals in her chapter, there was one alternative to the relief camps for unemployed single men. Under the terms of the federal-provincial farm employment plans, men were paid $5 a month to work on farms while farmers received a government allowance to help them pay for the room and board of those working under the plan. The program was seen as a means to both relieve unemployment, including the perceived threat posed by transient men, and provide support to farm families struggling under the dual burden of drought and low commodity prices. Since the program was less expensive than the relief camps, the federal government, particularly after Mackenzie King's Liberals defeated R. B. Bennett's Conservatives in 1935, tried to expand the plan so that it could begin to close down the highly unpopular relief camps.[18]

Back on the farm, the successive years of drought and depression drove farm families to leave the Palliser Triangle. Unable to pay their mortgages or taxes, a number of farmers simply abandoned their farms. They joined the mob of unemployed on the west coast of British Columbia or relocated to new homesteads in the forest fringe of Saskatchewan and the Peace River country of Alberta.

As John McDonald points out, the migration to forested areas of Saskatchewan took place in the absence of any coherent government policy in the early 1930s. The result produced enormous hardship for many farm families, in some cases much worse than what they had faced in the Palliser Triangle. The situation improved slightly with the provincial government's creation of the Settlers Re-establishment Branch in 1935. However, it would take the Second World War—new jobs and higher commodity prices—to make a major difference in the lives of these settlers.[19]

Using a biographical approach, Clinton Westman explores the lived experiences of a family—his own family—which relocated to the Peace River country of northern Alberta to escape the continual drought in the Palliser Triangle. As in the forest fringe of Saskatchewan, settlers depended heavily on hunting, gardening, and gathering to supplement their extremely meagre cash earnings from farming in the 1930s. Indeed, cash was so short that settlers often operated in a barter economy, trading their livestock and wild food for the goods and services they needed. Low prices for all agricultural goods during the Great Depression meant that subsistence farming became the order of the day.

POLICY, POLITICS, AND LASTING PERCEPTIONS

The exigencies of the Great Depression cried out for a collective response. However, the federal and provincial governments did everything possible to delay and limit their policy interventions as their revenues fell like a stone. Moreover, these governments felt overwhelmed by the administrative requirements of existing programs such as relief. As a consequence, they were only too willing to work with voluntary organizations to assist the human casualties of drought and depression.

Nancy Sheehan's chapter is a fascinating case study of the relationship between the Alberta division of the Canadian Red Cross and the provincial and federal governments. During the 1920s, the Red Cross worked closely with the United Farmer and Social Credit governments to deliver needed clothing and health services to those in desperate need in the Alberta Dry Belt. The way in which the Red Cross worked with the provincial government in the 1920s was a practice run for its much larger job as official agent of the federal and provincial governments to provide clothing relief in Alberta and other provinces in the 1930s.

Local governments were at the front line of the war to deal with the Great Depression. In the first years, no one, including those running local governments, could have predicted that the slump would persist for a full decade. Past experience said that it might be necessary to tough things out for a year or two. For this reason, a number of Prairie cities initiated public works projects to get men back to work and avoid civil unrest. Eric Strikwerda focuses on the public works projects initiated by the City of Saskatoon and the nature of the financing, including limited provincial and federal government contributions. Of course, the City eventually ran out of money for such projects and the Broadway Bridge, completed in November 1932, was the last civic project in Saskatoon to employ the jobless.

The next chapter focuses on the Depression-era policies of the Canadian government. Robert Weir was the Minister of Agriculture in R. B. Bennett's Conservative government from 1930 until 1935. Through Weir, we get a window on how the Bennett cabinet responded to the environmental and economic disaster in the Palliser Triangle. The first response was to contribute money for provincial relief efforts. However, as a mixed farmer from the Melfort area in Saskatchewan north of the Palliser Triangle, Weir seemed to have little understanding of the situation facing grain farmers in the blighted areas to the south. It was only in his last months in office that Weir put in place the Prairie Farm Rehabilitation Act, a set of programs and policies aimed at reclaiming and repurposing the most drought-stricken lands of the Palliser

Triangle, and facilitating the changes needed to make grain farming more sustainable in the rest of the Triangle. The farm dugouts, treed shelter belts, community pastures, and dam projects which the PFRA facilitated became a vital part of Prairie dryland agriculture for the rest of the twentieth century.[20]

The upheaval of the Great Depression would produce major changes in the political landscape of the Prairies. Two new parties opposed to the establishment, Liberals and Conservatives, emerged out of the chaos. While the Co-operative Commonwealth Federation (CCF) was relegated to an opposition force until it took office in Saskatchewan in 1944, Social Credit would gain government in Alberta in 1935. Alvin Finkel argues that Social Credit was much more radical in character in its first years in government under Premier "Bible" Bill Aberhart than it would become under his successor Ernest Manning. Beyond his "funny money" proposals,[21] Aberhart's policies—including a minimum wage, licensed trade requirements, and marketing boards, as well as a state medicine proposal—threatened Alberta's business and professional establishment. In some cases, Socred members were willing to forge temporary alliances with the CCF and even the Communist Party against the establishment parties.[22]

Novelists have likely had more influence than historians in shaping contemporary perceptions of the Prairie West during the 1930s. This alone justifies the subject of the last chapter—Victor Carl Friesen's essay on Prairie novels set in the Great Depression. These novels, including W. O. Mitchell's

Using PFRA machinery to dig a dugout. (PFRA 6118)

Who Has Seen the Wind, Margaret Laurence's *The Stone Angel*, and Sinclair Ross's *As for Me and My House*, are an indelible part of Canadian culture. Unlike iconic novels such as *The Grapes of Wrath* written by Americans during the 1930s, the Canadian novelists all wrote their books after the Depression. While it may make this body of work less overtly political, there remains considerable commentary on the politics of the time. These novels provide a valuable way to see and even relive the experience of a dust storm, the plight of strikers and the unemployed, and the promise held out by new political movements.

NOTES

1   Barry Broadfoot, *Ten Lost Years, 1929–1939: Memories of the Canadians Who Survived the Depression* (Toronto: Doubleday, 1973), and James H. Gray, *The Winter Years: The Depression on the Prairies* (Calgary: Fifth House, 2004, orig. 1966). Also see Pierre Berton, *The Great Depression, 1929–1939* (Toronto: Random House, 1990).

2   Dietmar Rothermund, *The Global Impact of the Great Depression, 1929–1939* (London: Routledge, 1996); Michiel Horn (ed.), *The Dirty Thirties: Canadians in the Great Depression* (Toronto: Copp Clark, 1972); Michael L. Cooper, *Dust to Eat: Drought and Depression in the 1930s* (New York: Clarion Books, 2004); and R. Douglas Francis and Herman Ganzevoort (eds.), *The Dirty Thirties in Prairie Canada* (Vancouver: Tantalus Research, 1973).

3   Gregory P. Marchildon, "The Great Divide," in Gregory P. Marchildon (ed.), *The Heavy Hand of History: Interpreting Saskatchewan's Past* (Regina: Canadian Plains Research Center, 2005), 51–66.

4   Gregory P. Marchildon, "War, Revolution and the Great Depression in the Global Wheat Trade, 1917–39," in Lucia Coppolaro and Francine McKenzie (eds.), *A Global History of Trade and Conflict since 1500* (London: Palgrave Macmillan, 2013), 142–162.

5   Irene M. Spry (ed.), *The Papers of the Palliser Expedition, 1857–1860* (Toronto: Champlain Society, 1968), and Irene M. Spry, *The Palliser Expedition: An Account of John Palliser's British North American Expedition, 1857–1860* (Toronto: Macmillan of Canada, 1963).

6   Donald Lemmen and Lisa Dale-Burnett, "The Palliser Triangle" in K. Fung (ed.), *Atlas of Saskatchewan: Second Edition* (Saskatoon: University of Saskatchewan, 1999), 41.

7   John H. Thompson and Allen Seager, *Canada, 1922–1939: Decades of Discord* (Toronto: McClelland and Stewart, 1985); H. Blair Neatby, *The Politics of Chaos: Canada in the Thirties* (Toronto: Macmillan of Canada, 1972); and Michiel Horn, *The Great Depression of the 1930s in Canada* (Ottawa: Canadian Historical Association, 1984).

8   Gerald Friesen, *The Canadian Prairies: A History* (Toronto: University of Toronto Press, 1987), 383–417. Gregory P. Marchildon, "The Great Divide," in Gregory P. Marchildon (ed.), *The Heavy Hand of History: Interpreting Saskatchewan's Past* (Regina: Canadian Plains Research Center, 2005), 51–66.

9   David C. Jones, *Empire of Dust: Settling and Abandoning the Prairie Dry Belt* (Calgary: University of Calgary Press, 2002, orig. 1987).

10 Also see Johanna Wandel and Gregory P. Marchildon, "Institutional Fit and Interplay in the Dryland Agricultural Social-Ecological System in Alberta, Canada," in Derek Armitage and Ryan Plummer (eds.), *Adaptive Capacity and Environmental Governance* (New York: Springer, 2010), 179–95.

11 Curtis R. McManus, *Happyland: A History of the Dirty Thirties in Saskatchewan, 1914–1937* (Calgary: University of Calgary Press, 2011).

12 Gregory P. Marchildon, Suren Kulshreshtha, Elaine Wheaton, and David J. Sauchyn, "Drought and Institutional Adaptation in the Great Plains of Alberta and Saskatchewan, 1914–1939," *Natural Hazards* 45, no. 3 (2008): 399–403.

13 See Stephen Endicott's *Bienfait: The Saskatchewan Miners' Struggle of '31* (Toronto: University of Toronto Press, 2002), and *Raising the Workers' Flag: The Workers' Unity League of Canada, 1930–1936* (Toronto: University of Toronto Press, 2012).

14 Tommy Douglas quoted in Stephen Endicott, "Bienfait: Origins and Legacy of the Coal Miners' Strike of 1931," *Prairie Forum* 31, no. 2 (Fall 2006): 228.

15 James Struthers, *No Fault of Their Own: Unemployment and the Canadian Welfare State, 1914–1941* (Toronto: University of Toronto Press, 1983).

16 See Eric Strikwerda, *The Wages of Relief: Cities and the Unemployed in Prairie Canada, 1929–39* (Edmonton: Athabasca University Press, 2013) and Michael Ekers, "'The Dirty Scruff': Relief and the Production of the Unemployed in Depression-Era British Columbia," *Antipode* 44, no. 4 (2012): 1119–42.

17 Bill Waiser, *All Hell Can't Stop Us: The On-to-Ottawa Trek and the Regina Riot* (Calgary: Fifth House, 2003); Victor Howard, *"We Were the Salt of the Earth!": The On-to-Ottawa Trek and the Regina Riot* (Regina: Canadian Plains Research Center, 1985).

18 Robert Wardhaugh, *Mackenzie King and the Prairie West* (Toronto: University of Toronto Press, 2000).

19 See Merle Massie, *Forest Prairie Edge: Place History in Saskatchewan* (Winnipeg: University of Manitoba Press, 2014) for a recent history of the forest fringe settlers.

20 Gregory P. Marchildon, "The Prairie Farm Rehabilitation Administration: Climate Crisis and Federal-Provincial Relations during the Great Depression," *Canadian Historical Review* 90, no. 2 (2009): 275–301.

21 On the theory and practice of the social credit dividend, see Bob Hesketh, *Major Douglas and Alberta Social Credit* (Toronto: University of Toronto Press, 1997).

22 Also see Alvin Finkel, *The Social Credit Phenomenon in Alberta* (Toronto: University of Toronto Press, 1989).

PART I

Drought in the Dry Belt:
Precursor to the Great Depression

1. The Dry Belt and Changing Aridity
in the Palliser Triangle, 1895–2000

Gregory P. Marchildon, Jeremy Pittman, and David J. Sauchyn

EARLY HISTORY OF THE DRY BELT

The Dry Belt has long been identified as the most arid portion of the Palliser Triangle. Straddling the border of Alberta and Saskatchewan, this dry core is a prominent geographical and historical feature of the western prairies. Located in the rain shadow of the Rocky Mountains to the west and the Cypress and Sweet Grass Hills to the south, the Dry Belt receives, on average, less than 350 mm of precipitation per year, considerably below the average of the Palliser Triangle. In addition, it is subject to high moisture loss because of the warm and dry winter winds known as Chinooks, as well as summer heat waves of great intensity. Finally, the soils of the Dry Belt are light and have low water retention, thus making the area more sensitive to long periods of moisture deficiency.[1] As the epicentre of drought and depopulation before the Second World War, the Dry Belt is often portrayed as a cursed land, a destroyer of families, livelihoods and dreams, as illustrated in David Jones's classic history of the Dry Belt.[2]

The Dry Belt lies within the Palliser Triangle, itself long recognized for its aridity and limited biodiversity.[3] The Triangle is named after Captain John Palliser, the leader of the British North American Exploring Expedition of 1857–60 sponsored by the British government.[4] Palliser viewed the region as a northern extension of what he called the Great American Desert. His "triangle" is actually more of a parallelogram extending up from the current Canada-U.S. border (Figure 1.1). Covering more than 200,000 square km of southern Alberta and Saskatchewan (including a tiny bit of southwestern

Manitoba), the Palliser Triangle encompasses what is now the single largest expanse of agricultural land in Canada.

Based on his observations of climate, vegetation and soil, Palliser concluded that the entire region was unsuitable for agriculture.[5] His findings were supported by Henry Youle Hind, a professor from the University of Toronto who had explored the western portion of the prairies for the United Province of Canada in 1858.[6] Hind referred to most of the Palliser Triangle as "Arid Plains," but he identified an arc of land directly to the north—"the fertile belt"—which he deemed as suitable for agriculture because it received more rainfall."[7]

What Palliser and Hind observed, however, was not merely the average aridity of the region, but its worst climatic feature—recurring drought.[8] From the mid-1850s until the mid-1860s, the southern Canadian plains were in the grip of one of the most prolonged droughts of the nineteenth century.[9] Based upon expedition recordings, the drought, at least during 1859 when Palliser traveled into the heart of the Dry Belt, was most severe in the western part of the prairies.[10]

Although most of the Palliser Triangle was opened for agricultural settlement in the late nineteenth century, the Dry Belt was settled by ranchers rather than farmers because of its high average aridity and continuing susceptibility to prolonged drought.[11] After the abnormally cold winter of 1905–06 which killed off approximately one-half of the cattle in the region, grain farmers

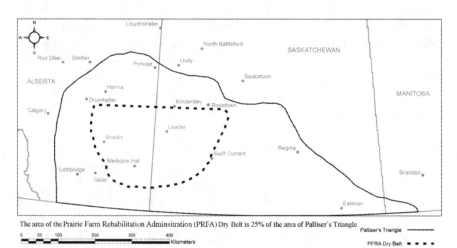

The area of the Prairie Farm Rehabilitation Administration (PRFA) Dry Belt is 25% of the area of Palliser's Triangle

Source: J. Palliser, *Exploration-British North America. The Journals, Detailed Reports and Observations* (London: Eyre and Spottiswoode, 1863). W. Namanishen, *Drought in the Palliser Triangle: A Provisional Primer* (Regina: Prairie Farm Rehabilitation Administration, Agriculture and Agri-Food Canada, 1998), 2.

Figure 1.1. The PFRA Dry Belt and the Palliser Triangle.

began to move into the Dry Belt.[12] Initially, Dry Belt wheat farmers enjoyed bumper crops. Beginning in 1917, however, grain farmers suffered a series of drought years.

Since farmers on the Alberta side of the Dry Belt suffered the most, the Alberta government was eventually forced to come to the aid of their bankrupt municipalities and help move thousands of drought-stricken farmers out of the Dry Belt, as well as administer the social and physical infrastructure of the region as a Special Area.[13] During the Dirty Thirties, the droughts expanded in size and intensity (at least in Saskatchewan) precipitating a major population exodus.[14] Although there have been severe droughts since the 1930s, in particular in 1961, 1988 and 2001–02, farmers in the Dry Belt have not suffered as prolonged (multi-year) droughts as they experienced from 1917 until the late 1930s.

VILLMOW'S DRY BELT

The location of the Dry Belt is not as precise as might be indicated by the Government of Canada's Prairie Farm Rehabilitation Administration (PFRA) in Figure 1.1.[15] The PFRA refers to the unique moisture characteristics of this region, and defines the boundaries of the Dry Belt based on a 350 mm precipitation isoline averaged over the period from 1961 to 1990. This raises the question of how, in more precise scientific terms, the Dry Belt should now be defined in light of this historical experience.

In 1956, an American geographer, Jack Villmow, published an article in which he provided an apparently precise description of the Dry Belt (Figure 1.2a) based on the best climate data available at the time.[16] Villmow analyzed surface meteorological data in a number of ways. He collected data from different climate monitoring stations throughout the region, and mapped out climatic isolines based on 25 to 35 year averages in temperature (T) and precipitation (P) as well as seasonal variability in climate. He also classified the climate of the area following the method developed by the pioneering geographer and climatologist C. Warren Thornthwaite.[17] Of particular interest is Villmow's application of the Thornthwaite model of potential evapotranspiration (PET) to differentiate regions using isolines based on the ratio of PET to P. He found that much of the Dry Belt had a PET to P ratio less than or equal to 1.75, which corresponds to a P to PET ratio less than or equal to 0.57.[18] He was able to combine these results to describe the static boundaries of the Dry Belt shown in Figure 1.2a. The boundaries Villmow used for the Dry Belt, however, differ greatly from those used by the PFRA (Figure 1.2b). The Dry Belt, as defined by Villmow, has twice the areal extent of the PFRA's version.

Villmow's work contributed greatly to knowledge of the Canadian Dry Belt. Villmow also acknowledged that "moisture characteristics form the primary basis for the contention that the Dry Belt is a unique and distinctive climatic region."[19] However, moisture characteristics must include both the amount of precipitation distributed both spatially and temporally as well as a measure of temperature as it relates to evapotranspiration (moisture in soil and plant life lost to the atmosphere). As noted by Villmow, both precipitation

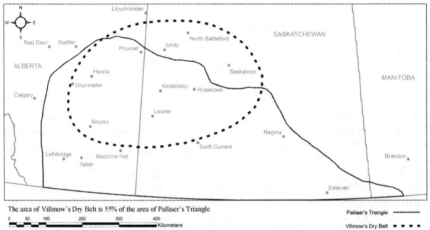

The area of Villmow's Dry Belt is 55% of the area of Palliser's Triangle

Palliser's Triangle ————
Villmow's Dry Belt ■ ■ ■ ■

Source: J. Palliser, *Exploration-British North America. The Journals, Detailed Reports and Observations* (London: Eyre and Spottiswoode, 1863). J.R. Villmow, "The Nature and Origin of the Canadian Dry Belt," *Annals of the Association of American Geographers* 46, no. 1 (1956): 211-32.

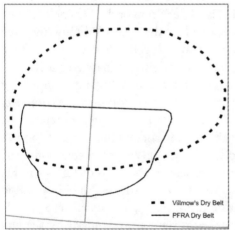

Figure 1.2a *(above)*. Villmow's Dry Belt and the Palliser Triangle.

Figure 1.2b *(left)*. Villmow's Dry Belt and the PFRA Dry Belt.

■ ■ Villmow's Dry Belt
—— PFRA Dry Belt

Source: J.R. Villmow, "The Nature and Origin of the Canadian Dry Belt," *Annals of the Association of American Geographers* 46, no. 1 (1956): 211-32. W. Nemanishen, *Drought in the Palliser Triangle: A Provisional Primer* (Regina: Prairie Farm Rehabilitation Administration, Agriculture and Agri-Food Canada, 1998), 2.

and temperature vary greatly seasonally, inter-annually and spatially in the area.[20] Since the boundaries of the Dry Belt are defined by these variables, the question addressed below is whether the boundaries vary appreciably over time and space when averaged over different periods.

NEW HISTORICAL MAPS OF THE DRY BELT

As illustrated in Figures 1.3 to 1.7, the boundaries of the Dry Belt vary significantly when based on mean conditions of different time periods. Drylands throughout the globe cannot be defined by static borders, and the Dry Belt is no exception.[21] To state the obvious, it is essential to specify the precise time period when mapping the Dry Belt because the boundaries will shift over time.

According to the United Nations Environment Programme's (UNEP) *World Atlas of Desertification*, drylands are areas with an average annual P to PET ratio of less than 0.65.[22] This definition and the P/PET data for the Canadian prairies were used to construct the maps seen in Figures 1.3 to 1.6. This definition also corresponds well with Villmow's pioneering work, since he obtained P/PET values within this range for his Dry Belt. PET was calculated using the Thornthwaite method from a gridded climate database of monthly precipitation and temperature produced by Environment Canada.[23] Although this method is simple relative to more complex techniques developed during the past half century since Thornthwaite's work, the method has proven itself in terms of delivering accurate results. As a consequence, it has been employed in similar studies, namely the *World Atlas of Desertification*.[24]

The map produced by Villmow is difficult to reconstruct given the lack of precise time constraints. Villmow used 25 to 35 year averages, but this varied from station to station. Sometimes, even less than 25 to 35 year averages were used, but this is difficult to determine because Villmow did not provide the exact years that were incorporated into his averages. It almost appears as though Villmow may have assumed that time was unimportant in defining the Dry Belt.

In his study for the PFRA, Walter Nemanishen acknowledges the significance of calculating the boundaries of the Dry Belt over specific time periods, but his exclusive use of precipitation to define the Dry Belt neglects the impact of evapotranspiration from the soil in determining the degree of aridity in the region. The use of the P/PET index accounts for this loss and provides insight into the amount of moisture available at the surface. Moreover, we were not limited to the 25 to 35 years worth of data that were available to Villmow. Our estimates are based upon historical data collected from 1895 until 2000. Different Dry Belt maps were produced corresponding to different periods of interest in the history of the area. Figure 1.3a illustrates the result for the full period from 1895 until 2000. Figure 1.3b shows this area in relation to the PFRA's Dry Belt and Villmow's Dry Belt respectively. The area with a P/PET < 0.65 is about half the size of the PFRA's Dry Belt and only about a quarter the size of Villmow's. What is noteworthy, however, is the extent to which the Dry Belt remains located almost entirely within the region originally identified by the PFRA and Villmow.

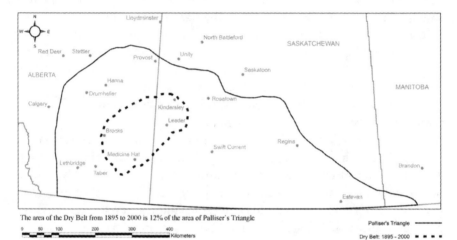

The area of the Dry Belt from 1895 to 2000 is 12% of the area of Palliser's Triangle

Palliser's Triangle ————
Dry Belt: 1895 - 2000 ■ ■ ■ ■

Source: J. Palliser, *Exploration-British North America. The Journals, Detailed Reports and Observations* (London: Eyre and Spottiswoode, 1863).

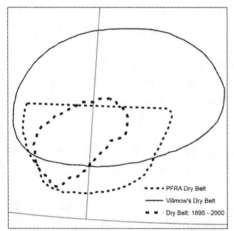

PFRA Dry Belt
Villmow's Dry Belt
Dry Belt: 1895 - 2000

Figure 1.3a *(above)*. The Dry Belt based on a P/PET < = 0.65 map for the period from 1895 to 2000 and the Palliser Triangle.

Figure 1.3b *(left)*. Dry Belt based on a P/PET < = 0.65 map for the period from 1895 to 2000, Villmow's Dry Belt and the PFRA Dry Belt.

Source: J.R. Villmow, "The Nature and Origin of the Canadian Dry Belt," *Annals of the Association of American Geographers* 46, no. 1 (1956): 211-32. W. Nemanishen, *Drought in the Palliser Triangle: A Provisional Primer* (Regina: Prairie Farm Rehabilitation Administration, Agriculture and Agri-Food Canada, 1998), 2.

The Dry Belt for the post-Depression years from 1939 until 2000 produces a very similar result—a comparably shaped but slightly smaller region as seen in Figure 1.4a. Since 1939, this has remained the driest part of the Palliser Triangle, the sub-region least conducive to crop-based agriculture. Although crop farming continues in the region, it is far more restricted. Ranching has again supplanted farming as the dominant form of agriculture within the Dry Belt, particularly on the Alberta side of the border, partly due to the

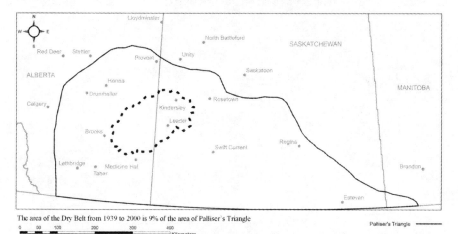

The area of the Dry Belt from 1939 to 2000 is 9% of the area of Palliser's Triangle

0   50   100   200   300   400
Kilometers

Palliser's Triangle ————

Dry Belt: 1939 - 2000 ▪ ▪ ▪ ▪

Source: J. Palliser, *Exploration-British North America. The Journals, Detailed Reports and Observations* (London: Eyre and Spottiswoode, 1863).

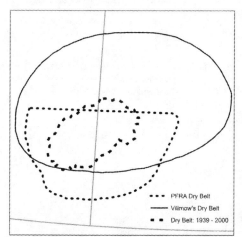

PFRA Dry Belt
Villmow's Dry Belt
Dry Belt: 1939 - 2000

Figure 1.4a. The Dry Belt based on a P/PET < = 0.65 map for the period from 1939 to 2000 and the Palliser Triangle.

Figure 1.4b. Dry Belt based on a P/PET < = 0.65 map for the period from 1939 to 2000, Villmow's Dry Belt and the PFRA Dry Belt.

Source: J.R. Villmow, "The Nature and Origin of the Canadian Dry Belt," *Annals of the Association of American Geographers* 46, no. 1 (1956): 211-32. W. Nemanishen, *Drought in the Palliser Triangle. A Provisional Primer* (Regina: Prairie Farm Rehabilitation Administration, Agriculture and Agri-Food Canada, 1998), 2.

efforts of the Special Areas Board in facilitating the shift from grain farms to ranches or mixed farm-ranches in the 1930s.[25]

The areal extent of the Dry Belt during the post-Depression years is considerably smaller than those proposed by Villmow and the PFRA. It is less than 40 percent the size of the PFRA's Dry Belt and less than 20 percent the size of Villmow's. Figure 1.4b illustrates these differences.

We should also expect the map of the Dry Belt to be quite different for the pre-Second World War era as a consequence of the prolonged droughts which

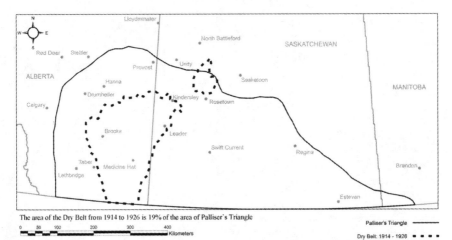

The area of the Dry Belt from 1914 to 1926 is 19% of the area of Palliser's Triangle

0   50   100   200   300   400
■■■■■■■■■■■■■■■■■■ Kilometers

Palliser's Triangle ————
Dry Belt: 1914 - 1926 ■ ■ ■ ■

Source: J. Palliser, *Exploration-British North America. The Journals, Detailed Reports and Observations* (London: Eyre and Spottiswoode, 1863).

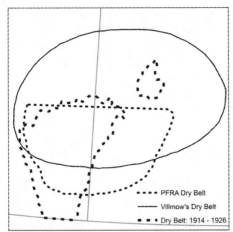

■ ■ ■ PFRA Dry Belt
——— Villmow's Dry Belt
■ ■ ■ Dry Belt: 1914 - 1926

Source: J.R. Villmow, "The Nature and Origin of the Canadian Dry Belt," *Annals of the Association of American Geographers* 46, no. 1 (1956): 211-32. W. Nemanishen, *Drought in the Palliser Triangle: A Provisional Primer* (Regina: Prairie Farm Rehabilitation Administration, Agriculture and Agri-Food Canada, 1998), 2.

Figure 1.5a. The Dry Belt based on a P/PET < = 0.65 map for the period from 1914 to 1926 and the Palliser Triangle.

Figure 1.5b. Dry Belt based on a P/PET < = 0.65 map for the period from 1914 to 1926, Villmow's Dry Belt and the PFRA Dry Belt.

devastated the farm families living in this part of the Palliser Triangle. In this case, it is worth examining the period beginning with the first recorded agricultural drought in 1914, and ending the year before the abnormally moist year of 1927. Figure 1.5a validates the considerable historical evidence of farmers in southwest Alberta suffering more from prolonged drought than their Saskatchewan neighbours over this time period. The Dry Belt was largely concentrated in southeastern Alberta, from south of Medicine Hat and Taber, Alberta, stopping short of Drumheller and Hanna, although it did swing northeast to include Leader and the region immediately west of Kindersley in Saskatchewan. In addition, the Dry Belt included a small patch in the central part of western Saskatchewan north of Rosetown and southeast of Unity.

The areal extent of our Dry Belt during this period begins to match that of the PFRA's Dry Belt but still is considerably smaller than Villmow's Dry Belt. Figure 1.5b shows our Dry Belt to be about three-quarters the size of the PFRA's Dry Belt and more than a quarter the size of Villmow's Dry Belt. In other words, there are major differences in the delineations of the boundaries between the Dry Belt for this period and these other two conceptions. The concentration of the drought during this period in Alberta, as discussed above, would not be easily inferred from the PFRA and Villmow maps but our map clearly shows the intensity of the drought in Alberta compared to Saskatchewan between 1914 and 1926.

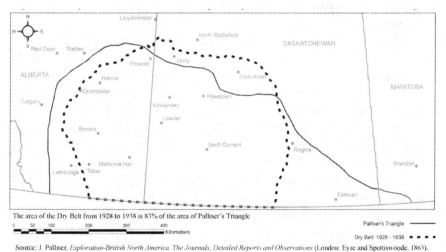

The area of the Dry Belt from 1928 to 1938 is 83% of the area of Palliser's Triangle

Palliser's Triangle ——————

Dry Belt: 1928 - 1938 ▪ ▪ ▪ ▪

Source: J. Palliser, *Exploration-British North America. The Journals, Detailed Reports and Observations* (London: Eyre and Spottiswoode, 1863).

Figure 1.6a. The Dry Belt based on a P/PET < = 0.65 map for the period from 1928 to 1938 and the Palliser Triangle.

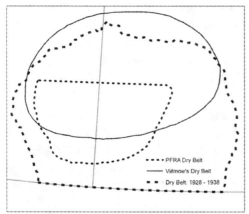

Source: J.R. Villmow, "The Nature and Origin of the Canadian Dry Belt," *Annals of the Association of American Geographers* 46, no. 1 (1956): 211-32. W. Nemanishen, *Drought in the Palliser Triangle: A Provisional Primer* (Regina: Prairie Farm Rehabilitation Administration, Agriculture and Agri-Food Canada, 1998), 2.

Figure 1.6b. Dry Belt based on a P/PET < = 0.65 map for the period from 1928 to 1938, Villmow's Dry Belt and the PFRA Dry Belt.

The era of the Dirty Thirties is captured in Figure 1.6a. We began with 1928, because this was the year that drought returned to the Dry Belt after the unusually wet year of 1927. We ended in 1938 because this is the last recorded year of extreme drought until 1961. The impact of prolonged drought can be seen in the extent of the Dry Belt extending from Saskatoon in the northeast, the U.S. border south of Regina in the southeast and south of Taber in the southwest, almost as far west as Calgary and northwest as Stettler. This huge territory constitutes well over one-half of the area encompassed by the Palliser Triangle. Our map of the Dry Belt covers an area at least three times larger than PFRA's Dry Belt and about one and a half times larger than Villmow's Dry Belt.

MAPPING HISTORICAL CHANGE IN THE DRY BELT
AND CLIMATE CHANGE IMPLICATIONS

When the P/PET calculations are averaged over the entire period—1895 to 2000—the mean position of the boundaries delineated for this period can be used as a reference to which we can compare the magnitude of the changes observed for the other periods, as illustrated in Figure 1.7. The Dry Belt during the pre-Second World War era was more than one and a half times larger than the Dry Belt during the full reference period. Amazingly, the Dry Belt of the Dirty Thirties is nearly seven times larger than the Dry Belt in the reference period. For the post-Depression period, the Dry Belt shrinks to a point where it is only a little more than three-quarters the size of the reference. Once again, the climate variability of the area becomes apparent through the shifting temporal boundaries of the Dry Belt.

The historical redrawing of the Dry Belt illustrates the extent to which a geographical area determined by climate is not static even within the confines of little more than 100 years of time. Although referred to in the historical literature as a relatively fixed area of geographical space, the Dry Belt has

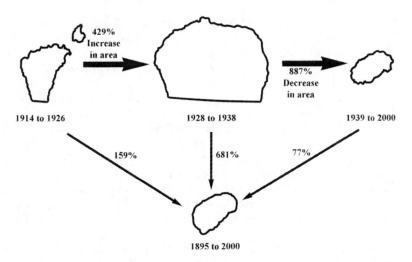

Figure 1.7. The areal change of the Dry Belt over three time periods relative to the reference period.

expanded and contracted over the past century. Understanding the shifting nature of the Dry Belt is particularly important given the forecasts of current global climate change models in general, and climate change scenarios for the Great Plains of North America in particular.

Most global climate change scenarios predict increased drying in continental interiors and greater risk of droughts for the twenty-first century.[26] Based on the expert opinion of the United Nations Intergovernmental Panel on Climate Change, there is a 66 percent probability of an increase in the area that could be affected by drought.[27] Using the history of the twentieth century as a guide, this could mean that the size of the Dry Belt for a significant period of the twenty-first century could be as large as that experienced from 1928 until 1938. If this occurs, then almost all the Palliser Triangle would be unsuitable for most types of non-irrigated grain farming, and difficult for ranching without appropriate provision for stored water.

The climate history presented here reveals the Dry Belt to be the vulnerable core of the Palliser Triangle. It should not be surprising if the size of the Dry Belt increases dramatically in the twenty-first century as a result of climate change.

NOTES

This article first appeared in *Prairie Forum* 34, no. 1 (2009): 31–44.

1   G. P. Marchildon, S. Kulshreshtha, E. Wheaton, and D. Sauchyn, "Drought and Institutional Adaptation in the Great Plains of Alberta and Saskatchewan, 1914–1939," *Natural Hazards* 45, no. 3 (2008): 399–411.

2   D. C. Jones, *Empire of Dust: Settling and Abandoning the Prairie Dry Belt* (Calgary: University of Calgary Press, 2002, orig. 1984).

3   D. Lemmen and L. Dale-Burnett, "The Palliser Triangle," in K. Fung (ed.), *Atlas of Saskatchewan: Second Edition* (Saskatoon: University of Saskatchewan, 1999), 41.

4   I. M. Spry (ed.), *The Papers of the Palliser Expedition, 1857–1860* (Toronto: Champlain Society, 1968). Also see I. M. Spry, *The Palliser Expedition: An Account of the John Palliser's British North American Expedition, 1857–1860* (Toronto: Macmillan, 1963).

5   Lemmen and Dale-Burnett, "The Palliser Triangle," 41.

6   H. Y. Hind, *Narrative of the Canadian Red River Exploring Expedition of 1857 and of the Assiniboine and Saskatchewan Expedition of 1858* (Edmonton: Hurtig, 1971, orig. 1860). Also see W. L. Morton, *Henry Youle Hind, 1823–1908* (Toronto: University of Toronto Press, 1980).

7   D. Hayes, *Historical Atlas of Canada: Canada's History Illustrated with Original Maps* (Vancouver: Douglas and McIntyre, 2002), 207.

8   According to Gerald Davidson, the recurring cycle of drought as much as high average aridity defines the prairie region: G. T. Davidson, "An Interdisciplinary Approach to the Role of Climate in the History of the Prairies," in R. Wardhaugh (ed.), *Toward Defining the Prairies: Region, Culture, and History* (Winnipeg: University of Manitoba Press, 2001), 201.

9   A. B. Beaudoin, "What They Saw: The Climatic and Environmental Context for Euro-Canadian Settlement in Alberta," *Prairie Forum* 24, no. 1 (1999): 1–40; D. J. Sauchyn and W. R. Skinner, "A Proxy Record of Drought Severity for the Southwestern Canadian Plains," *Canadian Water Resources Journal* 26, no. 1 (2001): 253–72.

10 W. F. Rannie, "Summer Rainfall on the Prairies during the Palliser and Hind Expeditions, 1857–59," *Prairie Forum* 31, no. 1 (2006): 17–38.

11 *Historical Atlas of Canada: The Land Transformed, 1800–1891* (Toronto: University of Toronto Press, 1993), plate 42. *Historical Atlas of Canada: Addressing the Twentieth Century* (Toronto: University of Toronto Press, 1990), plate 17.

12 O. E. Baker, "Agricultural Regions of America: Part VI—the Spring Wheat Region," *Economic Geography* 4, no. 4 (1928): 399–433; D. Breen, *The Canadian Prairie West and the Ranching Frontier, 1874–1924* (Toronto: University of Toronto Press, 1983), 141–2.

13 G. P. Marchildon, "Institutional Adaptation to Drought and the Special Areas of Alberta, 1909–1939," *Prairie Forum* 32, no. 2 (2007): 251–72; D. C. Jones and R. C. Macleod (eds.), *We'll All Be Buried Down Here: The Prairie Dryland Disaster, 1917–1926* (Calgary: Historical Society of Alberta, 1986); J. Gorman, *A Land Reclaimed: A Story of the Special Areas in Alberta* (Hanna, AB: Special Areas Board, 1988).

14 Marchildon et al., "Drought and Institutional Adaptation in the Great Plains of Alberta and Saskatchewan, 1914–1939."

15 W. Nemanishen, *Drought in the Palliser Triangle: A Provisional Primer* (Regina: Prairie Farm Rehabilitation Administration, Agriculture and Agri-Food Canada, 1998), 2.

16 J. R. Villmow, "The Nature and Origin of the Canadian Dry Belt," *Annals of the Association of American Geographers* 46, no. 1 (1956): 211–32.

17 C. W. Thornthwaite, "An Approach toward a Rational Classification of Climate," *Geographical Review* 38, no. 1 (1948): 55–94.
18 Villmow, "The Nature and Origin of the Canadian Dry Belt."
19 Ibid.
20 Ibid.
21 United Nations Environment Programme (UNEP), *World Atlas of Desertification* (Edward Arnold, London, 1992.)
22 Ibid.
23 R. Hopkins, *Canadian Gridded Climate Data* (Ottawa: Environment Canada, 2001). Thornthwaite, "An Approach toward a Rational Classification of Climate."
24 UNEP, *World Atlas of Desertification*. W. C. Palmer and A. V. Havens, "A Graphical Technique for Determining Evapotranspiration by the Thornthwaite Method," *Monthly Weather Review* 86 (1958): 123–8.
25 Marchildon, "Institutional Adaptations to Drought and the Special Areas of Alberta, 1909–1939," *Prairie Forum* 32, no. 2 (2007): 251–71.
26 R. Watson and the Core Writing Team (eds.), *Climate Change 2001: Synthesis Report, Intergovernmental Panel on Climate Change* (Cambridge: Cambridge University Press, 2001).
27 Intergovernmental Panel on Climate Change, *Climate Change 2007: The Physical Science Basis—Summary for Policy Makers* (Geneva: IPCC Secretariat, 2007).

2. Schools and Social Disintegration in the
    Alberta Dry Belt of the Twenties

David C. Jones

In the tumultuous years before World War I prairie society witnessed an overexpansion into marginal and dry areas. Unprecedented wheat prices and two mammoth harvests in 1915 and 1916 led farmers to overextend themselves, to double their equipment, and to brush aside the wiser policy of mixed farming. As land prices escalated immediately following the war a prolonged drought began in 1917 followed by a severe postwar depression starting in 1920. The cost of living rose and crop prices plummeted.

Everywhere the depression and drought of the early twenties was serious, but in the dry areas it was catastrophic. These regions in Interlake Manitoba, portions of southwest Saskatchewan, and the Dry Belt of Alberta, were the last settled and least stable regions of the prairies. The most extensive of these regions and the hardest hit was the Alberta Dry Belt.

Western Canadian historiography is strangely silent on the matter of the Alberta Dry Belt society of the twenties. Little is known about the magnitude of the calamity, about its effects on people or institutions. In particular, nothing systematic has been written about the Dry Belt school, its teachers, or their relationship with the land. Since the school was perhaps the most vital and powerful institution in that society and since it survived the catastrophe of the twenties it is a most instructive means of viewing the disintegration which occurred. This paper will try to clarify the extent of the disaster, to show how the school was affected by the economic hardship and depopulation, how the determination to maintain schools greatly intensified the sense of social dislocation and anxiety, and how teacher training, curriculum and social conditions further agitated this sense by moulding an institution alienated from rural life and unrelated to the fundamental agricultural activity of the land.

Significantly this interpretation of the school as a source of conflict, community discord, and social anxiety runs counter to the traditional view of the school as a community centre and a source of integration. Except where otherwise noted, specific school districts examined below were among the sixty-seven which eventually became the Berry Creek Consolidation in 1933. Centred in the Municipality of Berry Creek, south of Hanna, the region extended both east and west of that jurisdiction.

Consider first the extent of the dry belt problem. Between 1921 and 1926 the three census divisions constituting the dry regions lost 21 percent of their population. This figure greatly underestimates the exodus in the hardest hit

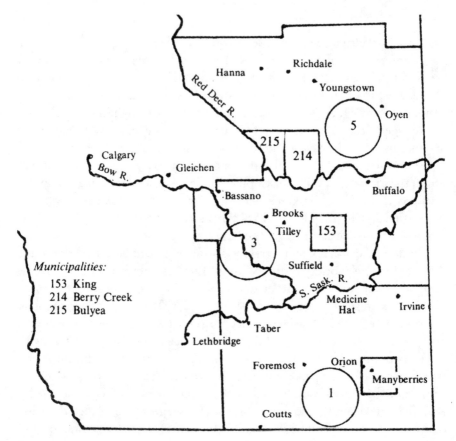

Figure 2.1. Alberta Census Divisions 1, 3 and 5 (1921–26).

regions. The local improvement district surrounding the towns of Manyberries and Orion, south of Medicine Hat, declined from 940 to 531 in the same period. Further north, the adjoining municipalities of Berry Creek and Bulyea dropped from 1369 to 534 and from 830 to 336 respectively. The municipality of King, between Brooks and Medicine Hat, literally wasted from 815 to 153.[1]

Accompanying this exodus was a dramatic decrease in the number of farms. The number in Manyberries district, for example, dropped from 213 to 96; that in King municipality dropped from 217 to 61; and that in Berry Creek dropped from 463 to 148.[2] Simultaneously farm abandonments rose. About two-thirds of the province's vacant and abandoned farms in 1926 were concentrated in the Dry Belt which involved only three of Alberta's seventeen census divisions.[3] The magnitude of the calamity in the twenties can be appreciated when one realizes that while there were 20,000 more farms in the province in 1931, there were 3,760 fewer abandonments than five years earlier.[4]

Farm sizes in the stricken area increased incredibly. By 1926 the percentage of farms in census divisions 1 and 5 over 480 acres was roughly twice the provincial mean.[5] While 71 percent of Albertan farms in 1926 were totally owned, only 56 percent of farms in the Dry Belt were totally owned. Some municipalities, of course, were much worse off. The most striking example, perhaps, was Bulyea where of 122 occupiers only 44 were complete owners.[6]

In view of these statistics, it is little wonder that two investigations were made into portions of the Dry Belt in the mid-twenties—one by the Federal Department of the Interior and another by the Alberta Government. The federal report indicated that of 2386 resident farmers in the area roughly between the Red Deer and South Saskatchewan Rivers east of the town of Tilley, only 645 remained at the end of 1924.[7] The Albertan study, known as the Tilley East Commission, estimated in early 1926 that there were then "well under 500" remaining. The Commission also estimated that no less than 3000 parcels of land, approximating 450,000 acres of 784,000 acres taken up, were in process of forfeiture.[8]

The economic catastrophe was accompanied by a series of nightmarish plagues—infestations of grasshoppers, Russian and Canadian thistles, army cutworms, pale western cutworms, wireworms and even rabbits. For farmers smitten by these, the drought and the hail, the destitution and the loss, it must have seemed that nature had run amuck, out of control.[9] In the Dry Belt of the twenties, indeed, the essence of life was this very sense of shattering uncertainty.

Under these conditions a key question was whether schools could exist. Clearly the costs of schooling were a major burden which threatened the community itself. By 1922 the story was grim. Inspectors at Hanna, Oyen, Irvine, Brooks and Foremost all remarked on the poor crops; in fact, by then their annual reports were more like economic resumés than pedagogical essays.[10] Tax collections in Hanna Inspectorate for the year probably typified the Dry Belt as a whole—5 to 40 percent of the amount levied.[11] Generally, the greater the disintegration of the community, the less collected. The next year, Inspector J. F. Boyce of Bassano noted of his dry area that "the people still residing in some of these districts are so discouraged that there is little evidence of inclination" to meet tax obligations. In the areas of worst depopulation, Bulyea and Berry Creek, twelve of the forty districts "failed even to requisition the Municipal Secretary for the annual levy in 1923."[12]

Where there were no people there were no schools. The demoralization noted by Boyce, however, occurred usually after persistent local effort to maintain the schools. School taxes were often collected more speedily than other forms of debt. At Chinook, east of Hanna, for example, Inspector J. W. Yake reported that ratepayers in some distressed municipalities had paid "70 percent and even 100 percent of their school taxes." Frustratingly for schoolmen and locals, the monies were poured into a common fund and used as security for municipal loans incurred at local banks.[13] Recognizing the propensity of locals to support the schools, municipalities even began to make school levies exceeding those required by local school boards in order to generate funds.

The effort to maintain the schools involved several strategies. All were problematic, all involved trade-offs, and all generated anxiety.

The first ploy entailed applying for loans. The experience of the Creole Bell school district, extending into both Bulyea and Berry Creek Municipalities, typified what happened when the municipalities failed to advance monies for school operations as required under the Rural Municipality Act. On 7 April 1919, the secretary of the school board was instructed to write to the Department concerning "the neglect of the Bulyea Municipal Council to supply our school with our estimate on time...."[14] A month later the secretary was asked to write again indicating "that the Board will be obliged to close the school unless it is forthcoming at once."[15] In August the secretary tried, apparently unsuccessfully, to arrange with the inspector a loan of $400 from the Department.[16] On 1 November the chairman and secretary were asked to interview the Bank of Toronto at Cessford, in Berry Creek Municipality, "to try and arrange a loan for $100 on a note for 60 days."[17] At a special meeting two weeks later more insistent pressure was placed on the inspector to provide a loan "as soon as possible...."[18] A week after, frantic and still unaided, the board decided to return to the bank at Cessford to sign a note for $225 in the names of the chairman and secretary and to have "the other members sign as collateral."[19] Two weeks later when the inspector turned down an application for a $500 loan, the board requested $550.[20] Beleaguered and unsatisfied, the board decided on May 29, 1920, after a few dollars trickled in, to pay the chairman and secretary "instead of paying Miss Ellsworth," the teacher. Ellsworth was "instructed to wait."[21]

Over the next few months the unnerving pressure increased. In March 1921, the Berry Creek Municipality failed to supply the money for schools and on May 1 the disconsolate board turned the school management over to an Official Trustee.[22]

Certain larger districts were more successful in exacting government assistance while the school board still operated. Efforts sometimes involved calling the government's bluff. Perhaps typical was the case of Bow Island, east of Taber. With poor crops and escalating costs, the school board held a special meeting on 29 September 1919, to consider finances. Since the Department of Education would not loan the money and since the town could not meet the requisition, the board decided to close the schools. The teachers and government were to be notified and correspondence with the latter was to be published. A week later Inspector Williams informed the board that he was recommending a government loan of $1965 to maintain the schools to the end of the year. Shortly thereafter Chief Inspector Gorman appeared on the scene, urging the town to assume responsibility for the schools. When the council refused, the government provided the assistance. The procedure was repeated in August 1920, involving this time the inspector, the chief inspector, and the deputy minister. Again, only after assurance that the Department would finance the schools till taxes came in, did the locals "consent" to operate the schools.[23]

By 1921 when the severity of the problem became more apparent the flow of loans increased. The relief was short-lived, for the next year, under insistent financial pressure, the government instituted retrenchments and loan cutbacks.[24] As a call to the locals to dig deeper, it was sometimes successful. "It would appear," said Inspector Cartwright of Irvine in 1922, "that substantial loans previously made had a tendency in many cases to cause ratepayers to make less effort to pay their taxes and school boards to exercise less pressure."[25] Inspector Scoffield of Foremost stated that "the refusal to grant increasing loans to School Boards, far from effecting the closing of schools, has been the means of rousing boards to increased activity in tax collection and in reducing operating expenditures."[26] The result was not everywhere the same, for Lethbridge Inspector A. J. Watson noted "more schools being closed during the fall term than at any other time since I have been in this district"—a period of five years.[27] The trouble with the government policy, as with all policies meant to apply to a vast region with districts in varying degrees of distress, was that it was never quite clear who the truly destitute were. While the locals sometimes blurred the distinction by painting a picture unduly black and by bluffing closure too often, over and over districts went through the terrifying process of discovering the limits of their ingenuity to provide funds. Few ever wanted to close the schools, but it began to dawn on the most resilient and forebearing that the harder they worked the less likely the government would help.

A second strategy involved the addition of territory in an effort to widen the tax base. Most districts liked the idea and many were even encouraged by inspectors to implement it. Unfortunately, school districts uniformly opposed giving up territory.[28] Nonetheless, a number of districts were carved out of existing ones during the period and in the fourth year of drought the new district of Forcina decided to build a $2170 school.[29] The consequences were devastating. Adjoining districts lost population and taxable land and the new district was submerged in debt. Month after month the board struggled— seeking loans everywhere, attempting to extend the period of debenture call, supplicating for the renewal of notes and the postponement of the teacher's salary.[30] Things hardly improved. Ten years later, as the secretary reviewed 1929 and thought of the future, he wrote dejectedly, "…I think to commence this term we really have nothing."[31]

A more viable solution to the problem of finance was the short term school. Thus the Arlington school board ruled on 20 January 1923, "that no levy be made this year." "Owing to the term being short last year," the secretary wrote, "there is enough money left to run the school seven months this year."[32] The Brown school board decided· to engage a teacher for only four months in 1923, opening school "on or about the 16th of April."[33] Sometimes more than finance was involved in the creation of short term schools. Thus the Jennings school board decided on 10 February 1919, that "owing to the fact that all children were small…to hold school seven months and more if [the] weather stayed good."[34]

While the short term school may have been a viable option for the locals and a means of maintaining local control, it was viewed by inspectors as the bane of the rural school, one of the chief reasons why rural education could never hope to approach urban education. Throughout the twenties as schoolmen sought to remedy the rural school problem they increased teacher certification requirements and length of normal school service and moved to terminate the "summer schools." Chief Attendance Officer D. C. McEacherne perused teachers' contracts and warned districts about infringing against regulations. "As...the School Act does not permit any board of a rural school district to grant more than ten weeks vacation during the entire year," he wrote the Dry Belt district of Keystone, "your board has no authority to grant a summer vacation as stated in paragraph five of the agreement submitted."[35]

By the late twenties local trustees had lost two or three lawsuits which were brought against them when they defied attendance regulations in sections 182 and 191 of the School Act. "I would suggest that your Board fall in line with the said sections," wrote Inspector J. F. Boyce of Bassano to L. E. Helmer, secretary of the Britannia school board, on 26 December 1927. "If it is the desire of the Board of trustees of Britannia to close down for the winter months please give me the details of their reasons, such as the size of the children, the number and names of the grades, the distance of the children from the school and their means of reaching the school, the number of pupils above grade v and the state of the finances of the district."[36] The reference to grades was motivated by an official feeling that where there were high school grades, or where the grade spread was such that the little children or the older ones might unduly suffer, or where there were many grades, the task of teaching was harder and the need for a longer term greater. The point of Boyce's letter was that the financial condition of the district was no longer enough to warrant a summer school. The letter indicated increased government attention as the traditional form of local control failed. For local trustees who survived, sometimes by dint of herculean effort, government standardization moves constituted a coup de grace. While professional schoolmen felt strongly that summer schools threatened the future of rural children and that a new form of administration was desperately needed, official intervention sometimes completed the breaking of the local spirit which the depression and drought had begun.

A fourth strategy for maintaining the rural schools in the Dry Belt involved the enforcement in 1923 of the Tax Recovery Act, the object of which was to bring in tax arrears from farmers, mortgages, and loan companies.[37] The operation of the Act had the same result as other forms of government intervention. Successful in continuing the operation of many schools which otherwise would have closed in the Lethbridge and Medicine Hat Inspectorates, the Act did much to destroy what was left of the local community.[38] Providing a speedy means of securing some unpaid taxes, it also assured widescale abandonment by the hardiest farmers left on the land. A single notice in the

Alberta Gazette in 1923, for example, listed 36 percent of the total land area in King Municipality under threat of forfeiture.[39]

The most common strategy of the locals was to try and cooperate. While some districts managed cooperative schools with minimal difficulty, the experience generally eroded the sense of community and set up a host of differences and antagonisms which were often difficult to eliminate. Districts which "cooperated" did not want to sell their school houses and did not want to change the district name.[40] Those who wanted to send their children into a neighbouring school had to await a report from that school regarding possible overcrowding and the always contentious issue of cost.[41] The decision of whether to send one's children to another school and renounce all further local control, or to operate one of the schools jointly and maintain a semblance of board input, was difficult to make.

The experience of the Arlington school district was typical. In February 1927 the board called a meeting to discuss the advisability of cooperating with Square Deal or Jennings districts "with the idea of reducing taxes," One trustee, F. Rudge, objected to school in either of these districts since the distance was too great for his children to walk. At the same time, the secretary presented figures which must have seemed very threatening to Rudge. The cost of running the Arlington school for a year, including teacher's salary, fuel, stationery, and audit was $740. The direct tax was $468. By cooperating with another district costs including half the teacher's salary, half the fuel, and rental of the school house, were $425. The direct tax was only $153.[42]

With difficulty the board decided against cooperation. The minutes, however, reflected an uneasiness and lack of decisiveness. At a meeting in January 1928, the board deemed "that as long as the number of children as at present remain…it would be advisable to run our own school."[43] Exactly one month later, the board reversed its stand and decided "to cooperate with the. Jennings School District for 1928…" It also decided to move the school house.[44] In January 1929, as the cooperation was extended another year, the board reported that Mr. Rudge had left the district.[45] While it was by no means clear that these school troubles had caused his departure, local histories of this period in the Dry Belt are sprinkled with cases of families moving in search of better schooling for their children. Also, as high school became more important toward the end of the decade, many families were split by the need to board sons and daughters in distant communities with high school facilities.

Not surprisingly, statements in board minutes like "Nothing was decided on," were common.[46] Yet decisions had to be made and the process was often agonizing. Once something was settled it had to be reconsidered each year.

Thus the Connorsville trustees agreed to pay the Corinth board twenty-five cents per day per pupil for the education of Connorsville children in 1923.[47] But a few years later the Connorsville people considered the cost "a little high."[48] As well, agreements were often jeopardized by the inability of boards to pay for the tuition of their children in outside districts. When the board of Moccasin Flat failed to pay the tuition of Una Hornby for the term ending 30 June 1919, at the Creole Belle school, the Creole Belle trustees decided five days later not to "consider entering into an agreement for the tuition of the children of Moccasin Flat…until the said bill be paid."[49]

It was the sad truth that the urgent need for money fragmented the community in every conceivable way. On 7 October 1922, the secretary of the Crocus Plains school board wrote an area resident:

> Some time ago we wrote you about your account with this district, but have received no answer.
>
> This school cannot be kept running without funds, so we have decided to give you until the end of October to pay this account. If it is not paid by then your children will be expelled.[50]

A sixth and sometimes terminal strategy for maintaining the schools in the burnt-out areas involved the assumption by inspectors of the role of Official Trustee. In 1923 Chief Inspector Gorman reported ninety school districts in the province in the hands of Official Trustees, "the greater proportion of which were in the southern inspectorates."[51] Official Trustees were appointed when there were no locals left to govern, or they did not want to govern, or they could not operate because of unremitting debt or internecine quarrels. Sometimes they were appointed where there was a particularly determined board which had stayed through thick and thin and discovered in the end that its self preservation formulae of summer school or low salaries for teachers was unacceptable to government. Official Trustees were the means by which control over schooling was transferred, sometimes wrested, from despondent, pathetic, bickering, fearful, and sometimes courageous locals. Trusteeships in the Dry Belt, however, were not the results of some conspiracy by professional schoolmen to impose a new system of administration involving consolidation upon unsuspecting or reluctant locals.[52] They were the results of an official policy buttressed by local sentiment to stabilize local school districts to regenerate collapsing school boards, and to restore the status quo before the drought.[53]

Unfortunately, many local school boards could not be resurrected. As Inspector Scoffield of Foremost said, "In a few cases successive crop failures have so broken the spirit and interest of these people that they will not stand for election to the school board nor attend school meetings."[34] Significantly when the Official Trustees were appointed they used the strategies that they as inspectors had devised in concert with the locals and that the locals had fashioned on their own. Thus they perpetuated the dramatic new alignments, fluctuating student dormitories, makeshift boundaries, and floating schools—ploys which were exceedingly disruptive and unsettling. The school might be retained, the Official Trustees began to see as the locals and the tax collectors had seen, but only by destroying the community.

In all the grasping to maintain Dry Belt schools the interrelationship between floundering locals and paternal government was profoundly complex. Occasionally the locals made threats they had little intention of carrying out, sometimes they cried and no one heard, sometimes as with the short term school they were willing to do with less than official policy permitted. For the government, extreme crises demanded extreme measures and some, like the Tax Recovery Act, were self defeating. As well, chaos demanded order and some forms of government order, like standardized attendance regulations, stultified local self determination.

From all this what can one infer about the Dry Belt state of mind? Almost for sure the locals did not know what to make of government attempts to help. The government swore that it was dedicated to the restoration of local control, but that rarely happened. The government promised to maintain the schools, but few provincial moves were as disconcerting for the locals as the one to reduce loans. Government policies regarding individual districts were ad hoc decisions, dependent upon inspectors, or Official Trustees, or provincial finances, and thus were never certain, never definite. These qualities were part of the legacy of strategies to keep the schools.

If these strategies heightened the lines of community division, the sense of anxiety and break up, the divisiveness was reinforced by the nature of what happened in the school, of the teachers, and of the circumstances under which they lived—all of which helped to produce an institution largely unrelated to the fundamental agricultural activity of the land and out of touch with rural life. Notwithstanding all the agonizing effort of government schoolmen and locals to provide schools, the kind of school provided was in a basic sense apart from the people, apart from the land, and apart from the community.

To understand how this happened one must review briefly the nature of teacher preparation in the period, contemporary curriculum reform, and teachers' living experiences in the Dry Belt.

The purpose of eight months of normal school training in the early twenties was the preparation of teacher trainees for instructing all subjects on the elementary school curriculum. A major weakness of teacher training institutions was that they failed to prepare teachers for rural conditions. "The teachers being trained here," said W. A. Stickle, Principal of Camrose Normal School in 1921, "will nearly all teach in rural schools, yet they get no opportunity to observe or to practise in a rural school." Without such practice, he concluded, trainees did not learn how to compose multiple graded timetables, how to group classes, how to keep students busy on different projects, or how to grade, teach or test such classes.[55] Principal E. W. Coffin of the Calgary Normal School, meanwhile, was pleased that his institution had an arrangement with two rural schools. Since only one was a single room school and since that meant that of the fourteen apprenticeship schools connected with the normal school only one was a bona fide country school, Coffin's elation was doubtlessly tempered.[56]

The next year unprecedented numbers of trainees flooded the teacher training institutions in response to a number of factors—the depression and lack of clerical jobs, departmental pressure to induce permit teachers to take regular training, and rumours that the government loan to students was to

Typical one-room schoolhouse in the Canadian Prairies (Courtesy of the Provincial Archives of Saskatchewan / R-A14580).

be withdrawn and that the normal school course was to be lengthened to two years.[57] Inundated at the height of drought in the Dry Belt, Coffin regretted that "we cannot hope to give every student the opportunity of apprentice work in either of our two rural schools."[58] At Camrose, Stickle again noted the "anomaly of training rural school teachers without observation or practice in a rural school"—especially considering the fact that "quite a large percentage of our students are wholly ignorant of the problems of the rural school or the rural community...."[59] Indeed, he stated that with the massive increase in enrolment and twelve public school rooms available, each room would have twenty-one student teachers in the 1922–23 school year![60] Hamstrung, Stickle did what he could "to put the students into touch with movements which concern the rural districts.... " Special speakers gave addresses on school fairs, the public health nurses, tree culture, municipal hospitals, junior Red Cross, and organized girls' work. "Students are encouraged," he said, "to identify themselves with rural organizations which aim to improve conditions, and to be real members of the community."[61]

What was needed was a broad knowledge of rural life, a spirit of enlightenment and willing leadership. Camrose Inspector J. W. Russell characterized the need well in 1921. "There is not sufficient effort being made by our teachers in leadership in community work," he said, "the majority being content...to accept the type and standard of community activity prevalent, rather than to aspire to leadership and to shape community life and activity."[62]

These exhortations and earlier ones from the normal schools, summer schools, and inspectors since before the war had been accompanied by demands that the curriculum be expanded. Significantly the disaster in the Dry Belt of the twenties occurred just as the most concerted attempt in prairie and national history to enhance agriculture on the school curriculum bogged down. Promoters of the subject had argued that school gardening and school supervised home gardening would bring the school and community together by engaging students and teachers in the essential activity of the land, by accentuating the dignity of labour and the work of the soil, and by encouraging farm children to stay on the land. In Alberta and other western provinces school gardening peaked about 1916 and in five years it was all but forgotten.[63] Many tragedies befell gardens in the period—drought, hail, frost, gophers, maggots, lack of summer care, and lack of leadership.[64] Generally, however, school gardens were worst where field crops were worst—in the Dry Belt.

The story of Miss Speiran is an example of what happened in Dry Belt school gardens. Arriving from Ontario in 1916, fresh from normal school and eager to plant a garden in the coming spring, Speiran went to a district near

Oyen, just then beginning the long drought. At her school in the spring of 1917 she carefully built elevated rows where her students planted their seeds. The notion of elevating seeds was current in Ontario where there was danger of flooding. Unhappily in the Dry Belt the major dangers of the next decade would be drought and soil drifting. In spite of massive intervention by students in lugging water to the garden, the plants were victims of the gophers and the hot winds. By mid-June she had abandoned the project.[65] Once was often enough. As Inspector M. E. Lazerte of Bassano wrote, "I have noticed that if the school garden is a failure the first year it takes a long time to win back the sympathy and cooperation of the parents...."[66]

Closely tied to school gardening was the school grounds beautification movement. Properly kept school grounds were part of the plan to bring school and home together by making the school a local shrine and by providing carefully landscaped models for home grounds maintenance and esthetics. "The natural features of the site and its surroundings," a Departmental bulletin said in 1916, "should be attractive and lend themselves to a landscape treatment that would cultivate a taste for the beautiful and make the school centre a place of which the district may be proud."[67] Nowhere in the province, however, were these purposes so thwarted as in the Dry Belt. There, upkeep was neglected, playground equipment was not bought, and fences were left down. No trustees ever illustrated the negation of the beautification movement better than the Lyman school board. None ever so poignantly depicted what the school meant to the sinking Dry Belt community. The scene was a meeting on 25 September 1926, the mood was deliriously comical, and the occasion was a sort of Last Supper, strangely jovial and insanely sardonic. The trustees began to talk of painting the school.

> Then followed a very heated discussion as to the colour, each trustee insisting on his national colours. Owing to the great diversity of opinion and the apparent hopelessness of arriving at an agreement, it was decided on the suggestion of the chairman to paint the school yellow, with the view of its blending with any deposit made on the door step or nuisance committed in the vicinity. Further that a white elephant to be painted on the front. This suggestion met with great enthusiasm and was immediately earned unanimously.[68]

The Dry Belt school and its grounds were neither a shrine nor a model, nor were they beautiful or enviable. For these tired trustees they were mostly a burden. Less than four months later there were only ten ratepayers in the district. On March 17, 1930, Lyman fell into the hands of an Official Trustee.[69]

Also related to school gardening, and to grounds beautification, but much more successful, was the school fair. Instituted in 1916 under the guidance of the School of Agriculture at Olds, school fairs spread rapidly across the province in the early twenties. By 1921 there were 89 school fairs and by 1922, 129.[70] Principal J. C. Hooper of Claresholm School of Agriculture explained that the purpose of fairs was "to stimulate in the children an interest in the activities of the farm and the home, to increase their knowledge of the principles and practice of farming and home-making, to encourage the teaching of agriculture and home economics in the rural schools, [and] to increase the interest of parents in the work of the school."[71] As R. M. Scott, Principal of Youngstown School of Agriculture, established in 1920, said, "They have promoted…loyalty to home and community."[72]

This role was enhanced in the Dry Belt when the regular fairs were cancelled and the agricultural societies died out.[73] For a time, in communities such as Orion, Manyberries, Irvine and Youngstown, school fairs took the place of the agricultural fairs as the major community celebration.[74] When drought cancelled the agricultural fair at Youngstown in 1922, for example, the secretary of the agricultural society reported that the society was banding "behind the school fair [to]…make it a success in every way."[75] Why school fairs could be held when agricultural fairs could not is explainable partly through the fact that exhibits of penmanship, manual training, or domestic science were less susceptible to the weather than purely agricultural products. As well, both the government and the locals were more determined to maintain the schools than the agricultural societies.

For several reasons school fairs never completely supplanted the agricultural fairs in the Dry Belt. First, most school fairs in the region became the responsibility of the new Schools of Agriculture at Raymond, Gleichen and Youngstown. Agricultural instructors had no sooner taken over the organization than the government closed the Gleichen and Youngstown schools in 1922.[76] Crop failure had reduced enrolment to unacceptable levels and the institutions created to combat farming difficulties in the dry areas fell victim to the problems they were to solve. Second, in May 1923, as an economy measure, the staff of school inspectors for the province was reduced from forty to twenty-five.[77] Since an integral part of the inspector's job was the adjudication of school fairs, the staff reduction at a time of fair expansion meant that the remaining inspectors were hard pressed to cover the fairs. As A. R. Gibson, Inspector for Red Deer, said, "the Inspector's work is now heavy and his being held responsible for…school fair work interferes with his itinerary …."[78] With less inspectoral interest, especially in the dry areas where problems of finance became critical, teachers had less reason to participate. Third, the success of school fairs depended largely, though not completely, upon good crops.[79] As Inspector John Scoffield of Foremost lamented, "On the eastern side of the Inspectorate the dry season of 1923 affected few school activities more seriously than the school fairs. Field and garden crops were a failure and no fairs were held."[80] Finally, those who taught for short terms had no time to prepare exhibits and sometimes their schools were not open when the larger fairs were held.

School fairs did not perish in the Dry Belt of the twenties, but they were increasingly limited to the bigger centres where the quality of agricultural exhibits was often pathetic. Under such circumstances the festivity could be a discouraging display of the land's intransigence, of man's subservience to nature. Clearly the fact that the school fair had a strong non-agricultural component allowed it to continue in the dry lands. It survived partly because it represented enterprises which were *not* related to the fundamental activity of the land. That is, the kind of fair which emerged in the Dry Belt could not inspire children with signs of progress, could not exact pride in the work of the soil, could not genuinely interest children in farm life, and could hardly speed their return to the land. Even in that school activity ostensibly most related to agriculture and rural life, there was thus a basic irrelevance, a counterproductiveness.

There was also something about the living conditions of school teachers which promoted the sense that the school was somehow apart from the people. Inspector F. L. Aylesworth of Oyen wrote in 1924 that

> the rural teacher is presented with perhaps only three really serious problems: (1) The location of a suitable boarding-house; (2) How to avoid being entangled with different factions, and in petty disagreements and quarrels rife under present economic conditions; (3) How to provide herself with suitable and adequate recreation and entertainment without acquiring the habit of attending six or more barn dances a week.[81]

A real attempt was made to solve only the first of these problems. When money was provided in 1919 for the construction of teacherages, it was hoped that the residential difficulties of teachers would be solved. Two years later, however, Inspector Dobson at Hanna felt that the "Departmental plan has not met with much success…since many teachers prefer to board."[82] The explanation for this preference is beginning to emerge from teacher biographies of the period and later. These show a life of hardship in the "residences"—stories of snowladen roofs caving in, of infestations of mice and vermin, of fear of foreigners in immigrant districts, of social isolation and abject loneliness.[83] Moreover, in the Dry Belt where funds were shortest, facilities were skimpiest and improvements were often put off indefinitely. Teachers might renovate, of course, but at their own expense. At Creole Belle district in 1919 the teacher was "allowed to buy [wall] paper for the residence," providing she "put it on" and agreed "to be paid…when there are sufficient funds available."[84] Characteristically, the teacherage more resembled a bare and secluded cloister than the headquarters of a community leader.

For those who boarded there was companionship—and suffering of another sort. The district of Crocus Plains had to "bear the loss in having bought furniture for the teacher's shack…when the teacher decided not to use the same."[85] In times of poverty teachers might regret such decisions. Sometimes local penury was so pervasive that the teacher had to board on a rotational scheme with every family in the district. While it was possible to know virtually everyone at least superficially, the scheme involved continual adaptation to changing routines, expectations, and degrees of destitution.

When Miss Speiran, the gardener, came to the Oyen district, she boarded with an English family in 1917. Farming on only a quarter section, the family was eager to board the teacher as a means of supplementing their income. Speiran ate in a separate room from the four children since there was not enough "quality" food to go round. Favored, she recalled her guilt as the children gazed ravenously at her plate. To reach her bedroom with its uncomfortable straw mattress, she had to pass through the main bedroom where the couple and their four children slept.[86]

Ten years later Norman Jackson Pickard began his teaching career in a German settlement sixteen miles south of Irvine. Following a diphtheria outbreak Pickard contacted Inspector Carr who ordered him to close the school. The locals, however, countermanded the order, voting to keep the school open. After a second outbreak Pickard took no chances and appeared on the scene with a Mounted Policeman to enforce the order. As Pickard's biographers have noted, the incident demonstrated the difficulty faced by young, inexperienced teachers in attempts to provide the enlightened community leadership the normal schools and inspectors advocated.[87]

In circumstances like these the school was in the charge of one who was forced to live a very restricted life, who often had the best interests of the locals at heart but who frequently knew nothing of their lifestyles, who had been exhorted to join the community but who remained in the end an outsider. In a very real way the school with its alien tutor was the symbol of what was left of the burnt out Dry Belt. It had been favored over the community by government and locals alike. In that it had not linked itself permanently with the fundamental activity of the land, it had survived. Its inability to become relevant was simultaneously the mark of its success and failure. Any educational institution designed to deal directly with or to improve life as it then existed on this dying land was doomed. The Agricultural Schools at Gleichen and Youngstown proved that. The school survived precisely because it represented a world far from the scorching wind, the dust and the thistles, away from the back-breaking labor, the hopelessness and the destitution.

As the relief in groceries, coal and seed escalated in the southeast in amounts which in some districts dwarfed similar measures during the Great Depression, the railroads were called in to assist the exodus.[88] By the end of 1926, 1,851 families totaling 3,179 carloads had been freighted out—some to Saskatchewan, many to the wetter west, and a few to the newer north. The experience of these and thousands of others who left in a more private manner, often with less, was utterly demoralizing.

This paper has argued that the kind of school that survived in the Alberta Dry Belt of the twenties contributed to the social malaise of the period and region. The fanatical determination to maintain the schools meant that they would exist in a way which heightened uncertainty, fear, dislocation, in essence, the Durkheimian sense of "anomie." The issue of schooling—when, where, with whom, and how—tore districts apart, neighbours apart, and families apart. Teacher training in the period bore little relationship to rural life in general and curricular reforms involving agriculture suffered grievously in the Dry Belt. These factors and social conditions intensified the teacher's determination to be gone after an apprenticeship in what must have seemed like purgatory. They thwarted many attempts at self sacrifice and service. The rotational boarding schemes left the school teacher in a constant state of stress and pity for her penniless hosts and herself, with variations to be heard on the lament of the farmer and new routines to be learned each month or two. Training and conditions had made the teacher an outsider, hardly capable of integrating a society which the school itself had done so much to fracture.

The experience of local school districts in the Alberta Dry Belt of the twenties set the scene and justification for the larger school districts in the thirties, for the Berry Creek area was the first major rural consolidation in the province.[89] Not surprisingly, Alberta pioneered the establishment of large school divisions. And importantly, the smaller steps which led to large-scale consolidation were often initiated by the locals themselves.

The decade in the Dry Belt witnessed the consequences of the overexpansion of prairie society, horrendous personal loss, and the accommodation of schools to a new social and demographic reality. The accommodation foreshadowed accurately the fate in store for much of the prairies during the Great Depression.

NOTES

This article first appeared in *Prairie Forum* 3, no. 1 (1978): 1–20. The author thanked Nancy M. Sheehan and Robert M. Stamp for their constructive comments.

1   *Census of Prairie Provinces 1926* (Ottawa: King's Printer, 1931), 518, 561–2. For relevant studies see Jean Burnet, *Next Year Country* (Toronto: University of Toronto Press, 1951); A. M. Pennie, "A Cycle at Suffield," *Alberta Historical Review* 11 (Winter 1963): 7–11; James H. Gray, *Men Against the Desert* (Saskatoon: Modern Press, 1967); W. A. Mackintosh, *Economic Problems of the Prairie Provinces* (Toronto: Macmillan, 1935); Wilfred Eggleston, "The Old Homestead: Romance and Reality," in *The Settlement of the West*, ed. Howard Palmer (Calgary: Comprint, 1977), 114–29.

2   *Sixth Census of Canada 1921*, Vol. v, Agriculture (Ottawa: King's Printer, 1925), 168–69; *Census of Prairie Provinces 1926*, 711–12; *Seventh Census of Canada 1931*, Vol. viii, Agriculture (Ottawa: King's Printer, 1936), 672.

3   *Census of Prairie Provinces 1926*, 702.

4   *Census of Canada 1931*, 695.

5   *Census of Prairie Provinces 1926*, 711–12.

6   Ibid., 716.

7   Report and Papers on East Tilley Drought Area (Tilley East Commission), microfilm BR 1943, Glenbow Archives, Calgary, Alberta, including Report on Southern Alberta Drought Area by B. Russell and W. H. Snelson, 6. See "Tilley East Area Act," *Statutes of Alberta, 1927*, ch. 45. See also Appendix B, "Problems of a Retrograde Area in Alberta," in Mackintosh, *Economic Problems of the Prairie Provinces*, 291–94.

8   Tilley East Commission, 11, 17.

9   See Helen D. Howe (ed.), *Seventy-Five Years Along the Red Deer River* (Calgary: D. W. Friesen and Sons, 1971), 152–53; Pendant d'Oreille Lutheran Church Women, *Prairie Footprints* (Val Printing, 1970), 96; Shortgrass Historical Society, *Long Shadows* (Bow Island: Commentator Publishing Co., 1974), 33, 71, 191, 192; Sunshine Women's Institute History Committee, *The History of the Border Country of Coutts* (Lethbridge: Southern Printing Co., 1965), 74, 84; Bow Island Lion's Club Book Committee, *Silver Sage: Bow Island 1900–1920*, (1972), 301, 311, 461; Alberta, *Annual Report of the Department of Agriculture 1920*, 9, 35, 36 (hereafter cited as ARA); ARA 1921, 7; ARA 1922, 7.

10 Alberta, *Annual Report of the Department of Education 1922*, 58 (hereafter cited as *ARE*).

11 *ARE* 1922, 58.

12 *ARE* 1923, 72.

13 *ARE* 1921, 57; *ARE* 1922, 60. Re: speedier collection of school taxes, note the Parr district minutes of 7 October 1922, which instructed the secretary to "write to each of the rate payers in the Parr S.D. and request the rate-payer, should his taxes be in arrears, to pay his school taxes at least, in order to keep the school in operation." (Berry Creek School District, Box 9, folder 51, hereafter cited as *BCSD*, Glenbow Archives, Calgary, Alberta).

14 *BCSD*, Box 4, folder 15, Creole Belle School Board Minutes, 7 April 1919.

15 Ibid., 3 May 1919.

16 Ibid., 23 August 1919.

17 Ibid., 1 November 1919.

18 Ibid., 14 November 1919.

19 Ibid., Special Meeting, 26 November 1919.

20 Ibid., 8 December 1919.

21 Ibid., 29 May 1920.

22 Ibid., 1 May 1921.

23 *Silver Sage*, 175–76.

24 The 1921 provincial deficit of $14.6 million was the greatest deficit in the period 1913–37 (*Royal Commission on Dominion-Provincial Relations*, Province of Alberta, Comparative Statistics of Public Finance, Appendix J., 8). The outstanding debt in the province in 1921 was $96.1 million. In 1925 it was $116.1 million, highest of all provinces in the west and second only to Ontario in the country (M. C. Urquhart and K. A. H. Buckley. *Historical Statistics of Canada* [Toronto: Macmillan, 1965], 221). For a good study of Alberta finances in the period see "Financial Position of Alberta," in Stewart Bates, *Financial History of Canadian Governments* (Ottawa: 1939), 256–83.

25 *ARE* 1922, 60.

26 *ARE* 1923, 71.

27 Ibid.

28 *BCSD*, Box 4, folder 21, Dry Coulee School Board Minutes, 14 January 1926; *BCSD*, Box 3, folder 13, Connorsville School Board Minutes, 16 March 1921.

29 *BCSD*, Box 5, folder 22, Forcina School Board Minutes, 12 May 1920.

30 Ibid., 12 May 1920–25 June 1921.

31 Ibid., correspondence, Charlie McLay to L. A. Thurber, 27 January 1930.

32 *BCSD*, Box 1, folder 1, Arlington School Board Minutes, 20 January 1923.

33 *BCSD*, Box 2, folder 9, Brown School Board Minutes, 9 February 1923.

34 *BCSD*, Box 6, folder 30, Jennings School Board Minutes, 10 February 1919.

35 *BCSD*, Box 6, folder 33, Keystone School Board Correspondence, D. C. McEacherne to C. F. Patterson, 10 March 1925.

36 *BCSD*, Box 2, folder 7, Britannia School Board Correspondence, J. F. Boyce to L. E. Helmer, 26 December 1927.

37 See *Statutes of Alberta, 1922*, "An Act to Provide for the Recovery of Taxes 1922," ch. 25. See also Alberta, *Annual Report of the Department of Municipal Affairs*, 1922, 7.

38 *ARE* 1924, 57, 51; see also *ARE* 1923, 71.

39 *Alberta Gazette,* vol. 19, 31 May 1923, 668–71.

40 BCSD, Box 3, folder 10, Cessford School Board Minutes, 9 February 1923.

41 BCSD, Box 3, folder 13, Connorsville School Board Minutes, 14 January 1922.

42 BCSD, Box 1, folder 1, Arlington School Board Minutes, 24 February 1927.

43 Ibid., 13 January 1928.

44 Ibid., 13 February 1928.

45 Ibid., 14 January 1929.

46 BCSD, Box 3, folder 13, Connorsville School Board Minutes, 2 December 1922.

47 Ibid., 20 March 1923.

48 Ibid., 22 January 1927.

49 BCSD, Box 4; folder 13, Creole Belle School Board Minutes, 5 July 1919; see also Box 6, folder 27, Homestead Coulee School Board Minutes, 16 April 1928.

50 BCSD, Box 4, folder 17, Crocus Plains School Board Minutes, 7 October 1922.

51 ARE 1923, 72. See also ARE 1924, 79.

52 This is an important point deserving amplification. The noted American historian David Tyack has identified a movement to "take control of the rural common school away from the local community and turn it over to the professionals...." "The impetus to consolidate rural schools," he says, "almost always came from outside the rural community." *The One Best System* (Cambridge: Harvard University Press, 1974,) 25. A close look at the period in which the sixty-seven districts of Berry Creek came to consolidation suggests that the impetus often came from *within* the community, that Official Trustees tried again and again to regenerate the local school boards, and that by the time consolidation had come in 1933 the natives generally recognized that local school governance was, for reasons quite apart from official propaganda for large administrative units, simply impossible and against their best interests.

53 ARE 1923, 72; ARE 1924, 72.

54 ARE 1924, 81. See also Burnet, *Next Year Country,* ch. 7.

55 ARE 1921, 45.

56 Ibid., 38.

57 ARE 1922, 43–44.

58 Ibid., 43.

59 Ibid., 45.

60 Ibid., 44.

61 Ibid., 45.

62 ARE 1921, 93.

63 See ARE 1913, 56, 57; ARE 1914, 82; ARE 1916, 47, 56. See also G. V. Van Tausk, "Development of School Agriculture in Alberta," *The Agricultural Gazelle of Canada* 10 (March–April 1923): 145–47, hereafter TAG; Van Tausk, "High School Agriculture in Alberta," TAG 10 (September–October 1923): 453–54; "School Gardens: Alberta," TAG 3 (February 1916): 170–74.

64 See ARE 1915, 122; ARE 1916, 93; ARE 1917, 44; ARE 1918, 37.

65 Jim Devaleriola, Teacher Biography, June 1978, in author's possession. For similar results in Hanna Inspectorate, see ARE 1918, 47; and in Jenner Inspectorate see ARE 1919, 80.

66 ARE 1915, 133.

67 *School Buildings in Rural and Village School Districts*, Bulletin (Edmonton: King's Printer, 1916), 8.

68 *BCSD*, Box 8, folder 43, Lyman School Board Minutes, 25 September 1926.

69 Ibid., 4 February 1927; 29 March 1930.

70 *ARE* 1921, 28; *ARE* 1922, 30.

71 *ARA* 1921, 152.

72 Ibid., 161.

73 See for example W. Holdsworth to Secretary, Manyberries Agricultural Society, 23 March 1927, Box 29, 234; Holdsworth to D. W. Nattrass, 23 January 1930, Agricultural Societies of Alberta, 1887–1955, Glenbow Archives, Calgary, Alberta (hereafter cited as *ASA*). See C. W. Whitney to W. Holdsworth, 25 September 1927, indicating the windup of the Foremost Agricultural Society, *ASA*, Box 15, 118. See also P. W. Johnson, Secretary, Dept. of Agriculture, Report re Irvine Agricultural Society, 15 April 1930, *ASA*, Box 21, 171.

74 *ARA* 1922, 162.

75 E. E. Maxwell to Alex Galbraith, 4 July 1922, *ASA*, Box 48, 409.

76 See E. B. Swindlehurst, *Alberta's Schools of Agriculture, A Brief History* (Edmonton: Queen's Printer, 1964), 78–82.

77 *ARE* 1923, 52.

78 Ibid., 79.

79 See for example *ARA* 1921, 161; *ARE* 1924, 83.

80 *ARE* 1924, 84.

81 Ibid., 70.

82 *ARE* 1921, 67.

83 Ted Hellard, Teacher Biography, April 1978; Anne Gagnon, Teacher Biography, March 1978, in author's possession.

84 *BCSD*, Box 4, folder 15, Creole Belle School Board Minutes, 4 October 1919.

85 *BCSD*, Box 4, folder 17, Crocus Plains School Board Minutes, 12 January 1920.

86 Devaleriola, Teacher Biography.

87 Fran and Tom Cormack, Teacher Biography, June 1978, in author's possession.

88 Re: relief, see *Story of Rural Municipal Government in Alberta: 1909 to 1969*, nd., 82, *et passim*; *Silver Sage*, 302–11; *Statutes of Alberta, 1922*, "The Drought Relief Act," ch. 8.

89 Note also the much smaller Turner Valley consolidation.

3.   Institutional Adaptation to Drought and the
     Special Areas of Alberta, 1909–1939

Gregory P. Marchildon

INTRODUCTION

Geographically, the Special Areas refers to a large (currently 2.1 million hectares or 5.2 million acres), sparsely populated region of southeast Alberta. Bordered by the town of Drumheller in the west and the province of Saskatchewan in the east, the Special Areas has been governed and managed by a provincially-appointed Board since the 1930s in response to the exigencies of prolonged drought. Replacing municipal local government, the Special Areas Board not only manages land and water resources throughout the region but also roads, schools and other physical and social infrastructure. Although the Alberta government has periodically investigated the unique status of the Special Areas with a view to re-instituting local democratic control through municipal government, the Special Areas Board continues to administer the region on behalf of the provincial government.

The Special Areas constitute the majority of the region known by both historians and climatologists as the Alberta portion of the Dry Belt.[1] The Dry Belt is the most arid portion of the semi-arid Palliser Triangle, itself long known to be highly susceptible to "cyclical prolonged droughts, lasting many years."[2] As can be seen in Figure 3.2, the boundaries of the Palliser Triangle as drawn by Captain John Palliser do not correspond precisely to more contemporary conceptions of the Triangle. The area of the Palliser Triangle has been re-interpreted over time based on different variables including: the low amount of moisture gain through precipitation (rain and snowfall); the high amount of moisture loss through evapotranspiration; and a thin topsoil that is prone to drifting after extensive cultivation.[3] Lying in the rain shadow of the Rocky Mountains in the west and the Cypress Hills and the Sweet Grass Hills in the south, the Dry Belt receives less than 325 mm of annual precipitation, considerably lower than the Palliser average. The Belt also suffers higher moisture losses because of summer heat waves and winter Chinooks.[4] Approximately 80 percent of the Alberta Dry Belt has a thin, light brown soil cover. Because the organic content and the nitrogen content of the soil is low, it is highly susceptible to erosion in conditions of low moisture and high winds after the natural grass cover is broken.[5]

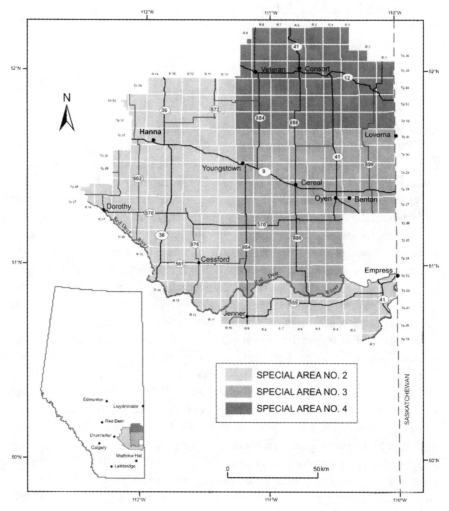

Figure 3.1. Special Areas of Alberta, 2006.

Despite the aridity and unsuitable nature of the soil of the Dry Belt in Alberta, it was nonetheless settled by grain farmers just before World War 1. After enjoying bumper crop years, these same settlers faced a series of successive droughts commencing in 1917. Over time, most left, eventually with the encouragement of the government of Alberta which concluded that settlement of the Dry Belt had been an enormous mistake. By the late 1920s, the Alberta government had begun experimenting with direct administration of the region through administrative boards in order to encourage further depopulation and to transform the abandoned farms into productive farming or livestock grazing adjuncts to surviving farms or ranches. These properties were either leased to ranchers or rancher-farmers at a low price or turned into community pastures that were available to all on the same terms and conditions. In this manner, farmers or ranchers could increase the size of their spread without taking on the risk of ownership.

This article begins with the agricultural settlement of the Dry Belt of southeast Alberta, and the impact of successive droughts on the region. This is followed by an examination of the government of Alberta's establishment of the administrative boards—eventually consolidated as a single Special Areas Board in the late 1930s—that would manage all the land, water and

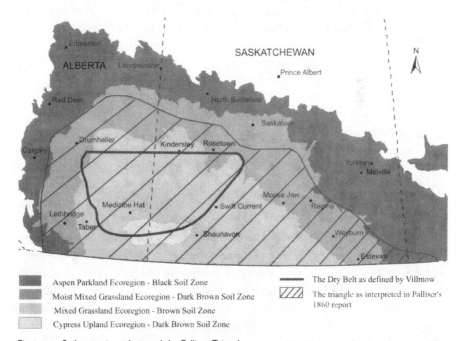

Figure 3.2. Soil zones in and around the Palliser Triangle.

infrastructure resources in the region. The article concludes with the impact of this institutional legacy on how the provincial governments of Alberta and Saskatchewan currently address the threat of drought and how they might address the threat of future prolonged droughts in the Dry Belt as a result of climate change.

AGRICULTURAL SETTLEMENT AND DROUGHTS IN THE SPECIAL AREAS

By the 1880s and 1890s, the large herds of buffalo that had once roamed southern Alberta and Saskatchewan had been killed off and the Aboriginal groups that had once lived on the buffalo faced starvation and marginalization as they were moved onto reserves.[6] By the early 1900s, ranchers had moved into the Dry Belt and were using much of the region for grazing. As a consequence of the bitterly cold and treacherous winter of 1906–07, however, these same ranchers saw at least half of their herds starve to death, and most were forced by bankruptcy to abandon their ranches in the area.[7]

With the Dry Belt largely swept clean of ranchers and cattle, the federal government in conjunction with the Canadian Pacific Railway and local real estate boosters unleashed an intensive publicity campaign to attract settlers into the region despite the fact that the region received less rainfall than other areas within the Palliser Triangle. In 1909, the Alberta Dry Belt was officially opened to homesteading. By 1910, farmers and their families were streaming into the region; by 1911, school districts had begun to be formed; by 1914, the municipalities and local improvement districts were established. From a population of less 800 people in 1906, the Alberta Dry Belt was supporting 24,000 inhabitants just ten years later. Almost all lived on newly-established farms with wheat as their principal crop.[8]

This new grain economy was propped up by temporarily inflated wheat prices induced by World War 1. Higher than average precipitation helped produce bumper crops in 1915 and 1916. However, this prosperity was brought to a sudden halt by successive droughts beginning in 1917 and continuing through to the abnormally wet year of 1927. After that short reprieve, the droughts came back with a vengeance during the 1930s.[9]

The Alberta Dry Belt would decline in population and its land tenure converted from pure wheat farming to larger livestock-grain operations, with far more emphasis on the livestock portion of the enterprise. As can be seen in Table 3.1, the Special Areas reached a peak of population in the 1921 census. By 1976, the rural population of the region was less than one quarter of what it had been in 1921. This depopulation was not simply the product of families abandoning their farms and moving to greener pastures on their own resources. It was also the product of a major institutional effort, spear-headed by the provincial government of Alberta, to depopulate its portion of the Dry Belt.

TABLE 3.1. RURAL AND URBAN POPULATION OF THE SPECIAL AREAS, 1916–76

Census Year	Rural	Urban	Total
1916	21,715	2,449	24,164
1921	26,031	3,658	29,689
1926	19,344	3,529	22,873
1931	20,320	3,754	24,074
1936	14,967	3,038	18,005
1941	11,794	3,325	15,119
1946	9,542	3,504	13,046
1951	8,430	4,076	12,506
1956	8,723	4,657	13,380
1961	8,799	5,256	14,055
1966	7,974	5,354	13,328
1971	7,050	5,250	12,300
1976	5,854	5,182	11,036

Source: L. S. Martin, "The Special Areas of Alberta: Origin and Development," report prepared for G. E. Taylor, Member of the Legislative Assembly of Alberta, July 1977, 49.

By the early 1920s, the new government formed by the United Farmers of Alberta (UFA) had concluded that the settlement of the Dry Belt had been an enormous mistake. Simply put, grain crops required more moisture than the natural grasses of the area, and this meant that ranching was inherently more suited to the region than farming.[10] The preamble of the 1938 legislation establishing the Special Areas commission and administration stated that the Dry Belt was simply incapable of supporting a viable crop economy.[11] At around the same time, a report to the provincial government on the Special Areas Act stated that the legislation was "designed" to "mend ... the mistakes of a land settlement policy which had placed thousands of settlers upon lands which were capable of sustaining only a small fraction of their number—the tragedy of Western Canada."[12] More than two decades later, in a 1961 review of the administration of the Special Areas, the view still held that the wheat economy of the region had been doomed from the beginning, and with it, a social and political infrastructure administered by local governments.[13] David C. Jones, the principal historian of the Dry Belt, wholeheartedly agrees with this view, arguing that recurring droughts from 1917 until the 1930s exposed the Dry Belt settlement as a "monumental blunder of western colonization."[14]

In 1921, the UFA government had been elected on the promise that it would address the drought catastrophe in southeast Alberta. In Jones' opinion, what to do with the Dry Belt "was perhaps the great single problem facing the United Farmer government in the twenties" and the problem "was constantly before the government until its defeat" by William Aberhart and the Social Credit Party in 1935.[15] Premier-elect Herbert W. Greenfield promised that his government would do everything possible to solve the problem, going so far as to say that should the southeast "fall" even after this, then his government was "prepared to fall with it."[16] In November 1921, the UFA government asked Charles Magrath, an entrepreneur and former mayor of Lethbridge, to do a study of the Alberta Dry Belt.[17]

To address the impact of successive droughts, the Magrath Commission recommended that the region be closed for further settlement and that Crown lands be expanded by taking over abandoned farms.[18] Since the Magrath report preceded the 1930 transfer of natural resources and Crown lands to the three prairie provinces, it called upon the federal government to conduct extensive soil and water surveys of the Dry Belt that would include recommendations on new weather recording stations as well as possible sites for irrigation projects and the "impoundment of water."[19] The Commission also urged the provincial government to provide loans to farmers with larger and more viable spreads so that they could purchase seed grain and horse feed in order to keep their farms going.

In response, the provincial government took two major steps. After brokering a deal with the federal government and the railways to each share one third of the cost with the province, the UFA government offered free transportation to destitute farmers to leave the drought-stricken region. Administered by the provincial government, the program paid for up to two railway cars per farm family to transport machinery, furniture and livestock. By 1926, 1851 farm families had taken advantage of the offer of free transportation.[20] Most moved north of Calgary or to the irrigated districts near Lethbridge.[21]

The second step was the Alberta government's introduction of the Drought Relief Act of 1922 (succeeded by the Debt Adjustment Act in 1923), which empowered a government commissioner to negotiate the settlement of debts, particularly land mortgages. After suffering five years of successive droughts, most farmers, school districts and municipalities in the region were unable to pay their respective debts. E. J. (Ted) Fream, the first secretary of the UFA, described by Jones as the "workhorse of the UFA government," was made Commissioner.[22] Fream's job was to travel throughout the Alberta Dry Belt negotiating settlements between debtors and creditors with a view to prolonging the life of at least some farms, schools and local governments. In the process, Fream came to know almost every aspect of the Dry Belt from the ranchers and farmers to the school teachers and local reeves.

THE EVOLUTION OF THE SPECIAL AREAS SOLUTION

Having Ted Fream working year after year to clear away a few bad debts only partially addressed the problems that were accumulating in the Alberta Dry Belt. By the mid-1920s, many were becoming impatient with what they viewed as a weak provincial response to the crisis, and the UFA government decided to try a new approach. In 1926, Fream was asked to head up a joint federal-provincial commission. The mandate of the Tilley East Commission was to study one of the hardest hit portions of the Dry Districts—the parched land between the Red Deer and Saskatchewan rivers, from the town of Tilley to the Saskatchewan border—and make recommendations on its future administration. Both governments were involved because the federal government, rather than the province, owned all Crown land within the province.[23]

The Tilley East Area may have been the hardest hit portion of what would eventually become known as the Special Areas but it also exemplified the problems affecting the entire Dry Belt. Settlers in the region had been encouraged by high wheat prices and bumper crops in World War I to buy more land and equipment on borrowed money. When the droughts came, farmers became increasingly insolvent but stubbornly continued to farm, hoping that each new season would bring rain and a bumper crop even as the mortgage companies and debt collectors closed in. By the early 1920s, however, it was too late for many farmers. No longer able to purchase seed grain or, in many cases, able to feed their families without relief, they began to abandon their farms and move away.

Covering 1.5 million acres, the Tilley East Area had lost approximately 80 percent of its inhabitants by 1926.[24] Average wheat yields had fallen like a stone after 1916, and some crop districts suffered complete crop failures that year and after.[25] Farms were being abandoned at a rate that threatened the viability of the remaining farms which were increasingly stranded and threatened by blowing topsoil from adjoining, untended fields.[26]

Although droughts were a recurring phenomenon directly east on the Saskatchewan side of the border, the droughts were far less severe than those on the Alberta side between 1917 and 1926. As a consequence, as can be seen in Table 3.2, vacant or abandoned farms in the Dry Belt region on the Saskatchewan side of the border covered only one-sixth the area of vacant or abandoned farms on the Alberta side of the border by 1926. The few farmers left in the Alberta Dry Belt were surrounded by almost 1.3 million acres of untended and drifting land. The extreme situation in Alberta goes far to explain the numerous provincial studies, commissions, laws and policies—all designed to address the drought catastrophe—compared to the relative lack of similar activity in Saskatchewan during the 1920s.

TABLE 3.2. VACANT OR ABANDONED FARMS IN THE ALBERTA AND SASKATCHEWAN DRY BELT BY CENSUS DIVISION, 1926

	Population	Vacant or abandoned farms (number)	Vacant or abandoned farms (acres)
Alberta Census Divisions 3 and 5	39, 365	5,124	1,287,594
Saskatchewan Census Division 8	44,667	916	212,091

Source: Derived from Tables 1, 3, 4 and 6 in David C. Jones, *Empire of Dust: Settling and Abandoning the Prairie Dry Belt* (Calgary: University of Calgary Press, 2002), 254–57.

Going further than the Magrath Commission five years earlier, the Fream Commission recommended that a single board manage all land and water resources throughout the Tilley East Area. Since the federal government still owned Crown land in the province, Fream envisaged a board established jointly by Ottawa and Edmonton. The whole idea was to encourage the continuing exodus of farmers while allowing the Crown to repossess vacant and abandoned land (through non-payment of back taxes) and then lease back some of this land to the few viable rancher-farmers left in Tilley East and create community pastures out of the rest.

In 1927, the provincial government passed a law putting the area under the stewardship of the Tilley East Board but without dissolving the existing municipalities, local improvement districts and school boards.[27] The new law was based upon three assumptions: 1) the "soil and climate" of the Tilley East Area was incapable of providing "human subsistence and economic security from ordinary farming based upon cereal production"; 2) further depopulation was required to ensure the "productivity" of those remaining; 3) the necessity of taking "lands out of private control" and publicly managing access to both land and water in a way to allow existing ranches and ranch farms to expand and thereby become more economically sustainable.²⁸

It took until July 1929 for the UFA government to actually establish the board. The delay appears to have been caused by the negotiations between the province and the federal government over the transfer of natural resources (including land) from the federal government to the province. Ultimately, the federal government decided that a federal-provincial board was unworkable and that it would be best for the province to operate on its own after it was clear that all Crown lands were about to be transferred to the province.²⁹ The UFA government appointed Ted Fream as Chair of the new three-member board.³⁰ Five months later, the UFA government signed the Natural Resources Transfer Agreement with the federal government, finally giving the government of Alberta, and by delegation Fream's new board, full jurisdiction over Crown land and water resources in Tilley East. This power was delegated, in full, to Fream's new board by virtue of the legislation establishing the Tilley East Area.³¹

Fream used the board's powers to bring vacant and abandoned lands under the control of the board. Since the property taxes on these lands were generally in arrears for years, the board initiated tax recovery proceedings in order to obtain default judgments through the courts and, ultimately, Crown ownership of the lands. Once under board control, these lands could then be used by the board in a way to shore up nearby ranches and farms through sale or, more commonly, lease, at very low prices. Some of the larger parcels of marginal land were transformed into community pastures so that a large number of ranchers or rancher-farmers in a given district would have access to additional grazing land for their livestock. The whole purpose was to encourage "the extension of ranching operations" or a "combination of ranching and farming rather than straight grain growing."³²

With the Tilley East experiment proving successful, the UFA government asked O. S. Longman to investigate the exodus of farmers from the Berry Creek Area northwest of the Tilley East Area. Longman recommended that Tilley East Area Board extend its control to the Berry Creek Area. "[I]t would appear desirable, if not essential, that all possible land within the area be brought under single control," Longman concluded, "to facilitate the organization and establishment of the farm-ranch unit."³³ In response to Longman's recommendations, the provincial government passed a law that put the Berry Creek Area under the administrative control of a single board composed of the same members as the Tilley East Board supplemented by an individual from the Berry Creek Area.³⁴

The Berry Creek Area administrative consolidation, however, went one major step further than Tilley East Area. Before consolidation, there were sixty-seven school districts in the Berry Creek Area south and east of Hanna.[35] Because of their destitution, municipalities voluntarily gave up their individual school boards in favour of a single large experimental school district under an official trustee. One municipal secretary summarized the dismal arithmetic: "No rain: No crop: No taxes: No school."[36] Initially, the provincial government had passed the Tax Recovery Act (1932) in an effort to facilitate recovery of unpaid taxes in part to allow municipalities to keep their schools open. Unfortunately, this also had the undesirable impact of bankrupting even more farmers and forcing them to abandon their lands, ultimately leaving municipalities in a worse position.[37] Something more radical was required if schools were to be kept open and teachers were to be paid.

The individual most responsible for the Berry Creek school consolidation—school inspector Lindsay Thurbus—would go on to manage similar school consolidations in the Acadia and Sullivan Lake school divisions that would become part of the Sounding Creek and Sullivan Lake Special Areas established in 1935. In effect, the large school districts—a response to the exigencies of drought in the Dry Belt—became the blueprint for education in postwar Alberta as fewer and larger farms as well as highly dispersed population became the norm for the rural regions outside the Dry Belt.[38]

Unfortunately for the UFA government, the droughts of the 1930s were not limited to the Tilley East and Berry Creek areas. With the entire Dry Belt suffering the impact of severe drought, the government was again pushed into a policy of encouraging the depopulation of the region and the province resurrected its program of free transportation for farm families and their machinery, livestock and personal effects. Between 1931 and 1935, almost 2,000 families moved out of the Alberta Dry Belt, the majority settling around Edmonton or in the Peace River country. In 1934, for example, 1,102 rail cars were paid for by government and the railway companies to relocate 601 farm families.[39] Ultimately, however, more than a program of organized depopulation was required to deal with the crisis.

In 1934, the provincial Minister of Agriculture appointed a committee of agricultural experts and farmers, again under the leadership of O. S. Longman, to recommend a policy solution for the entire drought area. The committee decided that the Tilley East and Berry Creek Area Act be amended to include other areas similarly deemed "unfit for agricultural purposes."[40] In 1935, the provincial government replaced the Tilley East and Berry Creek Area Act with the Special Municipal Areas Act, and brought in extensive new areas—Sounding Creek, Neutral Hills and Sullivan Lake—under the administration of the Special Municipal Areas Board as well as consolidated municipalities.[41] Two years later, the Bow West Special Area was added. This consolidation in effect created the boundaries of the original Special Areas, a region considerably larger than the current Special Areas.

In 1938, the provincial government took a further important step by eliminating all of the municipalities and improvement districts with the Special Areas. Before consolidation, there had been thirty-four separate governmental and administrative units managing some seven million acres.[42] The provincial government also established a new three-person Special Areas Board headquartered in Hanna to manage all land and water resources as well as roads, schools and other physical and social infrastructure throughout the Special Areas.[43] This Board, appointed by the provincial cabinet in Edmonton, was

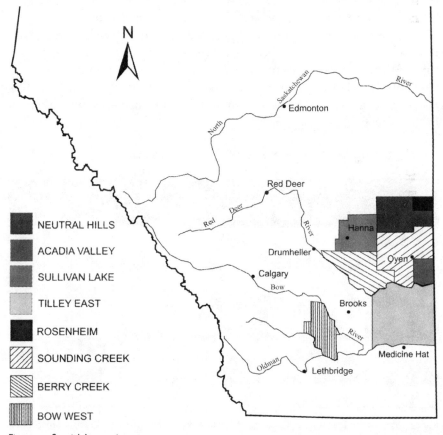

Figure 3.3. Special Areas, circa 1942.

conferred all the legal and administrative tools required to manage the Special Areas in the manner it deemed most efficient for the remaining residents.

ASSESSING INSTITUTIONAL ADAPTATION: THE
IMPACT AND SUCCESS OF THE SPECIAL AREAS

One of the main objectives of the Alberta government through its free transportation programs and the Special Areas form of administration was to reduce the population of the region while transforming land tenure—from small wheat farms to larger ranches and ranch-farms. In order to do this, private ownership was increasingly supplanted by Crown ownership under the control of the Special Areas Board. In effect, the Board offered an alternative to the risk of private ownership—and the debt that accompanied it. Access to land was increased through inexpensive Crown leases and community pastures. In 1938, for example, grazing lands were leased for 2.5¢ per acre while crop lands could be rented for a one-sixth share of the annual crop.[44]

As shown in Table 3.1, the rural population of the Special Areas, which reached a peak in the early 1920s, has been on a downward trajectory ever since. At the same time, the urban population has grown gradually since the late 1930s, indicating a small but viable service economy in the region. This decline in population is also reflected in the decline in the number of farms in the Special Areas (Table 3.3).

TABLE 3.3. FARM SIZE IN SPECIAL AREAS COMPARED TO THE PROVINCIAL AVERAGE, 1936–76

Census Year	Number of Farms	Special Areas Average Size (in acres)	Provincial Average Size (in acres)	Farm Size Ratio of Special Areas relative to Provincial Average
1936	4,319	697	404	1.7
1941	3,847	908	434	2.1
1946	3,449	1,188	464	2.6
1951	2,895	1,459	527	2.8
1956	2,384	2,074	579	3.6
1961	2,126	2,322	645	3.6
1966	1,927	2,631	706	3.7
1971	1,675	2,862	790	3.6
1976	1,556	3,085	864	3.6

Source: Derived from L. S. Martin, "The Special Areas of Alberta: Origin and Development," report prepared for G. E. Taylor, Member of the Legislative Assembly of Alberta, 59.

However, there is a legitimate question of whether both of these declines are simply part of a larger North American trend of depopulation and growing farm size throughout the Great Plains of North America.[45]

By 1936, farms in the Special Areas were already 1.7 times the size of the average Alberta farm, perhaps in part the product of the provincial government's active interventions beginning in 1921. The relative trend line is even more significant: Table 3.3 illustrates the fact that farm size in the Special Areas grew to 3.6 times the size of the average Alberta farm by 1956, a ratio that would remain stable for at least the next two decades. This means that, at least for the early history of the Special Areas, provincial policies seem to have had a substantial impact on increasing the size of farms in the region *relative* to the rest of Alberta even in an environment where rural population was decreasing and farm size was increasing as a general rule throughout the Great Plains of North America.

The fact that a Special Areas Board, rather than individual municipalities, continues to manage a huge expanse of southeast Alberta also speaks to the political success of the Special Areas. Despite the fact that there is, in effect, only limited democratic representation at the local level—an anomaly in terms of all other provinces in Canada—there has been limited political opposition to the continuation of the Special Areas administration.[46] This is no small feat given the fact that the Board has had, and continues to have, more decision-making authority than any elected municipal government and elected school board combined.

This anomaly continues even though the unique governance model of the Special Areas has been examined periodically by the provincial government. These re-examinations were triggered, in large part, because the interwar crisis caused by successive, severe droughts did not repeat itself in the postwar era. While droughts have occurred in the Alberta Dry Belt since the 1930s, the region has not experienced the magnitude of almost continuous drought exposure suffered between 1917 and 1939. As a consequence, it is less than surprising that the idea of disbanding the Special Area Board and reintroducing local government was raised on occasion. The first reappraisal occurred in 1953. Appointed by the Minister of Municipal Affairs, the three person committee chaired by O. S. Longman, by this time the provincial deputy minister of agriculture, concluded that while the Special Areas had made a dramatic recovery in economic terms, "the hazardous nature of the region and the possible recurrence of prolonged drouth" required the extraordinary administration of the Special Area Board.[47]

In 1960, Ernest Manning's government appointed a three-person Commission, chaired by W. R. Hanson, to determine whether: 1) the climatic and soil conditions that had led to the establishment of the Special Areas were "still sufficient to warrant the continuance" of the administration; 2) "the agricultural conditions in the Special Areas are of a sufficiently different character in comparison to other areas of the Province to warrant the special type of administration now in force in this area;" and 3) the unique conditions continue to warrant comparatively low rental rates and tax rates (subsidized by all Alberta taxpayers) for grazing leases and community pastures in the Special Areas.[48]

After numerous field trips as well as public hearings at the towns of Consort, Hanna, Oyen and Buffalo, the Hanson Commission came to the conclusion that, irrespective of improved change in circumstances, all of the verbal and written briefs and submissions "supported the continuation of the government by the Board as set up under the Special Areas Act." As the committee report noted: "[n]ever have members of the Committee found a people so unanimous in their approval of a form of local government, especially one in which all power is centralized in a Minister of the Crown with local self-government lacking." This view supported the Committee in its recommendation that, as an instrument, the Special Areas Act and Board were "well conceived to accomplish the job at hand" and the "administration has generally been well carried out."[49]

Despite this, the Hanson Committee still found it difficult to justify the lack of local self-government and the permanent continuation of the Special Areas Board. Concluding that the rehabilitation of the Dry Districts had been largely completed, the Committee argued for the restoration of local self-government and the disbanding of the Special Areas Board over a transition period of 10 years.[50] The recommendation was not implemented by the Manning government nor accepted by succeeding Alberta governments, perhaps because of the popularity of the Board among the remaining farmers and ranchers in the Special Areas.

THE POLICY LEGACY OF THE SPECIAL AREAS
AND FUTURE ADAPTATION TO CLIMATE CHANGE

What is the policy legacy of the Special Areas in the context of climate change as currently understood by a majority of scientists? There are a number of lessons that can be drawn from the historical experience of the Alberta Dry Belt. In terms of institutional adaptation, the creation of the Special Areas Board (and its predecessors) was a direct response to the inadequacy of local government. The municipalities and local improvement districts were simply too small and too bereft of social and physical capital to cope with the crushing impact of prolonged drought. Originally designed to serve a settlement pattern of one-quarter- to one-half-section (160–320 acre) grain farms, these local governments simply could not adjust to wholesale farm abandonment and the inability of most remaining farmers to pay property and education taxes because of successive crop failures. Little wonder that relief for the worst-off farm families and town residents, originally a municipal responsibility, had to be administered by the province and the federal government from the beginning of the crisis in the Alberta Dry Belt and in both Alberta and Saskatchewan during the drought and depression of the 1930s.

In contrast, the Special Areas Board had the size and the expertise to facilitate adaptation to drought. The Board (and its predecessors) rehabilitated abandoned land by planting crested wheat grass to stop soil drifting. It built and maintained the main roads while abandoning roads in the most sparsely populated parts of the Special Areas. It managed an enormous school district in which it could build a critical mass in terms of teachers and students to continue educating the children of dispersed farm-ranch families. It managed land resources in the most economic manner possible, ensuring that farmer-ranchers could obtain access to additional grazing land inexpensively and in as risk-free a manner as possible through the renting out of Crown land at low rates and through extensive community pastures. Indeed, the Special Areas Board and its predecessors in Tilley East and Berry Creek built up enough expertise that the provincial government felt free enough to reject the federal government offer to set up community pastures in Alberta through the Prairie Farm Rehabilitation Administration (PFRA) during the late 1930s.[51] The Board could also manage, even redirect, scarce water resources to best serve the farmer-ranchers in the region. This is a job it continues to do: in 2005, for example, the Special Areas Board launched a major study of a water diversion project on the Red Deer River which it perceived as a "long-term solution to recurring droughts in the Special Areas."[52]

Beyond adaptation, the Special Areas Board also reduced physical exposure to drought by converting land tenure from small wheat farms to large ranch-farm operations in which livestock—cattle and sheep—were central to the livelihood of those who remained. This required an active policy of encouraging depopulation, a policy initiated by the provincial government but eventually turned over to administrative boards in the Special Areas.

Historically, the Alberta Dry Belt experience contrasts sharply with that in the Saskatchewan Dry Belt. Because early exposure to drought was not nearly as severe in southwest Saskatchewan relative to southeast Alberta, the Saskatchewan government did not dismantle its local governments in favour of a centrally controlled administration. Nor did it actively encourage depopulation and a radical change in land use. As a consequence, when the more extensive droughts of the 1930s struck, no longer limited to a part of the Dry Belt and instead covering most of the Palliser Triangle, Saskatchewan wheat farmers in the Dry Belt were hardest hit. As a consequence, the Saskatchewan government—assisted substantially by the federal government— spent much more on relief than the Alberta government in a desperate effort to prevent starvation in the drought-stricken rural areas during the 1930s. The more senior governments were forced to act because of the inability of municipal governments to provide relief much less initiate any proactive efforts at rehabilitation.[53]

While land rehabilitation and water conservation eventually became the purview of the federal government, through the PFRA, in Saskatchewan, the provincial government did facilitate the northward exodus of those farmers completely broken by drought in the south. Unlike Alberta, however, there was no similar effort to convert small grain farms into large ranch-farm operations through the direct control and management of land resources. The municipalities continued to regulate (to a very limited extent) land resources, the majority of land remained in private ownership and grain farming continued in the Dry Belt of southwest Saskatchewan during and after the continuous droughts of the 1930s.

If climate change produces more severe and more prolonged droughts in the future than those suffered in the 1920s and 1930s, Alberta is currently better prepared than Saskatchewan to adapt. The historic experience of the Alberta Dry Belt has conditioned the provincial residents for a more interventionist approach by the Alberta government to deal with the crisis. Although the PFRA helped immensely in the rehabilitation of the Saskatchewan Dry Belt by the late 1930s (and continues to provide expertise and maintain infrastructure which ensures that farmers in southwest Saskatchewan are not as vulnerable as they would be in its absence), the fact remains that the rural municipalities are too small and too poorly resourced to deal with prolonged drought crises. In contrast, coping with and adapting to drought is the primary responsibility of the Special Areas Board in Alberta. As a special-built institution, it is in a much better position to help the communities and rancher-farmers of the Albert Dry Belt to deal with an extended drought than the many rural and urban municipalities in the Saskatchewan Dry Belt.

NOTES

This article first appeared in *Prairie Forum* 32, no. 2 (2007): 251–272.

1   D. C. Jones and R. C. Macleod, *We'll All Be Buried Down Here: The Prairie Dryland Disaster, 1917–1926* (Calgary: Alberta Records Publication Board, 1986). J. R. Villmow, "The Nature and Origin of the Canadian Dry Belt," in J.G. Nelson, M.J. Chambers and R.E. Chambers (eds.), *Weather and Climate* (Toronto: Methuen, 1970), 51–74. According to Villmow (52), the phrase "Dry Belt" can be traced to a 1938 article written by climatologist A. J. Connor who identified the boundaries of the Dry Belt and pointed out the reasons for its increased exposure to drought relative to the rest of the Palliser Triangle: see A. J. Connor, "The Climates of North America: Canada," in W. Köppen and R. Geiger (eds.), *Handbuch der Klimatologie, Bd. II* (Berlin, 1938), 359–64.

2   G. T. Davidson, "An Interdisciplinary Approach to the Role of Climate in the History of the Prairies," in R. Wardhaugh (ed.), *Toward Defining the Prairies: Region, Culture, and History* (Winnipeg: University of Manitoba Press, 2001), 102. For Captain John Palliser's own observations, see I. M. Spry, *The Papers of the Palliser Expedition, 1857–1860* (Toronto: Champlain Society, 1968). As Davidson (109) points out, Palliser traveled through the region during a drought that lasted from 1840 until 1865, a more severe drought than any experienced in the twentieth century, including the droughts of the 1920s and 1930s.

3   On the shifting boundaries of the Palliser Triangle, see L. Dale-Burnett, "Agricultural Change and Farmer Adaptation in the Palliser Triangle, Saskatchewan, 1900–1960" (PhD dissertation, University of Regina, 2002).

4   Prairie Farm Rehabilitation Administration, *Drought in the Palliser Triangle: A Provisional Primer* (Ottawa: Agriculture and Agri-Food Canada, 1998), 2.

5   L. S. Martin, "The Special Areas of Alberta: Origin and Development," report prepared for G. E. Taylor, Member of the Legislative Assembly of Alberta, 1977, 2–3.

6   D. Owram, *Promise of Eden: The Canadian Expansionist Movement and the Idea of the West, 1856–1900* (Toronto: University of Toronto Press, 1980). S. Carter, *Aboriginal People and the Colonizers of Western Canada to 1900* (Toronto: University of Toronto Press, 1999). J. R. Miller, *Skyscrapers Hide the Heavens: A History of Indian-White Relations in Canada* (Toronto: University of Toronto Press, 2000). O. P. Dickason, *Canada's First Nations: A History of Founding Peoples from Earliest Times* (Toronto: Oxford University Press, 2001).

7   D. C. Jones, *Empire of Dust: Settling and Abandoning the Prairie Dry Belt* (Calgary: University of Calgary Press, 2002), 9, 46–47. Glenbow Alberta Archives (hereafter GAA), M4454, a Glenbow Foundation Project, an historical survey of the Special Areas of Alberta by U. D. MacLean, 4 December 1959 (hereafter referred to as Glenbow History of Special Areas), 4–19. On the shifting ranching frontier, see D. H. Breen, *The Canadian Prairie West and the Ranching Frontier, 1874–1924* (Toronto: University of Toronto Press, 1983). S. M. Evans, "American Cattlemen on the Canadian Range, 1874–1914," *Prairie Forum* 4, no. 1 (1979): 121–35.

8   Jones, *Empire of Dust*, 21–24.

9   G. P. Marchildon, S. Kulshreshtha, E. E. Wheaton and D. Sauchyn, "Drought, Demographic Migration and Institutional Adaptation in Alberta and Saskatchewan, 1914–1939," IACC Project Draft Working Paper, 2006.

10   On 18 July 1921, the UFA government was elected with thirty-eight members compared to fifteen Liberals and eight independent and Labour Party members. On the rise of the UFA and their agricultural platform in the 1921 election, see B. J. Rennie, *The Rise of Agrarian Democracy: The United Farmers and Farm Women of Alberta, 1909–1921* (Toronto: University of Toronto Press, 1977).

11   "Whereas certain areas of the Province include a considerable amount of land which by reason of insufficient rainfall, inferior quality of soil and other causes, cannot by the use of ordinary methods of agriculture be made to yield over a period of years produce in sufficient amount to provide the persons farming such land with the means of livelihood..." Preamble quoted in R. S. Rust, "An Analysis and Evaluation of Land Use in the Special Areas of Alberta" (M.A. thesis, University of Alberta, 1956), 26.

12   Public Archives of Alberta (hereafter PAA), Department of Public Welfare fonds, 73.307, Box 7, Appendix on the History of the Special Areas (hereafter referred to as Appendix), 23.

13   PAA, 711456, Government of Alberta, Report of the Special Areas Investigation Committee [Chair, Wallace R. Hanson], January 1961, 4.

14   D. C. Jones in Jones and Macleod, *We'll All Be Buried Down Here*, xxix.

15   D. C. Jones, "A Strange Heartland: The Alberta Dry Belt and the Schools in the Depression," in D. Francis and H. Ganzevoort (eds.), *The Dirty Thirties in Prairie Canada* (Vancouver: Tantalus, 1980), 102.

16   D. C. Jones, "Herbert W. Greenfield," in B. J. Rennie (ed.), *Alberta Premiers of the Twentieth Century* (Regina: Canadian Plains Research Center, 2004), 61–62.

17   Jones, *Empire of Dust*, 120.

18   Given the dispossession of reserve lands throughout the prairie provinces in the decade following World War I, it is interesting to note recommendation number 7 of the Magrath Commission: "That the Dominion Government should be requested by the Alberta Government to arrange through it that such grazing as is available on Indian Reserves should be made available for 'community pastures' by farmers in adjacent areas." PAA, 73.307, Box 7, Appendix, 15.

19   PAA, Department of Public Welfare fonds, 73.307, Box 7, Appendix, 16.

20   Government of Alberta, *Department of Agriculture Annual Report, 1926* (Edmonton: Department of Agriculture, 1927), 14.

21   Government of Alberta, *Department of Agriculture Annual Reports, 1922–26* (Edmonton: Department of Agriculture, 1923–27).

22   Jones, *Empire of Dust*, 167.

23   E. W. Stapleford, *Report on Rural Relief due to Drought Conditions and Crop Failures in Western Canada, 1930–1937* (Ottawa: Minister of Agriculture, 1939), 77.

24   Estimate provided in Jones, *Empire of Dust*, 212.

25   On Alberta Dry Belt wheat yields from 1912 until 1921, see Table 11 in Jones, *Empire of Dust*, 265.

26 GAA, Glenbow History of Special Areas. According to this manuscript history, the Tilley East Area was the first of the Special Areas to suffer severely from drought (p. 47).

27 An Act respecting the Tilley East Area, S.A., c. 45, 1927.

28 PAA, Department of Public Welfare fonds, 73.307, box 5, Appendix, 23.

29 Stapleford, *Report on Rural Relief*, 77.

30 The other two members were A. Buckham of the Department of Muncipal Affairs, and John Barnes, a farmer from Bindloss. The work of the board was so extensive that the part-time members, including Fream, were replaced by full-time members-employees in April 1931. PAA, Department of Public Welfare fonds, 73.307, box 5, Appendix, 25–26.

31 On the signing and implementation of the Natural Resources Transfer Agreement and what it meant to the UFA government, see Franklin L. Foster, "John E. Brownlee," Rennie (ed.), *Alberta Premiers of the Twentieth Century*, 89–92.

32 Stapleford, *Report on Rural Relief*, 77.

33 O. S. Longman quoted in GAA, Glenbow History of Special Areas, M4454, 54.

34 An Act respecting the Berry Creek Area, S.A. c. 55, 1932. PAA, Department of Public Welfare fonds, 73.307, box 5, Appendix, 27. In 1934, the two Areas were consolidated into a single Area: An Act to amend and consolidate an Act respecting The Tilley East Area and The Berry Creek Area Act, S.A. c. 61, 1934.

35 Jones and Macleod, *We'll All Be Buried Down Here*, xliv.

36 D. C. Jones, "A Strange Heartland," in Francis and Ganzevoort (eds.), *The Dirty Thirties in Prairie Canada*, 93.

37 Jones and Macleod, *We'll All Be Buried Down Here*, xlvi–xlvii.

38 D. C. Jones, "Schools and Social Disintegration in the Alberta Dry Belt of the Twenties," *Prairie Forum* 3 (1978): 1–9.

39 Government of Alberta, *Department of Agriculture Annual Reports, 1931–36* (Edmonton: Department of Agriculture, 1932–37).

40 Stapleford, *Report on Rural Relief*, 79.

41 An Act respecting the Special Municipal Areas, c. 69, 1935. PAA, Department of Public Welfare fonds, 73.307, box 5, 29.

42 PAA, Department of Public Welfare fonds, 73.307, 67, brief report on work in Special Areas, date unknown. Jack Gorman, *A Land Reclaimed: The Story of Alberta's Special Areas* (Hanna, AB: Special Areas Board, 1988), 131.

43 An Act to Amend and Consolidate the Special Areas Act, S.A. c. 92, 1938.

44 Stapleford, *Report on Rural Relief*, 81.

45 M. Fulton, R. Olfert and M. Partridge, *Population Growth—Double or Nothing? Preparing for Saskatchewan's Next 100 Years* (Saskatoon: Canada Rural Economy Research Lab, Policy Brief, September 2005).

46 Advisory members to the Special Areas Board are elected. The Board Chair is appointed by the provincial government and reports to the Minister of Municipal Affairs. The Special Areas Board's approximately two hundred workers are employees of the Department of Municipal Affairs.

47 Government of Alberta, "A Preliminary Report on the Special Areas of Alberta," report submitted to C. E. Gerhart, Minister of Municipal Affairs, Government of Alberta, 4 November 1953.

48 Excerpt from order-in-council 1376/60, Government of Alberta, 13 September 1960, in PAA, Government of Alberta, Report of the Special Areas Investigation Commission, January 1961.

49 PAA, Government of Alberta, Report of the Special Areas Investigation Committee, January 1961, 21.

50 Ibid., 24.

51 G. P. Marchildon, "The Origins of the Prairie Farm Rehabilitation Administration," IACC Project Discussion Paper, draft, 2006.

52 Special Areas Board, *Special Areas Water Supply Project: Public Consultation Results—Summary, May to July 2005.* Hanna: Equus Consulting Group on behalf of the Special Areas Board, 2005.

53 B. Neatby, "The Saskatchewan Relief Commission, 1931–1934," *Saskatchewan History* 3, no. 2 (1950): 41–56. G. P. Marchildon and D. Black, "Henry Black, the Conservative Party and the Politics of Relief," *Saskatchewan History* 58, no. 1 (2006): 4–17.

4. History, Public Memory, and the Land
   Abandonment Crisis of the 1920s

Curt McManus

Thirty miles west-northwest of Maple Creek, there lies an enormous expanse of empty grassland. At first sight it is not exceptionally different from any other region in Saskatchewan: rolling plains and wild prairie are criss-crossed with interlocking grid roads. But here, in the middle of this quiet, arid, desert-like region, there stands an unassuming, forlorn relic of the past which hints at something untoward that happened on these heat-ravaged plains. The slightly crumbling remnants of a concrete bank vault stand just beside a conspicuously quiet and underused grid road. The first thought which springs to mind upon seeing this wreckage of the past is that it has absolutely no business being there, for there is no indication of human life for miles around. Further considerations, however, reveal a secondary depth to this sad, unintended monument; it represents, in the plainest fashion possible, one of the great tragedies which accompanied the settlement of western Canada.

The bank vault itself is all that remains of the tiny community of Tunstall. All around the vault is nothingness, a void: wild grass, unbroken prairie, and heat. It was a different matter, though, one hundred years ago. The vault, at that time, was lodged in a building which sat in the hamlet of Tunstall, located just a few miles up the road from the thriving town of Hatton, of which absolutely nothing remains. These two communities were, a century ago, located at the very centre of one of the largest movements of humanity the world had ever seen. But today, all that remains is the absurd bank vault.

The obvious question which naturally presents itself to the visitor to this area is the same one which might arise when coming across, say, a ghost town, or perhaps a sunken ship: What happened? In a word, the answer is abandonment. Starting as a trickle and ending as a flood, hundreds and then thousands of settlers fled this region between 1908 and 1939, as drought and then crop failure and bankruptcy took hold of their daily lives. The key part of the answer is "when" the abandonment occurred. For in considering that simplest of questions, new perspectives open up which call into question a number of assumptions which have underpinned much thought about the history of those settlement years.

Much of the abandonment of southwest and west-central Saskatchewan occurred during what is popularly known as the "Roaring Twenties." Whilst prosperity smiled gently on much of Canada, those who lived and farmed in the drylands had a somewhat different experience between 1917 and 1927. Settlers in the Mantario district some miles north of Tunstall, for example, found themselves, early on in the 1920s, eking out a precarious existence on the sharp edge of destitution, a life quite different from the promise of plenty which had lured them to western Canada. Unless something could be done to help, argued J. Evans Sargeant, the Secretary Treasurer of the rural munici- pality (RM), "some 1,500 people ... are faced with the prospect of starvation this winter."[1] The alarm Sargeant sounded occurred after what he called "the most complete crop failure that has been known" hit the district in 1921. The 1920s roared, certainly—just not in the drylands.

Drifting soil on homestead near Cadillac, in the southwest corner of Saskatchewan (Courtesy of the Provincial Archives of Saskatchewan / R-A16398-1).

The legendary crisis of farm abandonment in the 1930s is permanently etched into the collective consciousness of Saskatchewan. Rural Saskatchewan families grew up on tales of what it was like during those terrible years; it forms a basic part of the prairie mind. But consider that the worst of the drought which drove thousands from the land was largely limited to the southwest and west-central areas of the province; there were no dust-bowls in the Tisdale district, or in the parkland area of the province. The distinct regional flavour of the 1930s, then, raises some interesting implications.

Land abandonment in the dry areas was a staple feature of life, a consistent thread in the history of the region which seems to automatically deflate the exceptional nature of the 1930s. Rather than being a sudden and surprising aberration which caught thousands of settlers unaware, the Dirty Thirties was actually the final act in a three-act tragedy which started almost as soon as the region was opened up to settlement in 1908.

As matters stood in 1908, much of the land which lay between Calgary and Moose Jaw south of North Battleford was, for the most part, empty. A few frontier outposts like Maple Creek gave the region some semblance of civility, which hinted at the prosperous and energetic cattle industry which had thrived in the area for several decades. Cattle ranchers at the turn of the previous century had what amounted to almost exclusive rights to this region because it had long been widely assumed that the area was unsuited to agricultural pursuits.[2] The now famous phrase of Captain John Palliser contained, for the cattle ranchers at least, a modicum of truth: "this land is unfit for human habitation." This idea of Palliser's, first voiced after his journey through what was then the interior of British North America in the late 1850s, became the basic assumption for those who were charged with creating and developing Dominion lands policy during the settlement years.

The man who managed and directed the Dominion Government's land policy between 1896 and 1905 was Clifford Sifton. He was the architect of those policies which courted the cattle rancher, and he consciously avoided populating the region with "moss-backs" or "sod-busters," pejorative terms applied to settlers by the region's cattle ranching majority.[3] As long as Sifton exercised control over the Department of the Interior, settlers were not permitted in the drylands in any meaningful numbers. All of that changed quite abruptly in 1908.

Sifton's thoughtful and considered policy of caution was cast aside by the "cantankerous [and] rough hewn" Frank Oliver.[4] Oliver assumed control of the Department of the Interior in 1905, replacing the highly efficient and practical Sifton, and it fell to Oliver to be the man who would undo some

forty years of policy and conventional wisdom regarding the benefits of settling the drylands.

There were a number of reasons why Oliver wanted to jettison his predecessor's cautious approach to land policy. For starters, Oliver assumed control
of the Department at that moment in history when the image of the farmer
had assumed almost super-human qualities: Oliver and his contemporaries
viewed the settler/farmer as an almost separate being who, through dint
of his honest labour, somehow embodied man's essential goodness. Oliver
saw it as almost morally offensive that Sifton had in effect signed over some
twenty-eight million acres of land to the money-grubbing cattle rancher.
Historian Lewis Thomas explains that the settler "appealed to a morality
much more in step with the buoyant enthusiasm of nation building."[5] So, the
rancher became an easy and obvious target whose concerns could be brushed
aside. It likewise did not help the cattle-rancher cause that for decades they
had collectively maintained strong and amicable ties with the Conservative
party, a circumstance which no doubt rankled the delicate sensibilities of
Oliver, a lifelong Liberal.

In addition to the rose-colored notions Oliver held for the settler and his
role in nation building, the Dominion lands boss also faced the apparently
objective reality that settlement had, for all intents and purposes, drawn to a
close by 1905. Oliver's predecessor, Clifford Sifton, had succeeded beyond all
expectations in settling the west: the way it stood in 1905, there appeared to
be no land left. Settlement seemed to have run its course, or so the thinking
went.[6] When Oliver looked out from the insular yet commanding heights
of Ottawa, his eyes were drawn to the millions of acres of flat treeless land
sitting vacant and empty with the exception of the cattle ranchers, of course.
Making his own mark on history, Oliver promptly drew up a plan for setting
aside some forty years of conventional wisdom and public policy, and threw
open the drylands for settlement.

The way in which Oliver opened the drylands was deceptively simple.
A small bill was tabled in the House of Commons in 1908 which amended
the Dominion Lands Act, a many-headed monster which governed the use
and distribution of all Crown lands between 1870 and 1930. Oliver created
that now-famous formula for settlement: the free 160-acre homestead and
the "pre-emption." After paying a nominal $10 fee, settlers would select a
quarter-section of land, on which they and their families were expected to live
for six months in each of six years. At the end of this period, settlers could
"pre-empt" or have first-right-of-purchase on an adjoining quarter-section
or one located nearby.

The act, amended with all ease and dispatch, even included a provision aimed at satisfying the concerns of those who felt the area would sustain neither agriculture nor human life. The settlers would employ the new "summerfallow" method of farming, a technique in which half the land would be tilled while the other half would lie dormant or "fallow" for one season. Oliver reasoned that "if a man can only farm one half of his land, then he must have twice as much land."[7] Thus, fears over the possibility of maintaining a life in the drylands were allayed by faith in scientific farming.

What Oliver may not have known is that the same kind of "faith" had been embraced in the United States some years earlier. Right around the time Oliver was busy amending the Dominion Lands Act, state legislators in Nebraska were tinkering with the Kincaid Act. This act expanded the standard half-section settlement allotment to a full section because, despite the most intelligent methods of farming, Nebraska legislators discovered that no one was able to maintain a decent life on a half-section of land.[8]

Even though faraway clouds of doubt and fear accompanied the amendment, Oliver was insistent on the passage of the bill. The tremendous power Oliver wielded was a point not lost on his fellow parliamentarians: he was accused of being an "absentee landlord [with] practically despotic powers."[9] North York member of Parliament George Foster considered Oliver's power over timber, mineral, mining and grazing rights in addition to agriculture, and concluded that he was in fact "the boss of all of us."[10] Flattering though such comments must have been to Oliver's no doubt substantial ego, he insisted that "we are not closing anything to settlement."[11] And so it was.

The effects of the amendment were immediate and quite astounding, and indeed comparable to the wonders worked by Oliver's predecessor Clifford Sifton. It requires no little effort to imagine the effects of that simple amendment. As R. J. Thompson of Alsask puts it, "virtually every quarter or half section was taken up and homestead shacks sprouted like grain on the prairies."[12]

Dominion Lands offices, where settlers initially staked their land claims, were swamped by this sudden onrush of humanity. The harried and overworked land agent James Rutherford claimed that the year 1908 was "the most successful ever experienced" in the history of settlement[13]: he processed some 8,710 land applications (approximating some 20,000 people) that year. By comparison, the land office in North Battleford processed just 3,385.[14] In 1909, at the end of the first full year, 41,568 people filed claims in the preemption area, as it was known.[15] In 1907, prior to the amendment, there were only some 1,600 farms in the entire region; in 1909, there were over 6,000.[16] Total cultivated acreage increased from 106,000 in 1907 to 516,377 in 1908.

It was more than anyone could have hoped for; optimism reigned, and the naysayers who felt the area was unsuited to agriculture were, temporarily at any rate, proven wrong. The revenues for the Department of the Interior positively swelled with cash generated by the amendment. Interior Deputy W. W. Cory noted that these revenues had been pushed to $3.2 million, which was "the largest in the history of the department."[17] If initial and immediate results meant anything, Oliver's decision was wise and good; but, as Canada's first Prime Minister, Sir John A. Macdonald, was fond of saying, "the long game is the true one," and it did not take long at all for the shine of success to start rubbing off.

The years between 1908 and 1917 were uneven at best, and unevenness in the drylands could and usually did mean land abandonment. The climate showed beguiling promise one year, and in the next would lay waste all human endeavour. In 1909, for example, farmers in the drylands posted the highest yields in Saskatchewan, averaging 28 bushels per acre.[18] In 1910, the average yield was 7 bushels per acre in the RMs which made up the drylands.[19] The years between 1911 and 1913 demonstrated an average, mediocre stability with yields of twenty bushels per acre. It took the crop disaster of 1914 to destroy many of the illusions cherished by those who felt honest labour and intelligent farming methods could overcome any obstacle.

Deputy Agriculture Minister A. F. Mantle was forced to concede the point in 1914: total failure was achieved when the average wheat yields in the drylands bottomed out to two bushels per acre.[20] Of the 74 million bushels of wheat produced in the province that year, just 857,000 came from the area south and west of Swift Current.[21]

The problems posed by this failure were obvious. It seemed as though those problems revolved around the unstated and unappetizing question, "How can settlement be undone?" By the time of the 1914 failure, dozens of RMs had been established in the drylands; communities like Hatton were well on their way to maturity; and local improvements had been undertaken, elevators constructed, and rail line laid. As the point of no return had long since been passed, the government was left with only one option: step in and participate in the rescue of settlers in the drylands in order to prevent depopulation. There was no other answer.

The government immediately moved to staunch the threatened exodus out of the drylands by suspending homestead cancellations. Settlers were not allowed to cancel their claims during 1914–15: this was almost certainly a hardship in a region where cancellation claims, first and always, exceeded those of other regions in the province. In 1913 for example, 2,039 people filed homestead claims at the Swift Current office and 1,468 filed cancellations. Here one almost automatically conjures images of wide-eyed greenhorns flooding onto the deserts of the south whilst the worn-out veterans file past in the opposite direction in a blank stupor. Land agent Frank Forster viewed this early exodus as "a process of elimination": in Darwinian terms, it was the "survival of the fittest."[22] But the measure to suspend cancellations demonstrates the crucial point that both levels of government knew that the penalty for inaction was abandonment; if they did not move to stop the outflow of settlers, already at unacceptable levels, all of the work that had gone into settling the "Last Best West" would be undone.

In addition, then, to suspending cancellations, relief depots were established at key points throughout the region. These depots, located at Swift Current, Maple Creek, Lethbridge and Medicine Hat, provided fodder, flour and coal for stricken settlers.[23] This, the government noted, was to ensure that "there will be no hardship or suffering and no sacrificing of stock or implements necessary for work on next year's crop." The government understood that with no money, settlers' thoughts would quite naturally turn to selling stock and implements in order to survive. Subsidized train tickets were also provided to the men, which allowed them to get to work on threshing crews around the province at a reduced rate. The government went so far as to pledge it would purchase all horses necessary for the Royal North West Mounted Police only from stock growers in the drought-stricken area.[24] "This prompt action," the government assured, "successfully met a serious situation which threatened the depopulation of a large area in the west." And in some bizarre fashion which confounds all logic, Saskatchewan's Premier Walter Scott, whistling past the graveyard, observed that a "gratifying feature" of the crisis was that "our faith in the excellence of our soil ... is only strengthened by the experience of this year."[25]

Only six years had passed since settlers had been allowed into the drylands, and by 1914 the pattern of crop failure, relief aid, destitution and abandonment had clearly developed well in advance of the Dirty Thirties. Those broad themes of the Dirty Thirties—land abandonment, crop failure, destitution, and relief aid—would become a common and accepted way of life in the drylands by the early 1920s.

Settlers arrived in 1920 grimly trailing in the destructive wake of four successive crop failures. Still wrestling with difficult problems and questions which seemed to have no real answer, the province and the federal government established the Better Farming Conference in 1920. It was held in the heart of the drylands at Swift Current; the aim was to try and find some way out of the mess in which all parties concerned seemed to find themselves.

While there was talk of being at wit's end where better farming was concerned (summerfallow, as it turned out, was not a cure-all as imagined, but rather a suitable technique if it rained at regular intervals), the chief sentiment which arose from the commission was unambiguous: "to abandon such lands," commission chair George Spence observed, "would be the first step towards finding a way to use them."[26] Gone was the optimism of the early boom years; gone was the hope that farming could be made profitable on a half-section of land; gone were all of those illusions under which so many people had lived and worked for over a decade. It was time, the commission concluded, to cut losses.

And really it was quite difficult to take issue with the findings of the Commission. The settlers in the RM of Mantario, far removed from the Commission's home base in Swift Current, were operating under starvation conditions. Local organizations in the Kindersley district like the International Order of the Daughters of Empire established relief depots to feed and clothe settlers who have had "no crop or only a little for some years now"—and that was in 1924.[27] Down in the Senate district south of Maple Creek, forty-six farmers and their families were one of those early groups of a very few given this kind of help: they were evacuated by the province in one fell swoop and removed to the literally greener pastures of the Tisdale district.[28]

In some instances, destitute settlers volunteered for what amounted to a kind of indentured servitude, an 'Old European' notion quite out of place in the heady, egalitarian frontier of the Canadian West. Six German farmers who had hailed from colonies in Russia entered into a crop-share arrangement with Calgary-based Western Stock Ranches. The immigrants were provided with food, shelter and clothing, and in return they worked the company lands at Cluny, Alberta, paying off the debt with proceeds from farming.[29] Anything seemed better than what the Konschuhs had known: in the six years Philip Konschuh had farmed in the Maple Creek district, he had never grown a crop of more than three bushels per acre; the year he left, he somehow managed to grow nothing.[30]

Up towards the Alsask area, the situation was not much better. Local settler Anton Huelskamp reported that "hundreds" of families had lost everything; with no aid coming from the province, many were seen "walking out" of the district.[31] According to his own estimation, loan companies owned two-thirds of the homesteads in the district. The land Huelskamp and his luckless neighbours farmed is, today, a Prairie Farm Rehabilitation Administration pasture; PFRA land is land which was reclaimed by the government and turned back to prairie because all efforts at farming it proved useless.

For its part, the province remained reluctant until well into the 1930s to take an active role in helping drought-stricken settlers. True, the administration did participate in the early 1920s in an evacuation plan originally formulated by the Alberta government and the CN/CP railroads; but the Saskatchewan government did so grudgingly and under half-steam. As Premier Charles Dunning informed Huelskamp, "we have not been able to see our way clear to assume a responsibility which, properly speaking, belongs to the federal government in connection with opening up unsuitable lands for settlement."[32] This technically correct, though rather narrow, variety of reasoning excused the young province from assuming any real responsibility for settlers during the crisis: that, as will be shown below, fell instead to the infant RMs.

Unable to secure aid for removal (which, it is important to bear in mind, was one of the key findings of the 1920 Royal Commission), Huelskamp sold what he could, abandoned what he could not sell, packed the rest along with his wife and two daughters, and abandoned their home of six years in 1922. His daughter Polly, who would have been about ten years old at the time, recalls simply that those six years were not easy, as indeed settling virgin prairie anywhere was not supposed to be. Still, there remains a touch of humour and lightness in her memories, seemingly inconsistent with the larger tragedy which was enveloping thousands of settlers. She no doubt fondly recalled, for example, the evening when a John Deere collection agent appeared on the front step of the family's shack, and (perhaps giving credence to the rumours of starvation in the region) the luckless soul was fed a meal of porcupine stew on which he apparently gagged.[33] But where the province was concerned, and despite all seeming conventional wisdom to the contrary, it remained reluctant to move a finger. In the words of an unsigned internal Department of Agriculture memo, any further assistance by the province "seems as unreasonable as it is unwarranted."[34]

The province moved very sluggishly during the crisis when compared to Alberta, whose government was struggling too. The Alberta-Saskatchewan border runs precisely through the middle of the drylands but it is striking how differently each government responded to the crisis. Historian David Jones notes that Alberta's Premier Greenfield "was determined to save the capsizing south or go under with her."[35] Greenfield had organized the evacuation of thousands of drought-stricken settlers. The Saskatchewan government resisted such an approach and the result was what Huelskamp had seen: hundreds of people, bags on their shoulders, "walking out." This was years before the onset of the terrible droughts of the 1930s.

The role which Rural Municipalities were compelled to play during the crisis reinforces the idea that the province resisted any real involvement in this crisis. The RMS became responsible for bailing out drought-stricken settlers, and very quickly the crisis coiled itself tighter and tighter around the neck of the young RMS; it ultimately threatened to strangle the life out of these municipal districts which the province had established only a few years before.

Rural Municipalities provided flour, fodder, coal, and seed grains to drought-stricken settlers. RMS financed the relief by securing additional operating loans from financial institutions. On paper at least, the plan was simple: the costs of the relief were to be recovered when the settlers sold the following year's crop. Deputy Municipal Affairs Minister J. N. Bayne noted that "councils are wary of indulging in seed grain distribution owing to the difficulties so often experienced in securing payment."[36] But this was the course to which all parties were committed, and Bayne tried to reassure the RMS in a wonderfully Churchillian rhapsody that "while we have seen sunshine and shadow [those RMS] will be stronger whose fate it was to struggle."[37] And struggle they did.

Almost immediately, RMS were swamped by the sudden demand for assistance. The RM of White Valley, for example, approved a loan request in 1920 for six families.[38] One month later 94 families, approximating some 200 settlers, received aid in the amount of $16,490.75 which included seed and fodder.[39] And as January wound its slow and bitter way into February, another seventy-nine applications were approved for coal, flour and fodder, totaling $14,625.25.[40] In addition to all of this aid, thirty-three settlers were provided with $7,992.50 in seed. In the space of just two months, White Valley took on a debt of some $40,000.

The RM of Clinworth on the edge of the Great Sand Hills was likewise pushed to the brink of insolvency before quitting relief altogether. Councillor W. L. Lawton moved a motion in 1920 which limited aid to "extreme cases"; those who did receive it would be granted such "only after being interviewed and questioned by council."[41] The bank likewise took a stringent approach with the floundering RM. Running short on operating capital, Clinworth came to the sad realization that the bank was actually avoiding the RM; RM officials had apparently made several entreaties to the bank but received no response "despite repeated protests, interviews, telegrams and phone calls."[42]

The relief aid was meant as a temporary solution to a growing problem, but all solutions contain their own peculiar set of problems. Settlers, plainly put, could not farm without aid, and they could not repay the aid because they were not growing anything. When this wall was reached, the crisis then moved into territory no one had expected: as the 1920s roared, RM administrators busied themselves devising the best and most efficient ways of seizing the property of settlers.

The appropriately named RM of Big Stick, for example, tried gentle inducements at first to recover aid costs. Council magnanimously pledged to exempt from seizure "not more than 25 percent" of any crop planted with relief seed.[43] But as spring made its way into summer and monotonous failure loomed darkly, council agreed that the Municipal Collection Agent "be instructed to seize and sell anything on [a] farm" whose settler owed money to the RM.[44] Such pronouncements were posted up, in typically prairie fashion, throughout post offices and notice boards within the district demanding a settlement of accounts. Demanding is one thing, satisfying the demand is another: after failing in the latter, the RM took the unusual step of writing the province and asking for an amendment to the appropriate legislation allowing the RM to "seize at any time."[45]

As the soul-withering drought reached convulsive proportions, a frenzied Big Stick council seemingly toppled over into the deep end of frustration, and indiscriminately began shooting horses. First, council ordered the shooting of two wild horses which had been contentedly munching on public grass and apparently making "a public nuisance" of themselves. Then, in a delirious sweat and perhaps driven just slightly mad by the heat, council later on, at the same meeting and for no stated reason, passed a motion to "shoot the two horses" owned by the RM as well.[46]

And so it went in Big Stick and other RMs throughout the drylands. White Valley agreed to "seize [any] implements or buildings on skids" to recover aid costs.[47] Maple Creek RM councillor E. Suval favoured the exertion of "the full force of the law" to collect on bad debt.[48] Clinworth councillor Thomas Armstrong spoke for everyone when he said: "This municipality cannot carry them [settlers] any longer."[49]

The amount of land seized by RMs increased in direct proportion to the worsening crisis. Thousands of parcels of land were seized in the ten years between 1917 and 1927 by RMs eager to gain back some of what they had lost during the crisis. The tax sale registries of the RMs unflinchingly record the ultimate consequences of the crisis. Saskatchewan's Minister of Agriculture, F. H. Auld (a logician who took his degree in statistics), pointed out in a confidential memo to a peer in the Alberta Administration that the crisis did seem to have the practical benefit of "mak[ing] it easier for those who remain to establish themselves."[50] And, in a way, he was right: those who remained in the drylands were able to buy cheap land and expand their holdings. The RM of Reno, in what is today the virtually empty southwest corner of the province, seized and sold, for example, 419 parcels of land between 1921 and 1925.[51]

Tax sale registries are highly abstract, and indicate only that ownership of a certain parcel of land had been transferred from one party to another. But there can be a slightly chilling feel to such dry historical fare. In the records of the collection agent for the Department of Municipal Affairs, one is struck by the ghostly quality of his brief and summary reports about land abandonment: Paul Thack of Vidora, section 9-3-36-3, "back to the United States"; Wilson James of Govenlock, 21-2-39-3, "abandoned"; 27-2-29-3, "crop failure"; 1-3-29-3, "no answer to my letter"; 35-2-39-3, "this man is gone."[52] Hugh MacDonald told the agent that he "hasn't received a cent off that land since 1916." In 1926, the file closes out with the words "land abandoned; should be forfeited."[53]

Urban communities suffered a similar fate as did the individual settlers being flailed by the heat on the open prairie. Maple Creek saw its land forfeiture sales spike at 103 in 1924; that was the same year the Department of Municipal Affairs records the loss of some 500 people from the town.[54] Estuary, at one time a hub of activity in the early settlement years and located on prime land right next to the South Saskatchewan River, was all but obliterated during the crisis of the 1920s. Between 1920 and 1927, 302 people abandoned the once-thriving town.[55] Clinworth councillor James Wardell had no doubts about the wisdom of amending the Dominion Lands Act to open up the drylands for settlement. In a letter to the Department of Interior, he asked for help in removing liens from lands so that the RM might sell them. Wardell touched on the theme of responsibility, and indicated that perhaps the Department had more than a passing interest in assisting with his request since "in the first place [these lands] should have never been settled."[56]

In total the drylands lost an estimated 10,000 people between 1917 and 1927, though the worst of the land abandonment occurred after 1923, which is right around the time when most Municipalities stopped providing aid. The worst of the drought lasted seven years, from 1917 to 1923; the worst of the Dirty Thirties lasted eight years. This raises obvious questions which will now be addressed.

The Dirty Thirties occupies an ascendant place in prairie consciousness: few are those who do not have a passing acquaintance with that legendary calamity. But the crisis of the 1920s, by contrast, does not register in the Saskatchewan mind; it is simply not there. This absence seems to result almost naturally in the erroneous notion that there was relative prosperity on the plains up to 1930, when, suddenly, matters took a turn for the worse. In short, there is the belief that nothing exceptional occurred on the prairies until the Dirty Thirties struck. This unawareness of the past is most striking in the local community histories of the drylands. Valuable and accurate barometers of prairie consciousness, not one of the histories consulted for the purposes of this work pointed directly toward a crisis in the 1920s.

The history of Hatton, for example, includes the stories of men like Harrison Green and his family of seven, who farmed in the district for eight years, harvesting one crop before quietly leaving in 1922.[57] There are numerous other examples of men like Green in the Hatton history, and also examples of his opposite, men like Gottlieb Anhorn. Anhorn came to Hatton from Bessarabia. He was one of those hardy souls who elected to tough out the worst of the crisis, and "in the year 1925, when neighboring farmers began to move away owing to poor crop conditions, Mr. Anhorn bought and leased additional land."[58]

In compilations of local histories, individual family members submit these short stories to an editorial board, which then assembles the entries alphabetically and prefaces the final product with an introductory essay on the history of the district. So, for all intents and purposes, these books with their hundreds of entries each from a different person are assembled in different rooms, so to speak, and as a result no one has made obvious connections. The stories of Green and Anhorn restate in simple form the basic contours and elements of the entire crisis: settlement, crop failure, land abandonment, and land consolidation. But since these various threads lie unconnected on the page, there remains an unawareness of the crisis at the local level. It seems to be assumed that what happened in one family or district was strictly limited to that one family or district, related to nothing outside of it. A historical vacuum, as it were, has been created.

Academic historiography contains similar conceptual lapses. The very first historian to see, understand and write about the dryland crisis in its entirety was Chester Martin. He wrote the first (and what will likely remain the only) history of Dominion Lands policy. Martin saw the abandonment crisis as a problem peculiar to the regions settled in the second half of western settlement after 1908, and as a problem which transcended the 1930s.

Martin, for example, describes early trends of land abandonment this way: "In Saskatchewan, the net area pre-empted up to 1917 was five million acres. Thereafter, cancellations exceeded entries and reduced the net area pre-empted to about 3.7 million acres." Martin writes thus of land consolidation: "by 1921, the percentage of farms over 200 acres had risen from 38 percent in 1901 to 67.4 percent. The process continued, however, after 1918; by 1926 it had become over seventy percent."[59]

Certainly, one's lower lip trembles upon reading such dry historical fare: little wonder that further interest in the crisis was not piqued. But Martin's words crisply illuminate the essentials of the crisis. Martin, as well, offers this terse thought on the nature of the history of the settlement after 1908: it "presents a truly appalling list of casualties." But it was all numbers and figures and abstractions, and no one would pick up on those threads for another sixty years.

David Jones was the first historian to put flesh on the abstract bones of Martin's earlier work. Jones' work *Empire of Dust: Settling and Abandoning the Prairie Drybelt* is exceptional on a number of levels—thorough and exhaustive archival research and a fine prose style to name just two. But the primary focus of his work is Alberta and not necessarily Saskatchewan.

Jones argues that the crisis was, by degrees, worse in Alberta than in Saskatchewan. The implication seems to be that the crisis lessened or some-how changed itself at the Alberta-Saskatchewan border. Jones indicates that Saskatchewan lost some 3,000 people during the crisis, whereas Alberta lost some 17,000.[60] In Jones' earliest work on the subject, a 1978 article on school disintegration during the crisis, he notes that southeast Alberta lost just 1,851 people.[61] The difference between the numbers in the article and the numbers in the book were caused by the sources he used. Jones used the Canadian census in his book as the primary source for determining the number of people who abandoned or were evacuated out of the drylands. That same source also indicates that the population of Saskatchewan's drybelt region remained essentially stable during the crisis.[62] Thus, the Saskatchewan experience seems less important, less vivid because the crisis which claimed so many livelihoods in Alberta appeared not to have been registered here at all.

But records of the RMs themselves show otherwise and so do the tax sale registries. Records of the provincial Department of Municipal Affairs and the Department of Agriculture agree with this, too. An estimated 10,000 people fled the area between 1917 and 1927. In addition, more than one his-torian has questioned the accuracy of the Canadian census; Barry Potyondi and D. M. Loveridge both agree that the vast expanses of the area and the highly transient population of the drylands "make this source [the census] of limited value."[63]

The crisis of the 1920s in Saskatchewan was as tragic as that which occurred in Alberta. To argue otherwise is to argue that the problem somehow altered itself at the artificial border between the two provinces—a quite strange propo-sition. But, as stated previously, where the Alberta government took an active (one could argue excessive) approach to evacuating its settlers, Saskatchewan, by contrast, downplayed the problem and held a very tight rein on the numbers of people it evacuated. So, if the crisis was deemed unimportant at the time it happened, then it becomes easier to understand how it simply, quietly and quite naturally slipped away from the grasp of public consciousness.

Popular history forms much of the bedrock of common assumptions about the past. Hard-pressed would be the person striking out to find a rural Saskatchewan home which did not contain a copy of, say, Pierre Berton's history of the west (which does not mention the crisis), or James Gray's *Men Against the Desert*, a fine history but one which, however inadvertently, also helped to give form and shape to the idea that the 1920s roared. Gray argues that "good crop followed good crop from 1922 to 1928."[64] This statement begs reconsideration when it has been shown that the worst of the evacuation and land abandonment occurred in precisely those years. The crisis of the 1920s basically passes Gray by, as it did for other historians, both local and academic, in part because the contours of Saskatchewan history had long since taken shape, and because those who would speak of it, families like the Huelskamps or the Konschuhs or the Greens, were gone. Other historians agree that for a very long time there has been an obvious tendency in Prairie history "to exaggerate the well-being of prairie agriculture [prior to the Thirties]" because it makes the calamity of the Dirty Thirties seem that much more dramatic.[65]

The crisis of the 1920s has the power to subtly change the basic contours of Saskatchewan history. The connection between the crisis of the 1920s and what occurred in the 1930s is very real and very obvious. The connections between those two periods and the early failures and excessive abandonment and cancellations of the pre-1917 period likewise are obvious. When finally placed together and in context, a different picture emerges, a picture which portrays 1908–39 as one block of time which was characterized by steadily worsening degrees of land abandonment and destitution, finally and logically culminating in the calamity of the 1930s.

NOTES

This article first appeared in *Prairie Forum* 33, no. 2 (2008): 257–274.

1   Provincial Archives of Saskatchewan (PAS), R-261, 23-1-1, Sargeant to F. H. Auld, 14 July 1921.
2   David Jones, *Empire of Dust: Settling and Abandoning the Prairie Drybelt* (Edmonton: University of Alberta Press, 1991), 10, 21.
3   Lewis H. Thomas et al., *The Prairies to 1905: A Canadian Sourcebook* (Toronto: Oxford University Press, 1975), 225.

4   Pierre Berton, *The Promised Land: Settling the Canadian West, 1896–1914* (Toronto: McClelland and Stewart, 1984), 206.

5   Thomas, *The Prairies to 1905*, 226.

6   W. A. Waiser, *The New Northwest: The Photographs of the Crean Expedition, 1908–1909* (Saskatoon: Fifth House Publishing, 1993), 1, 9–11, 47–50.

7   Canada, *House of Commons, Debates*, 14 March 1907, 4690.

8   Chester Martin, *"Dominion Lands" Policy* (Toronto: McClelland and Stewart, 1973), 162–64. The Kincaid Act would be followed in the years to come with legislation which would actively encourage settlers to turn to cattle ranching in the American drylands. The experience of the settlers in the northern tip of the Great American Desert prefigured exactly what would occur in southwest Saskatchewan and southeast Alberta in the 1920s and 1930s.

9   Canada, *House of Commons, Debates*, 14 March 1907, 4699.

10   Ibid., 4715.

11   Ibid., 4727.

12   *Captured Memories: A History of Alsask and Surrounding School Districts* (Alsask: Alsask History Book Committee, 1983), v.

13   Saskatchewan, Department of Agriculture, *Annual Report* (1908), 93.

14   Ibid.

15   Canada, *Sessional Papers*, 25, vol. 45, no. 16, (1911), xx

16   Saskatchewan, Department of Agriculture, *Annual Report* (1907), 116. See also Ibid. (1908), 76.

17   Canada, *Sessional Papers*, 25, part 1, vol. 48, no. 19 (1914), iv–x.

18   Saskatchewan, Department of Agriculture, *Annual Report* (1909), 75 (the actual volume produced was 3.4 million bushels in a provincial total of ninety million).

19   Ibid. (1910), 68 (actual volume of wheat produced dropped precipitously to 170,000). There are sixteen RMs which constitute the drylands proper. The region resembles a triangle with its peak at the Kindersley Alsask district, stretching down to the American border just below Eastend. This article is based upon information gathered from locations in this general area, though the dry region is much larger and includes, for example, all of Grasslands National Park.

20   Ibid. (1914), 106.

21   Ibid., 113.

22   Ibid., 45.

23   Canada, *Relief for Western Settlers* (Ottawa: Federal Press Agency, 1914), 2.

24   Ibid., 1–2.

25   "Premier Scott Comes to the Aid of Farmers," *Kindersley Clarion*, 27 August 1914, 1.

26   Saskatchewan, "Report of the Royal Commission of Inquiry into Farming Conditions" (1921), 16. In saying this, Spence was simply restating the conclusion of another federal commission: the three-member Pope Commission had also concluded, in 1914, that millions of acres of land ought to be cut off from further settlement. Sadly, the commission's recommendations were not heeded, and settlement continued. Spence would ultimately have difficulty getting the province to evacuate settlers from the drylands in the 1920s. It was not until the province established the PFRA in the 1940s that officials began the process of reclaiming

millions of acres of land which two government commissions had agreed should not have been settled.

27 "Relief for Dried out Farmers," *Kindersley Clarion*, 28 August 1924, 1.

28 PAS, Agriculture 2.7, Papers of the Department of Agriculture, "Correspondence re: movement of settlers, 1922–1925," CNR Freight Agent E. A. Field to F. H. Auld, 25 July 1923.

29 PAS, Agriculture 2.7, Honens to the Department of Agriculture, 26 March 1923.

30 Ibid., "Application for the free shipment of settlers stock and effects from points in the dry area."

31 PAS, M-13, 14, f1, Huelskamp to Dunning, 8 July 1922.

32 Ibid., Dunning to Huelskamp, 14 July 1922.

33 *Captured Memories*, 304–05.

34 PAS, M13, 14, f1 "Internal Memo, Department of Agriculture," 10 November 1922.

35 Jones, *Empire of Dust*, 215.

36 Saskatchewan, Department of Municipal Affairs, *Annual Report* (1918), 8.

37 Ibid.

38 RM of White Valley Archives, "Minutes Book for RM of White Valley from January 1919–1924," #1 (hereafter White Valley Minutes), 174–75.

39 Ibid., 24 January 1920, 181–83.

40 Ibid., 21 February 1920, 193.

41 RM of Clinworth Archives, "Minutes of RM Meetings, 1912–1981" (hereafter Clinworth Minutes), 6 March 1920.

42 Ibid., 18 March 1922.

43 RM of Big Stick Archives, "Minutes of RM Meetings, 1920–1923," 4 February 1922.

44 Ibid., 5 August 1922.

45 Ibid., 3 February 1923.

46 Ibid., 5 July 1922.

47 White Valley Minutes, 288.

48 RM of Maple Creek Archives, "Minutes of RM Meetings," 7 February 1925.

49 Clinworth Minutes, 5 February 1921.

50 PAS, R-261, F23-1-1, Auld to G. R. Murdoch, 14 November 1921.

51 RM of Reno Archives, "Tax Sale and Redemption Record, 1921–1925." The figure of 419 is a simple tally of all of the entries in this log.

52 PAS MA-3, Records of the Department of Municipal Affairs "Seed Relief: 1921–1924."

53 Ibid., MacDonald to Smith 29 October 1922.

54 Saskatchewan, Department of Municipal Affairs, *Annual Report* (1926), 26–39.

55 Ibid. (1920), 26–37; ibid. (1926), 26–33.

56 Clinworth Minutes, 16 September 1924.

57 Laura Phaff, et al., *Prairie Echoes: A Story of Hatton, Saskatchewan and Surrounding Area* (n.p., 1983), 23.

58 Ibid., 3.

59 Martin, *"Dominion Lands,"* 164.

60 Jones, *Empire of Dust*, 220.

61 David Jones, "School and School Disintegration in the Alberta Dry Belt of the Twenties," *Prairie Forum* 3, no. 1 (Spring 1978): 16. (Chapter 2 in this volume.)

62 Jones, *Empire of Dust*, 245.
63 Barry Potyondi, and D. M. Loveridge, *From Wood Mountain to Whitemud: a historical survey of the Grasslands National Park Area* (Ottawa: National Historic Parks and Sites Branch, 1983), 175.
64 James Gray, *Men Against the Desert* (Saskatoon: Western Producer Books, 1978), 16.
65 Ian MacPherson and John Herd Thompson, "The Rural Prairie West, the Dirty Thirties and the Historians" (unpublished address delivered at a joint session of the Canadian Historical Association, Winnipeg, 1986).

PART II

Dislocation and Conflict

5. Bienfait: Origins and Legacy of the
    Coal Miners' Strike of 1931

Stephen Endicott

> *"I defy these operators to say that I am anything but an honest*
> *Englishman…but the way I have been used it is enough to make*
> *me a Red."* (Harry Hesketh, coal miner in Saskatchewan since
> 1903; Secretary-Treasurer Local 27, Mine Workers' Union of
> Canada, Bienfait, 31 October 1934)

> *"It appears to me that the moment a man submits himself to be*
> *appointed on a Committee or some position in a Union, and he has*
> *nerve to approach the Owners on behalf of the workers, he is imme-*
> *diately branded a Red. I have not yet interviewed the Owner or*
> *Manager of a mine in regard to the red element, that has not given*
> *me the names of all the men on the Pit Committee and the names*
> *of some Official of the Union…There is a Communist Movement*
> *amongst the miners, but in my opinion they are not all on the Pit*
> *Committees and with the assistance of —— [name of under-*
> *cover informer omitted] I will endeavour to have all Communists*
> *reported on."* (Detective Sergeant J. G. Metcalf, RCMP, Estevan
> Detachment, 3 December 1931)

The coal operators in the Souris River valley of southeastern Saskatchewan were accustomed to having their own way. For over thirty years, since deep-seam mining began in this district at the turn of the century, they had a short answer to any worker bold enough to express a grievance or to complain about conditions in the mine: "If you don't like it here, pick up your tools and get out!" And the owners generally had the provincial mine inspectors in their pocket as well—inspectors who made the most cursory of tests into safety conditions in the mines and then wrote skimpy, uninformative reports about their visitations.

Three times during the first three decades of the twentieth century the coal miners of Estevan-Bienfait tried to remedy their situation by collective action. The first time in 1907, they appealed for assistance to the United Mine Workers of America (UMWA). This union was organizing the more numerous coal miners in Alberta. However, it was part of the craft-orientated American Federation of Labor which was in the process of fostering conservative, business-style unions, and was unable to develop the strength to overcome the opposition of the Saskatchewan operators to any kind of unionization. The UMWA withdrew from the Saskatchewan field after several years.

When the Bienfait miners sought outside assistance again, in 1920, they turned to the more militant, syndicalist One Big Union. This union was also active in Alberta and had played an important part in the Winnipeg General Strike of 1919 as well. However, the coal operators were ready to block another attempt at unionization. When the OBU organizer came to

Coal miners near Estevan, Saskatchewan, 1912 (Courtesy of the Provincial Archives of Saskatchewan / S-B 472).

Bienfait, an employer-sponsored vigilante committee dragged him from his hotel room in the middle of the night, drove him over the American border and, in Ku Klux Klan style, threatened to tar and feather him if he ever returned. The Saskatchewan government sent its provincial police into the area and prevented the One Big Union from taking root.

The third attempt to raise the banner of the union in Bienfait, in 1931, was initiated by miners who had recently become members of, or were associated with, the Communist Party. They contacted the Workers' Unity League, a union centre whose western headquarters was in Winnipeg, and through it the Calgary-based Mine Workers' Union of Canada, requesting the assistance of organizers. Saskatchewan's daily newspapers soon headlined alarming reports of communist agitators infiltrating the coal fields. Prime Minister R. B. Bennett, on a western tour, conferred with provincial officials and had several "exhibits" of the communist paper, *The Worker*, submitted to him. *The Worker* shot back an angry, sarcastic reply, raising the level of rhetoric and helping to awaken the miners for struggle:

> The eastern reptile press reports all this in the usual tone of sensational discovery. When the revolutionary unions...organize the workers of an industry against the vilest forms of exploitation and victimization, the governments of the bosses and its sewer press always "discover" something. But when there is no Union, and the workers can be terrorized into subjection and forced to accept the terms of the bosses then the governments discover nothing, since they have no need to. [5 September 1931]

In the end, this third union drive also failed to establish a lasting presence in the Bienfait coal fields. But when the youthful organizers of the Workers' Unity League first arrived in August 1931—led by Martin J. Forkin and Sam Scarlett, and soon to be followed by James Sloan, president of the Mine Workers' Union of Canada, and Annie Buller, a union organizer in Winnipeg—the coal operators were caught off guard. After a successful work stoppage at the Crescent Collieries, all 600 miners joined the union within a few days, before the operators had time to react. For the first time the workers succeeded in creating an industry-wide union in the coalfields.

A week later, when James Sloan invited the operators to a conference at Estevan City Hall to negotiate a contract, the mine owners claimed that some sinister communist conspiracy was at work that was disloyal, unpatriotic and prone to violence. They refused to negotiate, forcing a thirty-day strike that has long been remembered in Canadian labour history because of the lives that were lost. Supported by their allies in the press and government, the operators publicized the idea of a Red conspiracy so well that it became, even to this day, a widely accepted version of the origins of the Bienfait coal miners' strike of 1931, shared even by some of the miners' descendants. In reality, while the Communists provided crucial leadership, it was the miners themselves, motivated to escape from abysmal living and working conditions in the coalfields that were the driving force behind the strike. Perhaps it is time for a look at the forces involved, and at the mix of time, place and circumstances that led the people co support a union drive in Bienfait. What strategy and tactics did the Communist organizers actually employ and what is their legacy to the union movement?

The village of Bienfait, located eight miles east of Estevan, was sandwiched between the station grounds of the CPR and CNR railways. It had eight short streets bisected by a provincial highway. Responding to efforts of the Canadian Pacific Railway's recruiting agents in Europe, the population grew after World War I, doubling in size to 500—almost one-hundred families. Yet even when these numbers were added to the larger surrounding rural municipalities of Estevan and Coalfields, where the mining camps were located, the census of 1931 showed a local rural populace not much in excess of 4,000 people.

The overseer (as he was called) of this small, intimate village community was A. H. Graham, manager of the Lake of the Woods grain elevator. He liked to boast that Bienfait, nestled on a deep seam of coal seven miles square and containing more coal than would be needed "in the next hundred years," was the most prosperous place of its size in Saskatchewan. For five months of the year, there were plentiful signs of activity, with four men and a locomotive working full-time in each of the railway yards making up trains. On average, during the winter months, they shipped out one hundred cars of coal per day. Even though the rail yards were virtually empty during the rest of the year, an annual payroll from the mines, amounting to $400,000 in 1930–31, provided the material base for a score of more-or-less successful businesses and community enterprises. As signs of Bienfait's vitality, the fledgling village Board of Trade cited the presence of a garage, hardware, five groceries, two butchers, a barber shop, pool room, drug store, several cafes, an electric shop under construction, a lumber yard, a machine shop under way, two amusement halls, and football, baseball and other organized sports, including a hockey team "that had figured in the provincial playdowns."

Perhaps the crown of this bustling community was the King Edward Hotel, a two-storey frame building on the corner of Main and Railway Streets.

It advertised itself as "the best equipped village hotel in Saskatchewan"—Simmon's beds, Slumber King springs throughout, hot soft-water baths at all times in connection, four first-class billiard tables, three bowling alleys, first-class two-chair barber shop, and electrical refrigeration. The proprietor, Gordon White, had his motto written large: "WHITE HELP—WHITE SERVICE." The village elite—mine managers and office staffs, pit bosses, the school principal, business people, and others largely from the Anglo-Saxon majority—gathered here for their smokers, their relaxation and social affairs and took their privileged standing for granted.

Other places that played an important part in village life at the time of the strike were two Ukrainian Halls and Boruk's Bakery and Boarding House. These were the gathering places of the "foreign born" in the parlance of the day, immigrants from Eastern Europe—Lithuanians, Poles, Ukrainians, Czechoslovaks and others who made up about thirty percent of the population. It was the men of these families who did most of the bone and muscle work down in the mines and who, according to Mervyn Enmark, a mine foreman in the 1970s, "were treated as Indians are treated today."

A large part of the "foreign born" in Bienfait had emigrated from the Western Ukraine, an area that was under Polish rule. Originally there was one Ukrainian Hall in Bienfait, built in 1921, where people celebrated the poetic works of Taras Shevchenko and conducted other social activities. But after the Bolshevik Revolution and news of developments in the Eastern or Soviet Ukraine filtered in from the large Ukrainian community in Winnipeg, the Bienfait Ukrainians became divided on how to view the experiment of building socialism in "the Old Country." The majority sided with the pro-socialist Ukrainian Labour-Farmer Temple Association of Winnipeg, and the minority stopped coming to the hall. A bitter law suit over the ownership of the building, sparked by a determined Ukrainian priest from Brandon, Manitoba, divided the community further. Eventually the court in Estevan awarded the building, with costs, to the nationalist, anti-communist group. From then on it was called the Green Hall.

"The enemy thought to smash us but they mistook our will," said John Bachynski, secretary of the Bienfait branch of the Ukrainian Labour-Farmer Temple Association. By the late 1920s, according to Bachynski, this group had rebounded and grown to 70 members. With the court costs paid off, they rented Sinclair's Pool Hall further up Main Street and cleared out the pool tables. Known as the Red Hall, it became an important centre for union organization during the miner's strike. As for Boruk's Bakery and Boarding House, perhaps its reputation is summed up best by James Cuddington, a

Main Street merchant in Bienfait who disparaged the owners of this establishment, saying they "held a number of questionable meetings in the other parts of the building" of which "the police would have knowledge."

During the hot, dry, wind-blown summer of 1931, many of the 600 Saskatchewan miners and their families in the Bienfait coalfields had hit rock bottom. Most were living at subsistence levels. According to some reports, there were people and livestock in this drought-stricken area close to starvation. Hungry farmers' sons provided a large pool of unemployed from which mine owners could pick replacement workers for any miners who expressed their discontent.

Outbursts by miners occurred against reductions in the standard of living, poor housing, wage-cuts of up to 26 percent for coal diggers in the spring of 1931, and against the deterioration of working conditions. However, these had little effect on the coal operators, who said they had $3 million of capital invested in the mines and owed it to their shareholders to make the mines more profitable. They insisted that miners' wages were at a "very fair standard" considering the depressed state of the economy in general and claimed to be losing money. That, however, was not exactly the case according to investigations of the Royal Commission into the Coal Mining Dispute. There were other options to wage-cutting, as the royal commission demonstrated. Nevertheless, spontaneous, individual remonstrations were futile against the power of capital.

One evening in mid-July 1931, about the time a devastating cyclone hit the Bienfait area, a dark-haired man of medium build and not yet thirty walked into Boruk's Bakery and Boarding House with his suitcase. The proprietors, Alex Boruk and his wife Tekla Scribialo, were expecting him, for this was Sam Carr, national organizer of the Communist Party. Carr had arranged to stay with them during the Bienfait leg of his national organizing tour. Combining a relaxed, easy-going manner with a persuasive speaking ability and an analytical mind, Sam Carr had a reputation that preceded him to Bienfait. For one thing, the Boruks and their close friends were aware that he was a recent graduate of the prestigious Lenin School in Moscow. There he had spent several years studying Marxism and building up his knowledge of strategy and tactics in the labour movement by exchanging experiences with revolutionary workers from over thirty countries. Now he was intent on building a party unit among the workers in Bienfait, and the Boruks, along with other members of the Ukrainian Labour-Farmer Temple Association, were willing to assist him. In recent months, Matthew Popowich and other national leaders of the labour farmer organization in Winnipeg had been pushing their membership to participate more actively in the class struggles of Canadian workers, urging that the plays, songs and music presented in concerts at the halls "should be chosen for their class content," and closely tied to the working class movement.

TABLE 5.1. PRODUCTION AND PROFIT AT BIENFAIT AND M & S MINES, 1929–31

Mine	Year	Net tons produced	Profits ($)	Profit Per ton (¢)	Capital	Profit as % of capital	Dividend paid
M & S	1929	100,605	18,137	18.13	$1,201,500	1.5%	Nil
	1930	92,179	7,871	8.54		0.7%	
	1931	105,478	7,098	6.72		0.7%	
Bienfait	1929	76,281	23,301	30.5	$100,000	23.3%	18%
	1930	75,933	18,650	24.6		18.6%	20%

Note: The profits of Manitoba & Saskatchewan Mining Co. are after payment of interest on $201,500 of 6% bonds outstanding. No reserves made for depletion. Mine managers' salaries were $5,000 to $6,500. There are two official government statistics for workers' average wages: $477 per annum (*Census of Canada 1931*) or $750 per annum (*Coal Statistics for Canada*). Bienfait Mines Ltd. had made adequate depreciation and depletion allowances. M & S Mines had 130 employees of whom 45 were miners or loaders; Bienfait mines had 110 employees of whom 75 were miners or loaders. SOURCE: J. Raffles Cox, "Confidential Report on an Inspection of Part of the Saskatchewan Lignite field, with special reference to: THE COST AND RATE SITUATION," Exhibit C27 at Royal Commission into the Mining Dispute, Estevan, 1931, Provincial Archives of Saskatchewan, Regina; Inspector F. W. Schultz, RCMP, "Strike Conditions, Bienfait, Sask" (Secret), 20 September 1931, H. V.7 file, Canadian Security Information Service (CSIS), RG176, National Archives of Canada, Ottawa.

After Carr left Bienfait he was able to write to Tom Ewen, a senior Communist Party colleague in Toronto, saying that he had formed a party unit there. Among those who met and became favourably influenced by Carr (some of whom joined the party) were the Boruks and their eldest daughter, Stella, 17; the already-mentioned John Bachynski and his wife Mary; Maria Germann, a miner's wife and women's leader; the brothers Alex and Fred Konopaki, who worked in the National Mine; William Choma of the Eastern Collieries; and John Billis, a daring immigrant from Lithuania also working in the Eastern Collieries at the time who was first radicalized in the Pennsylvania coal mines. In addition there was Martin Day, from Fyfeshire, Scotland, a miner for twenty-one years and head of the union committee at Crescent Collieries; John and Mary Harris, a Welsh couple with thirty-three years mining experience now at the Bienfait Mine; and Fred Booth, a British miner since the age of thirteen and a veteran of World War I who worked for the Manitoba and Saskatchewan Mining Co. Besides their long experience in coal mining, the Day, Harris and Booth families had something else in common: they had all migrated to Bienfait three years earlier after the bitter defeat of the miners' general strike in Britain. Lacking five years domicile in Canada, they were all blacklisted and, according to available information, deported after the Bienfait strike. The reason for identifying these people is not to embarrass their descendants, but to put a human face on a group or courageous people who, in the depths of the Great Depression, took a lead in fighting for workers' rights.

It is not likely that Sam Carr had to spend much time explaining to the miners the ideas of class struggle, the exploitation of labour by capital, the polarization of wealth and increasing poverty, or even about the Communist Party's program for a worker's government nationalizing the means of production along lines existing in the Soviet Union. The group gathered in the Boruk's living room knew all this. What they desperately needed at the time was practical help in dealing with the misery being created daily by the workings of capitalism in Bienfait. Carr came prepared. From his suitcase he produced the constitution of the newly formed Workers' Unity League and explained the revolutionary nature and program of this trade union centre.

The league's openly proclaimed revolutionary nature included three aspects: its purpose was to organize workers into industrial, rather than craft, unions, "with widest rank and file control" to fight for the defence of the Canadian working class "against the bandit raid of capitalism on living standards." It also wanted to organize Canadian workers "for the final overthrow of capitalism" and for the establishment of a workers' and farmers' government; and it was the Canadian section of the Red International of Labour Unions, headquartered in Moscow (in contrast to the international connections of the other Canadian trade unions with centres in the United States, in Amsterdam or in Rome). The main practical tasks of the WUL were to organize workers in the unorganized industries, organize the unemployed to demand non-contributory unemployment insurance and, lastly, to establish left-wing groups within existing craft, patriotic or business unions with a view to transforming them into revolutionary industrial unions.

All this was rather general, but Carr was also able to give the Bienfait miners encouraging specific news from Alberta. Two months earlier in a referendum, the coal miners there had voted three to one (1,727 in favour, 641 against) to have their union, the Mine Workers' Union of Canada, affiliate with the Workers' Unity League. He also probably shared with them, as a practical guide, the contents of another document, called the "Resolution on

Strike Strategy and Tactics." It had been adopted at a recent international conference sponsored by the Red International of Labour Unions and (for some unknown reason) it was called "the Strassburg Resolution."

The Strassburg Resolution, which summed up the recent experience of European workers, strongly warned against any conspiratorial approach by militants: the important decisions should be made by all the workers in a potential strike situation. It stressed that clear and understandable economic demands arising from the concrete situation in the mining pits "must be discussed by all workers." In the case of favourable conditions for a strike, the resolution stressed that a strike committee should be elected by all the workers: "workers of all beliefs and affiliations must be able to participate in these elections, the organized as well as the unorganized" otherwise the strike would fail. These were strong urgings for democratic participation by all involved. The Strassburg Resolution raised several other important questions. Consideration should be given to the offensive of the bosses, the diversionary tactics of the reformist, business-as-usual unions and how to paralyze these efforts in the course of the struggle. How were the unorganized, the unemployed, the youth and women workers going to be drawn into the struggle? How was the whole working class and its sympathizers in the wider community to be mobilized to aid the striking workers in achieving their demands? These were the challenging questions that the party club in Bienfait began to ponder as Sam Carr took his leave for the next leg of his tour.

The implication of Carr's outline was that they should try to include both Green and Red Hall members on the union committees, open the door to Anglicans, Catholics, United Church members and members of the Jewish faith, both the British and "foreign" sides of the village. They should concentrate on what everyone had in common and set aside differences. This was the meaning of the ringing phrases with which Marx and Engels had concluded their famous Communist Manifesto: "Workers of the world, unite! The proletarians have nothing to lose but their chains. They have a world to win."

By 6 August 1931, the district organizer of the Communist Party in Winnipeg heard that "the miners and unemployed at Bienfait, Saskatchewan, are in revolt," and Joe Forkin, area organizer of the Workers' Unity League, hurried over to Bienfait to carry on where Sam Carr had left off.

Forkin, 31, of Brandon, Manitoba, was an even-tempered man, tall, and slight of build but with abundant energy and possessed of a keen political sense. Although he was not a fiery speaker, his direct manner inspired confidence. As a three-year veteran of the Canadian Expeditionary Force in World War I, followed by a year's service in the Royal Canadian Mounted Police and then ten years or participation in the labour movement in Winnipeg, Forkin had a solid fund of background experience. Before long *The Mercury* of Estevan would, with good reason, be calling him "the generalissimo of the strikers' forces."

On his arrival in Bienfait, Forkin discovered that half the employed miners had already signed lists stating their desire to join a union. He immediately contacted the Mine Workers' Union of Canada in Calgary and requested that they send an organizer and bring union cards and books. In the meantime, to dispel gossip and hostile rumours, he decided it was important to make the presence of the Workers' Unity League publicly known in Estevan. For this purpose he organized an open air meeting in the fair grounds on Sunday, 16 August 1931, that was attended by about 140 people. There was a good deal of interest. After his address, poorly-paid workers employed in a CPR construction gang, a brickyard, as well as some unemployed workers—about one-hundred in all—joined the General Workers Union, the Lumber and Agricultural Workers Industrial Union or the National Unemployed Workers' Association—all of which, Forkin explained, were affiliated with the Workers' Unity League. An unemployed miner, John Loughran, now farming, was chosen as president of the General Workers Union.

Loughran, a boastful type who had worked around the mines for thirty-three years and now volunteered for all kinds of activities, turned out not to be entirely reliable from Forkin's point of view, but at least he was enthusiastic and, as a farmer, out of range of the employers. Perhaps for the reason of not wanting to expose any of the coal diggers active in forming a union to employer retaliation, Forkin also put Loughran forward as pro tem, acting-president of the still-to-be-announced miners' union.

In the next two weeks, events moved swiftly. On Tuesday, 18 August, the union cards and books arrived from Calgary and the committeemen started signing up the employed miners. Two days later Crescent Collieries fired John Adams, who, according to the local paper, was "organizing the foreign workers" in the mine. Martin Day, head of the pit committee there, promptly led a small delegation to call on the manager to see if he would reinstate Adams. The manager refused to give any reason for Adams' dismissal or to reinstate him. The next day all fifty workers at Crescent Collieries walked off the job and the workers in the other mines expressed their willingness to have a sympathy strike if necessary. The following Sunday, 23 August, Forkin and the committeemen organized a family picnic at Taylorton Bridge. It was located several miles south of Bienfait near the mining camps of Western Dominion Collieries and the Manitoba & Saskatchewan Mines, which were the largest employers in the district. Twelve hundred men, women and children turned out and heard speeches by Forkin and George Wilkinson, a veteran English miner employed at Western Dominion Collieries for eight years. Wilkinson was a meticulous, plodding sort, thorough and thoughtful, but he was not comfortable with the militancy of the Workers' Unity League. Perhaps the most important event for stirring up enthusiasm was a speech given by Sam Scarlett, "a ruddy-faced square-built worker with a husky voice" who had come from Saskatoon to give Forkin a band.

Sam Scarlett was a legendary working-class leader; so much so that the RCMP headed their whole file on investigations into the Bienfait strike as "Sam Scarlett—Communist Agitator." A skilled machinist who migrated from Scotland to Canada and then to the United States at the turn of the century, he had soon become involved in some of the epic struggles of the miners in the Mesabie Iron range in Minnesota with William D. Haywood, Joe Hill and others in the Industrial Workers of the World (IWW). Framed on a murder charge and accused of over one hundred separate crimes, he was imprisoned and then deported back to Scotland. He returned to Canada in the early 1920s as a harvester and later joined the Communist Party. Such a man inspired awe among fellow workers. The central theme of his speeches was that our society was divided into two classes, "the exploiter and the exploited [and] between them there is nothing in common..."and he would go on to trace out the pattern of another and better tomorrow. Older people in Bienfait still speak of Sam Scarlett with respect. His convictions were contagious and he could move people to laughter and to tears.

The picnic at Taylorton had its desired effect on the manager of Crescent Collieries. He caved in the next day and rehired Adams. Meanwhile, James Sloan, president of the Mine Workers' Union of Canada, arrived from the Calgary headquarters to address an open air meeting of a thousand people at Bienfait and another one in Estevan Town Hall. He declared that the conditions in Bienfait were the worst he had ever seen, and that one hundred percent of the miners had signed up for the union. With Sloan presiding, all the mine committees met together for the first time and Local 27 of the Mine Workers' Union of Canada was born. Dan Moar was elected president of the local, a bachelor and ex-serviceman working in the Crescent Collieries. John Harris, in the Bienfait Mine, was vice-president, and Harry Hesketh, a miner of the British Independent Labour Party tradition who had worked in the area since 1903, was secretary-treasurer.

The following week, both sides were frantically busy. The union activists met to investigate and gather material for a meeting with the operators. Mass meetings were held among the miners and their families in preparation for the possibility of a strike. Joe Forkin and Sam Scarlett explained how unions worked in other coal fields and promised the support of the Red International of Labour Unions, which they said had twenty-eight million members, including fifteen million in Soviet Russia. Sloan answered questions asked by the miners and their wives. He told them that they had the sympathy of the people, and "not to spoil this sympathy by violence."

The managers of the six deep-seam mines were also busy. They formed the South Saskatchewan Coal Operators Association, with an American, C. C. Morfit, manager of the largest colliery, Western Dominion, as president. They went to Regina for a meeting with the provincial cabinet and requested more police to deal with the threatened miners' strike. The cabinet, however, was non-committal on that score, preferring instead that the operators try to split the new union by fostering independent (company) unions, and suggested that they request a conciliation board to diffuse the situation. The government sent agents to Estevan to work with the operators' lawyer, W. W. Lynn, on the attempt to split the miners. These men approached John Loughran, who was greatly flattered by their attention. They developed the line that Sloan, Forkin and Scarlett were outsiders with "no right to be here" interfering in disputes, and that their union was unpatriotic because of its association with "the Red International of Labour Unions in Moscow." The provincial labour minister, J. A. Merkley, also journeyed to Estevan. From his discussions there he felt confident that should a strike take place, it would pass over quickly as "there are a thousand men ready to take the miners' places."

As a precaution and perhaps to mollify the operators, the government sent a detective to join the two-man RCMP detachment in Estevan to investigate "the alleged violence that was to happen at the mines of this district." After spending a couple of days making quiet enquiries in Bienfait and visiting the mines, Detective Constable Sincennes made a report that helps to explain the initial sympathy shown to the miners' cause by the RCMP:

> The Bienfait Mines are situated about one-half mile from the hamlet of Bienfait, Sask. There is no road other than a prairie trail leading to the mine or the houses. The miners live in small houses, about thirty-five of them, unpainted, which are owned by the mine owner. The company operates a store and the miners are obliged to buy at this store, if not they are threatened to be fired. The store prices are above any of the private merchants in the district.

The miners claim that they have to dig between 2,500 and 2,800 pounds of coal for every ton.

On one instance one of the operators opened a parcel addressed to one of the miners, and told this miner that if he ordered any more merchandise from Eatons he would be fired. The difference between the Eaton price and the Company's price was deducted from his miner's pay.

These are some of the grievances the miners have to put up with, and as there is no leader amongst them, President Sloan was certainly welcome in this district... It is my firm belief that there is, so far, no cause to worry, and that the miners will abide by Sloan's word who has so far told them that no violence must be used if they wanted to get somewhere with their newly born union. (File: Sam Scarlett—Communist Agitator [Secret]. 7 September 1931)

With this situation as background, it is understandable why the head of the Estevan RCMP detachment, Sergeant William Mulhall, a twenty-two-year veteran of the force, was cautious about acceding to the wishes of the operators for action against the union. "There is a noticeable feeling of sympathy in favour of the miners throughout the district," he told his superiors in Regina, and therefore "our investigation must be carried out with care and patience...I am satisfied that there is no immediate necessity for alarm." The majority of these miners are not in favour of communism, he went on, "though they believe that they have had unjust treatment and need a leader to guide them and air their grievances." Twice the union invited the operators to a conference to reach an agreement on wages and working conditions and twice the operators refused to attend. "We will not meet with the representatives of the Mine Workers' Union of Canada," said C. C. Morfit, president of the operators association, "because they are communistic," and the union "is an emissary of the Third Internationale."

The Estevan detachment of the RCMP was more than a little irked by Morfit whom they described as "an American with extreme ideas." This same man Morfit, who would not negotiate a contract with the Bienfait union because it was indirectly affiliated with Moscow, was himself a principal of Stuart, James and Cooke Inc., consulting engineers and efficiency experts of New York City, who held six contracts at the time to operate mines in Tomsk, Kharkov, Leningrad and Moscow. The hypocrisy did not pass unnoticed. Furthermore, Morfit told Sergeant Mulhall and others that when miners went on strike in

Pennsylvania, USA, they were literally mowed down with machine guns and he thought the present situation "should be handled by police in a similar manner." The RCMP believed that Morfit wished to force a strike.

Sergeant Mulhall's information was that, after convincing British investors to put half a million dollars into new machinery at the Bienfait Briquet Plant, the operation was proving to be a failure and, if the plant were forced to close because of a strike, it would form a loophole for the New York company to escape from investors' criticism. The RCMP kept in touch daily with Saskatchewan's attorney general, M. A. MacPherson, and his instructions to the police were that they should not interfere "until the men had committed some illegal act."

If the RCMP showed some sympathy for the ordinary miners, the same cannot be said of their attitude towards the organizers in the mines and those in the Workers' Unity League who were critical to making the union possible. The police had three undercover special constables who knew Ukrainian, one of whom rented a room in the Boruk's Boarding House "with a view to obtaining evidence against these agitators." The police also had two informers (called "stool pigeons" by the miners) who talked "Red," and pretended to criticize the police and the operators. These men knew many of the activists by name. They supplied the RCMP with separate lists of the British-born and the "foreign element" whom they considered to be radical and communist, as well as those they knew to be more reluctant participants in the strike, possibly willing to disown the union. On one such list bearing the names of ten "foreign element" miners, Sergeant Mulhall wrote: "believed to be 'reds'…and bear watching."

The stool pigeons, whose names remain protected in the police files, were not members of the union's leadership committee. They did, however, attend all the general meetings, reporting on the content of speeches and the gist of overheard private conversations. This sometimes caused the police to react to unfounded rumours. Apart from being able to anticipate the union's moves, the police hoped by these reports to catch the militant leaders advocating violent strike tactics, an act which could become the subject of criminal prosecution and possible deportation proceedings. In a gesture of prejudice, the stool pigeon from Taylorton commented that "I have noticed that all Jews in Estevan and Bienfait are 100 percent behind the Communist movement."

While the RCMP tried to undermine the union, the union leaders and the Workers' Unity League organizers expanded community support for the miners. Forkin and Scarlett went to local meetings of the United Farmers of Canada to describe the situation, to solicit food relief contributions and to ask the farmers not to engage in strike breaking. They sent telegrams to unions in Calgary, Winnipeg and Port Arthur, Ontario which brought financial contributions. They contacted other people in the community. Soon the Reverend H. Gordon Tolton, the young Baptist minister in Estevan, began espousing the miners' cause in his church and around the town. Tolton invited his colleague, the Reverend T. C. Douglas of Weyburn Baptist Church to come to Estevan to preach on the subject. As a result Tommy Douglas, who was yet to attain his future prominence, toured the mining camps with his wife. They were appalled by the poor housing and living standards of the miners. Alongside Forkin and Scarlett, Douglas spoke at a mass rally of the miners in Bienfait, representing the Independent Labour Party of Weyburn, and while he was not comfortable with the Workers' Unity League, he considered it a mistake to "give up on a good cause because there are a few communists in it." The next Sunday, on returning to Weyburn, he preached on "Jesus the Revolutionist. How would Jesus view the coal miners' strike in Estevan? Were he to come to Earth again would we crown him, crucify him, or merely deport him?" Douglas led a campaign to collect a truck-load of food for the miners and their families.

On Monday evening, 7 September, after the operators failed a second time to show up for negotiations, the union met to make final preparations for a strike. The men formed a strike committee composed of the executive

Miners in Bienfait being addressed two days prior to the Estevan strike (Courtesy of the Provincial Archives of Saskatchewan / Uncatalogued).

of Local 27 of the Mine Workers' Union of Canada, Joe Forkin, and four committeemen from each of the mines—twenty-eight in all. These men would be the picket captains. At the same time fifty women attended a meeting in the Ukrainian Labour Temple to form a women's auxiliary of the miners' union.

The strike began on Tuesday morning, 8 September. After making arrangements for adequate crews to maintain the deep-seam mines, the union established its picket lines. Only the Truax-Traer Coal Ltd., a recently-started surface strip-mining company (whose owners were connected to the gangster underworld in Chicago) remained open; its new technology—electric shovels, drag lines and bulldozers—were all from North Dakota, and many of the fifty workers were Americans without roots in the community. Eleazar W. Garner, a former mayor of Estevan and the general manager of the local operation, declined to recognize the union because of its affiliation with the Workers' Unity League, but for the moment, after the police refused him permission to hire guards armed with shotguns, he decided not to try to move any coal out.

The strike ended thirty days later without Local 27 being able to win union recognition. The miners could not withstand the combined pressures of Saskatchewan's political elites—including the premier, the attorney-general and others—(who arrived in Bienfait to establish a "patriotic" company union), the intimidation by armed posses of the RCMP (ninety red-coats led by Inspectors Moorhead and Rivett-Carnac) and their own inability to stop the shipment of 125 box cars of coal a day by the Truax-Traer mine, which was in full operation.

What then was the legacy of the Bienfait coal miners' strike of 1931?

In a few short weeks during that summer, the miners, led by the Workers' Unity League, managed to form a union encompassing the whole minefield; they brought the unemployed onto their side and won the sympathy of the farmers; they conducted a month-long strike against the deep-seam mining companies; and they forced the appointment of a Royal Commission to consider their situation. They wrested some concessions from the mine owners; and they made some mistakes. The tragic events of Tuesday, 29 September 1931, which became known as Black Tuesday in Estevan, have already become part of the lore of Canadian labour history, although opinion remains divided even yet on who was responsible. When the striking miners and their families drove into town to publicize their cause—with banners that read "We will not work for Starvation wages; We want houses, not piano boxes," and "Down with the company store"—armed police stopped their motorcade, and in the ensuing melee killed three men and wounded a score of others. The miners were driven helter-skelter back to the coalfields, their leaders and the wounded hunted down like criminals. In an atmosphere of police terror, the militant miners stood firm, raised $100,000 in property and cash bail for their arrested comrades, testified in court and appeared before the Royal Commission to state their woes and offer proposals to change the rules governing the mining industry. The next time around, a decade or so afterwards, the same miners' local union (under a new name) would win some strikes and take permanent root in Local 7606 of District 18 of the United Mine Workers of America.

Sixty-six years later, in 1997, when passions had subsided somewhat, the Saskatchewan Federation of Labour conducted a ceremony honouring the three martyrs: Peter Markunas, Nick Nargan and Julian Gryshko. The participants in this ceremony completed the ill-fated motorcade of 1931 by returning to the coalfields from Estevan in a solemn automobile procession, escorted this time by the RCMP at their own request. The procession stretched for over a mile across the prairie. It ended in a sudden windstorm that whipped up the prairie soil from the nearby fields, darkening the sky and enveloping the Bienfait graveyard. Amelia Budris, Peter Markunas' widow, who has lived in the village all her life, stepped forward with great dignity to unveil a memorial plaque on the martyrs' tomb. In the presence of a crowd of veteran miners, family members, local mayors and members of the provincial legislature and federal parliament, a Miner's Choir and other supporters, the Canadian labour movement paid tribute to "the fighting spirit of the 1931 strikers, and the courage of the three miners who gave their lives to better the lot of other workers." In the fullness of time the rumours and gossip, the usual account of the communist organizers as a group or violence-prone criminal conspirators has been redressed. Historians and the labour movement in Saskatchewan are coming to view the lead given by the Workers' Unity League and the activities of the group of Bienfait miners inspired by the ideas of Marxism in a more objective fashion: it was the president of the coal operators, not the union leaders, who advocated violence; it was the government's police who practiced conspiracy and used firearms. And it was the workers, and Sam Scarlett, Annie Buller and their comrades who went to jail or exile or on a blacklist for exercising their democratic rights.

Peter Gemby, 94, a miner and original member of the Red Hall in Bienfait who had participated in the 1931 procession and had been blacklisted for ten years, told the crowd in Estevan in 1997 that he'd been waiting patiently for this day. "In the long run, history is on the side of the people," he said. "I hope the young people here will feel encouraged by what can be achieved when the union makes you strong." The legacy and lesson of the strike, in short, was that history may be contested; nothing is inevitable or fixed, everything remains subject to challenge and change.

NOTES

This article first appeared in *Prairie Forum* 31, no. 2 (2006): 217–232.

SOURCES

This article is adapted from material in the author's book, *Bienfait: The Saskatchewan Miners' Struggle of '31* (Toronto: University of Toronto Press, 2002); sources for all quotations are there. Documentary resources include Records of the Royal Commission on the Estevan-Bienfait Mining Dispute, 1931 (Wylie Commission), Records of the Royal Commission on Coal Mining, 1934 (Turgeon Commission), transcripts of the trial *Rex vs. Anne Buller, Rex vs. Samuel Scarlett* and other related trials, transcript of *Harry Kaik et al. vs. Nick Boraska et al.*, over the ownership of the Ukrainian Hall in Bienfait, microfilm of *The Mercury* (Estevan), records of the Department of Labour, Deputy Minister's Office, Estevan Strike File, 1931; James H. Cuddington, "History of Bienfait" (typescript) all located in the Provincial Archives of Saskatchewan, Regina; microfilm of *The Leader-Post*, Regina Public Library; records of the Estevan Court House, Estevan, *Rex vs. Day et al.*, and other related trials; Estevan Municipal Archives, file on the Strike of 1931; Bienfait Village Office, Minutes of Council, 1931; Rural Municipality of Coalfields, No. 4, Bienfait, Minutes of Council, 1931; microfilm records of the Communist Party of Canada, RG4, microfilm of *The Worker*, *The Western Miner/Canadian Miner, Workers' Unity*, all located in the Ontario Archives, Toronto; Bill Bennett Collection, Angus MacInnis Collection, UBC Special Collections, Vancouver, BC; records of the Canadian Security Information Service (CSIS) in RG176, including Vol. 817, file H.V.7, parts 1 to 6 which is the Royal Canadian Mounted Police Correspondence on the miners' strike and personal history file 175/P2456 of Sam Scarlett, records of the Communist Party of Canada, MG28. IV.4, all in the National Archives of Canada, Ottawa; S. D. Hanson, "The Estevan Strike and Riot, 1931" (MA thesis, University of Regina, 1971); *A Tale Is Told: Estevan 1890–1980*, 2 vols (Estevan: 1981); Peter Krawchuk (ed.), *Our Stage: Amateur Performing Arts of the Ukrainian Settlers in Canada* (Toronto: Kobzar Publishing, 1984); Peter Krawchuk (ed.), *Women's Fate: Interviews with Ukrainian Canadian Women* (in Ukrainian, Toronto: Kobzar Publishing, 1973); *Almanac of the Ukrainian Labour-Farmer Temple Association 1918–1929* (in Ukrainian, Winnipeg: 1930): 177–78; Tom McEwen, *The Forge Glows Red* (Toronto: Progress Books, 1974), Annie Buller, "The Estevan Massacre," *National Affairs Monthly* (May 1949); Glen Makahonuk, "Trade Unions in the Saskatchewan Coal Industry, 1907–1945," *Saskatchewan History* 31, no. 2 (Spring 1978); Ovid Demaris, *Captive City* (New York: Lyle Stuart, Inc., 1969).

Oral history sources include taped interviews in the 1970s with Howard A. Babcock (camp cook), Peter Gemby (miner), Alex Konopaki (miner, small mine operator), Archibald MacQuarrie (miner) Jean Moroz (miner's wife), Harry Nicholson (town councilor, small mine operator, mayor of Estevan), Mervyn Enmark (miner, foreman), Thomas Hesketh, (miner), Sarah Prescott (blacksmith's wife), Leslie Kingdon (miner), Joe Pryznyk (miner, policeman), and others, in the "Estevan Strike and Riot, 1931" and "Sounds and Stories of Strip-mining Soft Coal in Southern Saskatchewan," all to be found in the Provincial Archives of Saskatchewan, Regina.

My special thanks to residents and former residents of Bienfait for agreeing to interviews in the 1990s and sharing with me their memories and thoughts about people and events surrounding the miners' strike: Mike and Helen (Hitchens/Pryznuk) Antoniuk, Tony Bachynski, Mike and Elaine Baryluk, Steve and Gloria Baryluk, William Baryluk, Ann Bozak (Elchyson), Amelia Budris (Billis, Markunas), Paul Carroll, Gene Choma, Wally Choma, Jim Davies, Donald Doerr, Sam Dzuba, Steve Elchyson, Peter and Stella (Bachynski) Gemby, Stewart Giem, Kenneth Hesketh, Mary-Jo Rohatyn, Tom and Mary Sernick, Anne Thompson (Billis), Norvin Uhrich, George and Olga (Boruk) Wozny. Bob Leslie, of Estevan, kindly shared his archives of the Estevan Labour Committee. And finally, thanks to Misha Korol, of Toronto, for his recollections about the Ukrainian Labour-Farmer Temple Association and for help with translations.

6. Unemployed Struggles in Saskatchewan and Canada, 1930–1935

Lorne Brown

INTRODUCTION

During the first five years of the Great Depression unemployment and the threat of unemployment became the most important issue facing working people across Canada. It was a national problem though it was worse in some regions than others. The Saskatchewan economy was especially devastated because of the collapse of agriculture, which affected not only rural communities, but also the cities where employment plummeted in the construction, transportation and service industries. The problem was national in scope and there was little a province like Saskatchewan could do to alleviate unemployment. The struggle around unemployment would be fought out on the local level by necessity within a national context.

One should begin by looking at unemployment as a political issue in mainstream politics during the first five years of the Great Depression. It was probably the single most important issue contributing to the defeat of Mackenzie King's Liberal government in the federal election of 1930. And it was undoubtedly the most important contributing factor in the annihilation of the R. B. Bennett government five years later. In the intervening five years, provincial Conservative governments were defeated in British Columbia, Saskatchewan, Manitoba, Ontario and Nova Scotia. Unemployment was a significant issue in all of the provinces but particularly in British Columbia and Ontario where Pattulo and Hepburn had emphasized the plight of the unemployed in their election campaigns. Both men represented an unorthodox populist variety of Liberalism. And in British Columbia and Saskatchewan, not only were the Conservatives annihilated but the newly founded Co-operative Commonwealth Federation (CCF) rose as the main provincial opposition. The rise of Social Credit in Alberta and the Union Nationale in Quebec also occurred in the mid-1930s and unemployment and related issues were factors in both cases.

From the time the Conservatives made unemployment a priority issue in the federal election of 1930, all parties, at both provincial and federal levels, either continually raised it or were compelled to respond to it as an important public issue. But while the two major parties treated unemployment in general as an important public issue, they did not regard the unemployed themselves as specific constituencies to be cultivated or organized. Most politicians considered the unemployed themselves to be almost outside the "body politic." Opposition politicians might tailor some of their propaganda towards the unemployed during election campaigns but even here, the appeal was more to the fear of unemployment among those who still had jobs than to the already jobless. Unemployment was generally treated as the symptom of an unhealthy political economy with little attention paid to the specific grievances and problems of the unemployed. This would change as unemployment increased and the unemployed developed organizations of their own.

At the beginning of the Depression, the Independent Labour Party (ILP) and other social democratic parties and formations in Canada also lacked an overall strategy for organizing the unemployed or appealing to them as a specific constituency. As the situation developed, the ILP and its successor, the CCF, would participate directly in unemployed struggles in some provinces and localities.[1] And in their Parliamentary work and their electoral campaigns, the CCF put more emphasis on unemployment and recommended more sweeping legislative remedies. But they never did develop a co-coordinated national strategy for day to day political work among the unemployed.

For the most part, the established labour organizations of the day, while concerned and even alarmed at the increasing unemployment, had no organizational or political strategy for dealing with the large number of unemployed workers. In the initial years of the Depression, many of the trade unions affiliated to the Trades and Labour Congress (TLC), the All Canadian Congress of Labour (ACCL) and the Canadian Catholic Congress of Labour (CCCL) were losing ground as many of their members lost their jobs. There was no consistent strategy for keeping in organizational touch with these ex-trade unionists let alone embarking upon campaigns to organize the great masses of unemployed—most of whom had never been organized into unions. Most established unions contented themselves with acting as pressure groups attempting to persuade governments to embark upon public works programs and to be more generous with their relief policies.

In general, the more conservative elements in the Canadian political community feared the very idea of an organized movement of unemployed. Most of those Liberals and social democrats who did sympathize thought only in terms of legislative solutions or palliatives. They did not view organizing among the unemployed as a priority activity and in many cases, they did not believe it was possible to organize the unemployed on any meaningful scale. This was true of most of the Trade Union leadership, probably the majority of ILP-CCF activists, and most left wing sympathizers in the churches and the intellectual community.

Before the 1930s, there had been sporadic attempts to organize the unemployed but with no success over any extended length of time or beyond scattered local areas. From a trade union perspective, the task would be even more difficult than attempting to organize unskilled workers in a locality where there was a labour surplus. The unemployed had no labour power to withdraw and hence no bargaining position. It was especially difficult with the transient, single, unemployed, because of their habit of moving from locality to locality in search of jobs. This made it difficult for the rank and file to develop organizational loyalties and experience and militated against the development of a stable leadership.

Historically, the unemployed had lacked status not only in the society as a whole but also within the working class and trade union community. They were often feared by trade unionists as potential strike-breakers during periods of class conflict. Prolonged periods of unemployment also sapped the pride of the jobless and some developed a "lumpen proletarian" mentality and lifestyle. Many who escaped this often developed a cynicism, which made them rebellious and contemptuous of constituted authority as individuals but with no consciousness of class solidarity. Organization and collective action were anathema to such individuals. Some became the proverbial "hoboes" of the popular imagination who were constantly on the move in search of casual employment and when not working obtained part of their sustenance from charity, begging and minor crime.

The above description of the "hobo" mentality would be inaccurate for the vast majority of those transient workers who would become unemployed during the first few years of the Depression. These people, the majority of whom were single and young, comprised an indispensable part of the Canadian work force during normal times. They were crucial in the forestry industries, road and railway construction and maintenance, agriculture, urban construction and often in mining and other resource industries as well. They were indispensable to the Canadian economy but suffered from a relatively high incidence of unemployment even during the most prosperous years. However, they constituted a disciplined, if unskilled, workforce and most had ambitions of eventually obtaining the type of permanent employment that would allow them to marry and settle down in one locality. While these people often suffered temporary periods of unemployment, they were not accustomed to lengthy periods of joblessness. They were accustomed to the status that comes from having a regular job. A small minority would have been members of unions at one time or another. They would be unlikely to tolerate the treatment historically accorded to "hoboes." Generalized discontent built up rapidly as the rate of unemployment got worse instead of better. The possibilities for organization would soon emerge for those with the imagination and dedication to attempt the very difficult task.

Few people who sympathized with the unemployed at the beginning of the Depression believed that a sustainable organization was possible, and they were inclined to virtually write off the single transient unemployed in this regard. They had developed ideas about the transient unemployed similar to those of Reverend Andrew Roddan who spent years working among the destitute in the "jungles" around Vancouver. Roddan claimed that Communists and others had made persistent efforts to organize such people but it was an impossible task:

> They will talk about aims and objectives and curse and damn
> the capitalist system, but when it comes to the actual working
> out of ideas, it is impossible to do anything with them. The boss,
> the Labour Party, the Capitalists and the Communists are all
> trying to put something over on them, which they won't stand.[2]

Roddan saw his role as providing practical relief and spiritual sustenance to the unemployed. He had never been a political or union organizer and he had obviously been jaded by years of work in what appeared to be a hopeless environment. Some people who did have experience at organizing were almost as pessimistic. The One Big Union (OBU) sent an experienced man named J. Terrill on a "scouting" tour of the Prairies and BC and he travelled those provinces from April through June, 1931. The OBU had been founded in 1919 during the great labour upsurge after World War 1. They were led largely by orthodox socialists though they also represented some radical syndicalist tendencies. They enjoyed a brief spectacular growth but were crippled by the state and the employers in the reaction which followed the Winnipeg General

Strike. By 1930, they were limited mainly to Winnipeg but enjoyed some presence in a few other localities. Terrill reported his findings in letters to the OBU office in Winnipeg and in a series of articles under the by-line "The Wayfarer" for the OBU *Bulletin*.³ Terrill encountered vastly more people "riding the rods" and in the "jungles" than at any time in his experience as a transient, which went back to 1908. He remarked on the large number of young men and youth on the move, most for the first time, and also of encountering for the first time unemployed women riding the rods.

Terrill was pessimistic about the political consciousness of the transient unemployed and claimed that those who thought unemployed youth were developing radical ideas "had better wake up and get in touch with reality."⁴ He claimed that they were merely trying to "get by" and were neither aware of political ideas nor interested in organization. "On the road today the old time criticisms of the existing order and the propaganda for the changed social relationship has ceased, and the anthems of rebellion from the 'Little Red Song Book' of the Wobblies are seldom if ever heard. The nascent hobo of 1931 knows nothing, and as yet desires to know nothing about his position in modern society"⁵

In one of his letters to OBU headquarters, Terrill claimed that 80 percent of the sawmills had closed down in the BC interior and demoralization had set in among large numbers of former loggers who had been unemployed for over a year. "Many of them are rapidly becoming unemployable and are degenerating both physically and mentally. Their backbone seems to have evaporated and their sole aim in life appears to be to get hold of a quart of whisky, a bottle of 'joky' or a tin of canned heat. This ideology, I am sorry to say, is general among the short logger today; of course there are exceptions but they are few and far between."⁶

In several of his letters, Terrill also claimed that racism was on the upsurge among both workers and the unemployed, many of whom blamed unemployment on competition from "foreigners," meaning immigrants:

> Naturally enough, there is discontent, any amount of discontent, but—in the main—their discontent expresses itself in the form of anti-foreignism, anti-Slovak, anti-Swede. In my opinion, it will take years of propaganda and education work to eliminate this feeling.⁷

He was also fearful of the rise of the Ku Klux Klan or a fascist anti-foreign organization among working people and the unemployed. "The time appears opportune for a fascist, anti-alien movement, because from nearly every English speaking person I meet I hear the same opinion expressed—'damn the foreigners!'"[8]

Terrill was pessimistic about the possibility of an immediate progressive organization among the unemployed and considered it more possible that there would be outbreaks of lawlessness by small groups of the desperate. He thought this likely to occur first in the BC interior where thousands of unemployed were travelling up and down the valleys of the province. He foresaw marauding gangs of the hungry and desperate raiding isolated farms and ranches and food stores and claimed there had already been some instances of ranchers with rifles driving off bands of hungry men. Terrill concluded one of his articles with the following warning:

> Granted a continuance of the present situation unrelieved, sooner or later—and possibly sooner—some groups of hungry desperate men will go off the deep end and challenge society's dictum that men must starve in the midst of plenty. And such an action may well spread like wildfire and all hell break loose. Gentlemen of the bourgeoisie, it is your next move.[9]

Though his letters and articles were generally pessimistic, Terrill did sound a couple of optimistic notes. He claimed that the general public was more sympathetic to the unemployed than in the depressions he had experienced in the past: "In British Columbia at least, there seems to be a full recognition of the present crisis, and a knowledge that those now unemployed are now so through no fault of their own."[10] From his experience as a transient worker and an OBU activist, Terrill also recognized that while such workers were difficult to organize, they had great potential during periods of intense class conflict. "By the very nature of the occupations they follow and the lives they lead, hard to organize and hard to keep organized. But once started, once on the upsurge, they are initiative by instinct and daring to a fault, and represent a part of the working class not lightly to be disregarded in time of political upheaval and dangerous in the extreme to those who are now enthroned in the seats of the mighty."[11]

EARLY UNEMPLOYED ORGANIZING

Events over the next couple of years would demonstrate the accuracy of Terrill's claim that there was substantial public sympathy for the unemployed. His assessment of the potential should these unemployed transient workers be organized was also borne out though they would not be organized under the auspices of the One Big Union. In fact organization among the unemployed had already taken root in many cities by the time of Terrill's tour in the spring of 1931, though such organization had not yet made much headway among single unemployed transients.

In scattered parts of the country the urban unemployed had been organizing since 1929. Some of this was done on a purely local and almost spontaneous basis by independents not associated with any trade union or party. Some of it was done by individuals or local groups associated with the ILP, the Socialist Party of Canada or the Communist Party. From mid-1929, *The Worker*, official organ of the Communist Party of Canada, was reporting periodically on local unemployed struggles and calling for the organization of the unemployed on a national basis.

The Worker of 10 August 1929 reported that two men named Plummer and Perkins, described as "two leaders of the unemployed", had been arrested during an unemployed action in Regina.[12] This was followed up on 17 August with a report that the two men were serving sentences on "trumped up" charges. The same article predicted that unemployment would get much worse in the coming winter because of poor harvest and other factors. *The Worker* headlined the article "Unemployed Must Organize Their Forces For Nation Wide Struggle."[13]

It mentioned that the Mayor of Toronto had declared that the unemployed could not expect much help in the coming winter and the existence of the Communist Party might make them dangerous.[14] The article claimed that the unemployed were still barely organized in most places and the issue of unemployment was an important one for the working class as a whole and would require organization which was national in scope. "It is necessary that the unemployed worker at once take steps towards organization. It is not sufficient that the unemployed workers of each city organize separately. The organization of the unemployed workers must be on a nationwide scale."[15]

Throughout the latter months of 1929, unemployed organizing was taking place in several of the major cities in Canada with much of it under the direction and encouragement of the Communist Party. The necessity for organization was constantly reiterated in *The Worker* in articles, letters and slogans. Their predictions of what was to come often turned out to be amazingly accurate. On 26 October, an item from Calgary entitled "Calgary Unemployed Must Organize and Fight" described rising unemployment in the city and the necessity for an organization to agitate for work and wages or full maintenance. "The time has now arrived where a National Unemployment

Organization must be built because stability of industry has reached its peak and is now on the decline. This means a permanent unemployment situation."[16] An item from Vancouver on 14 December described a conference of 500 who set up an unemployed organization in the city with plans to extend its activities into the surrounding areas. The meeting had been called by the District Executive Committee of the Communist Party and out of it would come the Vancouver Unemployed Workers Association which would become one of the most active and effective in the country.[17]

The attempt to organize the unemployed on a national basis got underway in earnest after the formation of the Workers' Unity League (WUL) in January 1930. The WUL was founded under Communist Party auspices and based on an expansion of, and new direction for, the adherents of the old Trade Union Educational League (TUEL), which had been in operation throughout the latter years of the 1920s."[18] The WUL reflected the new "class against class" strategy adopted by the Comintern in 1928 and was intended to be a revolutionary alternative to the mainstream trade union federations. Most unions in the WUL were affiliated with the Red International of Labour Unions (RILU) so that the new body was intended to be not only national but international in scope. Unemployed associations, women's organizations, and other bodies which were not trade unions in the strict sense of the term, could affiliate with the WUL. They could not affiliate with other labour federations.

From the beginning, the Workers' Unity League considered the organization of the unemployed to be a major priority. They established an Unemployment Commission to oversee their work and when the Southern Ontario Conference of the WUL met in Toronto on May 24–25, 1930, it was evident that these organizational efforts were already bearing fruit. In fact, in the few months since the formation of the WUL, they may well have made more progress with unemployed than with employed workers. Karl Steinberg, who made the report to the conference on behalf of the Unemployment Commission, emphasized that unemployment had become a permanent national question and one of the important branches of WUL activities. He also emphasized the common interests of the employed and the unemployed and the necessity for unity. "Clearly it is the task of the WUL to lead the fight of the jobless for 'Work or Maintenance'. Only the revolutionary section of the labour movement can and will achieve the unity of the employed and unemployed on the basis of the common struggle against capitalism."[19]

Steinberg reported that there were already unemployed associations, most under communist leadership, in a half dozen of the major cities of southern Ontario. They were about to appoint a full time organizer to tour the province in preparation for launching a province-wide unemployed association at a conference in Toronto in July. The National Unemployed Workers' Association (NUWA) had already been declared to be in existence though, as yet, it had few affiliations. On the second clay of the conference, Charles Sims laid out the immediate tasks facing the WUL in an ambitious four-point program. Point two was as follows:

> The organization of the unemployed workers, where we have the task of uniting the already existing associations of Toronto, Hamilton, Windsor, Brantford, East York, Sudbury, Twin Cities and starting a campaign to organize associations in every city and town in Southern Ontario into a powerful provincial section of the National Unemployed Workers' Association.[20]

By the summer of 1931, the NUWA had dozens of local affiliates and thousands of individuals who looked to it for direction. Most of the major cities of the country had unemployed associations as did many of the smaller cities and towns. There would be several in each of the large cities organized on a district basis. There would often be separate organizations for single unemployed, married unemployed, unemployed war veterans and wives and children of unemployed. Even small cities could generally boast more than one such association. Saskatoon, a city of fewer than 40,000 in a predominantly agrarian province, had six such associations.[21] Tom McEwan estimated there were 16,000 members in the NUWA by July 1931.[22]

Not all unemployed associations were affiliated to the NUWA by any means. But the NUWA was the only organization providing national coordination and a national focus to the unemployed movement. This was extremely important in mounting pressure on the federal and provincial governments. It made possible centralized propaganda and strategic direction and provided the resources for full time organizers. And NUWA influence went beyond affiliated associations to reach thousands of individuals who belonged to non-affiliated associations and in many cases, no organizations at all. There would be very few unemployed associations in any of the major cities where there would not be at least a few supporters of the WUL, and/or the Communist Party. Andrée Levesque mentions eleven unemployed associations in greater Montreal where Communist Party supporters were active, though in many cases they would have very limited influence.[23]

Most of the unemployed struggles were on the local level and varied according to the local regulations, the ideological complexion of local politicians, the strength of the labour movement in the region and other factors. Struggles over relief rates and whether they should be in kind or cash were among the most common. Other points of contention were residency rules and who qualified for relief and under what circumstances. Disputes and work stoppages on projects where people had to work for relief were common. Organized actions to prevent people from being evicted from their homes or having furniture seized for non-payment of rent or taxes were frequent. Parades, demonstrations, petitions, delegations, sit-ins and occupations were among the tactics employed. Riots, often provoked by police actions, were not uncommon.

Perusal of left and labour journals and the daily press of the period reveal that struggles involving the organized unemployed were taking place on an almost continuous basis from early 1931. And they were spread across the country from Cape Breton to Vancouver Island. One need only examine the memoirs and biographies of almost any of the political and labour activists of the early 1930s to get a conception of the breadth and depth of the day-to-day struggle. Excellent accounts are contained in *Recollections of the On-to-Ottawa Trek, Work and Wages!, Which Side are You On, Boys, George MacEachern: An Autobiography, A Communist Life*, and other works of this nature.[24]

ORGANIZED UNEMPLOYED BECOME A NATIONAL PRESENCE

Perhaps where the National Unemployed Workers' Association and the WUL played their most important role was in their ability to transcend the hundreds of local struggles and provide a national focus. They could launch national campaigns making demands of the federal government and undertake mass protest actions coordinated on a national and occasionally even an international scale.

A survey of some of the major campaigns and actions of the NUWA and the WUL from January 1930 can provide a flavour of what was taking place at the time. They launched a nation-wide petition campaign to demand a national non-contributory unemployment insurance program. This coincided with a simultaneous campaign demanding from both the provincial and federal governments either work and wages or full relief maintenance for the unemployed and their dependents. These campaigns involved leafleting, mass meetings, door-to-door canvassing, demonstrations and delegations waiting upon politicians at all levels of government. They drew in not just the unemployed organizations but also WUL unions and sometimes individual activists and union locals in the mainstream union federations as well as such organizations as the Ukrainian Labour-Farmer Temple Association, the Women's Labour

League and other groups associated with the WUL or the Communist Party. The demands were sometimes endorsed by local church assemblies, locals of the ILP and other moderate left groups and thus reached beyond the hard core base of the communist oriented left. The demand for unemployment insurance was known as the Unemployment Bill Campaign and the petition garnered 94,169 signatures by 15 April 1931.[25] This campaign continued for several years and various unemployment insurance schemes became the subjects of debate in Parliament and the press. It provided the unemployed movement with a forum among more mainstream circles in the country.

Some of the national protest actions mounted by the NUWA, the WUL and related organizations in the first few months of 1931 indicate that they were beginning to build a considerable base across the country. On 25 February, they took part in the International Day against Unemployment which was sponsored by the Comintern and the Red International of Labour Unions. Millions demonstrated in countries throughout the world. Avakumovic cites sources to the effect that 122,000 leaflets were distributed in Canada in preparation for the day and more than 76,000 participated in street demonstrations.[26] The turnout was estimated at 13,000 in Toronto, 12,000 in Winnipeg, 5,000 each in Montreal and Vancouver and smaller demonstrations in many other cities and towns. The issue most emphasized in the leaflets and slogans was the demand for non-contributory unemployment insurance. These events were covered extensively by most newspapers in Canada and often related to similar activities in other countries.

The 25 February day of protest was followed up on 15 March with a large demonstration of unemployed on Parliament Hill which sparked newspaper comments throughout the country. Nation-wide demonstrations of unemployed were mounted again on 15 April when a delegation interviewed Prime Minister Bennett with demands for unemployment insurance. On this occasion, there were clashes between demonstrators and police in Montreal, Ottawa, Sudbury and Winnipeg. Two weeks later, unemployment was one of the main issues emphasized at May Day demonstrations in most cities and many towns throughout Canada. On this occasion demonstrations were broken up by police in Calgary and Port Arthur and there were clashes between police and demonstrators in several other cities.

THE "IRON HEEL OF RUTHLESSNESS"

By this time, the federal government and many municipal and provincial officials across the country were seriously alarmed at the extent of unrest among the unemployed, and especially the single male transient unemployed. The situation was deteriorating. From the time of the so-called "great crash" of October 1929, unemployment continuously increased throughout Canada until it peaked in 1933. Most politicians and government officials throughout the country barely understood what was happening and had no adequate plans to deal with the crisis. The Conservative government in Ottawa was becoming particularly unpopular with many of the unemployed partly because Bennett had made unemployment such an important issue in the federal election of 1930. In fact, in a speech in Moncton on July 10, Bennett had made the rash promise to provide work and wages for everybody:

> The Conservative party is going to find work for all who are willing to work, or perish in the attempt—Mr. King promised consideration of the problem of unemployment. I promise to end unemployment. Which plan do you like best?[27]

Bennett had only two plans to end unemployment. One was for Canada to "blast our way into the markets of the world" by increasing tariffs and then negotiating bilateral trade agreements. The other was to provide matching grants to the provinces and municipalities for public works projects and relief. After winning the election, Bennett called a special session of Parliament in September 1930 to implement his employment policy. The government raised tariffs substantially across the board and in the fall of 1930 also provided for a $20 million grant for relief projects to be administered by the provinces and municipalities. Bennett assumed that this would be sufficient to relieve the situation until the tariff increases restored the economy to normal which he anticipated would be the spring of 1931.[28] When the situation got continually worse rather than better, both federal and provincial governments were compelled to provide more relief to stave off widespread starvation and the chaos that would result.[29] But it was woefully inadequate. James Struthers has described how governments lurched from crisis to crisis during the first few years of the Depression with no effective strategy for alleviating the plight of the unemployed.[30] The unemployed were being forced into an increasingly hopeless situation and this was especially true of the single transient unemployed who in many parts of the country were denied any governmental assistance whatsoever.[31]

Given the circumstances, the degree of unrest and disorder which had already developed by the spring of 1931 is hardly surprising. The response to this by the authorities was to attempt to control the situation by increasing repression, pending the recovery of the economy. This was the response of the police, the judiciary, the business community, most provincial and many municipal politicians, much of the press and the federal government in the first few years of the Depression. Prime Minister Bennett provided much of the leadership and a good deal of the direction for this repression and boasted that he would be applying "the iron heel of ruthlessness" in combating communism and all its works. And he made it clear that the state of the political economy necessitated such a policy. "Whenever the minds of the people are disturbed by economic conditions, there are always agitators who capitalize and exploit 'humanitarianism' and the sympathy which is latent in all of us for the underdog."[32]

It is beyond the scope of this paper to go into detail on the fierceness of the political repression which gripped Canada between 1930 and 1935. It has been well documented by scholars and in the memoirs of many of the political activists of the period.[33] It was the most severe and extensive repression in our country during peace time in the twentieth century. It included police attacks on demonstrations and meetings, smashing strikes, deportations, raids on the premises of a great variety of left wing organizations, prison sentences for activists, and official encouragement of right wing vigilante groups. Much of this repression was directed against the organized unemployed movement.

The unrest and repressive response could be seen building up throughout the winter of 1930–31 and, with the coming of spring and summer, demonstrations became larger and more unruly and their suppression by the police more severe. The newspapers were full of stories about confrontations with the police after May Day when tens of thousands demonstrated in the streets across the country. In ruling circles, demands were building up for a crackdown on the agitators allegedly responsible for the unrest.[34] These demands played a role in the escalation of the repression with the arrest, conviction and imprisonment of Tim Buck and other Communist leaders under Section 98 of the Criminal Code of Canada in the fall of 1931.[35]

Those government officials and editorialists who hoped that the onslaught by the state against the Communist Party would weaken the organized unemployed movement were to be sadly disappointed. Struggles on the local level increased in the latter part of 1931 and into 1932. And the NUWA and related organizations continued to mount actions which were province-wide and national in scale.

In 1932, the tactics of organizing what became known as the "Hunger Marches" became common with marches often being held in several cities simultaneously. On 22 February there were very large demonstrations of this nature in British Columbia. On 3 March there were cross-Canada demonstrations with a large one of several thousand in Ottawa where an unemployed delegation presented demands to the Bennett government. On this occasion, the massive use of force, with over 200 police and an armoured car on Parliament Hill resulted in embarrassing questions in Parliament and critical comments in the press. Mitch Hepburn, then the MP for Elgin West, led the attack for the Liberals:

> In view of the fact that Parliament Hill today has taken on the appearance of an armed camp, I would ask the Minister of Justice [Mr. Guthrie] whether his troops had been instructed to shoot the unemployed if necessary.[36]

Even some staunchly Conservative newspapers were moved to protest with the *Ottawa Journal* claiming that the scene "smacked more of Fascism than of Canadian constitutional authority."[37] The events of March were followed up with especially large cross-country May Day demonstrations in 1932 with some estimating that there may have been as many as one hundred thousand in the streets. Unemployment was again one of the main themes.

The Saskatchewan unemployed played a considerable role in this turmoil. There were unemployed organizations in the four major cities and a few of the larger towns. The federal and provincial governments had various schemes attempting to deal with the situation. These included a program to place single men and women on farms where they would work for room and board and $5 monthly. There were also federal work camps run by the Department of Interior in Prince Albert National Park and provincial work camps which at one time numbered twenty-three. There were also relief projects for the married unemployed in the cities.

As unemployment mounted the various schemes failed to put an end to the unrest. Demonstrations were frequent in 1931 and alarmed the Regina RCMP who requested and received an issue of 300 bayonets and 30,000 rounds of 303 ammunition that year. The May Day parade in Regina in 1932 involved 10,000 participants and spectators and resulted in scattered violence and nine arrests. In October 1932 there were strikes at several Regina relief projects. On 7 November, about eighty RCMP and city police dispersed a rally of unemployed in front of the Saskatoon relief offices which resulted in what the Canadian Press called "the bloodiest riot ever seen in this city."[38] Dozens of unemployed and policemen were injured and several people arrested.

The unrest in Saskatchewan increased in the first months of 1933. May Day parades were banned in Regina and Saskatoon and in Moose Jaw both parades and meetings were banned on May Day and a labour hall was raided.

On May 8 a clash between police and unemployed at a relief camp on the outskirts of Saskatoon led to the death of RCMP Inspector L. J. Sampson, several injuries and the arrest of about thirty people.[39]

One of the more publicized events of 1932 was the Workers' Economic Conference held in Ottawa in early August simultaneously with the Imperial Economic Conference hosted by the Bennett government. Bennett hoped to make the Imperial Economic Conference the centrepiece of his strategy of using economic nationalism to fight the Depression. He was proposing bilateral trade agreements between Canada and other Commonwealth countries with the idea of working towards a high tariff wall for certain products around the entire British Empire. The WUL took advantage of the occasion to sponsor the Workers' Economic Conference to press working class demands, including unemployment insurance, on the Bennett government. The conference was attended by 502 delegates representing more than 50 organizations from various parts of the country.[40] There were also large demonstrations of unemployed workers, most from Ontario and Quebec, who had made their way to Ottawa for the occasion. There were confrontations with police and several arrests. The Workers' Economic Conference received considerable publicity not only in the daily press and the WUL newspapers but also in intellectual journals like the *Canadian Forum*.

Another of the events of 1932 which received a great deal of attention was the Alberta Hunger March when thousands of farmers, workers, and unemployed from throughout the province converged on Edmonton on 20 December. This was broken up by police with dozens of arrests. The trials resulting from the arrests became the focus of further agitation throughout the province. There were additional Hunger Marches converging on Ottawa, Toronto and various other cities in January 1933.

UNEMPLOYED RELIEF CAMPS

By the fall of 1932 the federal government was under considerable pressure to take control over the single, transient unemployed males who were "riding the rods" across the country and accumulating in large numbers in many of the major cities.[41] These people were considered the most dangerous by the authorities because they were the most difficult to intimidate. The threat of being cut off relief, imprisoned or deported was a very intimidating prospect to married men with family responsibilities. These possibilities were a factor with single men as well, but most of them got little or no relief in any case and as they became more desperate the likelihood of imprisonment lost some of its terror, especially in the midst of a Prairie winter.

Several provinces were already operating work and/or holding camps for the single unemployed by 1932.[42] But they were a financial drain and centres of turmoil as well. And provinces like British Columbia were constantly complaining about being inundated by an influx of single unemployed from other provinces. It was General McNaughton, Chief of the General Staff, who convinced the Bennett government to embark on unemployment relief camps under the auspices of the Department of National Defence in the late fall of 1932.[43] By mid-1933 the federal government had concluded agreements with most of the provinces to assume responsibility for a significant proportion of the single, homeless, physically fit unemployed males in the country. From the beginning it was understood by both provincial and federal authorities that a primary purpose of the camps was to remove the single unemployed from the cities.[44] And for many single unemployed, the camps were compulsory as they were denied any relief in the cities and then forced either to enter the camps or face arrest for vagrancy.[45]

James Struthers has pointed out that when the federal relief camp system was first established the scheme received very widespread support from mainstream trade unions, daily newspapers, local politicians, social workers and the Parliamentary parties.[46] He then discusses some of the reasons why the camps quickly became one of the most unpopular institutions established by the Bennett government and contrasts this with the somewhat similar Civilian Conservation Corps operated under the auspices of Roosevelt's New Deal in the United States. Struthers demonstrates that the different nature of the single unemployed problem in the two countries and the different approach of the governments explain why such camps were a total failure here and a success in the United States.

While Struthers is correct in portraying the federal relief camps in Canada as being initially supported by most mainstream opinion groups they were unpopular from the beginning with many of the single unemployed themselves and almost universally so with those among them who were organized. This was bound to be the case given the fact that the Bennett government was already intensely unpopular among the unemployed. And, as Struthers points out, the way the relief camp system was designed and operated almost guaranteed it.[47] The regulations were authoritarian, the 20¢ daily pay was an insult, the work was done by the most primitive methods and was often merely "work for work's sake" on projects of doubtful social value, and many of the men were forced into the camps against their will.

In British Columbia, the establishment of the federal camps was denounced by *The Unemployed Worker* as "the militarization of the camps" even before most of the camps were in operation.[48] In many BC provincial camps, there had been "camp committees" which had been granted virtual *de facto* recognition for negotiating grievances with supervisors. Their rations and allowances had also been more generous than would be the case under the new DND scheme. The BC unemployed resisted going into the federal camps and staged a strike involving about five hundred people in several camps in July 1933. It was led by the BC Relief Camp Workers' Union which was just then in the process of formation and would soon become the Relief Camp Workers' Union (RCWU), which would attempt to organize on a national scale. Although these strikes lasted only a few days, they gained some support from mainstream trade unionists, some elements of the Socialist Party of Canada and the CCF and independent sympathizers in addition to the usual support from the Communists and the WUL. It was a sign of the shape of things to come. Brigadier J. Sutherland Brown, District Officer Commanding of Military District 11 in BC had previously warned that "[i]t will be a tremendous and possibly impossible job to get the unemployed out of the cities without powerful legal authority."[49] Brown resigned from the military shortly after the relief camp scheme began when his superiors rejected his suggestions for more generous rations and allowances.[50] He publicly criticized the relief camp system.

There was turmoil surrounding the establishment of DND camps in other provinces. Authorities experienced some difficulties forcing the single unemployed in Edmonton out of the city and into the camps. Dundurn federal camp in Saskatchewan was established after a major riot, described above, involving the death of a policeman at a provincial camp in Saskatoon. There was considerable resistance in Toronto and elsewhere in southern Ontario. Long Branch camp near Toronto was closed in September 1933 after a well organized and bitter strike by its seven hundred inmates.

The federal relief camps were off to a rocky beginning. The single unemployed were much easier to organize in the camps than they had been in the cities. Within a few months of their establishment, many of the camps were organized by secret "bush committees" under the direction of the Relief Camp Workers' Union (RCWU) which was affiliated with the WUL. This was particularly true in British Columbia where over one-third of the relief camps were located. General McNaughton reported that "[t]here is a very active organization known as the British Columbia Relief Camp Workers' Union which publishes a bulletin monthly and which in spite of all our efforts appears to reach most of our camps. I obtain copies from time to time and they indicate a pretty complete organization which has a foothold in practically every camp."[51]

That these relief camps were far from tranquil institutions can be gleaned from the number of disturbances recorded at National Defence Headquarters. General McNaughton left charts of all events of this nature large enough to report to headquarters. He recorded fifty-seven such disturbances between 27 June 1933 and 31 March 1934.[52] Up to 31 December 1933, McNaughton recorded 3,379 men who had been expelled for disciplinary reasons or left the camps in protest actions. Prime Minister Bennett would later quote figures to the effect that 12,601 were expelled for disciplinary reasons up to late June, 1935. The thousands of men who returned to the cities after being expelled from relief camps became a bone of contention between federal and provincial authorities. It was also in anticipation of this problem that the federal government made arrangements for the establishment of prison camps to be known as "Camps of Discipline."[53]

ORGANIZATION AND AGITATION

By summer of 1934, it was becoming clear that the single unemployed had made the DND relief camps virtually unworkable as institutions of social control. They had also become a political liability and Bennett seriously considered disbanding the relief camp system but was talked out of it by McNaughton and others. Authorities could not come up with any workable alternatives.

One of the reasons militant actions became so popular among the unemployed was that they often brought results. Those cities which had strong militant unemployed movements were often the ones where relief allowances were increased and the unemployed treated with more dignity.[54] Perhaps what drew the unemployed to the militant tactics of the WUL more than anything else was that it raised their morale. Peter Hunter, who was active among the unemployed in Hamilton, emphasized this aspect of the political psychology of the time:

> Under Communist leadership you didn't plead, beg, or humbly request, you demanded! How many people who at first lost their jobs, then their furniture, then their homes, then their pride, found this was a way of fighting back? In place of personal humiliation as relief recipients, The Movement gave them mass action for retaliation. It changed self consciousness to class consciousness. It provided a release from the humiliation of begging by providing the class struggle. It was much healthier to transfer criticism of the family head who could not provide for his family to criticism of the government heads who could not provide work or hope for the people.[55]

As they became more experienced, the leading activists of the WUL-led unemployed organizations developed a fairly sophisticated understanding of the psychology of their rank and file constituents. They proudly proclaimed themselves agitators determined to change the conditions facing the unemployed and became adept at portraying their agitation as the natural outcome of the conditions of the times. As time went on and neither the unemployment situation nor the solutions offered by the authorities changed very much for the better this portrayal rang more and more true. A superb example of this type of appeal was an editorial in *The Agitator*, which was begun as an organ of the RCWU in November 1935 as part of a campaign to organize the Dundurn relief camp in Saskatchewan:

> Adherents of the present system try to tell us that "Agitators" are people with a grudge against most everything and everybody. They claim we pop up out of nowhere, rant and rave just for the hell of it. Now, *we* know that if there were no grievances, an agitator would not get to first base. You don't find agitators living in Hotels York and Saskatchewan nor Chateau Laurier, nor in the comfortable homes where people enjoy all the attributes of present day productiveness, have social and sexual expression and scope for their personal character.
>
> No, comrades you don't, for the germs of agitation are found in bad conditions, where men, women and children suffer hunger, terror, and repression. The writer claims the honour of being an "Agitator" as do our comrades at present on bail, in jail, or otherwise victimized for their stand against our persecutors.
>
> Are we to blame for 20 cents slave camps? For the fear and suffering we see around us? For farmers, workers and professionals bumming hand-outs in the summer and living in slave camps in winter? For workers employed at semi-starvation wages, farmers, who slaved all their lives, now serfs on the land they broke, their families in rags, fearing eviction? For men exiled in slave camps, women in the streets? Did *we* cause this?
>
> No, but these conditions caused us to be what we are— "Agitators." We speak all languages. We were born in Canada; we came from the old countries full of hope, we are of all ages, all types. Race, religion, colour are nothing to us. We are humanity. Our forefathers suffered for the Rights of Free Speech, assemblage, organization. They needed these weapons

in their fight for a decent standard. So do we. Are we to rot or do we follow the basic class struggle law? We demand Work and Wages. To Live "Outside."[56]

The editorial continued with an exposition of the specific grievances in Dundurn relief camp. The specific and the general were tied together in a very effective manner.

The increasing sophistication of the unemployed movement resulted partly from trial and error experience. But it also reflected the leadership and support provided by the WUL. The WUL connection enabled the unemployed movement to tap into an array of other organizations, many with substantial resources and years of organizational experience. These included the Canadian Labour Defence League, the Ukrainian Labour-Farmer Temple Association, the Finnish Organization of Canada, the Farmers' Unity League, the Women's Labour League and a host of other organizations bringing together ethnic and/or economic groups. These contacts were invaluable in providing organizational muscle for demonstrations and marches and an effective network for publicizing events, producing and distributing propaganda, taking up petitions and lobbying governmental authorities. There was also considerable overlap of activists with a good many of the unemployed in the early 1930s having had previous experience in other organizations.

The Communist and WUL leadership played an invaluable role working with the national unemployed movement to develop new cadres out of the great pool of unemployed. And they succeeded, perhaps despite their sectarianism and occasional ultra-left excesses, in developing a secondary leadership who were dedicated, resourceful and fairly sophisticated political strategists. Considerable resources were directed to political education and providing the rank and file and local leadership with strategic and tactical direction.

An example of this type of direction was a thirty-two-page pamphlet entitled *Building a Mass Unemployed Movement* issued by the National Committee of Unemployed Councils in Toronto and dated 26 April 1933.[57] The pamphlet discusses various forms of organization varying from direct membership associations to block committees and neighbourhood councils. They advised people to choose the type of organizational structure most suitable to their situation and locality but highly recommended block committees tied together by neighbourhood and municipal councils as supplements to direct membership associations. Block committees were cited as the most effective means of identifying an array of grievances and bringing people together in a united effort to deal with their problems:

> Here we have a form of organization and work that is part of the
> workers themselves, a form of organization that can be effective in
> all the workers'problems from relief discrimination to an eviction,
> from a case of "lights cut off" to "deportation under Section 41..."

These block committees were well established in Vancouver where they did
effective work and for a time were active in Toronto and other centres.[58]

Building a Mass Unemployment Movement emphasized the necessity of the
"united front" between employed and unemployed workers so that the latter
could not be used as strike breakers, and cited examples of such united action:

> This movement needs the support of all the workers, *employed*
> and *unemployed*, whether they are conservatives, liberals, social-
> ists or communists, or profess no political affiliation. It must
> include all the workers, men, women, youth and children...

It sketched out a very ambitious plan for a movement national in scope but
organized down to each city block. The pamphlet went into great detail on
how to organize a block committee, tie it into local structure, fight grievances,
develop leadership, and so forth. Examples of victories won were cited with
emphasis on the fact that struggle brings results.

There had been several unemployed associations and organizations combining employed and unemployed workers which were part of the broad
unemployed movement and did not rely on communist WUL leadership. In
most cases they remained right outside the WUL structure though sometimes
they affiliated to the National Unemployment Council or local councils of
the same nature without owing any organizational loyalties to and remaining
skeptical of the politics of the WUL. It is difficult to gauge the number and
strength of these associations because they were not coordinated by, and did
not report to, any national office. But they often related to, and participated
in, struggles and protests beyond the local level. Many of them would have
supporters in the streets during provincial Hunger Marches and national
days of protest and thus related to activities centrally coordinated by the
WUL but on their own terms. There was, in fact, a sporadic united front of
various sectors of the unemployed movement though it did not take on any
permanent, recognizable form until after 1935 when sectarianism died down
among both communists and social democrats.

Some of the better known non-WUL organizations were the Vancouver Relief
Workers' Association, the Burnaby Workingman's Protective Association, the

East York Workers' Association and the Verdun Workingmen's Association, but there were many others. Some were organized by social democratic activists who were members of the ILP, the Socialist Party of Canada and later the CCF. Some were organized by activists independent of any party affiliation and in many cases, these people would be unemployed trade unionists. In Montreal, where there were unemployed associations in every district and suburb, members of l'Association humanitaire played an active role in organizing the unemployed.[59]

Individual members of the CCF sometimes played active roles in organizing the unemployed, particularly in the Vancouver and Toronto regions where CCF supporters provided much of the leadership in the Burnaby Workingman's Association, which endorsed the party at one time. Ernest Winch and other CCF MLAs in British Columbia also visited the relief camps and addressed the inmates from time to time much to the chagrin of the DND authorities.[60] And ILP-CCF members of Parliament, particularly Angus MacInnis, often raised the grievances of the unemployed in the House of Commons. Both Woodsworth and MacInnis were active in defending the civil liberties of the unemployed in House debates and in demanding, without success, that relief camp inmates be guaranteed the right to vote in federal elections.[61]

Though the CCF fought for the rights of the unemployed in provincial legislatures and the House of Commons and individual party supporters were active in some localities in day to day struggles, the party had no overall strategy for organizing the unemployed. This partly reflected the class complexion of the CCF. With the exception of British Columbia and scattered pockets elsewhere, the party was more agrarian than working class and many of its activists in the cities tended to be from middle class backgrounds. They were adept at lobbying governments and electoral campaigning but had no experience at working-class organizing. And the dominant wing of the CCF was almost exclusively Parliamentary oriented in their strategic conceptions. Woodsworth in particular had drawn conservative strategic conclusions from the experience of the Winnipeg General Strike. He was skeptical of extra-Parliamentary politics and particularly of the confrontational kind. This was reflected in the CCF emphasis on working exclusively within constitutional and Parliamentary norms.

The result of these factors was that the CCF as a party made no attempt to organize or provide leadership for the unemployed movement in contrast to the Communists who made it a priority and put full-time organizers in the field from the beginning of the Depression in 1930. The Communists also had the advantage of much experience at organizing unskilled workers and most of their members were working class themselves. In fact, during much of the Depression, half of the Communist Party members were unemployed. They were culturally attuned to the people they were attempting to organize and lead. And the Communists had already established a position close to hegemony over much of the unemployed movement by the time the CCF was founded in 1932. This left the CCF for the most part playing a support function rather than a primary role in the unemployed movement. They played their support role quite effectively through their Parliamentary connections and by providing crucial material and moral support and assisting in mobilizing public opinion during the great unemployed struggles in Vancouver in 1934 and 1935. The CCF provided the same kind of support in Saskatchewan during the On-to-Ottawa Trek. When the supporters of the two parties did manage from time to time to overcome sectarianism and work together their strengths complemented each other to the advantage of the overall unemployed movement.

By late 1934 the tide had turned against the federal government. The Conservatives no longer controlled a single major provincial government and the Bennett regime had become the most unpopular in living memory. The public were in a combative mood and this was shown by the massive public support for the relief camp strikers who walked out of the BC camps and congregated in Vancouver during December 1934 and early January 1935. This was the biggest offensive to date for the RCWU and over one thousand unemployed became the centre of attention in Vancouver for a month.[62] This time their support went much beyond the usual left communist and unemployed movement to include the mainstream trade unions and even into significant sectors of the middle class. For the first time ever, the daily press were beginning to suggest that not only were many of the demands of the organized unemployed justified but many of the extra-Parliamentary tactics should be supported as well:

> Ructions in relief camps, walkouts, committees of unemployed, are evidence of virility and independence that should be accepted with gladness and treated with patience, not frowned upon and suppressed.[63]

The relief strikers returned to the camps in January 1935 with few significant concessions but the events of December 1934 would prove to be the dress rehearsal for the much more massive walkout which would lead to the On-to-Ottawa Trek of 1935. It is not the intention of this paper to discuss the details of the Trek which have been written about extensively elsewhere.[64] The single unemployed became the centre of national attention, enjoyed overwhelming public support and, though they were routed at Regina, helped to drive the nails into the coffin of a discredited government and became a permanent part of the national consciousness.

THE LEGACY OF THE UNEMPLOYED STRUGGLES

What were the accomplishments and the legacy of the five years of struggle of the unemployed movement between 1930 and 1935? The immediate concrete achievements may seem modest in the overall scheme of things but they were crucial for hundreds of thousands of unemployed and their families. The intense struggles did lead to modest improvements in the level and conditions of relief in most parts of the country. Without organized pressure it is probable that desperate poverty and malnutrition would have taken even more lives. The organized unemployed can also take much of the credit for the abolition of the relief camps and rescinding of Section 98 by the Mackenzie King government in 1936.

While fighting for the immediate needs of the unemployed, the movement played the role of defending their dignity and keeping up their morale. These

Demonstration support On-to-Ottawa trekkers in downtown Regina just prior to the Regina Riot of 1935 (Courtesy of the Provincial Archives of Saskatchewan / R-A27560-1).

were the not easily measured accomplishments "of standing up to the state, of fighting for human rights rather than succumbing to resignation and defeat, of taking up the cause of those for whom no one battled."[65] For the most part, the unemployed did not succumb to the ugliness and the racism which J. Terrill feared might develop when he surveyed the scene for the OBU in 1931. The organized unemployed movement played a significant role in bringing people of different national backgrounds together when there were some who would have divided them against themselves. Ronald Liversedge captured this aspect of the struggle when he described the headquarters of the block committee to which he was attached on East Pender Street in Vancouver:

> The headquarters was a very busy place, as I believe everybody on the block was unemployed. It could also truthfully have been called the House of Nations, as in the council we had Japanese, Chinese, Scandinavians, Slavs, Russians, British and probably other nations represented as well.[66]

Similar observations can be found in the memoirs of others who were activists in the unemployed movement.[67]

The longer term political legacy of the unemployed movement is also difficult to measure but some of that legacy can now be discerned. The Communist Party owed much of its growth and influence in the later 1930s and early 1940s to the role the party played in the unemployed struggles before 1935. Many of the veterans of the unemployed struggles were later participants in the Mackenzie-Papineau Battalion and the great struggles to organize the CIO unions in the late 1930s and early 1940s. Some, like Pat Lenihan of Calgary, would play leading roles in organizing public sector unions in the 1950s and 1960s.[68] And the unemployed movement also intersected with broader constituencies of trade unionists, farmers, intellectuals and others who would achieve unemployment insurance in 1941 and begin the construction of the modern welfare state.

Though there have been several studies of aspects of the unemployed movement of the early 1930s the observation of Thompson and Seager that their experience "comprises a rich though largely unrecorded history" is still at least partly true.[69] Much remains to be done in studying the overall unemployed movement, its constituent parts and how various institutions, groups and parties related to it. Work has barely begun on the position of unemployed women and their role within the unemployed movement in the 1930s.[70] Much more work must be done on the role of the CCF and the mainstream trade unions in relating to the unemployment movement. More local and provincial studies are needed and the examination of many important episodes and confrontations has barely begun. Events like the On-to-Ottawa Trek and the Regina Riot were not nearly as unusual as they might appear at first glance.

NOTES

This article first appeared in *Prairie Forum* 31, no. 2 (2006): 193–216.

1   Supporters of the CCF were active in unemployed organizations in Toronto, Vancouver, Burnaby, Montreal and almost certainly other scattered centres as well.
2   The Reverend Andrew Roddan, *Canada's Untouchables* (Vancouver: Clark and Stuart Co., 1932).
3   National Archives of Canada (hereafter NA), Charlotte Whitton Papers, Volume 25. Whitton collected samples of what she described as "Communist Literature" which she forwarded to R. B. Bennett during her tour of the West in 1932. Included in this literature are several *OBU Bulletins* and letters from J. Terrill, one in his own handwriting, to OBU headquarters in Winnipeg. Whitton does not say how she obtained these letters, but it may have been from the police.
4   *OBU Bulletin*, 4 June 1930.
5   Ibid.
6   NA, Whitton Papers, Terrill to OBU Headquarters, 22 May 1931.
7   Ibid., Terrill to OBU Headquarters, 26 April 1931.
8   Ibid., Terrill to OBU Headquarters, 31 May 1931.
9   *OBU Bulletin*, 4 June 1931.
10 NA, Whitton Papers, Terrill to OBU Headquarters, 22 May 1931.
11 *OBU Bulletin*, 11 June 1931
12 *The Worker*, 10 August 1929.
13 Ibid., 17 August 1929.
14 See S. M. Skebo, "Liberty and Authority—Civil Liberties in Toronto, 1929–1935" (Master's thesis, University of British Columbia, 1968).
15 *The Worker*, 17 August 1929.
16 Ibid., 26 October 1929.
17 See Ronald Liversedge, *Recollections of the On-to-Ottawa Trek*, edited by Victor Hoar (Toronto: McClelland and Stewart, 1973), and Ben Swankey and Jean Evans Sheils, *Work and Wages!* (Vancouver: Trade Union Research Bureau, 1977).
18 Nearly all of the books dealing with the Communist Party of Canada and many dealing with the general labour history of the early 1930s devote some space to discussing the reasons for the formation of the Workers' Unity League.
19 NA, Communist Party Papers, Vol. 52, File 75, "Report of Workers' Unity League Southern Ontario Conference, 24–25 May 1930, Toronto."
20 Ibid.

21 Lorne Brown, "Unemployment Relief Camps in Saskatchewan, 1933–1936," *Saskatchewan History* (Autumn 1970): 84.

22 Ivan Avakumovic, *The Communist Party in Canada: A History* (Toronto: McLelland and Stewart, 1975), 75.

23 Andrée Levesque, "The Canadian Left in Quebec During the Great Depression: The Communist Party of Canada and the CCF in Quebec, 1929–39" (PhD dissertation, Duke University, 1973), 145.

24 Useful memoirs, biographies and autobiographies of the period include: Peter Hunter, *Which Side Are You On, Boys*, edited by Irving Abella (Toronto: Lugus Productions, 1988); Liversedge, *Recollections of the On-to-Ottawa Trek*; David Frank and Donald MacGillivray (eds.), *George MacEachern: An Autobiography* (Sydney, NS : College of Cape Breton Press, 1987); Jack Scott, *A Communist Life: Jack Scott and the Canadian Workers Movement, 1927–1985*, edited by Bryan Palmer (St. John's, NF: Committee on Canadian Labour History, 1988); Swankey and Sheils, *Work and Wages!.*

25 *The Worker*, 18 April 1931.

26 Avakumovic, *The Communist Party in Canada*, 77–78.

27 James Struthers, *No Fault of Their Own: Unemployment and the Canadian Welfare State 1914–1941* (Toronto: University of Toronto Press, 1983), 46.

28 Ibid., 48.

29 Hunter, *Which Side Are You On, Boys*, and Frank and MacGillivray, *George MacEachern*, cite instances of hunger and even starvation, which Hunter notes was more often politically referred to as "malnutrition," during this period. Wendy Johnson, "Keeping Children in School: The Response of the Montreal Catholic School Commission to the Depression of the 1930s," *Historical Papers* (1985): 193–217, discusses the desperate poverty and hunger facing the children of Montreal.

30 James Struthers discusses the situation in *No Fault of Their Own*.

31 The lack of assistance for the single unemployed is discussed in Liversedge, *Recollections of the On-to-Ottawa Trek*, Struthers, *No Fault of Their Own*, and Lorne Brown, *When Freedom Was Lost* (Montreal: Black Rose Books, 1987) and in two books published in the 1930s: H. M. Cassidy, *Unemployment and Relief in Ontario, 1929–1932* (Toronto: J. M. Dent, 1932) and L. Richter (ed.), *Canada's Unemployment Problem* (Toronto: MacMillan, 1939).

32 Brown, *When Freedom Was Lost*, 33.

33 Most works dealing with labour, communist and ethnic history in the 1930s put some emphasis on the repression which was so prevalent at the time. Examples would be John Herd Thompson and Allen Seager, *Canada, 1922–1939: Decades of Discord* (Toronto: McLelland and Stewart, 1985); Donald Avery, *"Dangerous Foreigners": European Immigrant Workers and Labour Radicalism in Canada, 1896–1932* (Toronto: McLelland and Stewart, 1979); Barbara Roberts, *Whence They Came: Deportation from Canada, 1900–1935* (Ottawa: University of Ottawa Press, 1988). See also J. Petryshyn, "Class Conflict and Civil Liberties: The Origins and Activities of the Canadian Labour Defence League, 1925–40," *Labour/Le Travail* (Autumn 1982): 39–63.

34 Brown, *When Freedom Was Lost*, Chapter 2, Struthers, *No Fault of Their Own*, Chapter 3.

35 Brown, *When Freedom Was Lost*, Chapter 2.

36 Canada, House of Commons, *Debates*, Vol. 1, 3 May 1932, 748.

37 *Ottawa Journal*, 4 March 1932, quoted in Canada, House of Commons, *Debates*, 17 March 1932.

38 *Regina Leader-Post*, 8 November 1932.

39 *Saskatoon StarPhoenix*, 9 May 1933.

40 Avakumovic, *The Communist Party in Canada*, 76.

41 Struthers, *No Fault of Their Own*, Chapter 3.

42 Brown, *When Freedom Was Lost*, Chapter 3.

43 Ibid., and Struthers, *No Fault of Their Own*, Chapter 3.

44 NA, Bennett Papers, Micro p. 494237. See also Brown, *When Freedom Was Lost*, Chapter 3.

45 Ibid.

46 Struthers, *No Fault of Their Own*, 96.

47 Brown, *When Freedom Was Lost*, Chapter 3 and 4.

48 *The Unemployed Worker*, 5 July 1933. *The Unemployed Worker* was the official organ of the Vancouver branch of the NUWA.

49 NA, McNaughton Papers, File 361 (1).

50 Ibid., Volume 58.

51 Ibid., File 361 (1).

52 Ibid., File 359 (1).

53 Struthers, *No Fault of Their Own*, Chapter 3; Brown, *When Freedom Was Lost*, Chapter 4.

54 The reminiscences of Liversedge, Lenihan and Hunter cite examples. See taped interviews of Lenihan by Levine, National Archives of Canada. See also Gilbert Levine (ed.), *Patrick Lenihan: From Irish Rebel to Founder of Canadian Public Sector Unionism*, with an Introduction by Lorne Brown (St. John's, NF: Canadian Committee on Labour History, 1998).

55 Hunter, *Which Side Are You On, Boys*, 26.

56 *The Agitator*, 25 November 1935.

57 NA, Communist Party Papers, Vol. 61, File 10.

58 The role of the block committees is discussed by Liversedge, *Recollections of the On-to-Ottawa Trek*.

59 Levesque, "The Canadian Left in Quebec during the Great Depression," 65, 146.

60 See Lorne Brown, "The Bennett Government, Political Stability and the Politics of the Unemployment Relief Camps, 1930–1935" (PhD dissertation, Queen's University, 1980).

61 Brown, *When Freedom Was Lost*, Chapters 4 and 5.

62 Ibid., Chapter 5.

63 Vancouver *Daily Province*, 8 December 1934.

64 Bill Waiser, *All Hell Can't Stop Us: The On-to-Ottawa Trek and Regina Riot* (Calgary: Fifth House, 2003). Waiser's superbly written book contains much new information on the Trek, the Regina Riot and its aftermath. Others include Victor Howard, *"We Were the Salt of the Earth!": The On-to-Ottawa Trek and the Regina Riot* (Regina: Canadian Plains Research Center, 1985), and Brown, *When Freedom Was Lost*.

65 Scott, *A Communist Life*, 32.

66 Liversedge, *Recollections of the On-to-Ottawa Trek*, 32.

67 Lenihan and Swankey and Sheils make similar observations about the multi-racial nature of the unemployed movement. It is no accident that Blacks, Chinese, East

Indians and Native Indians were among the crowd attending the funeral of Arthur Evans on 17 February 1944.

68 See Levine (ed.), *Patrick Lenihan: From Irish Rebel to Founder of Canadian Public Sector Unionism.*

69 Thompson and Seager, *Canada, 1922–1939*, 223.

70 Marg Patricia Powell, "A Response to the Depression: The Local Council of Women of Vancouver," in Barbara Latham and Cathy Kess (eds.), *In Her Own Right: Selected Essays on Women's History in B.C.* (Victoria: Camosun College, 1980) contains an interesting discussion on how various women's groups related to unemployment and other depression issues.

7.   No Help for the Farm Help: The Farm Employment
     Plans of the 1930s in Prairie Canada

Cecilia Danysk

When city streets and soup kitchens became crowded with the unemployed during the 1930s, the countryside took on almost mythic qualities. Urban centres found the financial costs of relief more than they could bear, and they faced the growing possibility of violence from angry men unable to find work. Rural Canada became, in the eyes of governments and citizens alike, the place that could provide economic and psychological shelter from the devastating and demoralizing effects of the Great Depression. In 1931, municipal, provincial and federal governments collaborated to work out a rural solution to the urban problem: send the costly unemployed, potential troublemakers out of the cities and onto the farms.

During the course of the decade, probably close to 200,000 jobless Canadians were placed on prairie farms during the winter months.[1] In exchange for their labour, they received room and board and five dollars per month under a series of what were euphemistically called farm employment plans.

Cities and governments saw immediate benefit from what was a politically, economically and ideologically sound method of dealing with the financial costs and the social hazards of chronic unemployment. According to officials, farms offered the unemployed "no better surroundings under the existing conditions of unrest."[2] Unemployed urban or transient workers placed on farms under the plan could become "rural minded" and "desirable citizen[s]." They could be "kept in good physical and 'mental' shape," and would not be "so apt to get the impression that the government owes them a living."[3]

For the rural communities where the plans were implemented, the benefits were uneven. Just how well the plans would work depended greatly on the extent to which rural and urban interests did, or could be made to, coincide. The plans were designed to solve two problems at once: relieve the cities of some of their burden and offer the suffering farmer low-cost labour. In the beginning the plans worked to the advantage of farmers and their employees. More often than not it was out-of-work farm hands who were brought under the plans. But as economic conditions and political relations changed during the decade, rural communities came to benefit less and less from this solution to city problems. Farm workers were excluded from the plans in favour of unemployed city men and transients, and farmers were saddled with inexperienced and often unwilling help. As the Depression deepened, the farm employment plans came primarily to benefit the cities.

Prairie cities, to a greater degree than those in eastern and central Canada, looked to the federal government to ease the problems of growing unemployment and an increasing relief load. They saw excessive immigration as the main culprit in the growing numbers of transients swelling their overburdened relief rolls, and since immigration was a federal responsibility, they called for federal assistance.[4] The provinces, too, agreed that the problem of transients was beyond their financial capabilities and insisted that the federal government deal with the unemployed men who travelled from province to province in search of work.

Saskatchewan had already had some success in tackling this problem. The Department of Agriculture had recruited single men congregating in the towns and cities and encouraged them to take farm work during the winter. The next step was to approach Ottawa. By the spring of 1931, both Saskatchewan and Manitoba were meeting with federal officials to work out a systematic plan. In April the Agricultural Bureau of the Manitoba Department of Labour put together a committee from a wide range of government and private agencies. It met in Winnipeg to form a "central organization to which all interested agencies can co-operate in the question of placing unemployed on farms."[5] Sitting on the committee were members of the federal Department of Immigration, the Employment Service of Canada, the provincial Department of Public Works, the Special Commission of Unemployment of the Winnipeg City Council, the Winnipeg Board of Trade, the Citizens' Committee on Unemployment, the Canadian Bankers Association, the Canadian Pacific Railway, the Canadian National Railway and the United Farmers of Canada.

Adopting a farm labour program was urged as the least expensive method of dealing with single unemployed men. Although it was designed primarily to relieve the problem of unemployment, the farm placement plan was also seen as an aid to the faltering agricultural industry, since it would provide a material advantage to farmers who could not afford the hired help they needed. As for the jobless men, it would confer the benefits of both a home and a job. In the fall of 1931, both Manitoba and Saskatchewan instituted farm placement plans.

The structure was fairly uniform in both provinces. The plans called for the placement of single unemployed men with farmers who would otherwise be unable to hire help.[6] They were strictly winter projects, in effect from November to the end of March, but it was hoped that men so placed would then be hired by the farmers for the summer months. Transportation was provided to the job, and men who stayed for ninety days were entitled to a reduced fare when they left.

In the winter of 1931–32, the federal and provincial governments financed the plans jointly. Under the Unemployment and Farm Relief Act of 1931 and the Continuance Act of 1932, each government agreed to pay 50 percent of the costs. Saskatchewan paid the full 50 percent, but Manitoba passed on 25 percent of its share to municipalities, and charged transportation costs to the town or village where the placement took place.[7]

Although this was a joint federal-provincial venture, the federal government strongly opposed moving into the field of responsibility for unemployment or relief, arguing that these were first of all municipal, and secondly provincial, concerns. Federal involvement was limited simply to providing the funds. Administration, including its cost, was left to the provinces. In turn, selection of the men destined for the plan was usually handed over to municipalities.

This created disparities. The one uniform provision was the $5 per month allowance to the man. Farmers also received an allowance to help pay for the costs of board. Manitoba paid its farmers $5 per month, with the suggestion that "because extra work necessitated through keeping the hired man on the farm falls on the farmer's wife, it might be mutually agreed that the monthly cheque should go to the farmer's wife."[8] Saskatchewan also paid most of its participating farmers the $5 per month, but raised it to as much as $10 in areas of three successive crop failures.[9] Manitoba extended its plan to the end of April, and Saskatchewan extended it for the summer months for men in the dried-out areas, but did not pay the farmers. During the first year of operation, 1,602 men were placed in Manitoba. The winter and summer total in Saskatchewan was 8,299 (see Table 7.1).

By late October of the following year, the federal government had reluctantly responded to nationwide provincial, municipal, and popular demands that it assume responsibility for the homeless, single unemployed, and so for the winter of 1932–33, under the Relief Act of 1932, it undertook the full cost of payments under the plans and 50 percent of transportation costs. It still left administrative costs to the provinces. Prime Minister R. B. Bennett was adamant that the federal government should limit its responsibility for relief for transients to providing funds. "We have not endeavoured to destroy the constitution nor to substitute a federal for a provincial administration," he declared, but simply to "cooperate and assist, and in some cases to suggest what should be done."[10]

TABLE 7.1. NUMBER ON FARMS DURING PEAK MONTHS

	Manitoba	Saskatchewan	Alberta	Total
1931–32	1,602	7,937	—	9,539
Summer 1932	—	362	—	362
1932–33	2,600	6,678	1,173	10,451
1933–34	4,681	10,033	1,350	16,064
1934–35	5,510	5,400	1,286	12,196
1935–36	5,298	6,371	2,417	14,086
1936–37	9,509	26,426	3,250	39,185
1937–38	9,350	26,925	3,411	39,686
1938–39	7,800	17,038	3,063	27,901
1939–40	2,148	—	1,300	3,448

NA, RG 27, vol. 213, file 617, Canada, Department of Labour, "Dominion Unemployment Relief: Relief Since 1930," January 1940, 37–39; Canada, Department of Labour, *The Unemployment and Agricultural Assistance Act 1939* Report of the Dominion Commissioner of Unemployment Relief, 1940 (Ottawa: King's Printer 1940), 34–35. These are the statistics officially released by the federal Department of Labour from reports submitted by the provinces, showing the numbers of persons on the plan during the month of greatest use (usually March), except for the 1931–32 and summer 1932 figures which are of cumulative placements, and for the 1939–40 figures which are of "numbers afforded employment." However, their accuracy is dubious. Statistics are inconsistent, with different figures turning up for different reporting agencies, or even from different offices of the same agencies. Some of the figures in this table have been reported in provincial tabulations as placements. Inaccuracies, especially under-reporting, appear as figures are sent to different agencies. In general, local figures are higher than provincial figures which are higher than federal figures. There are also problems with determining the numbers of persons actually using the plans. Some agencies reported the numbers of placements made each month, which could be considerably higher (by as much as 20 percent) than the numbers actually on farms at any time. Disparities resulted because not all those placed actually reached their destinations, some left before the tally at the end of the month, and some were placed more than once over the course of a winter. Those placed under the plan and later eliminated without payment appear not to have been counted. A breakdown by sex was not usually included in statistical compilations.

Full federal funding lured Alberta into the scheme. John Brownlee, UFA Premier of Alberta, had been opposed at the beginning, in keeping with the UFA policies of encouraging self-help among its constituents and of restricting government involvement in relief." However, when Harry Hereford, Dominion Commissioner of Unemployment Relief, wrote to Brownlee in October 1932 outlining the agreements with the other western provinces, and promising to foot most of the bill, Brownlee was persuaded. Alberta joined that winter.[12] The numbers making use of the plans grew. At its peak month that year, 2,600 went to farms under the plan in Manitoba, 6,678 in Saskatchewan and 1,173 in Alberta.[13]

Like other relief measures during the Depression, this was an ad hoc program, expiring every year on 31 March, and requiring a new federal provincial agreement every fall. The Relief Acts of 1933, 1934, and 1935 all contained similar provisions regarding the farm placement plans. But with administration in the hands of the provinces, there were bound to be variations. Women were included in Saskatchewan and Manitoba, but not in Alberta which argued that its plan did not apply to women since "very few are anxious to undertake domestic work in the country."[14] The question of including women was controversial, as women usually were not considered transients. Throughout the Depression, there were few provisions for the care of single women, and in at least one instance, the federal government demanded repayment of the $5 per month allowance from Saskatchewan for women placed under the scheme. In the records for the farm placement plans, even where women were included, the correspondence, statistics and other documentation usually refers only to men. Within a few years after the plans were underway, the allowance to farmers was quietly dropped by all the provinces, and the costs of transportation and clothing, where it was occasionally included, were subject to much negotiation among the various levels of government, each apparently trying to avoid the responsibility.

Funding remained in the hands of the federal government. Under the agreement of 1932, and through 1933, the provinces had a relatively free fiscal hand, since funding for transients was now clearly a federal responsibility. Provinces could concentrate on placing as many as possible on farms, a cheaper alternative than work camps, and a much cheaper alternative than municipal relief, of which the federal government was willing to pay only half, leaving provinces with a bill of about $6 per month for every unemployed man who stayed in the city. On the other hand, the federal government was apparently willing to pay almost the entire cost for as many men as could be sent to either a farm or a relief camp.

But this did not last long. Relief costs soared, charges of inefficiency and overspending abounded, and in July 1934, the federal government announced it would change its method of financing from unlimited funding to grants-in-aid. This was to be a fixed sum based on "proven need." The provinces at first approved of this change, since it would give them the ability to limit municipal relief spending, which inflated their own. But the provinces were shocked when the amount of the fixed sum was determined by Ottawa without consultation with the provinces. Calculations appear to have been arbitrary. Alberta and Manitoba faced cutbacks that amounted to only 3 percent, but Saskatchewan, with a larger relief budget and a newly elected Liberal Premier James Gardiner, long-time foe of the federal Conservatives, lost 11 percent, or $25,000 per month.[15]

More cutbacks followed. In October 1935, the government in Ottawa changed hands. After five years of criticizing Conservative wastefulness, Liberal William Lyon Mackenzie King was once again Prime Minister. For the winter of 1935–36, King was tied to the Relief Act of 1935, negotiated under Bennett's administration. Even with the funding switch the previous year to grants-in-aid, King felt relief costs were far too high. He quickly moved to establish the National Employment Commission with a mandate to examine ways to cut relief costs further. A key to this endeavour was the reinvention of the farm placement plan.

One of King's campaign promises had been to abolish the immensely unpopular work camps. He charged Norman Rogers, his new Minister of Labour, with making plans for the men from the camps. Arrangements were made to employ numbers of them on railway construction over the summer, but the problem of winter employment remained. King's rather grandiose vision for the expanded farm placement plan was that it should absorb all the unemployed men who had been inmates of the relief camps. In February, Rogers calculated that even if the farm employment allowance were to be doubled to $10 per month, it would be much cheaper than the work camps had been. He declared that the money spent on maintaining men in camps during 1935, for example, could provide for 73,000 on farms,[16] more than double the 31,322 counted in the camps at the end of March 1935.[17] On 30 April 1936, two months before the camps were to close, Rogers announced in the House of Commons that "it is possible that we should be obliged to make greater use of this Farm Placement Scheme."[18]

The National Employment Commission made the scheme a priority. King appointed Harry Hereford as Chairman of the Farm Placement Committee, and Humphrey Mitchell as Director of Labour Transfer, responsible for ensuring that the men made the transition from camps to farms. The makeup of the committee was heavily weighted in favour of Ottawa. In addition to three members of the National Employment Commission, there were representatives from the Employment Service of Canada, the departments of Agriculture and of Colonization and Immigration, the office of Soldier Settlement, and the Veterans Aid Commission. Each province had one delegate, representing offices ranging from departments of Agriculture to provincial branches of the Employment Service of Canada to Unemployment Relief Commissions.[19] In September the National Employment Commission announced the establishment of a farm placement plan, naming it the Farm Improvement and Employment Plan.

The new version of the plan had a larger scope than that of its predecessors. Although it was similar to the plans under the Bennett administration, King went to great pains to point out the differences: in order to ensure that men would stay on farms and not drift back into the cities before the winter was over, they were to receive a bonus of $2.50 per month if they remained until the plan ended in March. In order to encourage farmers to provide positions, they were offered $5 per month to defray the costs of room and board. The plan started a month earlier, in October instead of November, it was extended to all provinces that wished to take advantage of it, and eligibility was extended to all persons, including women, over the age of sixteen years.[20] It was also intended to be the major program to take care of the single, homeless, unemployed. The largest number of placements on the plans under Bennett's administration had been 16,064, but the new plan was expected to accommodate up to 100,000 men and women.[21]

And there were important changes in regulations. Although the agreements were still signed between individual provinces and the federal government, the contract in each case was now identical. Regulations, allowances, restrictions and stipulations were made uniform among all provinces that joined the program.

More significant, though, were changes in funding. King's first line of attack was the grants-in-aid. In November 1935, to ensure provincial cooperation with the new National Employment Commission, King increased the grants-in-aid for December 1935 to March 1936, as an interim measure.[22] This was followed by a downward revision. The new fiscal year saw cuts of 15 percent in the first three months, and another ten percent to the end of December.[23] Further reductions came in May of 1937 and again in the fall.

But the reductions were only part of King's solution; the other was a complete revision of the financial agreement. Under Bennett, the federal government had provided 100 percent of the allowances for men under the farm help schemes, as well as their transportation costs and clothing allowances. The provinces had only to cover administration costs, which amounted to about 20 percent of the total costs of the plans.[24] Under the new arrangements, beginning in the winter of 1936–37, Ottawa agreed to pay only half the costs the previous government had paid. This saddled the provinces with more than half the costs of the program, since they still had to pay all the costs of administration. At the same time, with the work camps closed, thousands more men were being sent to farms, with a consequent increase of provincial expenditures. During the winter of 1936–37, numbers using the plan in the prairie provinces jumped to more than 39,000. Although a far cry from the anticipated 100,000, this was an increase over the previous year of 178 percent. Saskatchewan received the largest burden, with a 315 percent increase.[25]

On the federal balance sheet, the farm placement plan was still the cheapest way of caring for the single unemployed. From the provincial point of view, however, the costs per individual, as well as the total costs of the program, skyrocketed. The prairie provinces simply could not provide this kind of financing. Their own economies were not only failing to share the recovery of the rest of the country, they were continuing to deteriorate. The provinces were sinking deeper and deeper into debt, and faced with bankruptcy, were forced to borrow ever more heavily from the federal government to finance their relief measures.

This enabled Ottawa to exert considerable pressure upon the provinces to make use of the farm placement plan to remove men from urban centres. With the plan as the only significant measure to take care of the homeless unemployed, who were becoming more organized and making greater demands, Ottawa felt it was a necessity. The revised funding and new regulations of the farm placement plan gave clear warning that it was henceforth to be used unequivocally for transients congregating in cities. The homeless unemployed were to be cleared off the streets and sent to farms.

The emphasis on curing the problems of the city by shipping the unemployed out to the country may have been most starkly illustrated with the change in government in Ottawa, but that change was only a more dramatic representation of the shift that had been taking place over the course of the Depression.

Just how well the plans served the rural community depended on a complex and shifting mix of imperatives: the responsiveness of provincial governments to their rural constituencies, the relationships among different levels of governments, the involvement of officials in partisan politics, the deepening financial crisis on the Prairies, and the relationship between urban centres and rural communities.

In the early years of the Depression, when the farm placement plans were being introduced and modified, their administration was controlled directly by the prairie provinces, all of which were primarily rural. Prairie farmers had a long tradition of organization and political action, so provincial governments tended to respond sympathetically to their problems. And because Ottawa wanted to avoid responsibility, the provinces were able to exercise considerable latitude. So for the first few years of the plans' operations, there were wide variations in the regulations and even wider variations in the interpretation of the regulations. How closely each province adhered to the regulations of the plans seemed to depend on its responsiveness to its rural constituency.

Saskatchewan is an interesting study. That province made the greatest use of the plan, both in sheer numbers, and in proportions. In 1936, for example, there was one placement from the farm placement plan for every seven farms in Saskatchewan, while in Manitoba there was one for every nine farms, and in Alberta only one for every twenty-five farms. In almost every year it had more placements than any other province.

The most agricultural of the three prairie provinces and the hardest hit during the Depression was Saskatchewan. At the same time, with agriculture far and away the major industry, most of its unemployed work force were agricultural labourers. Plans to place men on farms would work to the best advantage of both men and farmers if the men were experienced farm workers.

Leniency was an important feature of Saskatchewan's regulations. From the very inception of the plan, Saskatchewan had a high proportion of local placements, and always allowed it to be open to men in rural districts. According to its own regulations in 1931–32, Saskatchewan interpreted the plan as "A farm labour relief scheme...for the two-fold purpose of supplying needy farmers in the dried out area with necessary help and obtaining employment for qualified farm labourers unemployed in the urban centres of the province."[26]

The "dried-out area," the southern section of the province which had suffered from two or more successive crop failures, needed and received special consideration. Hired men, for example, were allowed to collect the allowance by staying on farms on which they had regular jobs. Farmers in areas of three successive crop failures were also granted an allowance of up to $10 per month toward the cost of boarding the men. Although regulations specified that men were to be taken from urban centres, the emphasis was upon the needs of farmers, who wanted qualified help, and those of farm workers who wanted to remain in farm employment. In this case, the aims of the farmers, the farm workers and the provincial government overlapped.

Provincial relief commissions could be responsive to rural conditions. In Manitoba, for example, application forms dated 4 November 1932 stated emphatically that "This plan shall apply to men now on relief in Urban Centres ONLY."[27] However, within three weeks, the relief commission in Winnipeg recognized "the problem of the [single homeless] man...who may now be in Towns and Villages," and issued a directive that "subject to very definite restrictions," the plan would be made available to "the man of this class."[28]

Manitoba was well aware that farmers needed competent and willing help. In response to suggestions that it cut men off relief who refused placements under the plan, it argued that "men compelled to go to farms would be worse than useless as farm labourers."[29] By 1934, Manitoba's regulations reflected this policy. "The plan is primarily intended for persons now on relief in urban centres," ran the new instructions to relief officers, "However, homeless persons located elsewhere may be given the privileges of the plan," although there were still restrictions.[30]

But not all provincial governments were responsive to their rural constituents. Alberta, despite having a farmers' government, was more concerned about the urban than the rural constituency. The UFA tended to be less sympathetic toward individuals in economic crisis, and more oriented toward encouraging self-help. In Alberta, too, the large cities were magnets for transients, and according to some mayors and the provincial government, for radical agitators. When the Social Credit government took over in 1935, there were few changes.

As a result, Alberta was more skeptical about the farm placement plan. The province joined only after the federal government agreed to cover all except administrative costs, and was always opposed to paying an allowance to farmers. It made fewest placements among the three prairie provinces, preferring to send men to the federal work camps and to the work camps it operated itself after the federal ones closed. It limited the plan to men, and was especially diligent to restrict it to men from urban centres, particularly transients.

Local placements, the ones most likely to be unemployed farm workers, were carefully restricted. Regulations specified that the "plan shall only apply to men now on relief in the cities," and stipulated that those men would be "selected by the Commission and sent out in response to approved application."[31] Unemployed men were recruited from among relief applicants, and were told that to refuse the placement was to be refused relief. Such reluctant workers were often no help to farmers, who, after 1936, were denied the board allowance unless they took men from the cities. Not surprisingly, this thwarted at least one aim of the plans—that men on the winter farm scheme would be able to negotiate a job for the summer. Of the three prairie provinces, Alberta had the lowest rate of men remaining on farms, and the lowest rate of men persisting for the entire winter.

But even rural-minded provincial governments were not immune to the effects of the rancorous federal-provincial relations of the decade. An incident in Saskatchewan in 1934 illustrates the fallout from one such confrontation. In 1934, Bennett switched from unlimited funding to grants in-aid, with a consequent severe cut in relief funds to Saskatchewan. Ottawa was hoping to force the provinces to reduce their own costs by a more stringent polic-ing of their relief distribution systems, which Ottawa believed were riddled with abuses.

The federal government had always insisted that the farm placement plans were to be used to relieve the cities of single unemployed men, and this stipulation was spelled out in the annual agreements. Saskatchewan had generally ignored it. But in the winter following the funding cuts, the new Liberal government in Saskatchewan decided to tackle the federal govern-ment head-on.

In the fall of 1934, as the plan was reinstated, men began to sign up as usual. There was a brief rush in early November when the plan came into effect, then a slowdown to the end of the year. By 1 January 1935, there were 5,300 persons on the plan. If this year were to follow the trend of the previous winters, numbers on the plan would peak in February or March.

But on 25 January 1935, Thomas Molloy, the Saskatchewan Minister of Labour and Welfare, announced that the farm placement plan was to be discontinued at the end of the month. He blamed Ottawa for the necessity of reneging on the scheme, stating that the federal government was demanding a very narrow interpretation of eligibility for the plan.

According to Molloy, the federal government would allow the $5 per month allowance to be paid only to "single homeless and destitute persons from the urban centres of the province." This, according to Molloy, would eliminate "any person who had been residing in a rural municipality, and particularly those who are continuing in the employ of farmers with whom they have been previously engaged." This apparently amounted to 90 percent of those working under the plan. Since it was the federal government that provided the money to pay the allowance, and since Saskatchewan had no funds to do so, the only solution was to terminate the scheme on 31 January.[32]

Ottawa retaliated by taking administration of the $5 allowance out of the hands of the provincial government and placing it directly with a representative of the federal treasury. It denied that it had any intention of cutting off payment to those eligible, and accused Saskatchewan of political partisanship. "I cannot recall a more flagrant case where the facts have been so subtly distorted as in the present instance," wrote W. A. Gordon, the federal Minister of Labour, to James Gardiner, hoping that "matters political could at least be for the time forgotten." Gardiner countercharged, accusing the federal government of making "political capital out of the incident."[33] The battle raged for several weeks.

The plan was eventually reinstated, but administrative machinery moved slowly. There were continuous warnings that the ineligible would not be paid. Those who were already on farms waited an anxious two months to find if they would receive their payments, and those who had not yet signed up before the end of January were reluctant to do so as they could not be sure of receiving any money. Farmers were equally reluctant to apply for help under the plan, since they did not want to accept the responsibility of paying wages if the government refused to do so. By the end of the plan year, only 5,400 persons had been placed,[34] and many were still trying to collect their allowance. From Dollard, Saskatchewan, farm worker Fred Ward wrote to Gardiner, speaking for farm placement workers who were still waiting for their $5 allowance. They were "just about fed up" with the run-around they were given, he declared, "We write to you, and are referred to Ottawa, they refer us back to Regina, and so it goes on." Ward expressed the frustration of both farmers and workers: "You don't seem to understand what us [sic] men are up against, no clothes boots, etc. to go to work with and the farmers no money or credit."[35] Rural people were caught in the middle of battles such as this one over relief jurisdiction, administration and funding.

The one area in which all levels of government could agree was the fear of social agitation and disorder. From their inception, the farm placement plans were seen as the ideal solution to the problem of unrest among the urban unemployed. In his recommendation that the rest of the country adopt the plan that his province had so successfully followed in 1931–32, the member of Parliament for Weyburn, E. J. Young, echoed a common sentiment when he declared that work on a farm would prevent the susceptible unemployed from being "herded in the cities in an atmosphere of discontent where unsound doctrines might be preached in their ears."[36]

From the outset of the Depression, the unemployed were remarkably successful in organizing themselves to protest relief rates and regulations. When the communists began to harness their discontent, governments saw an even greater danger. By the middle of the decade, the dire prophecies that the chronically unemployed and the never-employed youth of the nation would begin to expect government handouts as their right seemed to come true. The farm placement plan was seen as a corrective, able to counteract "the increasing susceptibility of youth to the influence of the hard-shell hobo and the communist." The only problem, according to J. Neish of the Employment Service of Canada's office in Manitoba, was to find "a supply of suitable homes and farmers who would be willing to take and teach inexperienced boys."[37]

After the closing of the work camps, with their own lesson in the contagion of radical thought and action, governments were even more on their guard. Hard work on an isolated farm was prescribed as a corrective. Not surprisingly, associations of the unemployed decried the plans as "part of a scheme of the Gov't clear across Canada to split up any movement of single unemployed."[38] They mounted vigorous protests against what they called the "slave labour"of the plans, and especially the arrests of men who refused to go out under the scheme. "DO YOU BELIEVE YOU HAVE ANY RIGHTS AS A CANADIAN SUBJECT?" asked a broadsheet announcing a meeting of the Single Unemployed Persons Association in Edmonton. "This $5.00 per month forced labour scheme is one which would almost make Hitler or Mussolini blush." The association called for direct action, warning that the plans "will be used as a weapon to cut thousands of single unemployed off relief unles [*sic*] we take immediate steps to protect our own interests."[39]

The radicalized unemployed could be a focus for the tensions between farmers and officials and between federal and provincial governments. A series of anxious letters from R. A. Rigg of the Alberta office of the Employment Service of Canada to W. M. Dickson, federal Deputy Minister of Labour, illustrates the clash. In October 1936, the first winter following the closure of the federal work camps, and in the aftermath of the Social Credit victory the year before and its promise of a social dividend to Alberta citizens, Rigg noted "how attractive this Province has become to the unemployed." He warned that the Single Unemployed Protective Association "is well organized [in Calgary] and will bring the weight of its influence to bear in Alberta." His particular concern was that the unemployed were demanding trade union wages, and "are bent upon defeating the purpose of the farm placement scheme." Reaction was strong. RCMP reinforcements were sent to Calgary, and radio station CJCH broadcast warnings of the "communistic minded and 'won't work' character of many of the relief-cared-for unemployed."

Not surprisingly, the reaction from farmers was to distance themselves from the fray. Rigg reported that applications were down, noting "some fear among farmers that if they apply for help under the plan, they may be saddled with lazy troublemakers."[40] In order to ensure that farmers complied with the aim to remove the unemployed from cities, the Alberta government refused to pay farmers the board allowance unless they took men from the urban centres. And in order to ensure that the unemployed complied, they were informed that those applying for relief in the cities who turned down placements under the plan "must either take those jobs or be struck off relief."[41]

The pressure to make farm placements from the urban centres increased as the Depression deepened. Even though 1933 was the peak year for unemployment, relief rolls in the cities continued to lengthen as more and more individuals and families moved to urban centres in search of work. The long years of depression took their toll upon the meagre resources of prairie people and their municipal and provincial governments. Funding cutbacks from the federal government forced a closer adherence to federal imperatives. As a result, the provinces took steps to increase the number of farm placements from urban centres and to limit those from rural areas.

In Manitoba at the end of November 1934, of the 2,102 placements, only 720 or a little more than one-third were sent from Winnipeg; the remaining 1,382, or two-thirds, were "country placements." But by the same date the following year, the proportion of placements had changed. A. W. MacNamara, Assistant Deputy Minister of Public Works for Manitoba, wrote to Minister W. R. Clubb: "I think we are doing all right on this plan, and you will note that we have kept the country placements down to about half what they were last year."[42] By February 1937, MacNamara was able to report to Humphrey Mitchell that "We are objecting to about 75 percent of the local Farm Placements being sent in."[43]

The increasing emphasis on farm placements for the urban unemployed came also from the new farm placement plan of the King administration. The National Employment Commission had recommended a broad interpretation of eligibility for the plan, arguing that since it was "imperative to have full co-operation of farmer employers…the scheme should include unemployed in smaller towns, villages and hamlets."[44] But King insisted that its prime objective was to dear the cities of transients. When the new farm placement plan was unveiled in 1936, with its uniform regulations, the most prominent specification was that it was only to apply to the unemployed from urban areas, in particular, single transients.

It was immediately apparent that this tightening of regulations would disadvantage rural farm workers and farmers alike. "We have a considerable number of experienced farm hands," wrote a local observer in the Portage district, as well as "good farmers who are willing to take these men as per the farm placement plan." The regulations would create a mockery of the system:

"I fear that if the present rigid rules are adhered to, these experienced farm hands will remain unemployed during the winter months[,] pitiful objects of relief[,] while there will be a constant parade from farm to city of those who are not fitted to engage in farm work."[45]

Regulations governing local or rural applications became more stringent. City applicants were faced with an investigation by a relief official, but local applicants were required to undergo a rigid check by three "responsible persons not related to the Applicant." Recommendations were only accepted from "Government representatives, Justices of Peace, Railway Agents, Clergymen, or R.C.M.Police Constables."[46] Farmers were informed that if they were "willing to take a man from the City of Winnipeg or other urban centres, the application might not be reviewed so rigidly as in the case of the farmer wishing to take a man already in the district."[47]

The time during which local placements could be accepted was restricted. Manitoba's W. R. Clubb explained that the new regulations for the plan underscored the relief commission's intention to deal with unemployment in the cities. "The Plan will commence on October 1st, 1938, but only men or women from the Urban Centers will be sent out at the start." It was with reluctance that local residents were to be allowed to make use of the plan. "It may be necessary, after November 1st, 1938, to consider unemployed necessitous single persons who are already residing in the Country."[48] After 15 January 1939, applications from local areas were no longer accepted, although farmers could still apply for men from the cities.[49]

When provincial officials, such as Saskatchewan's Tom Molloy, objected that "reasons for rejection are based on the narrowest possible interpretation of the agreement without any regard for the practical problems or conditions surrounding the placement of these men,"[50] they were reminded that strict regulation was necessary in order to ensure that the plan worked to take city men from relief rolls. Even Saskatchewan knuckled under. In 1937, of 80,000 applicants, 24,000 were rejected,[51] most from rural areas where residents were in desperate straits. Many of the rejected applications were from farmers seeking help for their sons and daughters, but more often they were from local hired hands who were seeking work for which they were well qualified, or from farmers looking for qualified help.

Farmers who sought help under the terms of the plan found themselves in a difficult position. Men who were sent to them from the cities were often not only unqualified, but, especially after the work camps closed, unwilling. A canvass of farmers' opinions on the placement plan in August 1936 in Manitoba revealed serious reservations. Most farmers wanted "careful selection" of the men sent to farms, and many wanted a "probationary or testing period."[32] They were not happy at the prospect of taking on "green farm hands from the city,"[33] who were often more trouble than they were worth, and who might not be willing to do the hard work of farming. As one disgruntled farmer said about the urban man who stayed only long enough to collect his clothing allowance and a meal: "The manure fork did not suit him."[34]

But farmers who complained that they were being saddled with incompetent help were reminded that the farm placement plan was designed to provide places for "Homeless men on relief in Urban Centres," and farmers were getting free help and thus had no basis for complaint.[55] By 1938, farmers were being informed that the plan "is not intended as a subsidy to farmers; it is simply a plan for placing men and women in employment who would otherwise have to have relief."[56] Local officials were instructed not to be "too particular about the type of man you send out," nor to "worry about his qualifications."[57]

Farmers knew the kind of workers they needed. Pickardville farmer John James Breadon took a man from the city relief rolls, but very soon sent a plea to officials to "send me up a rough looking man about 30 or 45 years of age a forner [sic] not a city man."[58] In Breadon's eyes, the placement plan worker was simply not willing to do normal farm work: "[Walter] was no good whatevery [sic] would not help me in the barn to feed my horses and cows only when I

Dust storm on farm (Courtesy of the Provincial Archives of Saskatchewan / R-A3524).

told him he could not see that horses and cows had to be feed [*sic*] I had to tell him everything." But the urban man had a different perspective. "O hell [he said,] I am not getting Ten Dallors [*sic*] a day to hurry."⁵⁹

Although many urban men were glad to take advantage of the plan, petitions and demonstrations against the "forced labour scheme designed to force the victims of unemployment into a twentieth-century adaptation of serfdom" attest to the widespread opposition.⁶⁰ While the relief camps still operated, men much preferred them to farm work, and placement officers had great difficulty inducing men to choose a farm over a work camp. "The men looked on this offer as heaping insult on injury," according to a Saskatchewan farmer's son, "and very few went along with the plan."⁶¹ As the camps closed, the National Employment Commission recognized the problem, noting that "homeless men who have enjoyed a more or less gregarious life in the National Defence Camps or in the cities in previous years [find] it difficult to 'stick out' life on a farm." Men unused to farm life faced a dreary prospect in "the isolation and loneliness of the farm home, the individualism of the farmer employer, not to mention the character of farm tasks and the hours of labour required to perform them."⁶² It recommended not only a "maximum incentive" to men to remain on a farm for the duration of the plan, but also suggested finding a new title for it, recognizing the "psychological value [that] might be achieved in selling the thought...to those who will be given the opportunity of getting homes and work this winter."⁶³

Urban men themselves had mixed reactions. Some men who signed up for the plan took the opportunity to pick up a set of clothes and disappear. But many were glad of the chance for "a comfortable bed and good plain food," and were satisfied to stay for the whole winter.⁶⁴ Still others stayed until spring, only for their bonus and because of the lack of other employment opportunities. But there were many who were not able to endure. They complained that the farm was "to [*sic*] lonesome," the weather was "too cold," the work was "a misery," the food "was fit for pigs," or that they "just don't suit farm work."⁶⁵ Still others clearly did not suit their employers:

> Tim did the work before breakfast but when he came into the house the farmer asked him to wash his face, and that started it. Tim said he would wash his face when the Boss did, and it went from bad to worse, so the final was he told Tim to go. Now this farmer did not bring Tim to the village, but Tim walked the seventeen miles, and now he has no money and is in the Village.⁶⁶

Urban men who were sent to do farm work under the plan had their protests ignored or discounted. The official purpose of the plan was not to satisfy the farmers or the unemployed, but to clear the city streets and relief rolls of "agitators and trouble-makers."[67] Under these conditions, relations between farmers and the men could be tense.

Farm workers, too, found themselves at an increasing disadvantage. Regulations were designed specifically to eliminate local residents, the ones most likely to be agricultural labourers. When farm worker Alfred McIntyre of Birnie, Manitoba, applied for a placement under the plan, he was rejected. His letter of appeal indicates the difficulties faced by local farm workers:

> I only received ten dollars ($10) a month for summer wages which you think is enough to cloth [*sic*] myself on I don't think it is hardly enough for both summer and winter clothing.
>
> In regards to my parents[,] my father was on relief this summer....The last I heard from them he was not working, so I could not very well go home expecting them to keep me. I can stay with Mr. Birch for the winter to do chores. But he does not want me to stay without getting some thing for working as there is [*sic*] too many chores and he cannot afford to pay me.[68]

His appeal was rejected, too, on the grounds that "there were earnings during the summer," that it was "not definitely stated that the applicant's parents cannot provide a home if necessary," and finally that it seemed likely that "a home on the farm is available even if the Dominion Relief Allowance of $5.00 per month is not approved."[69]

The greatest handicap to farm workers was their attachment to the agricultural community. If they remained in their home province and if they found work over the summer, they were almost automatically disqualified. Relief officials were instructed that "If the applicant has been working all summer and fall at reasonable wages, he or she should not be approved for placement unless an explanation can be given as to why sufficient of the earnings have not been saved to provide a living during the winter months."[70] In a general but unspecified way, farm workers were expected to fend for themselves.

While the cities were full of men who objected to farm work under the placement plans, there were many among the farming community who would have been only too happy to take farm work over the winter. On 15 November 1937, James Anderson began working for Harry Mason near Melita, Manitoba, under the farm placement plan. Anderson was a farm worker by trade, and as he had parents in the province, he was categorized as a local placement. He had long since moved away from home, proudly declaring that he had "been looking out for myself for 3 years now and until this winter have allways [sic] earned my way." Before signing up for the placement plan, he had managed to work at farms for either a small wage or for his board. But his status as a local placement, coupled with his season's earnings of $50, while "it wasn't enough to buy the clothes and nesassary [sic] things I needed for the winter," was enough to disqualify him for the plan. On 18 February, his placement was cancelled. Both Anderson and Mason wrote to the relief commissioner requesting reinstatement, and payment for the period Anderson had worked. This was refused. "I havent [sic] any other place to go if I am shut off on the Farm Plan," he wrote, "so I will be forced to go to the city and apply for relief."[71] By the time he made his way to the city, the farm placement plan had ended for another year. Anderson's dilemma was repeated countless times in rural communities across the Prairies.

In the eyes of farm placement officials, local farm workers such as James Anderson had the resources to be self-sufficient: "It is the opinion of the officials that the vast majority of such persons could look after themselves."[72] Under the restrictions of the farm placement plans, farm workers and farmers did indeed "look after themselves." Throughout the decade, rural people—farmers, sons and daughters, hired men and women—used the farm placement plans in ways that governments never intended, in ways that officials termed "abuse."

Abuse was a major concern of all levels of government, and changes in funding and regulations aimed to eliminate it. Administration was the area of greatest contention. In each province it was handled differently, but in each the greatest concern was to keep costs down. This sometimes resulted in a laxity over the regulations, particularly in the interpretation of the qualification requirements. As relief costs soared, the federal government attempted to control the plans by sporadic attempts to eliminate abuses. In 1934, an audit of provincial relief distribution caused Gordon to admit to the House of Commons that "it appeared there may have been a laxity in connection with certain municipalities."[73] King was scathing: "These reports show that much of the money was wasted, or worse than wasted; it has been distributed in ways for which even the municipalities and provinces cannot account."[74]

In the eyes of governments and placement officials, abuse included farmers hiring their own relatives, or taking a man under the plan when they could afford to pay a wage themselves; farm hands travelling to the city to register for relief and then for the farm placement plan in order to go back to the same farmer by whom they were regularly employed; or farm hands applying for the plan when they had a pocketful of harvest wages. From the rural perspective, however, misusing and manipulating the plans was often the only way they could be made to actually serve those in rural areas.

Ivan Schultz was in a position to judge. Schultz was a Manitoba barrister, and later the provincial Attorney General, who was one of the qualified references for men and farmers. For farmers, he was asked to vouch that they would indeed be creating new positions by taking men under the plan, and that they were unable to pay for help on their own. For the men, he was required to vouch that they were destitute and had no friends or relatives to take care of them. In 1935, the Manitoba Department of Public Works sent a circular letter to such referees, asking for comments on the effectiveness of the scheme and the extent of irregularities.

Schultz found that there was misuse of the plan, and although he sympathized with government watchdogs, his greater sympathies were with farmers and men. "I do not doubt there is a tendency to take advantage of it," he remarked, "because it is not always an equitable arrangement."

The problem, as he saw it, was in the leverage given to men by the availability of relief, whether direct relief in the cities or by the farm placement plans. Men who worked on a farm over the summer might normally be willing to work only for board during the winter months. However, direct relief in the cities and the farm placement plan made it "next to impossible to get any man to say he will work for his Board." The men's position was logical: "In a nutshell their argument is: Why should we work for our Board when we can get it for nothing in the City?" As a result, in order to obtain winter help, "the farmers of Necessity [sic] take advantage of this scheme." They felt justified in doing so "because a comparison of relief schedules as between cities and rural municipalities, and a comparison of their own conditions with those of the unemployed on relief in the cities convinces them they are entitled to help under this scheme."

Schultz sympathized with the farmers: "it is certainly not their fault if a man who would ordinarily [stay] for his board tells them flatly he will not stay unless the gratuity is secured." And he sympathized with hired men who took advantage of the plan. Local men were, after all, the best qualified to do farm work, and the least likely to be able to receive local municipal relief. They felt they were entitled to enrolment under the plan; otherwise, they would be forced to accept winter work for only room and board, while men from the cities were able to draw $5 a month. "To say the least," observed Schultz, "this situation is galling to these men."

It should come as no surprise to the authorities that there were abuses of the plan. Schultz declared: "If it grows to be a racket in the country, it will be through exploitation of the relief scheme for the benefit of local men." He continued, "it is certainly not an easy matter to reconcile an arrangement that gives $5.00 a month to an incapable and inefficient city cingle [*sic*] man employed on a farm and denies it to the trained farm hand whose misfortune is that he was born in a locality that is rural rather than urban."[75]

The farm placement plans of the 1930s, part of the larger government strategy of seeking a rural solution to an urban problem, served the rural community poorly. But rural people retaliated by using the plans in ways that government policy makers and watchdogs had never intended. To the dismay of officials, it became "practically impossible to convince either the farmer or the man that they [were] doing anything wrong."[76] From the rural perspective, however, the farm help plans best helped those who helped themselves.

NOTES

This article first appeared in *Prairie Forum* 19, no. 2 (1994): 231–251.

1   Author's calculation based on average percentage discrepancy between recorded placements and reported numbers at work. See note to Table 7.1.

2   Glenbow Archives (hereafter GA), BN.C212G/41/476, Canadian Pacific Railway Papers, memo for Gordon, 28 August 1931.

3   Provincial Archives of Manitoba (hereafter PAM), RG18 A4, box 27, file: Farm Placement (DPW), H. B. Wallace to A. MacNamara, 23 January 1937.

4   John Taylor, "'Relief from Relief': The Cities' Answer to Depression Dependency," *Journal of Canadian Studies* 14, no. 1 (Spring 1979): 17.

5   PAM, RG14/AL/1, Department of Labour, W. B. Pickard to members of the Committee on Unemployed, 18 April 1931.

6   In Saskatchewan, women were also eligible, but available records do not indicate that any took advantage of the plan during its first year of operation.

7   PAM, MG13/12, John Bracken Papers, file 764, Manitoba Relief Commission, circular letter, 23 November 1932.

8   PAM, MG13/12/G581, file 548, circular letter from A. MacNamara, 9 November 1931.

9   Saskatchewan Department of Railways, Labour and Industries, *Annual Report*, 1932, Supplement, p. 39.

10   House of Commons, *Debates*, 10 October 1932, R. B. Bennett, p. 51.

11   Susan M. Kooyman, "The Policies and Legislation of the United Farmers of Alberta Government, 1921–1935" (M.A. thesis, University of Calgary, 1981), 90.

12   GA, BN.C212G/96/887, CPR Papers, Hereford to Brownlee, 22 October 1932. British Columbia also joined the plan in 1932.

13 See Table 7.1.

14 Provincial Archives of Alberta (hereafter PAA), 65.118/124, Superintendent to T. Hodgson, 14 October 1936.

15 James Struthers, *No Fault of Their Own: Unemployment and the Canadian Welfare State, 1914–1941* (Toronto: University of Toronto, 1983), 117–18.

16 House of Commons, *Debates*, 17 February 1936, N. M. Rogers, 244.

17 *Labour Gazette*, 1935, 477.

18 Ibid., 30 April 1936.

19 National Archives of Canada (hereafter NA), RG 27, vol. 3382, file 3, memo "National Employment Commission's Conference on Farm Improvement and Employment," n.d.

20 NA, RG27, vol. 3193, file "Relief Settlement. Farm Placement," memo from Dominion Commissioner re: Farm Placement, 14 October 1936, 6.

21 Struthers, *No Fault of Their Own*, 159.

22 H. B. Neatby, *William Lyon Mackenzie King, 1932–1939: The Prism of Unity* (Toronto: University of Toronto Press, 1976), 151.

23 *Canada Year Book, 1937* (Ottawa: King's Printer, 1937), 761.

24 Albert S. Duncan, "Unemployment Relief in the Prairie Provinces, 1930–37" (M.A. thesis, McGill University, 1938), 110.

25 Author's calculations from NA, RG 27, vol. 213, file 617, Department of Labour, "Dominion Unemployment Relief: Relief Since 1930," January 1940, 37–38.

26 Saskatchewan, Unemployment Relief Report, Supplement to *Fourth Annual Report of the Dept. of Railways, Labour and Industry*, 1932, 39.

27 PAM, RG14/Al/3, Department of Labour, ESC, Provincial Superintendent Correspondence, application form, 4 November 1932.

28 PAM, MG13/I2, John Bracken Papers, file 764, memo from W. H. Carter, 23 November 1932.

29 PAM, RG14/Al/3, Department of Labour, ESC, Provincial Superintendent Correspondence, form letter from Local Superintendent, 20 January 1933.

30 PAM, RG18/A4/27, Department of Public Works, Ministers Office, Correspondence and Papers, memo to relief officers, 1934.

31 PAM, RG14/Al/5, Department of Labour, ESC, Provincial Superintendent Correspondence, file: "Alta.," Unemployment Relief Commission, application for farm worker, 1935.

32 Provincial Archives of Saskatchewan (hereafter PAS), X3D/19, Newspaper clippings: Relief, "A Brazen Trick," *Regina Daily Star*, 4 March 1935.

33 PAS, R-1022.1, file 32, J. G. Gardiner to W. A. Gordon, 24 April 1935.

34 See Table 7.1.

35 PAS, R-1022.1, file 32, Fred Ward to Premier of Saskatchewan, 29 April 1935.

36 House of Commons, *Debates*, 11 October 1932, E. J. Young, 92.

37 PAM, RG18/A4/27, Department of Public Works, file: Farm Placement, J. Neish to A. MacNamara, 21 April 1936.

38 PAM, RG18/A4/27, Department of Public Works, file: Single Men's Relief Commission H. J. Martin "Secret Report," 9 October 1936; ibid., T. Dann, "Secret Report," 13 October 1936.

39 PAA, 65.118/124, broadsheet, action committee SUPA "IMPORTANT MEETING SINGLE MEN," 11 October 1936.

40 NA, RG 27, vol. 2249, File: Farm Settlement and Single Unemployed, Calgary, R. A. Rigg to W. M. Dickson 19, 21, 23 October 1936.
41 PAA, 65.118/122, *Edmonton Journal*, 24 October 1936.
42 PAM, RG 18/A4/27, Department of Public Works, file "Farm Placement," A. MacNamara to W. R. Oubb, 4 December 1935.
43 Ibid., A. MacNamara to H. Mitchell, 25 February 1937.
44 NA, RG 27, vol. 2249, file: Farm Settlement and Single Unemployed, NEC Memorandum, "Committee on Farm Placement," 10 August 1936.
45 PAM, RG 18/A4/27, Department of Public Works, Minister's Office, Correspondence and Papers, Unknown to the Unemployment Commission, 9 October 1936.
46 PAM, RG 18/A4/27, Department of Public Works, Ministers Office, Correspondence and Papers, Application Form Farm Improvement and Employment Plan, 1936–37.
47 PAM, RG 18/B3-2, Department of Public Works, Relief Commission, Farm Help Plan, form letter from W. R. Clubb, 23 November 1938.
48 Ibid., form letter from W. R. Clubb, 1 October 38.
49 Ibid., memo from A. MacNamara, 11 January1939.
50 PAS, R6.30/1, Bureau of Labour and Public Welfare, Relief Records, T. Molloy to P. Symons, 26 June 1936.
51 PAS, R6.31/27, Bureau of Labour and Public Welfare, Relief Records, Farm Bonus Correspondence: General 1937–38, "Farm Improvement and Employment Plan," [Report], 27 January 1938.
52 Of the 154 farmers who gave their opinion of the plan, forty-three were in favour, twenty-three opposed, and 154 "neutral [with) various suggestions and views." NA, RG 27, vol. 2088, file Y21-0, Committee of Farm Placement, Correspondence, A. Purvis to H. Hereford, 4 August 1936.
53 PAM, RG 18/A4/27, Department of Public Works, Minister's Office, Correspondence and Papers, Unknown to the Unemployment Commission, 9 October 1936.
54 PAA, 65.118, box 35, file 277, AES Papers, W. A. Boyle to A. A. Mackenzie, 15 December 1934.
55 PAM, RG 18/A4/27, Department of Public Works, file "Farm Placement," A. MacNamara to W. Clubb, 25 November 1935.
56 PAM, RG 18/B3-2, Department of Public Works, Relief Commission, Farm Help Plan, form letter from W. R. Clubb, 23 November 1938.
57 PAA, 65.118/126, H. Robertson to A. A. Colquhoun, 6 January 1938.
58 PAA, 65.118/271, John James Breadon to [Patterson), 24 December 1934.
59 Ibid.
60 PAA, 69.289/1019, circular issued by Single Unemployed Protective Association "THE $5.00 PER MONTH FARM SCHEME," n.d.; and see also PAM, RG 18/ A4, box 27, file: Single Men's Relief Commission, RCMP Reports; NA, RG 27, vol. 2249, file: Farm Settlement and Single Unemployed.
61 PAS, A/169, Alex Cunningham, "The Biography of the Cunningham Family," p. 215.
62 NA, RG 27, vol. 3365, file: "In favor of a bonus system in respect to Farm Placement Plan," NEC, n.d.
63 NA, RG 27, vol. 2088, file Y21-0, Committee on Farm Placement, Advisory to NEC, A. Purvis to H. Hereford, 12 July 1936.

64   PAS, R-281.5, Saskatchewan Relief Commission, m/f C 13-15, "Letters of appreciation."

65   Ibid., m/f B 2-10, "Letters of complaint"; see also PAA, 65.118, boxes 35 and 36, files 277, 278, 279.

66   PAA, 65.118/125, R. B. Langley to office of Secretary-Treasurer, Unemployment and Relief Commission, Drumheller, 9 December 1937.

67   PAM, RG 18/A4, box 27, Department of Public Works, file: Farm Placement, J. Neish to A. MacNamara, 30 April 1936.

68   PAM, RG 18/B3-2, Department of Public Works, Relief Commission, Alfred McIntyre to Employment Service of Canada, 23 November 1935.

69   Ibid., J. Neish to Alfred McIntyre, 18 November 1935.

70   Ibid., form letter from W. R. Clubb, 23 November 1938.

71   Ibid., James Anderson to Commissioner, 23 February 1938; ibid., Harry Mason to A. MacNamara, 23 February 1938; ibid., A. MacNamara to Harry Mason, 30 March 1938.

72   Ibid., form letter from W. R. Clubb, 1 October 1938.

73   House of Commons, *Debates*, 22 March 1934, W. A. Gordon, p. 1731.

74   Ibid., 6 March 1934, W. L. M. King, p. 1820.

75   PAM, RG 18/A4/27, Department of Public Works, file: farm placement, Ivan Schultz to the Minister, 18 November 35.

76   PAA, 65.118/126, memo from W. E. Patterson, 14 December 1935.

8. Soldier Settlement and Depression Settlement in the Forest Fringe of Saskatchewan

John McDonald

INTRODUCTION

This article provides a review of soldier settlement and depression settlement in the forest fringe of the prairies, and especially Saskatchewan (Figures 8.1 and 8.2), between the two World Wars. Although a certain amount of research has been done into this topic, there has been much more emphasis on the grasslands and park belt. This study reviews existing information on the two rapid influxes to the forest fringe which eventually resulted in considerable overpopulation relative to its true agricultural potential. Much poverty was experienced here in the 1930s, largely as a result of over-optimistic appraisal of the quality of farmland in the region.

BACKGROUND

The role of agriculture in the forest fringe along the northern extremities of the "park belt" of the prairies prior to World War 1 was minimal. Only in the Shellbrook and Preeceville districts (Figure 8.1) of Saskatchewan had any substantial progress been made. In these districts wheat was produced for export, but all other districts in which any farming had emerged were dominated by the production of oats and barley for local consumption; the lumber trade remained an important occupation. Little interest was shown in the encouragement of extensive settlement in the forest fringe of Saskatchewan prior to World War 1, and the Great War slowed settlement in the forest lands almost to a standstill. During 1913–1919 no new rail was laid on the pioneer fringe of Saskatchewan although construction remained active in both the

Peace River district of Alberta and the Interlake region of Manitoba.[1] In Saskatchewan, extension of the existing rail network was contemplated but the railways were hesitant to invest capital in lines which would serve only a small, scattered population.

Nevertheless, during the war both the Dominion and provincial governments conducted surveys whereby the agricultural potential of unsettled lands across western Canada was assessed. As the availability of arable land on the prairies and in the park belt diminished, the agricultural role of the forest fringe in Saskatchewan would soon increase. Optimism was high in regard to the forest fringe, as officials were generally convinced that problems encountered prior to the war had been caused mainly by the settlers' own ineptitude. Despite a greater awareness of the conditions peculiar to the north it was believed in official circles that these could be easily overcome, and that rapid and successful settlement was possible along the forest fringe.

SOLDIER SETTLEMENT

As the Great War drew to a close, the Dominion Government recognized that both the Canadian economy and the returning veterans would be subject to a period of readjustment. Concerned about the potentially high rate of unemployment amongst returned soldiers, the Dominion Government promulgated plans whereby many of them could be settled on the land. An outcome of this was the passing of the Soldier Settlement Act in 1917 which was described as: "An Act to assist returned soldiers in settling upon the land and to increase agricultural production." This Act provided for a maximum loan of $2,500 which would be used to assist soldiers in settling on free Dominion lands, on lands already owned by soldiers, or on land purchased on their behalf. Twenty years were allotted for repayment of the loan which was to be used only for the following purposes as prescribed in the Act:

a. The acquiring of land for agricultural purposes;
b. The payment of encumbrances on land used for agricultural purposes;
c. The improvement of agricultural land;
d. The improvement of farm buildings;
e. The purchase of stock, machinery and equipment; and
f. Such other purposes as the board may approve.[2]

During 1918 the Soldier Settlement Board was established and Dominion lands were reserved for soldier settlers. Eleven district offices to deal with applications were opened across the nation, three of which were in Saskatchewan, at

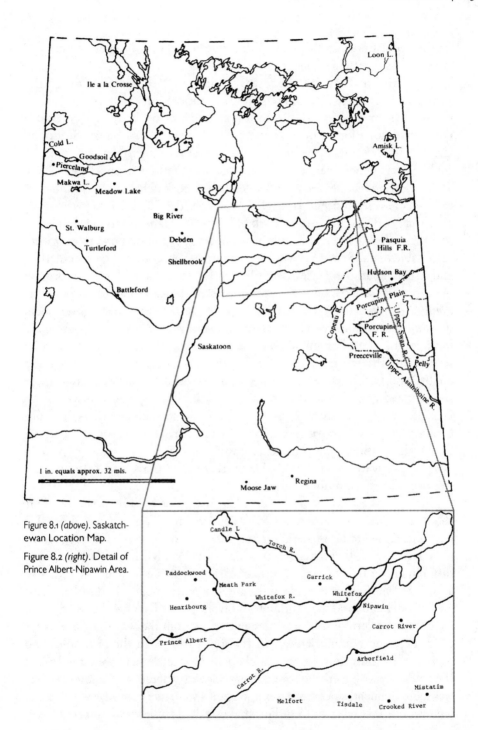

Figure 8.1 *(above)*. Saskatchewan Location Map.

Figure 8.2 *(right)*. Detail of Prince Albert-Nipawin Area.

Regina, Saskatoon, and Prince Albert. By the fall of 1918, these offices had issued loans in excess of one million dollars.

The Board had initially stated that it did not "...contemplate the settlement of soldiers as pioneers in remote locations or under isolated conditions, removed from markets, in virgin forest lands, or on lands not cultivable without reclamation or other development."[3] Despite the reservation of all Crown lands within fifteen miles of every railway for the exclusive use of soldier settlers, however, it was soon apparent that a land shortage existed. This condition had been acknowledged by the Saskatchewan government as early as 1916 when it declared that "There is considerable doubt as to the availability of good land in northern Saskatchewan.... Transportation facilities are poorly developed and it is almost impossible to get a good homestead within reasonable distance of a railway."[4] The shortage, accentuated by speculation, and also acute in the Peace River district, led to demands for the allocation of land from sources outside the confines of the existing Act, and to the eventual distortion of the Board policy quoted earlier. The federal government was forced to announce as early as November 1918 that land contained in the Pasquia Hills and Porcupine Forest Reserves was to be allotted for soldier settlement. This move was "justified" by declaring the land to be of the finest quality and within close proximity to rail transportation.[5] Although these were indeed good lands, they required much clearing, and transportation facilities were seriously lacking. The placement of soldier settlers at Pouce Coupe and Sunset Prairie in the Peace River district, however, was preposterous; the minimum distance to a railway was eighty miles and grain could be moved only over winter trails. Under these conditions land abandonment was exceedingly common.

The federal government also decided that lands held by private owners should be made accessible to returned soldiers under a purchase policy. This was determined to be a federal matter, and consequently the federal government was given full purchase powers under the War Measures Act by Order-in-Council on 11 February 1919. Legislation to this effect in July 1919 also authorized the Soldier Settlement Board to acquire uncultivated Indian lands and school lands, and to withdraw land from Forest Reserves.[6] A distinctive trait in the pattern of soldier settlement stems from the withdrawal of lands from these sources, particularly in the forest fringe. In the grasslands and park belt, the only new tracts of land opened for settlement were the Indian Reserves. However, in the forest fringe block settlement of soldier settlers was more frequent, since free Dominion lands were more readily available and land was also withdrawn from Forest and Indian Reserves. Land purchased by the Soldier Settlement Board in the forest fringe was also generally a little cheaper than lands purchased further south—probably a reflection of the inability of the forested land to quickly produce a cash crop.

Soldier settlers were involved in a considerable degree of pioneering activity along the forest fringe of Manitoba, Saskatchewan and Alberta. In Manitoba pioneering was particularly common in the Interlake region, north and east of Dauphin Lake and along the fringes of the Swan River district.[7] Much of this land was partially wooded and in many cases stony, particularly between Lakes Winnipeg and Manitoba where settlers were also blessed with frequent untimely frosts. Pioneering by soldier settlers in Alberta was particularly common in the Peace River district but was also found north and east of Edmonton. In Saskatchewan, soldier settlement across the park belt and the forest fringe took place to the north and south of Tisdale and Prince Albert, in the Porcupine Forest Reserve and at Melfort, Shellbrook, Battleford and Turtleford.[8] The settlement at Paddockwood north of Prince Albert and particularly that on land withdrawn from the Porcupine Forest Reserve involved pioneering. The latter case is used here as an illustration of the conditions experienced.

The Porcupine Soldier Settlement was created in 1919 on 200,000 acres of land which had been withdrawn from the north, northwest, and southeast sections of the Porcupine Forest. Although the Dominion advanced the necessary loans to enable the rudimentary beginnings in agriculture, further aid to the community was limited, such that "the building of schools, churches, a hospital and any progress made, could be achieved only by their own individual and/or collective effort."[9] The lack of familiarity with the forest fringe environment displayed by many authorities of the Soldier Settlement Board is exemplified by the comment of R. J. Shore, its Assistant Director of Lands, that "while some of it (the Porcupine Forest) is heavily timbered…there is a way of clearing this without very much trouble by employing fire"[10]—an unrealistic comment as far as much of the area was concerned. The land was predominantly characterized by stands of poplar, willow and scattered spruce interspersed with innumerable swampy sloughs which posed a frost hazard and necessitated draining. Consequently the years 1919–1925 were characterized by the initial clearing and breaking of the land. By December 1920 there were 101 established settlers and by December 1923, 175, of whom twenty-five had abandoned their property. Only one hundred of these settlers were actually in residence on their property.[11] This can probably be attributed to the lack of clearing and the subsequent reliance upon lumbering during these early years. Indeed, settlers were encouraged to obtain outside employment in order to supplement their finances. Through the efforts of the Soldier Settlement Board many were able to find employment in the lumber camps along the railway between Tisdale and Hudson Bay Junction.

By 1925 the Porcupine Plain settlement found itself in difficulty in its attempt to finance a school, due in part to owner absenteeism and to the fact that not enough soldier settlers had arrived to create an equitable tax base. Considerable criticism was consequently directed towards the Soldier Settlement Board for not permitting the area to be opened up to settlers other than returned veterans. This criticism disappeared when the federal government ultimately annulled the exclusive settlement rights of soldier settlers in the Porcupine Forest Reserve in February 1926. This move was prompted by the fact that, whereas settlement had earlier peaked at 355 settlers, by 1 October 1925 there had been 216 abandonments, leaving only 139 settlers. The major problem had been the settlement's distance to market, coupled with the fact that "prior to 1929 not a road worthy of the name (existed) in the whole district."[12]

PROGRESS OF SOLDIER SETTLEMENT

By the end of November 1920, 19,771 soldier settlers had established themselves on the land in Canada, about 70 percent of them in the three prairie provinces. There were 3,231 in Manitoba, 4,927 in Saskatchewan and 5,785 in Alberta.[13] Although these figures are by no means overwhelming, difficulty in finding suitable land leads one to believe that government officials were on the whole over-optimistic about the agricultural potential of the north. In 1916, for example, the Saskatchewan government, although acknowledging that there was a shortage of agricultural land in the vicinity of railways, "believed that 100,000 homesteads may be available—almost entirely in the north."[14] However, the difficulties encountered in placing the soldier settlers upon the land probably did much to dispel the myth of the north's vast agricultural potential.

On 1 May 1921 the reservation for soldier settlers of all Dominion lands within fifteen miles of a railway in the four western provinces was annulled. This annulment was, however, exclusive of the lands withdrawn from the Porcupine and Riding Mountain Forest Reserves, Hudson Bay Lands, Doukhobor lands and any other lands specially reserved for soldier settlement purposes.[15] Although the soldier settlers had been more or less successfully settled, they were no less immune to problems and setbacks than were ordinary settlers, and the period after 1921 was a difficult one.

The post-war economic depression had the effect of deflating the artificially buoyant economy of the pioneer fringe. There followed a time of retrenchment. Across the northern agricultural frontier, land had been purchased for soldier settlers when prices were at their peak. Deflation associated with the post-war recession had, by 1921, made it exceedingly difficult for many veterans to pay off their loans. Their property devalued until it was worth less than the government had charged them for it. Stock purchased prior to 1921 had a value of $13.5 million but by 1925 its value had fallen to less than half of that amount.[16] In contrast, there was little or no decrease in the cost of implements and building materials. As the 1920s evolved and soldier-settler tenure became longer, there were fewer soldier settlers on the land each year. Economic and environmental problems took a large toll. The failure rate of soldier settlers, for all reasons, rose from 7 percent in 1921 to 21 percent in 1924, and to 31 percent by 1926.

In response to demands by the soldier settlers for a solution to the cost-price squeeze, the Dominion government passed an amendment in 1922 which enabled the Soldier Settlement Board to consolidate all indebtedness into one loan payable over twenty-five years and to grant an interest exemption of from two to four years depending upon the date of occupancy of the land.[17] Not until the 1927 session of Parliament was the long-awaited amendment to the Soldier Settlement Act which provided for the revaluation of soldier-settler lands finally passed. It applied only to those settlers who were still in active occupancy of their lands; an average devaluation of 24 percent was achieved for those eligible for readjustment under the terms of the amendment. Further changes continued to be made in response to adverse conditions in the forest fringe, particularly after the onslaught of the "Dirty Thirties."

As the 1920s progressed, the Soldier Settlement Board's responsibility to the veterans was diminished as the successful settlers became established and the unsuccessful ones were weeded out. On 17 August 1923 the Board was transferred from the Minister of the Interior to the Minister of Immigration and Colonization, and was given new responsibilities.

> Knowledge gained by the Soldier Settlement Board could be passed on in the form of a 'Land Settlement Service' to newcomers whereby the inexperienced immigrant has a disinterested source of advice on farming districts and land values which will afford him a means of protection, which in the past he has been without, against unfair exploitation and his own ignorance of local conditions.[18]

By 1926 this new Land Settlement Branch of the Department of Immigration and Colonization had become involved in a series of settlement schemes and other activities, including the investigation of applications by aliens or on behalf of aliens for entry into Canada.[19]

Despite the influx of soldier settlers into the Saskatchewan forest fringe, the region still represented only about 4 or 5 percent of the provincial total population in the 1920s.[20] Homesteading had become common near Meadow Lake and Makwa Lake in the lower valleys of the Torch and Whitefox Rivers east of Prince Albert. Yet by the mid-1920s, apart from the Turtleford Plain, parts of the Debden-Big River Plain, Upper Swan-Upper Assiniboine Plain and to a lesser extent the Saskatchewan Lowland, the forest fringe was primarily dependent upon alternative sources of income in lieu of market-oriented grain production. For the majority of settlers, conditions had not substantially improved over those of the pre-war era. The predominance of oats and barley as the primary crops was indicative of the continued persistence of subsistence farming. Indeed, throughout the 1920s over 85 percent of the settlers did not usually market a crop. Bartering, such as that at Porcupine Plain in the form of "cord wood currency," was very common, and relief payments were made throughout the decade. Requests were also made to hunt game out of season in order to supplement food supplies.[21] However, for the most part there was little serious deprivation or suffering.

During the 1920s the greatest concentration of failure of soldier settlers was in Manitoba, due in all probability to the marginal condition of the land. The instability of the northern agricultural fringe in Manitoba was highlighted when in its Eighth Report in 1929 the Soldier Settlement Board complained that there was a good deal of abandoned land which was depressing prices and that the municipalities were dumping farms at only a fraction of their value.[22]

All in all, however, the introduction of over ten thousand soldier settlers into the northern agricultural fringe had been accomplished relatively successfully. By the end of the 1920s their transformation into farmers was all but complete, and the civilian succession of soldier settlement was well under way. Soldier Settlement loans fell from a high of 12,695 in 1919 to 29 in 1927. Although the degree of scientific planning which had both preceded and accompanied the soldier settlers was questionable, the cumulative total of soldier settlers did not, in the main, exceed the capabilities of the government to secure them land through one source or another. Where suitable Dominion lands had been lacking the shortage had been met with privately purchased land, uncultivated Indian Reserve lands, Forest Reserve lands, and Doukhobor, Hudson Bay and school lands. Through its ability to obtain suitable land, the Board was largely successful in limiting the advance of the soldier settlers on to the poorer grey-white podzolic soils. This movement, however, in combination with that of the civilian settlers, had enveloped the vast majority of agriculturally suitable land in the forest fringe. Although a quiet optimism existed in regard to the future, the succeeding decade would witness an uncontrolled land rush which would tax the forest fringe beyond its potential agricultural capability.

PRELUDE TO THE DROUGHT MIGRATION

By the end of the 1920s, the transfer of jurisdiction over the natural resources of the prairies from the Dominion to the provincial governments was imminent. In September 1929 the Department of the Interior withdrew all unoccupied Crown Lands from homestead entry in order that each of the three prairie provinces might promulgate a policy toward northern settlement. When the transfer of jurisdiction was made, the consensus of opinion was that, whereas the free homestead system had been useful in the past, "most of the land which could be selected by individual settlers without the guidance of the government had been taken up."[23] Consequently Saskatchewan and Manitoba discarded the policy of free homesteads in 1930. The retention of the free homesteading system in Alberta was indicative of the fact that the majority of the remaining agriculturally suitable land in the prairies lay within that province, particularly in the Peace River district.

The cessation of the homestead policy in Saskatchewan was based on the report of the *Saskatchewan Royal Commission on Immigration and Settlement, 1930*, which recommended "that the remaining Crown Lands where immediately available for agriculture be sold (a) to residents of the province (b) to other Canadians (c) to British settlers (d) to other immigrants."[24] The Saskatchewan Government subsequently refused to subsidize any new migrants and all remaining former homestead lands were to be classified and disposed of at a minimum price of one dollar per acre. The remainder of the Crown Lands were to be permanently closed to settlement. Yet despite these regressive policies the same Royal Commission optimistically concluded that settlement could, perhaps, eventually extend as far north as a line drawn northwest from Amisk Lake and running just north of Île-à-la-Crosse,[25] a line far to the north of the belt of reasonably fertile black and transitional soils. Despite the recommendations of the Royal Commission for planned and orderly settlement in combination with detailed investigations pertaining to soil, climate, and topography, the northern settlement of the 1930s, much of it spawned by the Depression, would proceed in an *ad hoc* fashion. The consequence of this was the placement of many settlers on submarginal lands which bred both turmoil and deprivation for years to come.

The migration to northern Saskatchewan was, in part, based on the belief that the land was capable of allowing someone a new start. Many half-truths about conditions in the north continued to be circulated, engendering an optimism in many drought-stricken farmers which was based on a distorted image of true environmental conditions in the forest fringe. "There was no doubt in the minds of some farmers, even before 1930, particularly those from southwest Saskatchewan, that the north came to be regarded as some type of mecca in which solutions to all problems could be found."[26] There was some foundation for this optimism. Whereas in 1931 crop returns in the four large southern crop districts averaged between 1.8 and 5.7 bushels per acre, in the Carrot River Valley and North Battleford districts crops of 23 bushels per acre were harvested.[27] In June 1931 a report from the Nipawin Tisdale area stated that: "pastures are good, and there is a good supply of water."[28] Nevertheless, the migration of drought-stricken farmers was only a trickle at first. It took some time to shake the faith of the population at large and to uproot any significant segment of it. Consequently, although immigration to the northern agricultural fringe steadily increased from 1929 to 1931, little of it was due to drought. However, by the fall of 1931 the movement of drought-stricken southern farmers had become the most important segment of the northern migration.

Moving from southern Saskatchewan to Meadow Lake in northern Saskatchewan, 1935 (Courtesy of the Provincial Archives of Saskatchewan / S-B257).

NORTHERN SETTLEMENT DURING THE DROUGHT ERA

In Saskatchewan at least, the period commonly referred to as the "Dirty Thir-ties" can be divided almost equally into two distinct phases. The first half of the decade witnessed a relatively uncontrolled and continuous in-migration to the northern agricultural fringe. In contrast the latter half of the decade witnessed the implementation of cohesive government policy which sought to revive the equilibrium of environment and settlement, and which resulted in a process of population consolidation accompanied by an out-migration.

The deterioration of conditions across the prairie and park belts created a renewed interest in the forest fringe. Yet the people who were drawn to this region came from a variety of sources. Some were the unemployed from the lumber camps, the rural communities or the cities. "A great many people who had homesteaded within the forest years before were now forced back to the land by urban unemployment."[29] This diversity in background, combined with the shortage of agriculturally suitable land which was under increasing pressure from an ever-growing number of would-be settlers, eventually culminated in widespread deprivation as bad as that which the settlers had sought to leave behind. By the fall of 1931 the migration of drought-stricken farmers neces-sitated the promulgation of more comprehensive relief measures. Through the initiation of these early settlement schemes it was hoped that the relief problem in southern Saskatchewan could be alleviated or, depending on the success of the scheme, even solved. However, these schemes were in variably designed around the assumption that the settlers would locate on agriculturally acceptable land. Yet conditions in the north dictated that farming practices must differ from those in the south. "Often non-agricultural opportunities were neglected, the result, at least in part, of misdirected encouragement given in the first years of occupancy."[30]

Despite the grim realities of the forest fringe, the attraction of an ever-increasing number of migrants indicated that optimism was buoyant in rela-tion to the perceived capabilities of the region. Between 1929 and 1931 several crucial rail lines were completed which greatly facilitated the movement of settlers into new parts of the forest fringe. The Nipawin-Henribourg line, the Carrot River and Arborfield branch lines and the line to Meadow Lake, which was completed in 1931, opened up vast stretches of territory (Figure 8.1). D. P. Fitzgerald, in *Pioneer Settlement in Northern Saskatchewan*, credits the completion of these lines with the altering of the pattern of population distribution.[31] The most rapid development of new farms on the forest fringe took place on the Beaver Plain, between the Torch River and the Whitefox River and east of the Copeau River, accessibility to each of these areas being directly associated with the completion of the new rail lines. Yet, despite the obviously beneficial impact of the railroad, the volume of passengers and their possessions transported fell between 1933 and 1935. This was caused by the fact that, as the Depression dragged on, new arrivals were less and less able to pay for either the rail fare or for the freight charges, even at subsidized rates. Despite the declining rail traffic, the importance of the railroad was indicated by the clustering of settlement within twenty to thirty miles of the railhead, with the exception of Big River which was surrounded by poor soil and dependent on the lumber trade.

The vast influx of settlers tended to increase the population all across the forest fringe, with the exception of already established districts such as that around Shellbrook. Settlers who came on their own took up land all across the frontier, and as their numbers increased small service centres such as Carrot River, Garrick and Mistatim developed in order to serve them. In eastern Saskatchewan the agricultural frontier was extended to the east into the forested lands between the Carrot and Assiniboine Rivers. Farther to the north, the Carrot River valley also attracted settlement, as did the Whitefox River valley between Prince Albert and Whitefox. Big River, to the north-west of Prince Albert, and Crooked River, east of Tisdale, attracted settlement because they were established lumbering centres although the agricultural quality of the land was poor.[32]

The majority of migrants located under the various assisted settlement schemes were placed on improved or partly improved lands. Thus in this case the availability of Crown lands was not as critical as it was with the drought refugees. Settlement under these schemes tended to occur wherever idle farms were available, thus nullifying to a great degree the extension of the frontier on to new lands. The Beaver River valley of Saskatchewan and Alberta was, however, the scene of much intermingling between assisted settlement and the arrival of unassisted drought refugees.

The settlement of relief recipients through the Saskatchewan Relief Commission was a very important feature in the extension of northern settlement. The Meadow Lake region was host to a great influx, as was the Loon Lake area on the east shore of Makwa Lake. The Pierceland-Goodsoil area north of the Beaver River contained excellent soils but was even more isolated than was Loon Lake, for it was served by railheads at Meadow Lake and St. Walburg in Saskatchewan and Bonnyville in Alberta. Extensive settlement in this region had, by 1935, forced homesteading beyond the Beaver River as far north as Cold Lake and as far west as the Alberta boundary.[33] Group settlements such as those found near Turtleford, St. Walburg, Pelly and Loon

Lake were also associated with the arrival of relief recipients. Government schemes associated with these movements, particularly the one to the Loon Lake area, did much to place newcomers beyond the limits of the agricultural frontier as it then existed.

The impact of immigrants upon the north was minimal at this time due to the restrictive immigration policies of the government. However, twenty German families arrived in the Loon Lake area in 1929, encountering extremely heavy bush, contrary to what they had been led to believe. By 1938 almost all of them were still on relief, whereupon they returned to Germany, their farms being purchased by German refugees forced from the Sudetenland in Czechoslovakia following its annexation by Germany.[34] The Beaver River area in total witnessed the arrival of several hundred German immigrants who settled on Crown Lands.

Despite the influx of settlement into the forest fringe, the growth in population cannot be entirely attributed to in-migration. The spread of settlement was, in some instances, associated with the indigenous growth and expansion of previously established localities. This was particularly important in the case of central Europeans such as Ukrainians who tended to cluster in tightly knit communities. The expansion of second-generation Ukrainians on to unalienated land was responsible for a large proportion of the population increase in certain areas. In Saskatchewan the Hudson Bay Junction and St. Walburg areas were affected, as was the Beaver River valley of Alberta and Saskatchewan where by 1935 nearly one-third of the population was of Ukrainian origin.[35]

The impact of the in-migration upon the population density of the forest fringe was uneven, such that although the average density had been pushed to between two and five people per square mile it ranged as high as seventeen people per square mile in certain areas. Land in the vicinity of Prince Albert, west of Nipawin and around Preeceville and Meadow Lake was inundated in this manner.[36] The impact of this settlement upon the north was such that 154 new school districts were formed through homesteading, with school enrolment reported as 4,801—an average of about thirty students per school.[37]

This deluge of population into an environment with which the majority were unfamiliar was accompanied by a host of problems. Whereas in the early 1920s the government had made every effort to purchase land directly for the soldier settlers, thus limiting the role of the intermediary, such was not the case during the "Dirty Thirties." In many instances settlers found themselves on unproductive land due to insufficient caution and, in part, to the unscrupulous habits of real estate agents who easily misled many of the drought refugees.[38] Perhaps the greatest hindrance to progress was the inability of the settler to clear and break an adequate amount of land. Many settlers arrived in the north destitute. Prior to 1935 there was no direct government assistance given in clearing the land, and thus the settler became dependent, in many cases, upon relief for survival. "A policy of direct relief, far from providing an effective remedy, had served to aggravate the worst features of the situation. Direct relief, although suited to the south, was totally inapplicable to northern settlement where even the basic rudiments of farming necessities were lacking."[39] Consequently the removal of forest cover was slow, indeed negligible, across much of the forest belt.

The settler's ability to utilize the natural resources of the land (such as fish, game, fur and timber), which were undoubtedly beneficial and in some cases vital to his survival, was limited by his own lack of resources. Often there was a lack of sugar needed for preserving purposes, and many could afford neither ammunition nor a gun for hunting game. Destitution was further enhanced as prairie-bred horses died of swamp fever and as crops were destroyed by recurrent frost, rust and sometimes even drought.[40] Indeed, some of the worst cases of deprivation during the 1930s occurred in the north, accompanied by extreme cases of loneliness caused by isolation. It was noted by a former provincial civil servant that northern settlers had a "regular route to the mental institution at North Battleford."[41]

By 1934 conditions in northern Saskatchewan were chaotic. The period was marked by destruction of survey stakes, refusals to pay taxes, illegal entries on homesteads, school and grazing lands, and an increasing incidence of attempted eviction being met by force. The tremendous surge of people into the forest fringe strained the capacity of its environment. There was a distinct relationship between the vast influx of migrants and the serious depletion of fish and fur-bearing animals, as well as the loss of much valuable timber due to forest fires. Whereas the reaction of local inhabitants had originally been one of sympathy and surprise as to the size of the migration, this attitude eventually turned to one of anger as the ever-increasing number of migrants taxed the resources of the land and the ability of the municipalities or Local Improvement Districts to meet their needs.[42]

With the continuation of the Depression and the land shortage the number of people on relief continued to rise. The number of families in Saskatchewan receiving direct relief including food, clothing and hospitalization rose from 3,789 in September 1934, to 5,911 in September 1935. Consequently in the fall of 1935 requirements for the acquisition of land were reduced, so that land could be obtained without a thorough survey. The establishment of the 1935 Homestead Act was further indicative of the acute land shortage and the need to alleviate it. By the time the Northern Settlers' Re-establishment Board assumed jurisdiction in 1935 it was determined that 40 percent of the Saskatchewan forest-fringe settlers were in the Meadow Lake-Loon Lake region, 40 percent were northeast and northwest of Prince Albert, and the remaining 20 percent were in the Hudson Bay Junction area. The 1941 Census of Canada later revealed that the population of the forest fringe exclusive of Prince Albert exceeded 80,000, just over half of whom had migrated north during the 1930s.[43]

By 1937 virtually all of the available Crown and private lands in Saskatchewan had been settled. Although the cancellation of homestead entries began to grow in Saskatchewan at this time, the majority of those cancelling did not leave the north but rather were re-located through efforts of the Northern Settlers Re-establishment Branch.[44] However, as conditions slowly improved elsewhere, the hardships of life in the forest fringe began to loom larger. The cost and labour of breaking land, the lack of services, the unpredictable climate, coupled with forest fires, disease and the increased costs of marketing a crop, slowly engendered a feeling that perhaps life could be more pleasant elsewhere. The resulting outward migration, although not very conspicuous until after World War II, witnessed the depopulation of the forest fringe as people forsook their temporary refuge and again returned to the farms and cities of the south. This movement helped to restore an equilibrium between the forest-fringe population and the supporting environment. It was with this equilibrium in mind that government policy in the form of the Northern Settlers' Re-establishment Board approached the problems of the south in the late 1930s and launched the north on the road to a long overdue recovery through planned utilization of the area's resources.

GOVERNMENTAL ACTIVITY IN RESPECT TO NORTHERN SETTLEMENT DURING THE "DIRTY THIRTIES"—THE CASE OF SASKATCHEWAN

In 1929–30 the Saskatchewan government had guaranteed municipal loans for relief to the amount of $1,731,717. The adversities of 1930–31 caused the municipalities to advance a further $2,725,683 for relief.[45] In December 1930, in response to the rapidly deteriorating conditions, the government announced the new Relief Settlement Plan, the aim of which was the transfer of people on relief to farms in the north.[46] Potential settlers were not required to have had previous agricultural experience, and a grant of up to $300 was made available for each successful applicant.

The United Farmers of Canada (UFC) were responsible for the administration of relief in the northern half of Saskatchewan. Consequently they were one of the first groups to show concern for the movement by the government of destitute settlers into the north and thus into their domain of responsibility. Although UFC officials sympathized with the government over the issue of unemployment, they were nevertheless opposed to further settlement in the north until an impartial yet thorough investigation of agricultural conditions had been conducted. As early as 1931, A. J. Macauley, the UFC president, warned that much of the land being occupied was unsuitable for farming and predicted, very accurately, that some of the settlers would be worse off than if they stayed in the south.[47] He was further critical of the small amount of assistance given to families who moved from the cities.

The need for further assistance to settlers after their arrival led to the passing of the Land Settlement Act, a joint federal-provincial effort which came into effect in May 1931. The purpose of this Act was to advance the capital needed to assist Saskatchewan citizens who were experienced in farming to settle on provincial lands. In the first month 231 farmers took advantage of this scheme.[48] Concentrations of migrants ultimately occurred at Loon Lake and in the Pelly district, settled by people from the Saskatoon and Moose Jaw districts respectively. The summer of 1931 also witnessed a withdrawal of land from the proposed Candle Lake Indian Reserve and from the Pasquia and Porcupine Forest Reserves in an attempt to fulfill the need for more land. Despite these efforts the shortage of suitable land led to the penetration of settlers on to parts of the Missouri Coteau and the Shellbrook-Meath Park Plain, both areas which had been formerly avoided.[49]

The attitude of the federal government played an important role in the determination of provincial relief policy, due to the fact that the provincial government was dependent upon Ottawa for financial support. Relief of poverty had traditionally been a municipal concern. Thus the federal government in the Depression assumed only a "temporary" role in contributing to relief.[50] The federal government was totally unprepared to bend its views in order to remedy the deteriorating economic situation on the prairies. In the absence of a constructive federal agricultural policy, the federal government's solution to the economic plight of the nation was the protective tariff, a measure which offered no solution to the problems of the agrarian-based economy of the prairie provinces.[51]

Other assisted land settlement schemes were worked out in 1932 and 1934 as part of federal relief policy. Under these Acts the Dominion contributed one-third and the province, together with the originating municipality of the settler, the other two-thirds of a sum not to exceed $600. Although advances were limited in 1932 to $300, due to the province's inability to contribute, this was rectified by 1934. About a thousand families received assistance under the back-to-the-land schemes and one of a similar nature in 1937.[52] However, the rate of abandonment under these schemes was high.

In August 1931 the provincial government took steps to set up a centralized and comprehensive Saskatchewan Relief Commission. This commission facilitated the northward migration by providing for the transportation of farm equipment and livestock. In response to what appeared to be a productive federal back-to-the-land scheme, the provincial government in April 1932 announced the creation of a provincial scheme. A board to administer it was subsequently established on May 12, 1932. This move was accompanied by the passing of the Saskatchewan Relief Act, a measure which gave the Commission absolute jurisdiction over people on relief. Both measures were also designed to cut costs.[53] However, the overall impact of this provincial back-to-the-land scheme was negligible due to its sudden termination a scant two months after its inauguration.

Financial restrictions tended to limit the size of the movements under provincial back-to-the-land schemes. The earliest schemes had allowed urban unemployed on to the land, but later provincial schemes were altered in such a manner as to limit their value to the urban centres. While in Saskatoon, Premier Anderson told the city that whereas "the provincial government was prepared to assist the unemployed to establish on land if they had farms selected, it was not the intention of the Co-operative Government to enter upon any large farm settlement scheme...."[54] This statement represented at least a partial change in government policy towards northern settlement.

The extent of government participation in the northward migration was in fact relatively small. Although figures vary, perhaps ten thousand families were involved in the northward movement.[55] In 1931–32 the Saskatchewan Relief Commission shipped 1,852 carloads of settlers' effects, in 1934, 662 carloads and in 1935 one thousand carloads.[56] Under the Relief Settlement Plans of 1932 and 1934 the three levels of government had participated in moving 920 settlers as of 30 April 1937. Of these a number moved to better land in the south or to the park belt, although the majority migrated north.[57] The great majority of farmers appear to have moved on their own, not participating in any of the maze of assisted settlement and loan schemes.

Beginning in the autumn of 1932, and due to stricter government control there was an actual decrease in homestead entries in each month until the spring of 1934. This resulted from the government's attempts to stem the tide of settlers moving on to sub-marginal land. Only those with sufficient equipment and finances were allowed to register a homestead entry. However, with pressure mounting for more land, a change in policy was urgently required. All unalienated provincial lands suitable for settlement had previously been classified and sold in 160-acre lots at prices ranging from one to three dollars per acre, depending on geographical location and land quality. This classification system was abandoned in April 1934 when only third-grade Crown lands remained unalienated. Under this system only 4 percent of the first 7,000 entries had occurred on lands classified as valuable settlement lands. Upon abandonment of the land-classification system, all provincial lands were sold for settlement purposes if so requested. Applicants had to swear that they had personally inspected the land and that in their opinion at least 50 percent of it was arable. Under this policy, settlers were given four years to break fifteen acres whereas previous requirements had stipulated that twenty acres be broken in three years.[58]

Government assistance in the early 1930s was plagued by a serious duplication of agencies, reflecting a confusion of policies which lacked both the cohesiveness and the power to dictate the pattern of settlement in the forest fringe. The majority of the various schemes emphasized merely the placement of settlers, paying little attention to the needs arising after their establishment in a new environment. Government efforts were also limited by the fact that many of them were halfhearted ventures meant to be nothing more than stopgap measures. It was not until after it became apparent that the Depression would not be an overnight phenomenon that the province began to develop a more cohesive set of policies through which to deal with the problems of settlement in the north. This development, however, had to await the return to power of the Liberals in 1934.

In June 1935, a Liberal amendment to the Provincial Lands Act restored the policy of free homesteads. All surveyed lands classified as suitable for homestead entry were made available to the first eligible applicant upon payment of a fee of ten dollars. Most squatting became legal under this Act, and a land patent could be applied for after three years if all requirements were met. The majority of outstanding loans against settlers were also cancelled. The pressure for land was revealed when 10,700 inquiries were made in the first year. However, although this Act gave the settler a firm legal right to his land, it still offered him none of the assistance which was needed if self-sufficiency was to be attained.

THE NORTHERN SETTLERS RE-ESTABLISHMENT BRANCH

A new era in the development and utilization of the forest fringe was initiated in September 1935, when the Northern Settlers Re-establishment Branch of the Department of Municipal Affairs was established.[59] This Branch was responsible for supervising settlement and the distribution of capital and relief assistance. It immediately began an economic survey of all settlers who had moved into the forest fringe in the 1930s and who were dependent on relief. It was found that about 7,800 settlers, some of whom had been in the area prior to the 1930s, were in need of some form of assistance; that 90 percent of these settlers had formerly farmed in the south, the balance coming from urban centres; and that many of them lacked both stock and equipment. Thus one of the major tasks of the Re-establishment Branch in its early years was to promulgate self-sufficiency amongst the settlers which, in many cases, required their re-establishment on suitable land.

Upon assuming responsibility for northern settlement, the Board found itself serving a population which was scattered through a belt across the entire east-west extent of the province, with an average width of about 100 miles. Providing services to such a population was very costly. Thus consolidation of population became part of the Branch's policy:

> [The Branch]...depends upon land being secured in blocks of
> a size that will at least accommodate the minimum number
> of settlers necessary to support the education, medical and
> transportation facilities essential to the well-being and progress
> of a community.[60]

This was a difficult task, for pockets of good land were surrounded by much poor land. Nevertheless, six blocks of land involving nearly 100,000 acres were taken over from the Department of Natural Resources and prepared for settlement by Re-establishment authorities.

The strong intent of the government to rectify the inequities of the forest fringe became exceedingly clear through the powers which were granted under the Land Utilization Act to the Northern Settlers Re-establishment Branch. The Land Utilization Act had given broad powers under which the Branch could declare any specified part of the province to be under the jurisdiction of the Act. Any lands within any declared area which were found to be unsuitable for agriculture could be converted to public lands. Data were subsequently collected on lands within each municipality, and the municipalities in their turn were required to sever assistance in the form of supplies to occupants of inferior lands.[61]

By 1936 the Branch was active in seventy-two Local Improvement Districts and Rural Municipalities. In 1937 the Branch commenced its own breaking of land, whereby 40,000 acres were cleared by 1939; in 1938 responsibility for the construction of market roads was assumed from the Department of Highways.[62] Rapid clearing and breaking of land and the construction of suitable roads were at last recognized as crucial. Thus the scope of the Branch expanded until it was participating in all aspects of northern settlement. It now possessed both the intent and the ability to manipulate and restructure the pattern of settlement in the forest fringe, much of which dated only from the early 1930s. It had taken half a decade to progress from the makeshift federal and provincial loan and settlement schemes, which failed to adequately recognize the nature of the forest-fringe environment, to an administrative body which could begin to rectify matters in an orderly and convincing fashion.

CONCLUSION

Settlement in the northern forest fringe of the prairie was, in the main, a gradual process. Yet the area was also host to two abnormally large movements of settlers in the twentieth century. The first movement, of soldier settlers, while not without its problems, was relatively successful. The second migration, in the "Dirty Thirties," occurred under an entirely different set of conditions. Depression and drought drove a substantial number of people northwards, many of whom were thankful merely to escape the drought. Their numbers exceeded the availability of Crown land and the ability of the government and the environment to meet and absorb their needs.

The relative success of the federal government in establishing the machinery necessary to administer the first movement is indicated by the fact that the Soldier Settlement Board was able to turn its attention to a range of diverse activities as early as 1923. In contrast, the almost uncontrollable influx of settlers to the Saskatchewan forest fringe in the early 1930s took place in the absence of cohesive governmental policy. This resulted in considerable deprivation in the forest fringe during the Depression. Both the authorities and the general population shared a false optimism about this region; the great difference between the forest fringe and the prairies was only slowly appreciated by the government. This is exemplified in the initial programs of providing direct relief to the northern settlers rather than practical aid in clearing land for farming. Only with the formation of the Northern Settlers Re-establishment Branch in 1935 did things begin to improve. Somewhat ironically, it was the Second World War which finally dissipated the excessive population of the forest fringe by prompting the return to buoyant economic conditions elsewhere.

NOTES

This article first appeared in *Prairie Forum* 6, no. 1 (1981): 35–56.

1   B. C. Vanderhill, "Settlement in the Forest Lands of Manitoba, Saskatchewan and Alberta: A Geographic Analysis" (M.A. thesis, University of Michigan, 1956), 95.

2   Government of Canada, *Report of the Soldier Settlement Board of March 31, 1921* (Ottawa, F. A. Acland, 1921), 24.

3   Ibid., 10.

4   Denis Patrick Fitzgerald, "Pioneer Settlement in Northern Saskatchewan," Vol. 1 (Ph.D. thesis, University of Minnesota, 1965), 180. Contained in Archives of Saskatchewan, Regina, N.R. 4.1.

5   "Indian Reserves To Be Given Soldiers," *The Morning Leader*, Regina, 30 November 1918, 22.

6   E. C. Morgan, "Soldier Settlement in the Prairie Provinces," *Saskatchewan History*, Vol. 21 (1968): 41–55.

7   Government of Canada, *op. cit.*, 88.

8   Ibid., 94.

9   Herbert R. Harris, *Porcupine Soldier Settlement and Adjacent Areas* (Shand Agricultural Society, 1967), 7.

10 "Advises Soldiers To Take Up Land In The Porcupine," *The Morning Leader*, Regina, 17 July 1919, 12.

11 Harris, *op. cit.*, 9.

12 Ibid., 63.

13 Morgan, *op. cit.*, 44.

14 Fitzgerald, *op. cit.*, 180.

15 Government of Canada, *op. cit.*, 152.

16 Government of Canada, *Third Report of the Soldier Settlement Board of Canada, December 31, 1924* (Ottawa, F. A. Acland, 1925), 9.

17 Morgan, *op. cit.*, 45.

18 Government of Canada, *Third Report...,op. cit.*, 9.

19 Government of Canada. *Sixth Report of the Soldier Settlement Board of Canada, December 31, 1927,* (Ottawa, F. A. Acland, 1928), 5.

20 Fitzgerald, *op. cit.*, 215.

21 Ibid., 237–47.

22 Government of Canada, *Seventh Report of the Soldier Settlement Board of Canada, December 31, 1928* (Ottawa, F. A. Acland, 1929), 12.

23 Vanderhill, *op. cit.*, 119. Quoted from letter by R. W. Gyles, Director of Lands, Manitoba Dept. of Mines and Natural Resources, Winnipeg, 27 May 1950.

24 G. E. Britnell, *The Wheat Economy* (University of Toronto Press, 1939), 203. Quoted from *The Report of the Saskatchewan Royal Commission on Immigration and Settlement,* 1930, 15.

25 Fitzgerald, *op. cit.*, 297.

26 Ibid., 304.

27 Britnell, *op. cit.*, 51. Quoted from *Annual Report of the Secretary of Statistics, 1934*, Dept. of Agriculture, Saskatchewan, 94.

28 George Joseph Hoffman, *The Saskatchewan Provincial Election of 1934: Its Political, Economic and Social Background*, 5. Quoted from *The Leader Post*, Regina, 2 June 1931, 14.

29 Vanderhill, *op. cit.*, 126.

30 Fitzgerald, *op. cit.*, 305.

31 Ibid., 309.

32 Vanderhill, *op. cit.*, 122.

33 Ibid., 126.

34 Jonathan F. Wagner, "Heim Ins Reich—The Story of Loon River's Nazis," *Saskatchewan History* 29 (1976), 48.

35 Vanderhill, *op. cit.*, 130.

36 Fitzgerald, *op. cit.*, 354.

37 Britnell, *op. cit.*, 210.

38 Vanderhill, *op. cit.*, 130.

39 *Britnell. op. cit.*, 213.

40 Ibid., 210.

41 Hoffman, *op. cit.*, 39–40. Quoted from an interview with L. R. Blakely conducted by E. C. Morgan, 2 February 1970.

42 T. J. D. Powell, "Northern Settlement, 1929–1935," *Saskatchewan History* 30 (1977), 95.

43 Information sources for this paragraph include Britnell, *op. cit.*, 209–11, and Fitzgerald, *op. cit.*, 346.

44 Fitzgerald, *op. cit.*, 336.

45 Max Wolfe Rubin, "The Response of the Bennett Government to the Depression in Saskatchewan, 1930–1935: A Study in Dominion-Provincial Relations" (M.A. thesis, University of Regina, 1975), 74.

46 Fitzgerald, *op. cit.*, 306. The Saskatchewan government had already formulated a plan to assist the movement of livestock from drought-stricken areas and to help farmers move to northern Saskatchewan. See P. A. Russell, "The Co-operative Government's Response to the Depression," *Saskatchewan History* 24 (1971), 86–87.

47 Hoffman, *op. cit.*, 37–38. Quoted from *Regina Leader Post*, 17 July 1931, 12.

48 Rubin, *op. cit.*, 48. Quoted from *Regina Leader Post*, 14 November 1933, 13.

49 Powell. *op. cit.*, 90–91.

50 Russell, *op. cit.*, 82. The federal Unemployment Relief Act of 1930 and the succeeding series of Unemployment and Farm Relief Acts were renewable annually with no guarantee of continuity.

51 Rubin, *op. cit.*, 27.

52 Britnell, *op. cit.*, 207.

53 Rubin, *op. cit.*, 135 and 149–50.

54 Ibid., 79. Quoted from *Regina Leader Post*, 4 April 1932, 2.

55 The number of people who migrated to northern Saskatchewan and just when they did so have been matters of intense debate. The lack of records for the myriad of government schemes coupled with the number of people who simply packed up and left on their own leaves no positive way of precisely determining just how many people

actually migrated to northern Saskatchewan. Britnell, through the use of statistics from the provincial Department of Natural Resources, estimates that 35,937 people entered the north. From these same statistics he concludes that the years of greatest migration were 1931 and 1932 (see G. E. Britnell, *The Wheat Economy*, 203). In contrast to this, D. P. Fitzgerald refers to the summers of 1933–34 as those forming the apex of the migration which he says has been described as the "great exodus." He further feels that the greatest advance took place in the years 1933–35. However, he states that at least 45,000 people moved into northern Saskatchewan from 1930 to 1936 (see Fitzgerald, *op. cit.*, 314). James Gray (*Men Against the Desert*, Western Producer Prairie Books, Modern Press, Saskatoon, 190) says that 10,000 families migrated, whereas Vanderhill (*op. cit.*, 121) estimates that 4600 families migrated north from the prairie farms, two-thirds of which came from Alberta, the majority of whom settled in Saskatchewan. George Hoffman (*op. cit.*) feels the number of migrants was in excess of 35,000. He further reports that in the 1934 Throne Speech it was announced that 4,000 settlers with their families had moved north since 1930, increasing the northern population by 20,000. John Charnetski, in his M.A. thesis, "A Study of Settlers' Progress in Northern Saskatchewan for the Period 1935–39" (University of Saskatchewan, 1940), like James Gray at a later date, estimated that about 8,000 families were involved in the migration. Estimates from articles contained in the *Regina Leader Post* on 17 July 1931, and 8 March and 2 April 1932, vary too widely from more properly conducted research to be given much credibility. This also holds true for a number of articles contained in the publication *Maclean's* during the first half of the 1930s.

56 Britnell, *op. cit.*, 206.
57 Powell, *op. cit.*, 93.
58 Information sources for this paragraph include Fitzgerald, *op. cit.*, 321, and Britnell, *op. cit.*, 205.
59 Britnell, *op. cit.*, 212.
60 Fitzgerald, *op. cit.*, 338. Quoted from *Annual Report of the* [Saskatchewan] *Department of Natural Resources, 1940–41* (Regina, 1941), 7.
61 Powell, *op. cit.*, 96.
62 Charnetski, *op. cit.*, 8.

9. Homesteading in Northern Alberta during the
    Great Depression: A Life History Approach

Clinton N. Westman

INTRODUCTION

My grandmother, Mrs. Alberta Elizabeth (Hughson) Knox, was born during World War I and remembers life on the prairie before tractors and combines. Her family, the Hughsons, homesteaded the northern prairies near Veteran in the pre-World War I period. They then moved to the Peace River country, via a circuitous route, at the advent of the Great Depression. She lived in the Debolt District (a bush region 80 km east of Grande Prairie, across the Smoky River valley) for most of the next seventy-five years. In an oral narrative about her life, which I taped in November 2003, the journey to Debolt advances the Hughson family through time and space, but also functions symbolically as an interstice between the mythological "Roaring Twenties" and "Dirty Thirties." Her narrative provides insights on family life and economic relations, the migration process, subsistence in the Depression, urban working class life during World War II, and the resource economy in northern Alberta. Settlement of the Peace River region marked the close of the agricultural frontier in North America; settlers' life stories are a valuable record of this singular period. Representation and analysis of Grandma's story forms the bulk of the present paper. I also use inter-textual analysis with other oral and written texts from family and community members.

HOMESTEADING

I once had the opportunity to discuss inter-war farm life with Alberta's sister, my great aunt, Ruth (Hughson Moore Thorpe) Patterson, while looking at family photos taken in the 1920s and 1930s. Aunt Ruth told me then: "It was homesteading! You young people have no idea what it was like." I was stung by this but saw that she was right. My experiences with farm and wage labour had been relatively easy compared to those of my parents and grandparents. This encouraged me to study my family's history more closely. As Aunt Ruth said then, the story of our family is the story of homesteading. "Homestead-ing" refers to taking up and improving free land from the government. "Filing on land" carried certain conditions of occupancy, construction and overall "improvement" (all quotes are from Knox, 2003). Old-timer Charlie Moore (Ruth's former brother-in-law) referred to homesteading as his $10 bet with the Alberta Government (Moore, 1978: 116).[1] As old-timers use it, the word "homesteading" connotes challenge and adventure, being an original settler and "proving up" country, community and self.

Today in northern Alberta, prospective farmers can still file on land, although for the most part what remains is undesirable bush country. However, the luster is off agriculture in the popular mythology. It was not always so. The rapid expansion or Euro-Canadian agricultural settlement in the Peace River Country (beginning prior to World War 1, culminating in the late 1920s and

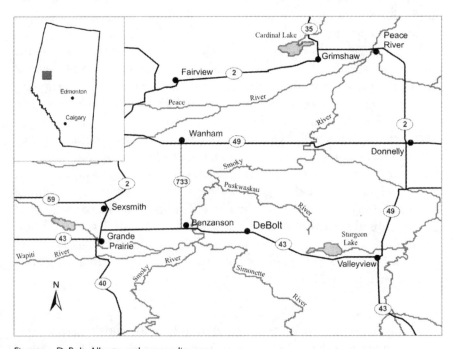

Figure 9.1. DeBolt, Alberta, and surrounding area.

continuing into the 1930s) represents the last, best example of a great western pioneering rush into a relatively cohesive "new territory."

The Peace River settlement rush represents both a response to, and a continuation of, problems evident in the agricultural settlement of the prairies generally. Climate conditions in the dry Palliser Triangle had already given a few hints of the drought to come in the 1930s. In spite of advances in genetics, technology and technique, farming on the southern prairies was "a bitter experience" for most (Easterbrook and Aitken, 1988: 479). Paul Voisey's exemplary book, *Vulcan: The Making of a Prairie Community* (1988), provides abundant information about the west as a whole, through focusing closely on change in one community. Voisey remarks on the extreme mobility of farm families between 1896 and 1929. During this period, western wheat was the central pillar of Canada's growth and prosperity (Easterbrook and Aitken, 1988: 476). Canada had a strong interest in settling the west: to provide markets for Central Canadian goods, to overwhelm the Indian population, to provide through wheat a trade surplus supporting subsidized industry and to siphon off excess labour(ers).[2] Settlement of the north and west was an official manifestation of a racist ideology, which explicitly envisioned the British Empire as a White Empire, with a duty to settle the west to counter Asian expansion (Wetherell and Kmet, 2000: 252) and assimilate Aboriginals.[3]

Settlement and marketing were both premised on the railway; in spite of this, costs or shipping and problems or access were major concerns for farmers (Easterbrook and Aitken, 1988: 491). Technology transfer problems were an even greater detriment to early settlers than transportation problems. Key technology and materials existed, but were not widely available in farming regions: this resulted in an artificially prolonged period (including the interwar era) or subsistence-style farming on the prairies—a condition that was exacerbated and prolonged in northern regions.

Often, prairie land originally selected proved unsuitable for farming. Government promotions and the promise of free land kept people moving, particularly in times of prosperity such as the pre-World War I years and mid-1920s. While many settlers arrived from eastern Canada and Europe, many people also moved extensively within the west to speculate or find superior land, often moving as a family to get land for their adult sons. People often moved in times of good crops and prices, such as during the late 1920s: this provides context for the Peace River land rush. This myth of the frontier served the influence of the state and capital in eastern North America, in the sense that it promised a land of milk and honey, while offering land which in many cases was ill-suited for agriculture. As good land on the prairies filled up and problems in areas such as the Palliser Triangle became more apparent, Canada looked north for more arable land.

Prior to 1930, the federal government[4] aggressively recruited settlers to the Peace region and invested in agricultural research, which ultimately belied the propaganda of a northern farming Eden. Many settlers came north during the period of record crops on the prairies, the late 1920s; more fled north to escape prairie drought in the 1930s. The calamitous experience of settlement on the southern prairies was repeated in the north, as infrastructure development was not able to meet growing demand. Desperate for clear arable land in a country with little of it, many settlers took land far from the railheads that were vital to transporting grain (a bulky, relatively low-value staple). Distance, shipping costs and isolation, as well as poor conditions and undercapitalization, made farming difficult (Wetherell and Kmet, 2000: 239–41). In spite of its dependence on rail shipping technology and its relatively recent history, life during this period for many homesteaders was remarkably anachronistic. Indeed, farm life for many in interwar and postwar northern Alberta recalled the lives of their nineteenth century pioneering predecessors more than those of contemporaries in other regions of North America. Also, settlers were poignantly aware of their relative deprivation, due to the first-hand experience which many had had with life in urban centres or established farming communities.

Moving the farm (Courtesy of the Provincial Archives of Saskatchewan / R-A4287).

This settlement rush marks the last manifestation of the agricultural frontier myth in North America, as described by U.S. historian Frederick Jackson Turner. Turner saw the frontier as a romantic, democratic entity. A competing myth, Harold Innis' "staples" theory, may have more utility than the frontier myth when considering the marginal and dependent nature of the subject region. Real control of the economy lies outside of the hinterland, and diversification of staples production is not necessarily an effective solution to this structural problem.

The Peace River Country became well known for agricultural potential in the early years of the twentieth century; by 1942, farming communities in the more arable parts of the Peace were well established. On the other hand, the relatively remote Debolt District was initially settled by Euro-Canadians[5] prior to 1918, but remained a fringe periphery of bush farmers until at least 1950. 1928 was a boom year for settlement in the Peace Country, which continued to grow in population through the 1930s. Between 1926 and 1931, the Peace Country's population increased from 2,800 to almost 7,000. In 1928, 4,400 new homesteads were filed in Peace River's and Grande Prairie's Dominion land offices, comprising 34 percent of all western Canadian homesteads filed that year. Settlement in this period was a function of the "boosterism" of government and corporate promotion, including "phrases such as 'Inland Empire' and 'The World's Bread Basket...the Last...Best West'" (Wetherell and Kmet, 2000: 243).

The reality of farming in the isolated Debolt Region did not meet this promise. To a large extent this is due to geographic remoteness: the Smoky River (a major northern river rising at Mt. Robson, the height of the Rockies) was not bridged until the 1940s; the community also lacked rail access until this period. Poor soil and climate were also factors. This lack of access, together with climate and geography, rendered farming in the district a marginal activity at best. Nonetheless, the settlers came. In 1942, Acton and Spence conducted a survey for the Department of Agriculture of "fringe districts" in the Peace Country, including Debolt (published 1947, quoted in Wetherell and Kmet, 2000: 269). This study found that, years to decades after original settlement, these "subsistence farmers" remained undercapitalized, having less money, less cleared workable land and poorer equipment than other "commercial farmers" in the Peace, for whom they often worked.[6] Subsistence farmers were more likely to rely on livestock than grain, and on oats rather than wheat. As a result, they had lower income and cash flow than commercial farmers in established districts around Grande Prairie and Peace River.[7] Horses and manual labour were critical to early settlers in this region, even as tractors and combines became more common elsewhere. Subsistence farmers were unlikely to have the means to harvest, and mainly had threshing work done by custom crews. People brought in income through a wide array of pursuits. This household economy is referred to as "makeshift" (Wetherell and Kmet, 2000: 269); all this is consistent with Grandma's narrative and the life experiences of other settlers:

> These subsistence farms demonstrated great variety, and it was evident that there was a greater range of pioneer experience and tactics employed to make ends meet than in the more established districts. (Wetherell and Kmet, 2000: 269)

Anyone who saw the men and women of the district at work got a glimpse of this "pioneer experience and tactics," as I myself can attest: many could work hard into their seventies and eighties, using skills they acquired as pioneers.

Today Debolt is well past the pioneer period, but still has a population of just several dozen. The hamlet supports a gas station, hotel/bar, convenience store, curling rink, library, two churches, seniors' housing and a cafe (no school), serving a rural hinterland of a few hundred. The region is a beautiful mix of woodlands, fields, creek valleys and hills. The core farming area around the hamlet is intermittently disturbed by bush, swamp and ravines, and is surrounded by wilderness on three sides. Game and bears thrive in the region. The town *qua* farm community is in decline, in spite of the overall prosperity of the Grande Prairie area and of Alberta as a whole. This is emblematic of natural resources having displaced agriculture as the economic mainstay of life in rural Alberta. Indeed, Debolt (which is located near a large forested Indian Reserve, against which it defined itself as a White farming community) is being repopulated by Cree seeking cheap housing close to the reserve. Overall, the area has been in decline in some respects since the 1950s, despite periods of prosperity. As Wetherell and Kmet state (2000: 239):

> As the place where most homesteaders settled in northern Alberta after 1920, the Peace River country was shaped by the economic expansion or the late 1920s, the collapse of the 1930s and dislocations of World War II. Settlers were first drawn by optimism, then by failure, and then as part of the post-war reconstruction or the Canadian economy.

This article is a close examination of one family and community during this timeframe.

TOWARDS A LIFE STORY

Those who remember first-hand the homesteading era in this fringe community are passing from us, but some remain. Their life stories represent important historical documents, the collection and analysis of which is urgent. They provide not only information about daily life in northern Alberta specifically, but also, perhaps, a template for understanding life as lived by settlers and colonists to remote regions generally. In line with this, I also draw from a suite of written texts to supplement Grandma's narrative, and to enhance our understanding of it. Local people's writings are from the community history book, *Across the Smoky* (Moore and Moore), published in 1978 by the Debolt and District Pioneer Museum Society. While using other secondary resources for context, I concentrate on developing an understanding of these primary sources. These popular oral and written texts recast history as the lived experience of farmers and workers.

There is a tension between oral and written texts provided by different family and community members, which I shall address where appropriate. In general, the twenty-five-year-old written selections lack the vibrancy and force of Grandma's oral performance. Also, both sources leave out key details by accident or design. In spite of these obstacles, my selection of texts brings different perspectives to light; overall, the stories complement one another and build a unified understanding of settler life in a newly colonized region. I believe this ensemble of texts is representative of homestead life in a fringe district of the east Peace. This reflects a flexible understanding of the life story, as discussed by Charlotte Linde (1993). Linde views stories as the primary means by which people understand both history and their own identity. Propriety, pride or propaganda may change the nature or theme of a person's "life story" while the narrator is hardly aware of it.[8] Linde's approach recognizes and accommodates the different approaches to framing a life story, which may cause different individuals to tell different "true" stories about events. This also applies to the same individual telling the same story differently in a different temporal or spatial setting, in a different medium or to a different audience. As a beloved grandchild, I am well placed to receive and understand the stories my grandmother chooses to share with me. In this respect, I have both an insider's (rural-born family member with farming knowledge and experience) and an outsider's (twenty-first-century urban academic) perspective on the story and its meaning.

EARLY YEARS AND CONTEXT

Alberta Elizabeth Hughson was born on July 3, 1918, near Veteran, Alberta. Her father was James Austin Hughson, of Cornhill, New Brunswick. He had come to Alberta in 1910,[9] and a few years later homesteaded near his sister, Ella (Clarence) Dafoe's family at Veteran. In 1914, James married Emily Orilla Hazelton; Emily had come from Minnesota, to be with her sister Cora's family, while having her son Roy,[10] whom James later adopted. The three other Hughson children were Ruth, Alberta and Owen. They homesteaded south of Veteran at Hemaruka on the dry prairie. Through the 1920s, their modest home grew into a good farm. Grandma spoke fondly of these years on "the prairie," where the wind through the fields sculpted huge snowbanks, upon which they would sled. Later, she would compare the depression dust dunes to these banks.

Grandma talked about a major childhood memory: going by train to visit her grandmother, Elizabeth Hazelton, in Minnesota in 1925 and seeing big cities like Winnipeg on the way. Periodically, problems with roads or medical emergencies highlighted the relative isolation of the northern plains[11]; nevertheless, the family was in touch with a broader world through a road system, telephone, rail and telegraph. They had some up-to-date access to medical care, including public health programming and drugs shipped by rail. In spite of the available technology, farming implements were in short supply. Alberta Knox saw her first tractor and her first combine harvester in 1928 (though use of these implements was not common until much later, particularly at Debolt). It is difficult now to imagine the labour of farming without these key implements.

Before the advent of the combine and tractor, there was a lot of work for hired help on farms, especially at harvest. This was one factor which helped homesteaders such as Jim Hughson get set up, as men who were still breaking or clearing their own land could work for more advanced farmers to earn cash or goods. A parallel labour market existed for frontier women and girls, who worked as domestics for established households. Moreover, farm families lived closer together than they do today, given that intensive manual labour necessitated smaller farms; this created a high level of community interdependence among new settlers and an overall farm-focused (as opposed to town-focused) community life. These traits are less evident today in rural Alberta, but still exist to some extent.

THE PEACE RIVER LAND RUSH

Since Alberta was settled largely after Turner had pronounced the supposed closure of the American frontier, many Americans settled in Alberta. This anti-nationalist tendency of people to keep moving as long as an agricultural frontier was open anywhere in the west led thousands to flood into the Peace

River Country during the 1920s, from across the west and elsewhere. This was the last great land settlement rush in North America. Settlement around Grande Prairie proper and Peace River proper had begun prior to World War I and was beyond the pioneering stage by the time of the Hughsons' arrival. However, homesteading continued in fringe districts of the Peace in the interwar period.

The forested country at Debolt was not consistent with government development literature about Peace River, which emphasized heat units, good soil and open land, associated with the core Grande Prairie area. Debolt was too remote to participate prominently even in regional agro-capitalism because of its distance from Grande Prairie. This localized collapse of the market economy during the 1930s and earlier led to a subsistence lifestyle for settlers. Still, the myth of the frontier was strong enough to draw settlers—mostly destitute ones; later, the Depression left them nothing to return home to. As we shall see, Grandma's life story demonstrates these points.

For many, the rush to the Peace River Country was caused by the drought of 1929. This was due to the marginally better soil and climate conditions prevailing in the Peace *at that time*, and also to the region's bounty for hunters, fishers and trappers. But actually, the Hughsons left the prairie in 1928, before drought and depression. Why? What drove someone to leave an established farm, friends and family? Grandma said:

> But, dad was always talkin' about the Peace River Country. The government were sending out literature and advertising a lot of these homesteads in the Peace River Country. He didn't seem to be quite satisfied with the farm he had or…although it seemed to me like we always had a good living. So in October 1928, he had his farm sale and we sold everything. He had a fairly good crop that year. And towards the end of October, we loaded everything into this Ford car, the four kids in the backseat covered up with a robe.

As her sister Ruth wrote of life in southern Alberta (Thorpe, 1978: 150):

> Things prospered and communities were formed, until the drought came in the early 20s. The Peace River Country was receiving lots of publicity. Dad wanted "greener pastures." Many people were leaving southern Alberta, 1928 saw our family on the way to Grande Prairie. Some household effects were shipped

by rail, but Mother, Dad and four "boisterous kids" were on their way in a 1927 Ford touring car.

It is interesting to note that these two narratives provide corroborative account of most details. This is in spite of having been collected from different sources (both of whom were young girls at the time of the experience), in different media, decades after the fact, and twenty-five years apart. This gives us a sense of the power of oral/popular history. In particular, both women mention the role played by government promotions in selling the Peace. Existing conditions around Vulcan made this an easier sell: James and Emily homesteaded relatively late in southern Alberta terms, and this may account for their settling in an arid region[12]; so, we might see their move north as a move from one marginal area to another which, while more remote, seemed to offer better opportunity.

The Great Depression of the 1930s was not a unique phenomenon. Depression in 1913–15, followed by further depression and drought in the early 1920s, had caused many to consider relocating away from southern Alberta as soon as they became able. Boom years in the mid-1920s and a record crop in 1928 brought about the prosperity required for James, Emily and family to buy a car and journey north. This was to be the last year of both Canada's wheat economy (Easterbrook and Aitken: 490–91) and of life as they had known it.

In Grandma's story, the journey chapter is long and functions as a bridge between dualities: prosperous/poor, bounty/depression, car/horse, agrocapitalism/subsistence agriculture, 1920s/1930s, metropolitanism/isolation. The journey itself is a liminal space between the opposites; broadly defined, it was over three years long. Leaving Veteran after harvest in late October, they stayed with "neighbours" (a term which may not imply geographic proximity) and family en route, also passing through Edmonton. Grandma remembers looking out the car's isinglass windows at the country, towns and city; the roads were poor but "at least there was no snow," as she once told me pragmatically. Nevertheless, they arrived at Athabasca too late for the ferry to the Peace River region; they faced the choice of shipping the car by rail or staying. Because of the cost of shipping the car, they sent for their household effects and lived in town that winter. Roy and Jim worked in a logging camp, but Jim was called back to Athabasca when Emily became "ill." After a time, Emily recovered; the family rented a small farm near Athabasca that spring and got some horses and cows. They sold milk in town, and Roy and Jim worked at a sawmill that summer.[13]

Following her recovery, Emily was homesick and determined to return to the Veteran district, where she had spent most of her adulthood. She and her daughters went south to bitter disappointment:

> That summer then, this is 1929, Mother was so upset, home-sick, she wanted to go back to the prairie…We were going to stay with Uncle Clarence. Roy and Dad were going to stay at Athabasca and take off the crop. Roy was working at the mill yet…and then *they* were coming. When we got back to the prairie in '29, there wasn't a *thing* growing…the *wind* blew and the *sand dunes* were just like snowbanks…there was *nothing*…There was *nothing* growing…I don't know how the cattle and horses survived. But anyway, we only stayed for three weeks when Mother took the train and took us back to Athabasca.

This sobering vision of the blighted prairie strengthened the Hughson Family's resolve to "come *on*" north.[14] They returned to Athabasca, where they had already given up the rented farm and had to live in another place for the winter of 1929:

> And then, Dad decided. All winter he was thinking about it, that we would come *on* to Peace River. So we sold our household possessions…and, in April, we left Athabasca and drove on our way to Grande Prairie.

This tortured decision—forced by the reality of drought in the south, shows the half-heartedness with which many settlers viewed their journey.

Grandma spoke of terrible roads on this circuitous two-week journey, which they began in April so as to drive on frost. They drove along the south shore of Lesser Slave Lake, with no proper road there. They camped in places, stayed at Immigration Halls in Peace River and Grande Prairie, and relied on the generosity of "neighbours": such as in one instance where they stayed in an abandoned home while waiting at Dunvegan for the Peace River to clear of ice. While Jim and Emily made this house ready, the kids waited in warmth and comfort at the neighbours' new house.[15] Again, Aunt Ruth supports the story of this two-week journey in many details.

Arriving in Grande Prairie in spring 1930, James and Emily demonstrated further their ability to form strong relationships with other pioneers. Through acquaintance with local farmers, merchants and real estate salesmen, brothers

Charlie and Norman Moon, they found a place to live, occasional work, and a source of material and information about real estate opportunities. Working with the Moons and another man, Bill Nicholson, James saw the country and acquired cattle, chickens, a chicken house, a stove, a team and sleigh.[16] The government had promoted the Peace River Country throughout the 1920s, and indeed there was land left to be settled. However, the classic dark-soil open land around Grande Prairie, which had attracted original settlers, had been settled prior to World War I. What remained in the Peace by 1930 was fringe land, small clearings and poplar groves away from established settlements. This "fringe" land had grey, wooded soils, requiring more labour to break and clear, which would produce poorer crops than the dark soil around Grande Prairie and the fertile central prairies (Wetherell and Kmet, 2000: 268).

In marginal regions, site conditions and microclimate are everything: James and Emily found themselves faced with a critical choice as to where to homestead in the new country. James in particular traveled extensively around the Grande Prairie area. As Aunt Ruth wrote of this period (Thorpe, 1978: 150), "Dad was always on the alert for a homestead to build a new home." The iconic importance of creating "home," in a building and a community, would be the focus of the next several years.

BUILDING FARM AND COMMUNITY

With Bill Nicholson and the Moons, James Hughson traveled around the country looking for land. He rejected poor land south of the Wapiti River that was suggested by an agent and finally homesteaded near Debolt (SE-23-71-1-W6) in 1930, where their friends the Moons and Bill Nicholson also took land. The family remained at Bezanson, on the Grande Prairie side of the river, until early 1932; there they lived in a nice house owned by Norman Moon. During this period, Roy, James and Emily continued to work for the Moons sporadically, and prepared their new homestead. But it was only in 1932, more than three years after first leaving Veteran, that the family finally moved to the homestead; this underlines the slowness of the journey and its preparations:

> So the next year or so Dad took these cattle from Bill Nicholson,
> on shares and we pastured them in Pete Moon's pasture. Sss,
> and uh, then he's got to move them if he's going over to the
> homestead...So, they started in February or before that. And,
> Bill Nicholson had a homestead over at Debolt by this time
> and he was over there. And him, and Jimmy Airth, and Dad,

Dad using some horses from Moons, went out and back and they hauled feed over there to where we were going to move into a house that Norman Moon had on his second homestead over there at Debolt, so that he got the feed piled up. And… they put up a barn, and that was with a lot of help; there was the Fehr family lived just across the creek from us. Put up a log barn, with all the neighbours' help. And they made many trips with the feed to get the feed over there, straw and that. So in March, Dad and Roy took the cattle. We had a team and sleigh by that time, too…had some horses…I don't know whether he bought them from Moons or…And anyway we had four horses. And, they took the cattle across there. I don't remember how long it took them. I wish I knew more about that. Anyway, Mother and the rest of us stayed with Mr. and Mrs. Ferris for a day or two and then we took the team and sleigh and went over there. There was no ferry, still frozen; this was March…So, you still went on the snow. And, they moved over a building too, from where we were living there, at Bezanson, because it was a chicken house, and we took chickens…Yep, building on sleighs, ahem…

It is most interesting to note that Aunt Ruth's written text (Thorpe, 1978: 151) supports not only the details of this narrative, but also uses similar phrasing in many cases: "cattle and horses on shares," "log barn," etc. In one case, the sisters even use a similar sentence: Aunt Ruth writes, "By now the depression of the '30s was well established"; compare Grandma's later remark, "By this time, the depression was really set in." Whether this is based on Grandma's prior knowledge of Aunt Ruth's text, or some deeper structural affinity is unknown.

The family built their own home (a small frame house) in 1933, and later changed homesteads to sw-22-71-l-w6,[17] land which would remain in the family for more than fifty years. In fringe areas such as the Debolt district, farming technology and transportation infrastructure were even more limited than in the west as a whole. As Grandma said, "Got over there and, well, *there we were.* There was no school, and…*there wasn't much!*"

As Grandma and my mother have told me, Emily may have come to resent James for bringing her and her daughters to a frontier region full of bachelors, hard work and basic conditions. Things were brightened by the presence of neighbours. Others coming into the country during this period later touched our family. These other families included the Knox brothers (five, including my Grandfather Pete, Alberta's future husband), the Moore brothers (including Tom, who was briefly married to Aunt Ruth and whom I knew as an uncle, and Charlie, one of my chief informants through his writing), and Charlie Coulter (later, Grandma's companion for over forty years). Knowing these original settlers and hearing their stories has always helped give me a sense of perspective about my own life and its labours; more, it gave me a respect for the toughness, ingenuity and pride of rural people.

SUBSISTENCE FARMING/FORAGING IN THE 1930S

During the Depression, families in this semi-isolated fringe district lived in a subsistence-oriented farming/foraging mode of production. Grandma's sister-in-law, Aunt Florence, has written (Knox, 1978: 108):

> Five Knox brothers came to Debolt from Manitoba. Frank, Lester (Slim), Gifford, Hugh and Norman (Pete). Frank [Florence's husband] was the only one married. I came from Senlac, Saskatchewan. The men homesteaded and moved here in 1929. I came in January of 1930 with a two-month old daughter...
>
> Times were hard in the '30s, but I realized how lucky we were when I made a trip home to the prairies in 1935. The men were all good hunters, so moose meat was a daily diet, and after we got land broke we had good gardens, and almost every year I crawled for miles picking berries...
>
> Most things we grew or made or traded for, but money was so scarce.

Aunt Ruth wrote (Thorpe, 1978: 151):

> The drought of southern Alberta and Saskatchewan was bringing in many families, and we were a young family always ready for adventure. Roads were only trails...
>
> By now the depression of the 1930s was well established. There was no market for produce. So perhaps the depression had more to do with the struggle to get ahead than the method of homesteading. Land clearing was slow as it was done with an axe by hand. But gardens grew well and there was an abundance of wild fruit. So the summers were spent picking and canning.

Uncle Gifford Knox (my grandfather's brother) wrote (1978: 108):

> During the next few years [after 1929], we did considerable log work, building houses for Nowrys, Diemerts, Pete Doerksen, church and manse (which is now the museum) and several others…Money was very hard to come by, so we got three pigs from Pete Doerksen for our log work.

Many men marked the measure of their time in the country by the log homes and buildings they had laboured on, both for personal profit and community advancement. In many cases across the north, roads and public works also were constructed by volunteer labour (Wetherell and Kmet, 2000: 193).

Grandma also remarked on the work, ingenuity and cooperation of these years:

> Anyway…we seemed to survive it…There was people around that, well, everybody hunted…And there was neighbours give us moose meat right away. Ha ha. My dad never hunted, never …Well he had a few pigs too. We had pigs and chickens and these cows…All to no avail… By this time…the depression was really set in…This is spring of '32, summer of '32…We had these cattle. We milked the cows and they didn't have a creamery at Grande Prairie. You couldn't ship the cream and, mother made lovely butter, but, so did other people and there was nobody buying butter at the store. You couldn't sell things and by the time you brought an animal from Debolt, that had to be shipped by rail to *Edmonton* then to be sold…you generally got a bill for shipping it. Didn't have enough land to be growing any grain…and that summer dad broke seven acres… it was an open area…but you know with horses that was an awful job. The harness was always breakin and you'd just go two feet ahead and a foot back. Ha ha. Broke that seven acres and got it worked down and…next spring, that'd be '33…The next spring, he seeded it to oats. He just seeded it by hand. Beautiful crop. Grew up about *six feet high,* and froze right down in August. Wasn't even good feed…And he had to borrow a mower, and he cut hay wherever he could find a slough to cut hay in, to put up for the cattle in the winter. And still we had all these cattle and there's no market for them, well nuthing.

There's no market for pigs either. Well if you *butchered* them, and brought them in [to Grande Prairie] and peddled them, which he did, some. But, you see, you had to get here, you had to...It was a two day trip, practically; well, if you left early in the morning you'd get here at night. He stayed at Reverend Waterman's a time or two and brought in meat and sold it. And things didn't begin to pick up very much until...well, seems to me that by 1935, it seems to they were beginning to be able to sell...Well there was no money, hahahaha, there was just *no money*...The *men* would come away, all the way here across the river to work in the harvest fields, or you come in the spring time and you worked for different farmers. There was well to do farmers out around Grande Prairie area. They had the land cleared...And in the fall of the year, they'd walk over here. Uhh...*Dad* (Knox) [my grandfather, Pete Knox], and *his* brothers generally went back to Saskatchewan and harvested. They did that for quite a few falls.

The above texts demonstrate the importance of livestock, subsistence plots, wild food resources and itinerant labour to the homesteading economy in the east Peace. Also, we see the centrality of animal care and feeding to homesteading, and the complementary roles of men and women. This reflects several characteristics of "fringe" districts, relative to the more established agricultural regions within the Peace.[18] This "makeshift" (Acton and Spence, 1947, cited in Wetherell and Kmet, 2000: 269) economy also included limited wage labour on projects such as road and dam building as well as forestry.

Throughout this period, the Hughson and Knox families demonstrated a very diverse household economic strategy. Grandma worked for neighbours as a teenager, and was paid in oats! We also see the continued hard work of Roy to support the family throughout their homesteading period. The labour of young people was a key factor in supporting the family as a whole: the whole family pulled together, as did, in many respects, the whole community. The community improved throughout the late 1930s, as stores, schools, a United Church,[19] and amenities such as halls, a cheese factory and a curling rink were constructed. In spite of disparities and hardship, the developing community saw itself as part of a broader world: for instance, Grandma's dream as a teenager was to play basketball for the famous Edmonton Grads.

Looking at history allows us to see our families' choices in broader context, with finance, depression and war having deeply personal impacts in a context of extreme mobility. Even in these personal decisions, we can see our family members responding to the tug of history and economics. For example, when asked about her marriage to Pete Knox, Grandma began by mentioning the price of wheat! She said the Knox brothers' years in the country were starting to pay off, as they had more land cleared and a spare house. Pete got a good crop just as the price came up, and on top of this had spent the winter trapping and the spring using a team to rebuild a bridge that had flooded out. Grandpa demonstrated his diverse talents that year! After seven years in the Peace Country, he had finally a little money.

In 1936, Grandma and Dorothy Debolt were cooking for a threshing crew at the Knox boys' "shack." Later, she and "quiet" Pete went to a Halloween dance on a snowy night and got married three weeks later. Grandma and Grandpa moved into the Knox boys' "old house," a log cabin which they had built when they came to the country, with a nice cabinet that the boys had had made. Gradually the couple moved to a new log house and homestead; there they had the use of a hired steam engine for breaking land, as more capital and technology became available in the household and district during the mid/ late-1930s. There Marion and Margaret were born. While Marion was born in a hospital, my mother, Margaret, was born (in 1939) at home with the help of a neighbour, by light of a coal oil lamp which malfunctioned. The Doctor had told Grandma to go home from the hospital, that she wasn't ready yet...[20]

WAR, WORK AND OIL

My detailed transcription of Grandma's interview concludes in 1935–36, although the actual recorded interview is somewhat wider ranging. Following this period, the family changed and grew. Emily moved to begin 'housekeeping,' ultimately marrying Mr. Brown; she would have limited contact with the family for the next years, although James remained a central figure. Ruth and Alberta both married, to Tom Moore and Pete Knox respectively. Then the war came and Owen, Roy and Tom Moore all left the Peace Country for good.[21] During the war, the lure of high wages took Pete, Alberta and other Knox's to the west coast, where Gary, Arlene and William (who died as a baby)[22] were born. They lived in Duncan, New Westminster and Victoria from 1941 to 1944; Grandpa worked at a distillery, a cement plant and later at a shipyard for $1/hour. That was big money, Grandma said. These jobs ultimately contributed to Grandpa's deafness.

They had a nice house in Victoria, where the Knox brothers would gather on days off from labouring. But all this time, Grandma was homesick and the men kept saying, "There's nothing here, we've got to get back to the land."

Foreseeing this, Pete had kept his farm and his good team together to return to farming. When he was offered $1,000 for their farm in 1944, he chose not to sell; so they did return to Debolt and continued to farm. (Ila and Heather were born during this period.) The decision to return shows the lure of the land in the Peace River country, which many characters in these stories had a hard time beating, in spite of the hard lessons of experience. This also may be due to the relatively poor wages and treatment of workers on the coast, which grandma commented on. But also, they both were homesick and loved the north, so they returned north to farm. The relative isolation of the area made it difficult to adequately address Marion's polio, which developed in the 1940s: this necessitated her leaving the community for hospitalization for long stretches. Marion and Margaret later went to high school at a boarding school in Grande Prairie, since there was no high school near Debolt until the 1960s.

Grandma said the arrival of the oil patch in northern Alberta in 1950 changed things a lot: oilfield work led to a source or capital for farms as people became farmer/workers and then, often, just workers. Grandpa was able to begin working heavy equipment, building roads, etc. Grandma herself worked as a cook on oil rigs in Alberta, and offshore NWT and Nova Scotia. During the late 1950s Grandma and Grandpa separated; he moved to BC to work in the resource sector.[23] Nevertheless, Grandma and Ruth stayed in the Peace Country for the long term with their subsequent partners, Charlie Coulter and Garfield Thorpe (Ruth would also later marry Art Patterson).

In spite of challenges, our family succeeded in the new community. Grandma says her father, James Hughson, in particular was "well thought of wherever he went." My Aunt Dorothy told me that James had made a name for himself as a "quiet leader" in the new community. My mother, Margaret, said that he was a very nice man, well respected and soft-spoken. He ran for the CCF, and was involved in cooperatives, the United Farmers' movement, the local school board and the hospital board. Although he was raised a religious Baptist (for instance he and Emily did not play cards), he was not a churchgoer in his old age. In his story I can see examples of leadership and drive. He passed away in 1965, aged seventy-five years.[24] As Charlie Moore wrote (Moore 1978: 116):

> Our area was blessed in having men like Jim Hughson and others with his ability to uplift the ego of most of those he met…the principles [these original settlers] introduced into our community linger on.

In looking for meaning in the remarks of Grandma and others here, we see the emphasis on homesteading, family, neighbours, improvement, progress and community. These ethics are emblematic of Alberta's pioneering spirit.[25] As Grandma's long-time partner, the late Charlie Coulter, wrote of the changes in his community (1978: 140):

> I still reside in Debolt. I am happy to say that our community has grown from pioneer days to a thriving agricultural district with many modern up-to-date farms.

Aunt Florence Knox wrote (1978: 108):

> I think people were better neighbours. We needed each other. If one woman heard how to can or dry in a different way, she told us all about it.

This underlines the cooperative nature of rural community life in the pre-1950 period, at least as this period is understood in the reminiscences of original settlers. Unfortunately, many settlers found farming in a sub-arctic region to be a bitter experience. This fringe region was not naturally suited to agriculture, however well it was suited to absorbing surplus population in a time of poverty and militancy. As Carl T. Peterson wrote (1978: 22) of his father, Walter, an early homesteader in the Debolt District:

> There is a lot more I could write since I have been in Debolt, but my story has already gotten too long. One more remark and with that I will close: my father never found the spot in the Peace River Country that was flowing with milk and honey. He was a hard-working man but never got the breaks to put him on his feet.

The legend of the Peace, promoted by state and speculator, had made fools of many dreamers.

Surveying the depopulated rural countryside around Debolt (and, indeed, elsewhere in Alberta), one senses that the senior Peterson's experience was widespread and manifold. Many settlers left the north as soon as possible; others slowly drifted away from farming, or moved to big cities over the generations. Ongoing difficulties with agricultural markets and weather underscore the marginality of farming in the Peace region. Depression or no depression, the Peace River land rush was, in many respects, a great fraud on settlers and their descendants; this is particularly true of those in fringe districts. That many made a life of it and built progressive communities through solidarity and hard work is a testament to the strength of their spirit.

CONCLUSIONS

Since her separation from Pete in the 1950s,[26] Alberta Knox has been very active in her family, community and churches. She was a cook, chicken farmer and bingo player, who lived in a "shack" (with outhouse) by the highway until the mid-1970s. At this time, she built a beautiful house in Debolt and developed several lots there, which she sold as real estate. She also was a leader on seniors' housing in Debolt. She has traveled to Arizona, California, Mexico and New Brunswick, as well as other locales. She enjoyed many years with Charlie Coulter, and fellowship with family and people in the community, including her sister, Ruth, who resided close by her for years. The loss of Charlie and Ruth, in recent years, has been difficult for her. Grandma has lived in Grande Prairie since 2003, but still considers Debolt home. In looking back at her life to date, Grandma stressed her thankfulness for "the Lord's blessings," chiefly her children who "mean everything" to her.

While I respect her framework for understanding her life, my own approach to understanding her life story is necessarily somewhat different. Certainly it is not my intent here to dismiss or deconstruct grandma's experience or insights. And yet, I look back at this period with a sense of awe and despair. As a leftist looking back at a period of material hardship and social dissent, in which the consensus of the postwar welfare state was forged, I see both a triumph of common people working collectively to survive, but also a lost opportunity for radical change.

I share Grandma's joy in our family, but in seeking to understand the broader history in their stories, I focus tentatively on material conditions. In line with this, economic, political/military and climatic factors drove many of the major decisions taken by characters in this story. Yet they were also able to struggle as agents, envisioning better life circumstances for themselves and their loved ones, then working towards goals. As I have noted, in the case of many characters in this story, love of the north, the bush and the frontier were major symbolic reference points, which became important to their identity.

Just as Grandma's recorded narrative omits some sensitive or tragic material, she also does not address explicitly racial, gender and class differences. Grandma is interested in politics. As a progressive prairie populist, influenced by the social gospel movement, she has supported since the 1930s populist movements in the guise of a range of political party labels. Grandma chooses whom to vote for each election, based on a mix of conservatism and communitarianism, which often has led to her supporting social democratic parties as well as more conservative ones. While she does not self-consciously employ a left-wing perspective to support her narrative, she nonetheless spoke of the radicalized politics of the 1930s with sympathy for the common person caught up in a crisis of capitalism. Aunt Ruth writes (Thorpe 197: 151) that both technology and fanning know-how were available, but that capital was lacking and therefore commercial forming could not succeed. Grandma reiterated this view, saying

Grandma Knox.

that people believed corporations and the government caused the Depression to keep farmers and workers poor; this view underlines the radical nature of politics in this period. Similarly, Charlie Coulter remembered hearing about mass riots of the unemployed, and the electric climate generated by the "On-to-Ottawa" Trek by unemployed men from the prairies.

Grandma emphasized the importance of cooperation in community life. Her father, her husband and others developed this theme into an overtly leftist political stance during this period, while grandma poured her energy into building relationships and community institutions. Nevertheless, one senses in her narrative the power of the deradicalizing trends in Alberta politics, active since the 1930s: the Social Credit and Conservative governments and the increased prosperity caused by the development of the oil patch. Note that these trends did not fully address the problems of rural poverty, inequality or dependence in northern Alberta.

Likewise, Grandma's narrative underlines the solidarity between female relatives, and the many ways in which women and girls contributed to family survival. She notes that Ruth could farm and work as well as any man. Indeed, Ruth and Alberta both endured the loss, absence and infirmity of partners, and the challenges of farming for a woman. She and other narrators also draw attention to the medical issues (such as childbirth, disease and mental health) facing women in frontier communities (cf. Peterson, 1978: 22). The life of Alberta's mother demonstrates the bitterness with which many women viewed the frontier. However, Grandma would most likely not describe herself as a feminist. Clearly, in the end, class and gender politics are not her dominant concerns. Rather, family, religion and community are the main values.

In this respect, the absence of Aboriginal peoples in Grandma's narrative is striking. This is also true of Moore and Moore's (1978) contributors, and of countless other small-town history projects, which either omit or caricature Aboriginals. These gaps are surprising in the case of Debolt, however, because many Aboriginals continue to live in both the Debolt and Grande Prairie regions. Indeed, a large reserve is located within a few kilometres of Debolt. Aboriginals are not absent from her family's experience; indeed our extended family includes Aboriginal people. Nevertheless, they are largely absent from local history, as exemplified by life story narratives and popular history projects such as museums and community history books. This underscores some of the limitations of popular and oral history.

Ironically, as Michael Asch (1990) points out, it is not at all clear that agriculture will, could or should inevitably and permanently succeed foraging modes of production in northern Alberta: indeed, for many early settlers, homesteading took the form of a reversion to the foraging mode of production. During this period, Whites and Natives worked together on agricultural and public works projects. It is hardly necessary to point out that this did not result in a broad-based alliance between Natives and poor Whites in Alberta; neither did the strong labour movement and Farmer/Progressive political stance of the province's population in the 1920s and early 1930s result in a radical restructuring of economic relations; nor did the strength of the province's early women's movement manifest itself as a major force in post-Depression Alberta. These facts of history cannot be taken as inevitable; things could have been otherwise. For those who remember this period, narrative and life story become tools in aid of understanding these contradictions. Many settlers experienced this period as a seemingly relentless series of hardships and tragedies; their narratives both reflect and obscure these material hardships, as well as the class, gender and racial divides at their root.

NOTES

This article first appeared in *Prairie Forum* 32, no. 1 (2007): 167–190. The author thanked Alberta Knox, Margaret Westman, Arlene Logan, Heather Sagan, Andie Palmer, Michelle Daveluy and an anonymous reviewer for their comments on earlier drafts of this paper.

1   Charlie's bet was a success. After years of poverty and isolation, he became a successful seed-farmer and community leader. His son, Marvin, became a provincial cabinet minister and close advisor to Premier Ralph Klein. Marv had a campground named for him in Grande Cache to commemorate his services as MLA. As it happened, it was Marvin who eulogized my Aunt Ruth (who was also his aunt).

2   During the 1930s depression, both the federal and provincial governments, as a matter of official policy, viewed Peace River settlement as a means to reduce dependence on relief and to redistribute internally both the rural and urban poor. In other cases, government and corporate promotions low-balled the advised amounts or savings and equipment required to survive while bringing land into productivity (Wetherell and Kmet, 2000: 24–29).

3   In this respect, the settlement of Peace River is nothing more than the last gasp of the National Policy, which was actually a colonial policy to the extent that it constructed Western Canada as a dependant colony of Central Canada.

4   Alberta did not take control of natural resources (or settlement policy) until 1930. Its 1930s policy generally mimicked that of the federal government (Wetherell and Kmet, 2000: 241), reflecting the Peace River country's status as a dependent hinterland of Edmonton.

5   The area was mainly settled by British and Americans (as well as Northern Europeans including many German Mennonites), many of whom had previously farmed elsewhere in the Prairie Provinces or the U.S. (cf. Wetherell and Kmet, 2000: 239).

6   Note that the entire Peace Region was undercapitalized and horse-dependent during the 1930s, relative to the southern prairies (Wetherell and Kmet, 2000: 271). This underscores the anachronistic nature of farming in the Debolt district especially.

7   See Grandma's remark: "the *men* would come away all the way here across the river to work in the harvest fields. Or you come in the spring time and ya worked for different farmers. There was well-to-do farmers out around Grande Prairie area."

8   This is particularly the case when writing, for official posterity, the 'family story,' as in community history books such as Moore and Moore.

9   James may have come west before 1910 on harvest excursions, and gotten a taste for the prairie.

10   Grandma did not mention this detail in her narrative.

11   This included the death of her beloved Aunt Ella Dafoe from an ectopic pregnancy (in spite of the men having "carried the car" over bad roads to the hospital) and the subsequent dispersion of the Dafoe family, which Grandma discussed with obvious emotion more than seventy-five years later.

12   As Voisey points out, after 1910 only the most northerly and arid lands remained to homestead in the prairie provinces.

13   Work in sawmills and forestry tided many destitute migrants en route to the Peace. As Elmer Nystrom, of Debolt, told Mrs. Knox (Nystrom and Knox, 1978: 159): "I was farming fifty miles east of Saskatoon when drought hit the area. I drove a car to the Peace River country, my brother Gus and a cousin were with me. I worked that winter in the bush in Burnt Hills, for Evans Lumber Co." Such migrations were common in the Depression. Each of my four grandparents' families experienced major migrations during this period, from farm region to farm region, within the prairie provinces.

14   It is interesting that Aunt Ruth did not mention this return to the prairies in her written text. Nevertheless, this jarring return to the dustbowl was a common theme in local life stories. As Aunt Florence Knox wrote, "Times were hard in the '30s, but I realized how lucky we were when I made a trip home to the prairies in 1935." Oral historian Barry Broadfoot (1985: 37–38) quotes others who remember well this "hot sucking wind," harder on women than men, "…blowing hard. Blowing the goddamned country right out from under our feet and there was nothing we could do about it…"

15   Many others wrote later of the way generous strangers had helped them come into the country. Some others were not so lucky. As Debolt settler Belle Swann wrote of her family's 1930 journey from Champion: "One thing that plagued us every night at camping time was that no one wanted us to camp on their property. Each and everyone complained about weed seeds, even after we assured them that we had no grain or straw and that our beds were factory-made mattresses. Some even ordered us to 'Move on' until we passed entirely beyond their property. As a result, we often had to find government or railroad land to camp on."

16   At this point in the narrative, cars become less significant for transportation relative to horses, which Grandma mentions frequently.

17   I visited these homesteads, and the later homesteads where she lived with Grandpa Knox, with grandma and other family members on a recent Thanksgiving visit. Her animated narration during these visits (which I did not record) underscores the importance of site visits for oral history fieldwork. These trips were also intrinsically rewarding: the land retains its stark beauty, with open fields against forest, ravines, muskeg and moody sky.

18   Even Bezanson, several kilometres from Grande Prairie, but on the same side of the Smokey as that city, was well ahead of Debolt in terms of development: by 1919, Bezanson had stores, a restaurant, a blacksmith and a flour mill (Doerksen, 1978: 23); Debolt was just becoming established at this point.

19   Catholics received spiritual services from the missionaries at Sturgeon Lake Indian Reserve; Anglicans traveled to Goodwin. The transition of sectarian allegiance has been marked: today the United Church still functions, but the main church in town is the Gospel Light Chapel. This is reflected in Grandma's own spiritual journey from her Baptist upbringing, through decades in the United Church, to the more evangelical Gospel Light Chapel.

20   My mother, born in a log cabin, went on to nursing school, living and working in Edmonton, Calgary, Vancouver and Europe. We settled on a farm west of Bowden, Alberta, in the 1970s. She nursed while my father, Norman (originally from a farm near Kenaston, Saskatchewan), farmed and worked in the resource sector. My mother never returned to live in the north.

21   I knew all these men as great uncles. Tom Moore in particular, though no blood relation, lived near us in his old age and made a profound impression on me, a boy of five or six.

22   William was not mentioned in our tape-recorded interview.

23   Many log buildings constructed by Grandpa, his brothers and other early settlers stand today. My family continues to celebrate his works through photos, discussions and visits to these sites.

24 Grandma's mother, Emily (Grandma Brown), is also remembered well by members of the family today. She was musical, relatively highly-educated and a good public speaker, who spoke a little German! She later lived in southern Alberta and BC, as well as Sangudo, Mayerthorpe and Ridge Valley. She passed away in the mid-1980s, aged over eighty-five. My mother said she was an excellent grandmother, although they did not get to know each other much until adulthood. Ironically, Emily spent many decades in the north in spite of her early aversion to it.

25 As Charlie Moore wrote (1978: 120): "The future generations of this family may never again find space for homesteading anywhere in this world. So may we remember that we did not inherit this land from our parents but rather we have borrowed it from our children."

26 My grandfather, Pete, went on to reside in BC and Alberta, working as a heavy equipment operator. In his old age, he worked with my father and me on our farm. He passed away in 1994, aged eighty-five.

REFERENCES

Acton, B. K. and C. C. Spence. 1947. *A Study of Pioneer Farming in the Fringe Areas of the Peace River, Alberta, 1942*. Ottawa: Department of Agriculture.

Asch, Michael. 1990. "The Future of Hunting and Trapping and Economic Development in Alberta's North: Some Myths and Facts about Inevitability." In Patricia A. McCormack and R. Geoffrey Ironsides (eds.), *Proceedings of the Fort Chipewyan and Fort Vermillion Bicentennial Conference*, 25–29. Edmonton: Boreal Institute for Northern Studies.

Broadfoot, Barry (ed.). 1985 (1975). *Ten Lost Years 1929–1939: Memories of Canadians Who Survived the Depression*. Markham: Paperjacks.

Coulter, Charlie. 1978. "Coulter, Charles Robert (Charlie)." In Winnie Moore and Fran Moore (eds.), *Across the Smoky*, 140. Debolt, AB: Debolt and District Historical Society.

Doerksen, Peggy. 1978. "Dana-McLennan." In Winnie Moore and Fran Moore (eds.), *Across the Smoky*, 23–24. Debolt, AB: Debolt and District Historical Society.

Easterbrook, W. T. and Hugh G. J. Aitken. 1988 (1956). *Canadian Economic History*. Toronto: University of Toronto Press.

Knox, Alberta. Oral narrative recorded by author, November 2003.

Knox, Mrs. Frank. 1978. "Knox, Frank." In Winnie Moore and Fran Moore (eds.), *Across the Smoky*, 108. Debolt, AB: Debolt and District Historical Society.

Knox, Gifford. 1978. "Knox, Gifford." In Winnie Moore and Fran Moore (eds.), *Across the Smoky*, 108. Debolt, AB: Debolt and District Historical Society.

Linde, Charlotte. 1993. *Life Stories: The Creation of Coherence*. Oxford: Oxford University Press.

Moore, Charlie. 1978. "The Moore Family at Debolt." In Winnie Moore and Fran Moore (eds.), *Across the Smoky*, 115–120. Debolt, AB: Debolt and District Historical Society.

Nystrom, Elmer and Berta Knox. 1978. "Nystrom, Elmer." In Winnie Moore and Fran Moore (eds.), *Across the Smoky*, 159. Debolt, AB: Debolt and District Historical Society.

Peterson, Walter. 1978. "Peterson, Carl T." In Winnie Moore and Fran Moore (eds.), *Across the Smoky*, 19–22. Debolt, AB: Debolt and District Historical Society.

Thorpe, Ruth. 1978. "Hughson, James A." In Winnie Moore and Fran Moore (eds.), *Across the Smoky*, 150–51. Debolt, AB: Debolt and District Historical Society.

Voisey, Paul. 1988. *Vulcan: The Making of a Prairie Community*. Toronto: University of Toronto Press.

Wetherell, Donald G., and Irene R. A. Kmet. 2000. *Alberta's North: A History, 1890–1950*. Edmonton: University of Alberta Press.

PART III

Policy, Politics, and Lasting Perceptions

10.   The Red Cross and Relief in Alberta, 1920s–1930s

Nancy M. Sheehan

The Red Cross to most of us elicits thoughts of blood donor clinics and swimming lessons at the local level, of emergency shipments of medical supplies, resources and personnel on the occasion of a spectacular disaster somewhere in the world, and of support and care for sick and wounded soldiers and for prisoners during times of hostilities. The first Red Cross organization arose out of a meeting held in Geneva in 1864 at which "The Convention for the Amelioration of the Condition of the Wounded and Sick in Armies in the Field" was born. Canada, as a colony of Great Britain, was bound by its provisions. The symbol of a red cross on a white background was first worn by a Swiss physician on the battlefield in 1864 during the Prussian/Danish conflict.[1] The Canadian Red Cross was organized as an overseas branch of the British Red Cross in 1896 and incorporated as an autonomous national Red Cross society by an act of Parliament in 1909.[2]

By the end of World War 1 the Red Cross had gained world-wide recognition. Millions of prisoners of war had been visited by delegates of the International Committee of the Red Cross in 524 internment camps and, through Red Cross channels, had maintained communication with their families. Military hospitals had been built and equipped by Red Cross funds. Red Cross nurses, aides and relief teams had worked among the refugees, the sick and the destitute from Siberia to Palestine. In thirty countries, national Red Cross societies had spearheaded and coordinated the auxiliary war effort, raising funds, rolling bandages, knitting socks, recruiting nursing personnel, and transporting the sick and wounded.[3] The Canadian Red Cross was no exception, and in addition organized (particularly in Saskatchewan) classroom Junior Red Cross units to enable school children to do their share for the war effort.[4]

These accomplishments throughout the world and the belief that this had been "the war to end all wars" spearheaded a peacetime move to federate the Red Cross societies of the world into an "international league of Red Cross Societies which, in the humanitarian field, would parallel the League of Nations in the political field." With the support of the medical and allied health professions the League of Red Cross Societies was organized with the mandate to work for "the improvement of health, the prevention of disease and the mitigation of suffering throughout the world." An amendment to the Act of Incorporation of the Canadian Red Cross Society was passed in 1919, giving the Red Cross the additional mandate to carry on in times of peace.[5]

From the beginning the Canadian Red Cross has been governed by a central council composed of up to sixty voluntary members who elect the officers and the executive committee. Divisions are organized provincially, and include all the branches within each province. Revenue has been derived mostly from the proceeds of an annual national campaign for funds and has been controlled by the central council. This policy has enabled the society to provide a uniform standard of service across the country, regardless of variations in economic status. It has also allowed it to respond quickly to regional and world-wide disasters.[6]

With the end of World War I, the Red Cross faced the challenge of becoming an effective peacetime organization, and the generally appalling health care conditions existing in Canada at that time provided a worthy target. Approximately fifty thousand Canadians died annually from tuberculosis alone—equal to the four-year wartime total of servicemen killed—while influenza, pneumonia, heart disease and infant mortality raised the toll even higher. Rural areas lacked hospitals, doctors and nurses. City schools which had begun medical examinations for entrance reported that approximately 50 percent of the children had defects of one kind or another. No federal department of health existed in 1918, the allied health organizations were not coordinated and physicians generally worked alone and with individual patients.[7]

The Red Cross confronted the health care issue in several ways. First, it endorsed the classroom-based branches of the Junior Red Cross, which focused on health, citizenship and service. Second, the central council held two conferences in 1920 which were attended by representatives from the newly formed Dominion Department of Health, the Department of Soldiers' Civil Re-Establishment, provincial departments of health and national voluntary health agencies. The various representatives outlined their programmes and described how the Red Cross had already assisted or could assist them. There was no doubt about the number and variety of needs, each of which warranted priority. The Canadian Red Cross made it clear that it did not wish to undertake or compete with work already being carried out by government or other organizations but that it wanted to strengthen and assist such activity and to coordinate voluntary efforts.

As the national organization was establishing its guidelines and policies each of the provincial branches was already at work extending its war-related efforts to peacetime activities. In Alberta this meant activity on several fronts. In common with other Red Cross branches Alberta encouraged the organization of Junior Red Cross units in classrooms. The more traditional role of serving sick and wounded soldiers was continued by supporting the Department of Soldiers' Civil Re-Establishment. By October 1920 the Alberta division was operating two hospitals in outlying areas, had plans to increase the number of these units, and had given supplies and/or financial assistance to eight struggling municipal hospitals.[8] The society was therefore active in the improvement of health and prevention of disease, and in the care of sick and wounded soldiers. Its ability to mitigate suffering, also a part of the peacetime mandate, was soon to be put to the test in Alberta. Although the Red Cross was not designed to be a relief organization in the usual sense of the word, events in Alberta in the 1920s and 1930s tested its ability to coordinate efforts of volunteers and to work in close cooperation with government authorities.[9]

The pre-war period on the Prairies witnessed large-scale immigration, a land rush and expansion into marginal and dry areas. Escalating land prices, a prolonged drought, and a post-war depression created hardship for many westerners, but especially for new immigrants who had not had time to establish their roots and for those living and fanning on marginal land. The most extensive Dry Belt area and the one hardest hit by fluctuating crops and prices was that of southeastern Alberta. Many settlers in this region just gave up and moved on. Others either could not or stayed hoping that "next year" would be better. As crop failure occurred year after year, the problems of the people who remained became more acute. Schools and hospitals were closed because of dwindling clients and eroding resources. Financial institutions recalled loans and foreclosed mortgages. Adequate food, clothing and shelter became more difficult to procure. Taxes were left unpaid and municipalities were forced to curtail services. The Alberta division of the Red Cross became involved in relief work almost by default since there was little in the way of social services operating at the end of the war.[10]

The first years of the 1920s found the members of the Alberta division active on several fronts in support of drought-stricken residents. They participated in the government conference on unemployment and relief held in August 1921. This was followed by a government questionnaire sent to municipalities asking for information on the percentage of residents who would need help, the reasons for their destitution, the kind of support anticipated, suggestions as to who should provide this and the names of any groups or agencies in the area which were active in social service.[11] Besides this assistance to individuals and families by local branches, the provincial organization surveyed the Dry Belt to identify conditions and needs, made suggestions to government on relief policies and implementation, and acted as coordinator for all clothing relief.

Farmer standing in a windswept grain field (Courtesy of Archives of Manitoba / N18333).

SURVEY OF CONDITIONS

The *Report of Survey Made by the Alberta Red Cross of Conditions in Crop Failure Districts September 13th to 24th 1921* was presented to the government of Alberta on 1 October 1921.[12] The *Report* listed the centres visited, assessed the conditions in each area and concluded that the Retlaw-Lomond section was in very poor shape. The *Report* noted:

> Conditions very bad. Immediate help needed, especially cloth-
> ing. This is already being distributed by Red Cross. These
> conditions are the worst of any visited.
>
> The question of securing medical aid for the Retlaw district
> is urgent. The local drug store was burned three weeks ago, so
> that not even drugs are available. The train to Medicine Hat
> passes through the town only twice a week. There is no hospital
> closer than Medicine Hat or at Taber. The people cannot afford
> to call the doctors from Taber. The Municipality are doing
> their best to secure the services of a medical man. A bonus
> of $1200 a year has been proposed....Mr. Podal, Secretary of
> Municipality, also stated that he thought the doctor might oper-
> ate a drugstore if he wished to do so as there was no prospect
> of a local druggist re-opening.
>
> Mr. Allan. Manager of the Bank of Commerce and Chairman
> of the District Red Cross, stated that it would be impossible for
> any donor to collect fees in and around Retlaw district under
> present conditions....[13]

The *Report* also included a list of the schools visited and a chart detailing the percentage of school children suffering from malnutrition and physical defects and classifying those defects. It noted that the general appearance of the children was poor. "Many of them lacked vitality...had round shoulders and narrow chests. Most of the children were poorly clothed, footwear especially was bad." Cases of children with tuberculosis, infantile paralysis, crippling injuries, harelip, chorea, eye disease, and nose and throat problems, which required either hospital or special medical treatment, were also listed. Two examples indicate the difficulties:

> Beth Cutler, Gold Coin School District, age six. This child is
> deaf. Parents have been planning to send her to Winnipeg so
> that she may be taught to speak. Four years' crop failure have

reduced them to extreme poverty and they have been unable to send the child away. Father and mother brought her to be examined. A bright and pretty little girl. Father broke down completely when speaking of their inability to have her trained.

William Johnston, age 6. Enchant School—suspected T.B. Very weak and pale, pulse feeble, breathing rapid. Coughs incessantly. Parents cannot afford hospital treatment....[14]

PROVISIONS FOR RELIEF

Suggestions for relief identified three areas of concern and assumed that suggestions made at the unemployment and relief conference would be followed, specifically that the government would take responsibility for the distribution of food, feed and fuel through either the municipality or district committees.[15] Clothing, medical service and malnutrition in children were areas the Red Cross thought needed coordinated action and it proposed that distribution of clothing be made through its district branches acting in cooperation with local committees composed of Red Cross members and representatives from any local organizations such as the United Farmers of Alberta (UFA), United Farm Women of Alberta (UFWA), and women's institutes. Decentralizing relief in this way and registering relief cases were seen as the best methods to reach deserving cases and to avoid overlap.[16]

Proper medical attention for families, particularly women and children, was not easy to supply. Since there was no adequate hospital accommodation between Medicine Hat and Lethbridge on any of the three railway lines, and beds at the Taber and Foremost hospitals were insufficient, it did not seem feasible to have doctors and dentists visit central points. Besides, families could not afford the railway fare to enable them to travel to a central point. The Red Cross suggestion was a novel one. It wanted to secure the loan of two ambulance cars from the Department of Militia and Defence, and to request the Canadian Pacific Railway to attach these cars to freight trains travelling through the crop failure district and park them on sidings of the various towns. Equipped with supplies of linen and clothing donated by the Red Cross and with personnel arranged between the government and the society, a travelling clinic would serve the whole district.[17]

Malnutrition among children, the Red Cross reported, was the result "not so much of lack of food as to lack of variety also ignorance and in certain cases, indifference on the part of some of the parents." It was suggested that in town and village schools additional nourishment be provided by issuing cocoa, soup or milk to all children at the morning and afternoon recess. Children in rural schools, where a box lunch was the norm, should have soup, milk/cocoa or some similar form of nourishment provided to supplement the noon meal. Red Cross committees and Junior Red Cross units would organize such a scheme if the government agreed to pick up the cost.[18]

ORGANIZED CLOTHING RELIEF

Although the Red Cross in Alberta had been distributing relief in southern Alberta since 1918 it was only in the fall of 1921, after the unemployment and relief conference and the Red Cross survey of the dried out districts, that the relief efforts of the Red Cross became organized. Division headquarters in Calgary became responsible for "collecting, purchasing, fumigating, sorting and shipping of all clothing for relief purposes."[19] In a report on relief distribution for 15 September 1921 to 30 April 1922, statistics for southern Alberta were noted.

Large donations of secondhand clothing were made by the Kiwanis and Rotary Clubs of Calgary, the Grand Lodge of Alberta, and locals of the UFA, UFWA and women's institutes. New goods at reduced prices were purchased from wholesale and business houses in Calgary and Edmonton. Through the cooperation of the Manufacturers Association and business firms of eastern Canada and the railway companies, purchases made at minimum cost and secured through fast freight helped emergency orders. It was estimated that a one-third to two-thirds saving was effected on goods ordered this way through national Red Cross headquarters in Toronto. In cases of extreme emergency, branches had the authority to purchase locally.[20]

Financial support for these activities came from both the provincial government and the Red Cross. The province's contribution was based on the understanding that the Alberta division would reimburse the government if its campaign for funds was successful. In forwarding a receipt for $23,918.01 that the government had made available to the Alberta division "on the understanding that if at all possible the money will be refunded," Mrs. Waagen, vice-president and honourary secretary, warned the government that "our appeal is meeting with very little success." She concluded that there was general willingness to support Red Cross activities in relief work but a lack of money made this difficult for many residents.[21]

The Red Cross appeal at the national level was much more successful. Financial support was contributed by the national office and bales of secondhand clothing by the Ontario division.[22] In a statement to the Honourable R. G. Reid, Minister of Municipalities and Health, total relief distributions of $105,166.36 were noted by the Alberta Red Cross. Of these, $65,391.36 was charged to the government and $42,513.30 received as contributions for relief purposes. Not included in this overall amount were secondhand clothing distributions valued at $38,775.00.[23] Besides these expenditures in the area of direct relief the organization also found that rural hospitals needed support. Those at Foremost, Hanna, Consort and Altario had between four and twelve beds each and cared for hundreds of patients each year. The inability of patients to pay hospital fees and the difficulties municipalities had in attempting to support hospitals when tax revenues were greatly reduced caused some hospitals either to be closed or taken over by the Red Cross. In 1922 hospitals at Taber and Strathmore were closed; that at Empress was given a loan to enable it to continue while at Foremost the debt was taken over by the province and the hospital was operated by the Red Cross.[24] As the relief crisis became more acute and the Red Cross found its funds depleted, a decision was taken to withdraw support slowly from rural hospitals. It was hoped that this decision would spur the government to become involved in rural hospital policy.[25]

The government was slow to act. It was 1924 before a municipal hospital policy was adopted for the purpose of affording hospitalization to residents in the rural districts and country towns of Alberta. The services of the Red Cross in this respect were to be to outlying and pioneer districts, and in other areas as an emergency and temporary measure.[26] The difficulty in Alberta had been, of course, that the emergency caused by drought was not temporary and the Red Cross found itself without enough clothing, supplies or cash to fulfill emergency requests from individuals, municipal officials and hospitals.

Early in April 1922 the UFA government decided to stop clothing relief measures at the end of the month. The Red Cross, however, which had been designated early in the preceding autumn as the agency for clothing relief, continued to receive requests which became more difficult to meet without any provincial assistance. With the onset of colder weather in the autumn of 1922, following another summer of poor crops, the situation was again becoming acute. Several times the Alberta division pleaded with the government to make a decision regarding relief, suggested a scheme for relief on a limited scale, and requested a grant of $2,000 for the purchase of relief materials. "Limited scale" meant the purchase of flannelette, wool, stockings, moccasins and blankets for use in urgent situations, with the great majority of requests being filled with secondhand clothing. Although Junior Red Cross branches were busily knitting mitts, stockings and jerseys, and women's sewing circles and church groups were offering assistance, Mrs. Waagen argued that it was absolutely essential that government get involved.[27]

Finally, in January 1923, the government established a relief policy:

> All applications for clothing relief received by the Red Cross Society to be forwarded immediately to the Hon. R. G. Reid. Minister of Public Health.
>
> Each application will then be investigated by us and instructions sent to the Red Cross Society at Calgary, as to what articles or materials are to be forwarded to the applicant.
>
> All buying and distribution to be done by the Red Cross Society and grants will be made from time to time to cover costs of goods distributed by the Red Cross Society.[28]

This policy was a fairly radical shift from the previous year since the government rather than the Red Cross was now deciding who should receive what in the way of clothing relief. The Red Cross thus became a collection and distribution agency only. The well-established network of Red Cross centres across the drought area, working in cooperation with local organizations, lost the ability to provide input and decisions on relief became centralized in the hands of the provincial government. This brought clothing relief more in line with the administration of other forms of relief under the Drought Relief Act.[29]

The Red Cross acquiesced to this decision and in a letter to the premier Mrs. Waagen indicated that all applications for clothing would be forwarded and she offered to place at the disposal of the government all reports and information connected with relief. As in the previous year government relief was curtailed in the spring and the Red Cross again felt pressure to respond, particularly as winter approached. Having reviewed the manner in which the government policy had worked in the early months of 1923, delegates to the Red Cross convention in the autumn agreed that the policy "was detrimental to the government itself, to those receiving relief, and also to the Red Cross."[30] A special committee of the provincial council of the Red Cross made several recommendations to improve the investigation and distribution methods. In essence, Red Cross committees in each area would investigate all applications, and make a recommendation to the reeve of the municipality or to the provincial police in an unorganized territory. An official signature would be necessary before the Red Cross could issue relief. In areas where no Red Cross committees or representatives were present the provincial police would take on the investigative task. The decentralized methods of the Red Cross which had operated in 1921–22 were being advocated.[31]

At approximately this time the UFA government decided that clothing relief could be handled by voluntary agencies, and it terminated the arrangements which had been made with the Red Cross. For the rest of the 1920s the organization acted under the terms of its charter—improvement of health, prevention of disease and mitigation of suffering. Improved crop conditions in some years allowed the Red Cross to concentrate on the crippled children's hospital, hospital outposts, radio shows and other educational functions, particularly for women and children. Relief action tended to be responses to emergencies such as fires or floods. In 1926 a committee was formed to survey conditions throughout the province, meet the executives of the various organizations and strive to define policies whereby the province might best be served in food and clothing relief and in health needs. Red Cross officials were concerned that time, money and effort were wasted because of duplication.[32]

In some ways the disaster of the Dry Belt is an example of the reluctance of governments to get involved in what previously had been the responsibility of the private sector. This division between public and private responsibility was also evident in the decision to phase out Red Cross assistance in the mid-1920s, at a time when other relief was being consolidated through the Debt Adjustment Board. This experience proved useful to the Red Cross during the more widespread depression and crop failures of the 1930s. Working with government, organizing municipal committees, coordinating the work of other agencies, investigating applications, establishing price lists for clothing, arranging bulk and wholesale purchases, negotiating government loans and grants and justifying its administrative and other costs helped develop the expertise of the organization.

Although the Alberta division of the Red Cross was well established and accepted by the people in the province the depression and drought of the 1930s went far beyond the experience of a still fledgling peacetime organization. Not only were the effects more widespread in the province, necessitating more relief, but investments of the Red Cross, which were used for operating capital, had been caught in the collapse of the money markets.[33] The national state of emergency declared by Prime Minister R. B. Bennett, the greater difficulty in attracting support through the annual Red Cross drive, and a new Alberta premier all helped to make the role of the Alberta division more difficult during the 1930s.

ORGANIZATION OF CLOTHING RELIEF

As in the early 1920s, the Alberta division eventually became the designated agent for clothing relief in the province. Unlike the earlier arrangement, the government was now more directly involved from the outset, but the role of the Red Cross was not always clear and it certainly was not always smooth. By December 1930 conditions in Alberta were strained, the Depression was into its second year, and there had been widespread crop failures. On 30 December the premier wrote to D. M. Duggan, second vice-president of the Red Cross in Alberta:

> a very complete organization has been arranged to take care or any relief problems throughout the Province.... Having already completed these arrangements... it would not be desirable to have another organization working along similar lines, thus duplicating expensive organization as well as undoubtedly, in many cases, duplicating relief issued to individuals. It has, therefore, been very difficult for us to see how the Red Cross organization can be fitted into our plans without the danger of this duplication.[34]

However, from mid-December to mid-January the Red Cross received 97 applications for relief, including 91 adults and 349 children, and it seemed obvious that more needed to be done.[35] Throughout the early months of 1931 the Red Cross and the government negotiated the conditions and terms to be met and the grants to be made available. At a meeting on 11 February 1931, an eleven-point programme was recommended to enable the Red Cross to act as the clothing relief agency for the province. The scheme allowed municipalities and the provincial police in unorganized districts (in cooperation with officials of the Soldier Settlement Board and the Canadian Legion) to investigate applications for relief and to requisition the necessary clothing. This was supplied to the municipalities from the stock in the Red Cross store which had been purchased with a government grant.[36] Projecting requirements to 15 May, the Red Cross executive estimated $15,000 were necessary, and asked for an additional $5,000 to help carry on the traditional work of the Alberta division. As an indication of the scope of its work and to support its request, the executive noted that more than $750,000 in Red Cross funds had been spent in Alberta since 1919.[37]

Correspondence in March and April showed little progress: the circular covering arrangements had not been distributed throughout the province; a grant had not been forthcoming from the government to the Red Cross, so no money was available to supply clothing relief; and some criticism of the Red Cross from the Department of Militia and Defence, the Soldier Settlement Board, and the Royal Canadian Legion was beginning to surface.[38] Mrs. Waagen noted in a letter to the premier:

> The Red Cross is, after all, in a different position to that of other organizations in that its undertakings, in peace-time are not wholly optional but were guaranteed under the Peace Treaty by governments signatory to the covenant of the League of Nations, Canada no less than others.[39]

Conditions in the first half of 1931 and the delays experienced by the Red Cross in trying to work out an agreement were repeated in the autumn after the federal government became directly involved. Prime Minister R. B. Bennett, declaring a state of national emergency, launched a drive for clothing and funds for the work of the Red Cross, designated the Canadian Red Cross as the agency to receive and distribute clothing relief, and agreed to help provinces with the cost of relief.[40] Under this arrangement federal, provincial and municipal authorities would share the burden of relief equally, with one exception. In a telegram to Premier Brownlee of Alberta, the prime minister said: "We have agreed to provide for the entire cost of relief measures where three successive crop failures have created a condition which may be regarded as a national calamity."[41] By 1 October, the Alberta division of the Red Cross became the agent for the provincial government for the accumulation of a reserve store of clothing. Under the arrangements the Red Cross was to receive a $500-a-month administration fee, purchase clothing and shoes up to a sum of $20,000, furnish the government with a price list of all articles of clothing, and distribute clothing once applications from municipalities had been approved by the new relief division of the Department of Municipal Affairs, under the direction of A. A. Mackenzie.[42] An additional $10,000 was approved to handle requests from cities and a loan of $10,000 was authorized to allow the Red Cross as an organization, not as the government agent, to supply certain relief items not covered by government regulation. The $500-a-month administration fee was to be recovered by placing a 5 percent charge on all orders. One further condition was that these arrangements were to be considered confidential, a public announcement indicating only that "clothing is to be distributed as direct relief through the municipalities."[43]

ORGANIZATIONAL FRUSTRATIONS

From 1931 until 1936, except for several interruptions caused by the hoped-for return of good times and good crops, the Alberta division acted as the agent of the government in the purchasing, warehousing and distribution of clothing under direct relief. It also continued its other activities, which included distribution of clothing to people who did not qualify as destitute according to the terms of direct relief. For the Red Cross this was an immensely active but difficult period.

From the beginning some local merchants felt they were unable to compete with the prices obtained by the bulk and wholesale buying practices of the Red Cross. The organization bought factory-made goods from eastern manufacturers and transported them by rail at reduced prices. Local merchants and manufacturers, unable to match the terms supplied by these larger outlets, thought that much-needed sales and work were being lost to eastern Canada.[44] There were many complaints of delay, with the Red Cross accused of not responding quickly enough to requests for aid. In turn the Red Cross made constant pleas to the government to act: to decide about the administration fee through the summer months; to settle Red Cross accounts which were overdrawn and causing credit to be refused; to authorize lower prices for left-over winter clothing; and to indicate what decisions were being made for the next fall and winter. The Alberta division's arrangements with the government were usually for the winter months only, causing the organization some problems. The government, of course, was hoping each year for an end to the drought.[45]

The Red Cross argued that the government's criteria for receiving relief were too strict, that owning a few stock did not necessarily give a farmer cash. Slaughtering a head or two might supply meat but not clothing unless cattle could be sold. A residency requirement in a municipality, agreement by the municipality to pay one-third of the costs involved, and a complicated application form all aggravated the situation.[46] Mrs. Waagen wrote that many individuals and families were suffering because municipalities could not afford or refused to pay the one-third cost of relief. Although an agreement had been reached with the federal government about such municipalities, no list exempting certain areas from payment had been received.[47]

A. A. Mackenzie criticized the attitude of the Red Cross, and Mrs. Waagen in particular, on the matter of distribution. He believed that she did not realize that some rural areas were not going through the Red Cross for relief because local merchants were willing to match Red Cross prices.[48] Mrs. Waagen replied that Mackenzie thought that "all foreigners should not be allowed to live in the country" and was turning a blind eye to their desperate situation.[49] She maintained that her organization was receiving up to twenty applications a day from people who did not qualify under the Relief Act,[50] some of whom lived in unorganized districts up to fifty miles from the nearest police depot. Mrs. Waagen indicated that Mackenzie's solution was for such cases to "walk" to the depot to have their applications investigated.[51] The Alberta provincial police thought there was too much publicity regarding relief and were flooded with applications from people in non-organized districts. The investigation of these was both time-consuming and expensive and the police argued that "some people, not destitute, wanted something for nothing."[52] There was some feeling in official circles that the women involved with the Red Cross were too soft. Nonetheless, internationally the Red Cross was the official organization to be activated in times of disaster, and despite "soft" women volunteers it was not a women's organization and could not be easily disregarded or dismissed as unimportant.

Statistics supplied by the Red Cross from November 1931 to August 1932 indicate that clothing valued at $42,840 had been distributed under government regulations and a further $32,921 from Red Cross reserves. The numbers for southern Alberta, excluding Calgary, were approximately one-half those for an equivalent period in 1921–22.[53] As David Jones has argued, farm abandonments in the 1920s meant that fewer people were still living in the southeast portion of the province. In the 1930s, the difficulties were spread throughout the entire province, and the cities in particular bore the heavy brunt of unemployment. The applications from the southeastern, non-urban communities stressed the need for clothing to allow the children to attend school. Although adult clothing would be useful, letter after letter indicated that the real need was for coats and shoes for school-aged children. Teachers, Alberta provincial police detachments, women's auxiliaries of the United Church, school board officials, and local relief committees emphasized that children were being kept out of school because of inadequate clothing.[54]

Although letters from most recipients were full of gratitude,[55] there were complaints about poor quality clothing from the superintendent of the Gleichen Eventide Home for men and J. J. Mott, who represented ex-servicemen. The Red Cross policy to purchase better clothing so that it would last longer, and the confidential and "hidden" 5 percent surcharge to cover administrative costs caused the mayor of Calgary to complain that the Red Cross prices were higher than necessary.[56] A. A. Mackenzie also believed that Red Cross prices were too high and he felt that many of the clothing purchases were not necessary for relief; only useful clothing should be distributed. His definition of useful is not available, but his list did not include coats, jackets, pants, scarves or shoes—all of which were available from the Red Cross.[57]

By 1936 the Depression was easing across Canada, productivity was increasing, and unemployment had begun to decrease.[58] An order in council was approved on 10 August 1935 which was to have been the last payment to the Red Cross for its clothing relief work.[59] This turned out to be premature. Despite recovery elsewhere the Prairies still experienced agriculture failure. Continuous drought in some areas, and hail, grasshopper plagues, early frosts and so forth in others, meant that in 1936 conditions were worse than in 1933, the year considered nationally to be the depth of the Depression. Under the Agricultural Relief Advances Act of 1936 a municipality had to furnish seed grain, fodder, feed grain, fuel oil or lubricating oil to farmers needing assistance.[60] As well, the Social Credit government, like the UFA before it, found it necessary to continue to use the services of the Red Cross for clothing relief.[61]

This look at the role of the Alberta division in supplying clothing relief during the Dry Belt disaster of the early 1920s and the depression and drought of the 1930s is instructive in understanding the development of government policies in relief situations. It is also, and perhaps more so, indicative of a changing attitude toward relief—from one of charity and individual benevolence to the notion that relief should be financed by governments. It can be argued that the Red Cross, despite its voluntary nature, and its appeals for funds and support nationally and in each province, by its very existence pushed governments into coordinating and financing relief. The election of a government sympathetic to farmers in the midst of the Dry Belt disaster and the depth of the Depression also contributed to this change in attitude.

One mandate of the Red Cross in times of peace, accepted by national governments, was the mitigation of suffering. Generally this meant that the Red Cross was activated in disaster situations such as earthquakes, floods, volcanoes and fires where individuals and sometimes whole communities lost everything. At such times the Red Cross disaster emergency team went into full gear directing relief operations and coordinating government and private donations. Before August 1921 this team dealt with disasters such as the Leduc fire and the influenza epidemic. Although the Dry Belt area was disastrous, the Red Cross activity there was individual and local. The Liberal government under Premier Stewart first signed a relief agreement in 1920 which included provisions, fuel and fodder for animals as necessities.[62] The election of the UFA government and the unemployment and relief conference resulted in the emergency relief team of the Red Cross being called upon to coordinate the Dry Belt clothing relief effort. The Red Cross coordinated with other organizations, worked with local committees to assess applications, and operated with a loan from the government. As the drought continued and more applications were received, the government became more directly involved, supporting the Red Cross with grants rather than loans. The Red Cross, with its knowledge of local conditions and its mandate to relieve suffering, urged the government to take measures in the areas that the Red Cross was unable to cover. In doing so the government insisted on control and accountability to the dismay of the Red Cross leaders.

The notion that governments had a role was well established by the end of the Depression. The Brownlee government went further than its predecessor with an administration grant, a scheme of one-third contribution from each level of government, and no liens in return for relief. By this time, of course, R. B. Bennett, former president of the Alberta division of the Red Cross, was prime minister and made the federal government responsible for relief and directed the Canadian Red Cross to be the clothing relief agency for the country. Total government relief for municipalities with three successive years of crop failure was a part of Bennett's scheme.

Besides urging the government to accept responsibility for relief the Red Cross also acted as a watchdog in areas beyond its responsibility for clothing. For example, the prominence afforded the Red Cross and its widespread organization meant that it became aware of a variety of problems and drew them to the attention of the government. Because textbooks were not supplied free of charge to schoolchildren, some students, especially in the more senior grades, could not attend school. School inspectors suggested to parents that they should appeal to the Red Cross, which immediately pleaded with the government to supply free texts.[63] The idea of the hot school lunch was also presented to the government as a way of ensuring better health.[64] Complaints about the low nutritional value of foods on the food relief list were also made and the Red Cross appealed to Irene Parlby to bring this matter to the government's attention.[65] What appeared to be a huge markup for clothing sold to men in work camps on the Banff-Jasper highway was another example of a problem that needed attention.[66] It was also suggested that participation in the Vacant Lot Garden Club Movement should be compulsory rather than voluntary for those on relief.[67] A scheme was advanced to reduce the cost of relief in cities and to assist the drought districts by securing produce from districts in which it was so abundant that it would go to waste. A *quid pro quo* arrangement of needed clothing for the donation of produce was suggested.[68] In essence the Alberta division prodded the government to become involved in areas that previously were not within the accepted mandate of governments, nor did the Red Cross hesitate to condemn practices it felt were deficient.

In 1936 the federal government initiated relief measures for the fifty thousand families in the drought area of the three prairie provinces. The announcement and the resulting effort indicate the changes that had taken place since 1919 and the beginnings of the peacetime mandate of the Red Cross. Instead of prodding the government to get involved, the process in 1936 consisted of the government asking "the Red Cross Society to assist it in its task of providing the necessary relief... by undertaking the distribution of bedding and other household necessities." The end result was that the Society was able to provide 290,361 articles of bedding, clothing and household materials to some 250,000 individuals in the drought area of the west at a cost of only a little more than one-third of ordinary prices. Premier Aberhart, in thanking the Red Cross in Alberta for its work in this particular campaign, also expressed gratitude to the Ontario, Quebec and British Columbia divisions of the Red Cross which had contributed generously.[69]

Two conclusions stand out. First, the disaster of the Dry Belt helped the Alberta division to gain experience in the area of relief and prepared it for the more widespread disaster of the 1930s. The assistance provided by the Red Cross provincially and nationally helped establish its reputation across the country as a valuable peacetime organization, a reputation it still holds today. Second, the relationship between the Red Cross and the government highlights the tension in the area of public versus private responsibility for social welfare. On the one hand the widespread nature of the depression disaster probably helped the development of a social welfare mentality in Canada, a mentality which has increasingly called on the government to provide assistance. On the other hand a voluntary agency such as the Red Cross, by its existence, assistance and expertise, allowed the government to limit the amount of official support it provided to those in need and to make temporary *ad hoc* arrangements for government assistance, thus curtailing and delaying its responsibility.

NOTES

This article was first published in *Prairie Forum* 12, no. 2 (1987): 277–293.

1   P. H. Gordon, *Fifty Years in the Canadian Red Cross* (n.p., n.d.), 11–12.

2   Canadian Red Cross Society (hereafter CRCS), *The Role of One Voluntary Organization in Canada's Health Service* (Toronto: Canadian Red Cross Headquarters, 1962), 1.

3   Ibid., 6; P. H. Gordon, *Fifty Years*, 78–80.

4   For information on the beginnings and growth of the Junior Red Cross in Saskatchewan, see Nancy M. Sheehan, "The Junior Red Cross Movement in Saskatchewan, 1919–1939: Rural Improvement Through the Schools," in David C. Jones and Ian MacPherson (eds.), *Building Beyond the Homestead* (Calgary: University of Calgary Press, 1985), 66–86.

5   H. P. Davison, "Address to Opening Session of the General Council. 2 March 1920," *Bulletin of League of Red Cross Societies* 1 (April 1920): 6–9.

6   CRCS, *One Voluntary Organization*, 1–2.

7   Ibid., 12; J. Riddington, "The Role of Voluntary Societies in the Care of Public Health," *The Public Health Journal* 11 (October 1920): 437–43; Dr. A. F. Miller, "Community Responsibility with Regard to Tuberculosis," *The Public Health Journal* 14 (March 1923): 99–100; G. D. Porter, "The Nineteenth Annual Report of the Executive Council of the Canadian Association for the Prevention of Tuberculosis," *The Public Health Journal* 10 (December 1919): 551–55.

8   CRCS, *One Voluntary Organization*, 16–17.

9   *Canadian Red Cross in War and Peace* (Toronto: n.p., n.d.), 30; Public Archives of Nova Scotia (hereafter PANS), MB 20, 1369 #76.

10   David C. Jones, "Schools and Social Disintegration in the Alberta Dry Belt of the Twenties," *Prairie Forum* 3, no. 1 (Spring 1978): 1–19. See also. David C. Jones, "An Exceedingly Risky and Unremunerative Partnership: Farmers and Financial Interests Amid the Collapse of Southern Alberta," in David C. Jones and Ian MacPherson (eds.), *Building Beyond the Homestead*, 207–27. In 1929 the hospital at Foremost had been closed for eighteen months. Others, at Consort and Hanna, only managed to stay open with the support of the Red Cross.

11   Provincial Archives of Alberta (hereafter PAA), 75.126, file 3295b, Attorney General Records, General Administration Branch, questionnaires in Drought Area Correspondence.

12   PAA, Red Cross Files #437 (hereafter RCF 437), Premiers' Papers 69.289. Letter from Mary E. Waagen to Premier Herbert Greenfield, 1 October 1921.

13   Ibid. *Report of Survey Made by the Alberta Red Cross of Conditions in Crop Failure Districts September 13th to 24th 1921. Prepared for Consideration of the Government of Alberta*, 6.

14   Ibid., 10.

15   Ibid. *Recommendations of Special Committee appointed at Government Conference on Unemployment and Relief, Edmonton, Aug. 23rd to recommend to the Government, methods of distributing Relief.*

16   Ibid. *Relief Regulations for the Information of Red Cross Branches or Communities*, 1–2.

17   Ibid. *Report of Survey*, 11–12.

18   Ibid., 12–13.

19   Ibid. *Report on Relief to Date*, Alberta Division, Canadian Red Cross, 31 December 1921. This report includes the organization set-up, the rationale, the distributing centres and the distribution of clothing to date.

20   Ibid., 9–10; *Report on Relief Distribution*, 4; untitled, undated two-page letter from Mary Waagen, circa late autumn 1921.

21 Ibid. Letter from Mary Waagen to the Honourable R. G. Reid, Minister of Municipalities, 3 February 1922.

22 Ibid. Telegram from Mary Waagen to Premier Greenfield, 28 January 1922, and from Greenfield to Waagen, 30 January 1922.

23 Ibid. Letter from Mary Waagen to the Honourable R. G. Reid, Minister of Municipalities, 22 May 1922.

24 Department of Public Health, *Annual Report for 1922* (Edmonton: King's Printer, 1923), 13, 38.

25 D. Geneva Lent, "Alberta Red Cross in Peace and War (1914–1947)" (unpublished manuscript), 43, 49; letter from Mary Waagen to Premier Greenfield, 16 February 1922; PAA, RCF 437. *Memorandum re Rural Nursing and Hospital Service*, Alberta Division, Canadian Red Cross, and *Statement of Finances of Hospitals*.

26 Ibid., 47.

27 PAA, RCF 437. Letters from Mary Waagen to Premier Greenfield, 18 October and 18 November 1922.

28 Ibid. Letter from Premier Greenfield to Mary Waagen. 6 January 1923.

29 For example, the Debt Adjustment Board established by the government in 1923 took on the responsibility for the operation of a number of relief acts, including the Feed Grain Relief, Binder Twine Relief and Bankruptcy Acts. See PAA, Department of Municipal Affairs Records, Administration Files, 74.6, file 3, "Instruction of Relief Agents," and *Statutes of Alberta, 1923*, "An Act to Facilitate the Adjustment of Agricultural Debts," 21 April 1923.

30 PAA, RCF 437. Letter from Premier Greenfield to Mary Waagen, 26 November 1923.

31 Ibid. "Relief," *Annual Report for 1924*, Canadian Red Cross Society. Alberta Provincial Division.

32 *Calgary Herald*, 10 March 1926.

33 PAA, RCF 438. Letter from Mary Waagen to the Honourable George Hoadley. Minister of Health and Agriculture, 16 February 1931.

34 Ibid. Letter from Premier Brownlee to D. M. Duggan, 30 December 1930. The complete organization eventually was as follows: all mailers pertaining to relief were placed under the Honourable O. L. McPherson, Minister of Public Works; A. A. Mackenzie, Department of Municipal Affairs, was appointed Director of Charity and Relief and was responsible for rural relief; Mackenzie's office was also responsible for the cost of administration of the Feed Grain Act (Department of Agriculture), the Unemployment Relief Commission (Public Works), Medical Attention and Hospitalization (Public Health), Debt Adjustment Board (Attorney General), and Direct Relief to Cities (Bureau of Labour). See PAA, 65.118, file 228, Alberta Unemployment Service Papers, 1920–1941, and letter from A. A. Mackenzie to O. L. McPherson, 1 March 1934, *Annual Report on Unemployment Relief*, Bureau of Labour.

35 Ibid. Letter from Mr. D. M. Duggan to Premier Brownlee, 15 January 1931.

36 Ibid. Memo, "Re: Red Cross Clothing Relief," circa mid-February 1931.

37 Ibid. Letters from Mary Waagen to the Honourable George Hoadley. Minister of Health, 12 and 16 February 1931.

38 Ibid., 7 March 1931.

39   Ibid. Letter from Mary Waagen to Premier Brownlee, 8 April 1931.

40   Known as the Relief Act, 1931, this act was passed for a year at a time. See for example, *Statutes of Canada, 1932*, chapter 36, "An Act respecting Relief Measures," 99–101, and *Statutes of Canada, 1933*, chapter 18, "An Act respecting Relief Measures." 89–91.

41   PAA, RCF 438. Telegram from Prime Minister R. B. Bennett to Premier Brownlee, 12 September 1931.

42   Ibid. Letters from Premier Brownlee to Mary Waagen, 1 October 1931, and from R. English, Department of Municipal Affairs to Premier Brownlee, 22 October 1931.

43   Ibid. The loan of $10,000 was made on the understanding that the first $10,000 raised in the national drive would be used to reimburse the government. See letter from Premier Brownlee to Mary Waagen, 24 November 1931; see also letter from E. J. Fream, Sec. Board of Public Utility Commissioners, Edmonton, to Premier Brownlee, 16 November 1931.

44   Ibid. Letter from Mary Waagen to Premier Brownlee, 12 September 1931; see also editorial in *The Drumheller Mail*, 17 September 1931.

45   Ibid. Letters from Mary Waagen to Premier Brownlee, 4 April, 10 and 28 May 1932; James C. Thompson, Provincial Auditor to Mary Waagen, 7, 8 and 12 April 1932; R. English, Deputy Minister of Municipal Affairs to Premier Brownlee, 5 and 20 May 1932; A. A. Mackenzie, Supervisor, Charity and Relief to R. English, 19 May 1932.

46   Ibid. *Report of Emergency Relief As At August 31st, 1932*, Canadian Red Cross Society, Alberta Division.

47   Ibid. Letters from Mary Waagen to Premier Brownlee, 22 December 1931 and 17 October 1932.

48   Ibid. Memorandum from A. A. Mackenzie to Premier Brownlee, 23 February 1932.

49   Ibid. Letter from Mary Waagen to Canon C. F. A. Clough, President, Canadian Red Cross Society, 1 March 1932.

50   Ibid. Letter from Mary Waagen to Premier Brownlee, 5 March 1932.

51   Ibid. *Report of Emergency Relief*, 5. For other incidences of Mackenzie's attitude see letter from A. A. Mackenzie to the Honourable Mr. Lymburn, Attorney General, 28 December 1932, and from George R. Walshaw, Independent Labor Party to Premier Brownlee, 17 November 1933. PAA, 83.212, file 119, Papers of J. F. Lymburn as Attorney General.

52   Ibid. See Report from J. C. Scott, Inspector, Commanding "D" Division to The Commander, Alberta Provincial Police, 4 November 1931, and from K. V. Shaw, Constable, Lomond Detachment, same date. See also letters from J. E. Woodhead, Paymaster Sergeant, Alberta Provincial Police to Secretary, Red Cross Society, 17 December 1931; Mary Waagen to J. F. Lymburn, Attorney General, 24 February 1932, J. F. Lymburn to Premier Brownlee, 27 February 1932.

53   Ibid. *Report of Emergency Relief*, 8–9.

54   Ibid. See *History sheets, Alberta Provincial Police Reports* and letters.

55   Ibid. Letters from J. J. Mott to Lieutenant Governor Maloh, 9 December 1931 and Hector C. Habkirk, Salvation Army to S. C. Jones, Department of Municipal Affairs, 15 February 1932.

56   Ibid. Letters from D. H. Tomlinson, Secretary and Acting Manager to Mayor Andrew Davison, Calgary, 27 February 1933, and Andrew Davison to Premier Brownlee, 6 March 1933.

57 Ibid. Memorandum from A. A. Mackenzie to James C. Thompson, Provincial Auditor, 27 May 1933.
58 Public Archives of Canada. RG 27, Vol. 2096, File Y40. J. K. Houston, *An Appreciation of Relief as Related to Economic and Employment Tendencies in Canada*, 31 October 1936, pp. 1–7; for details on Alberta see p. 14.
59 PAA, 65.118, Box 36, file 313. Alberta Employment Service Papers, 1920–1941, *Orders in Council, Relief Grants*, 10 August 1935.
60 For the terms of the Agricultural Relief Advances Act see *Commentary*, PAA, 74.437, Department of Municipal Affairs papers.
61 See J. K. Houston, *An Appreciation of Relief*, Table 12, p. 28; D. Geneva Lent, "Alberta Red Cross in Peace and War," 66; PAA, RCF 1224, and Canadian Red Cross Society, Alberta Division, *Report of Executive Officers*, October 1937 to September 1938, p. 8.
62 Order in Council 1863/19; Memorandum of Agreement signed by Arthur C. Meighen, Minister of the Interior, and Premier Charles Stewart; Order in Council 20/20, 7 January 1920, PAA 75.126, file 3379, Alberta Attorney General Papers, General Administration Branch.
63 PAA, RCF 438. Letter from Mary Waagen to Premier Brownlee, 20 September 1932.
64 PAA, RCF 437. *Report of Survey*, 12–13.
65 PAA, RCF 438. Letters from Mary Waagen to the Honourable Irene Parlby, 25 October 1932 and to Premier Brownlee, 25 October 1932; Government of the Province of Alberta, Department of Municipal Affairs, *List of Goods Which Can Be Purchased By Those Receiving Direct Relief.*
66 Ibid. Letters from Mary Waagen to Premier Brownlee, 26 May and 29 June 1932, and Premier Brownlee to Mary Waagen, 7 July 1932.
67 Ibid., 10 May 1932.
68 Ibid., 19 September 1931.
69 PANS, MG 20, Vol. 322. *Annual Report of the Canadian Red Cross Society*, 1936, 30–31.

11. From Short-Term Emergency to Long-Term Crisis:
Public Works Projects in Saskatoon, 1929–1932

Eric J. Strikwerda

The Broadway Bridge, connecting the Nutana residential area with the downtown core in Saskatoon, Saskatchewan, officially opened to public traffic on 11 November 1932. Constructed entirely by labour from the ranks of the city's unemployed, the bridge marked the end of a distinct period in Saskatoon's Depression experience; it was the last in a series of public works projects designed to provide work relief to the city's resident jobless. Although projects like the Broadway Bridge successfully created some useful work for the urban unemployed until 1932, their effectiveness at addressing the unemployment problem crumbled under the weight of economic exigency for the remaining years of the Depression. On one level, Saskatoon's public works projects created badly needed work for hundreds of the city's jobless and, with provincial and federal financial aid, contributed useful infrastructure works at a reasonable cost to the city. On another level, however, the projects revealed Saskatoon's initial understanding of the Depression in its earliest stages and illustrated the city's first response to the emerging unemployment problem.

Saskatoon had, of course, faced recessions before—one beginning in 1913 and the other in 1920—but the Depression's proportions in both severity and length were entirely unprecedented. In the first instance, the onset of the Great War in August 1914 curtailed potential economic and unemployment disaster. As the nation geared up for total war in a flurry of domestic war-time production activity, concurrent recruitment for overseas service turned unemployment into labour shortage. In the second instance, the economic difficulties caused in part by rapid demobilization after the war and intensified by American protectionist tariffs gave way to economic expansion and a corresponding return to prosperity by 1924. That the comparatively brief economic downturn between 1920 and 1924 had given way to substantial growth through the latter half of the 1920s seemed to offer testimony to the fundamental strength of the market economy and its self-corrective ability. It appeared as though traditional responses to periods of economic and employment uncertainty—including unemployment relief work programs— constituted effective measures in addressing urban unemployment problems. It should come as no surprise, then, that Saskatoon's initial response to the sudden increase in the numbers of the unemployed during the autumn of 1929 echoed the city's response to similar conditions in the past.

In early November 1929, municipal authorities in Saskatoon could not help but recognize the looming unemployment problem despite federal assurances to the contrary. Indeed, members of Saskatoon's city council, along with similar representatives from Moose Jaw and Regina, demanded some form of provincial unemployment aid even while Peter Heenen, the minister of Labour in Mackenzie King's cabinet, insisted that employment levels for November "had never been higher."[1] If the level of unemployment appeared troublesome at all, the minister suggested, then it had more to do with anomalous crop conditions than with the stock market crash in the United States or any longstanding economic collapse. And yet, Saskatoon's city council had good cause for concern. The city recorded fifty-six families on relief in December, more than twice as many as for the same month one year before. The recorded number of families on relief, however, disguised a much larger unemployment problem simmering just below the surface. Saskatoon's chief engineer estimated that at least 350 married men were actually unemployed in the city but had not yet applied for relief.[2] With at least four months of winter ahead, the unemployment situation seemed unlikely to improve before spring. It is hardly surprising that Saskatoon's municipal authorities recognized an unemployment problem at a time when the federal, or even provincial, governments did not. After all, while Canada's federal politicians and businessmen, bankers and economists buoyantly talked of a "fundamentally sound" economy, Saskatoon's City Council and residents alike watched revenues fall, local businesses fail, and unemployment numbers grow. Like other Canadian cities held under the yoke of local responsibility, Saskatoon was on the front line of a growing emergency.

Still, the Saskatchewan government had serious reservations about establishing any real and far-reaching unemployment policy that would undoubtedly set dangerous precedents for the future. At the same time, provincial authorities reasoned that some limited funding of municipal public works modeled after a federal emergency relief scheme of the early 1920s would not only ease the urban unemployment problem and pacify municipal demands, but would do so at a small political and economic cost to the province. The provincial cabinet viewed aid in small enough doses toward what was traditionally a local concern as nothing more than an emergency palliative, an explicitly short-term cure for a short-term ill.

That the emergency palliative should take the form of work relief rather than direct relief was nothing new. Conventional wisdom relied on during the recession of the early 1920s dictated that work relief was preferable to direct relief.[3] Little had changed in this wisdom by 1929. "The main question is already settled," the Saskatoon *Star Phoenix* editorialized on 8 November 1929; "[i]t is agreed that work is the best solution of any unemployment problem and public authorities should, so far as possible, spread their spending programs over the winter season."[4] Saskatoon's city council shared this perspective, viewing public works relief as the only legitimate means of alleviating the unemployment problem.

On 16 December 1929, the Saskatchewan government offered firm provincial commitment to Saskatoon's unemployment relief programs. The province promised to bear two-thirds of the extra costs associated with winter public works construction as opposed to the less expensive summer construction.[5] Although local improvements were generally more efficiently undertaken during the summer months, efficiency was not the main design behind the provincial work relief scheme. Winter construction, the province reasoned, would not only provide more men with more work, but also provide more work when it was needed most—namely during the winter months when unemployment levels were higher.[6]

On the surface, the provincial scheme was more than what was required of the province. According to a January 1922 federal order-in-council, unemployment became a provincial responsibility only when the municipality was under such extreme economic hardships that it could not possibly care for its unemployed residents.[7] The provincial scheme, moreover, was unveiled at a time when even the prime minister denied the existence of an unemployment problem. But despite the seemingly strong provincial commitment, the scheme failed to address the shadowy causes and implications looming behind the growing numbers of the unemployed. Essentially, the provincial scheme constituted little more than an incentive for Saskatoon to undertake routine public works immediately rather than wait until the summer, when the government expected unemployment numbers to fall.

In the end, the provincial contribution to the relief of Saskatoon's jobless fell far short of the city's need. The city itself could scarcely provide for those with little or no income teetering on the brink of total destitution, let alone the hundreds of jobless without food or lodgings.[8] From Saskatoon's perspective, although the unemployment situation was still viewed as a temporary problem, it was no longer a matter of purely "local" concern. Saskatoon's local resources, nearly tapped as a result both of the city's continued deficit financing for relief and core services as well as the debt carried over from the boom years earlier in the century, placed severe limitations on the city's unemployment strategy—a strategy based almost entirely on public works projects. This strategy demanded new funds, and with the provincial contributions already directed elsewhere, Saskatoon turned to the next source of unemployment relief—the federal government.

Other major urban centres in the West endured frustrations similar to those facing Saskatoon in early 1930. Hoping to strengthen municipal appeals for federal funding of urban public works relief through collective rather than individual action, Winnipeg mayor Ralph Webb organized an unemployment conference of provincial and municipal officials as well as trades and labour representatives from the Great Lakes to the West Coast. Held in Winnipeg in early January 1930, the conference adopted a series of resolutions aimed at securing greater federal involvement in the unemployment crisis facing western cities. The delegates agreed to three principal arguments. First, Port Arthur mayor George Gibbon argued that because the present unemployment situation was more widespread and acute than it had been during the recession of the early 1920s, the federal government should "again assume their share of the cost of unemployment relief" under the same conditions. Secondly, Calgary mayor Andrew Davison contended that owing to federal immigration policies, the dominion government had an obligation to take full responsibility for the care and maintenance of unemployed immigrants. Finally, the conference as a whole argued that the dominion-wide nature of the jobless situation afforded the federal government reason to intrude on provincial jurisdictions on the issue of unemployment relief.[9]

Armed with the resolutions adopted at the conference and the support of the western representatives, Webb led a delegation of more than twenty-five western politicians, businessmen, and labour leaders to Ottawa. Saskatoon's contribution included two delegates—the recently elected Mayor John Hair and Alderman A. M. Eddy—and a jobless figure of more than nine hundred married and single men. On 25 February 1930, the delegation met with Prime Minister William Lyon Mackenzie King and several members of his cabinet. After brief statements by the western delegates, most of which invariably referred to the poor state of affairs in prairie and coastal cities, Mayor Webb summed up succinctly the delegation's position: "We believe that the Government, in view of policies with regard to unemployment relief which were in effect some years ago, will recognize the nature of the problem. We do not want investigations, commissions, and the like, but assistance."[10]

An unmoved Mackenzie King responded that "[w]ith the possible exception of France, actual figures, if available, would show that the unemployment situation in Canada was better than that of any country in the world." He went on to suggest that the level of unemployment was comparable to any other winter, observing that "at no time was any country without unemployment," and reiterating the concept of local responsibility. In fact, so cold was King's reception of the delegation that he even questioned the sincerity of the municipalities and provincial governments, accusing them of asking for relief for themselves rather than for the unemployed.[11] Mayor Webb's active Conservative Party membership, moreover, helped convince King that the "alleged" unemployment condition was little more than a "Tory device to stir up propaganda against the government."[12] By the end of the meeting, King offered the delegation exactly what it did not need—a vague plan whereby "[e]mployers and employed, the provinces and the municipalities might consistently get together and study the problem to see whether [an unemployment insurance] scheme could be introduced."

Thoroughly rebuffed by the federal government, the delegation's members returned to their respective municipalities with only the empty promise of a possible investigation into an unemployment insurance scheme that, judging from experience, would probably never come to fruition.[13] Municipal authorities in Saskatoon once again faced the city's jobless with sympathetic words, but empty pockets. The few relief works still providing some of Saskatoon's jobless with employment, including water main extensions, boulevard and sidewalk work, and various odd jobs for the city's Engineering Department, never seemed to provide enough work. The lack of federal support and the nearly completed provincially supported works forced Saskatoon's city council to take steps aimed at reducing relief costs. One such step was to organize the unemployed along lines of less eligibility for whatever municipally funded work relief the city could afford. Designed to limit the number of jobless residents who qualified for work relief, the concept of "less eligibility" essentially divided the city's jobless into decreasing gradations of eligibility for work relief. Mayor Hair curtly described the formal organization in a letter circulated among Engineering Department foremen on 27 April 1930:

> Unless under very exceptional circumstances, only those who
> are at present time British subjects, either by birth or natural-
> ization or those who have applied for naturalization papers will
> be employed…preference [should be] given to married men
> and other things being equal, those with families [should be]
> given preference.[14]

The attention afforded British subjects was in direct response to a reported
five hundred immigrants who had arrived in the city earlier in the month.[15]
Saskatoon's Engineering Department could offer the city's estimated seven
hundred married and single jobless little more than small projects able to
employ only a fraction of their number as it was; providing relief to another
five hundred newcomers was simply out of the question. In any case, it is
doubtful whether Saskatoon would have offered relief to the new immigrants
even if municipal finances permitted. If Saskatoon's municipal authorities
viewed the recent immigrant unemployed as *bona fide* residents—and therefore qualifying for municipal relief—the city would surely have forfeited
one of its strongest arguments in favour of direct federal involvement in
municipal unemployment relief costs. Saskatoon's municipal authorities still
maintained that because immigration was a federal initiative, the federal
government should assume all responsibility for the care and maintenance
of the immigrant unemployed. In other words, and as Mayor Hair argued,
"those responsible for bringing newcomers should be responsible for finding
them employment."[16]

The lack of federal support for municipal unemployment relief expenditures,
combined with the rapidly disappearing provincial supplements to Saskatoon's
winter construction projects, forced the city to further divide its unemployed
population into married and single men. That municipal authorities considered single unemployed men as less eligible for relief work employment than
married men with families should not be surprising, particularly in view of
the social mores prevalent in Canada during the 1930s. Mayor Hair provided
an adequate illustration of such mores, along with a bit of advice for several
single unemployed men waiting on him for relief: "I explained to them the
first principles of manhood was [*sic*] to recognize women and children first.
Until we have taken care of women and children I had no authority to deal
with men such as they."[17] Hair's comments reveal some of the city's assumptions about the nature of work, gender and familial obligation. By recognizing
"women and children first," Hair implied that married men would use their
relief wages to provide for their wives and children because the city did not

offer relief work to women. This implication was of some benefit to the city. By offering work relief only to married men with wives and children, the city effectively stretched its relief dollar further than it could by giving that relief dollar to a single man.

Some unemployed women in Saskatoon resented such attitudes. During the summer of 1931, for example, Lily Whaley requested that she be considered for employment on the city's work relief programs: "My circumstances place me on the same level as a man," she wrote to Mayor Hair, "and I will be glad if it could be possible for the city to provide manual labour as far as these unemployed men for myself at the same low salary rather than be compelled to ask for relief."[18] Although Hair was sympathetic to Whaley's request and promised to make inquiries as to the feasibility of offering some light gardening work to the city's unemployed women, Chief Engineer Archibald warned against such a measure:

> I might say that it is probably quite true that there are many unemployed women in the city that could perform manual labour just as well as many of the men who are at present time engaged on this sort of work. However, I do not think that the city should take any step in this direction, as I am quite sure there would be a very serious revulsion of feeling on the part of the public if women were to be engaged on even lighter forms of labouring work.[19]

If letters from various residents are any indication of a "serious revulsion of feeling on the part of the public," then such letters generally confirm Archibald's warning. "The great majority of [employed] married women are working just so they can get away from their husbands and have a good time," one concerned citizen wrote in a letter to the city council in October 1931. "Supposing we all practiced the selfish economy of married couples working," another asked the editor of the *Star Phoenix*, "what would be the result? The world would sink into oblivion."[20] Although not necessarily constructed with a view toward saving the world from oblivion, Saskatoon's work distribution policies nevertheless confirmed the notion that women should not participate in the city's work relief projects.

Saskatoon's relatively minute efforts at reducing relief costs were no match for the 710 jobless men desperately seeking some form of municipal aid. On July 7, 1930, an indignant delegation of unemployed men appeared before the city council demanding "that immediate steps be taken to provide employment for those out of work."[21] But the city's beleaguered Relief Department could offer little more than small projects able to employ a total of only 167 men. Saskatoon's municipal authorities, meanwhile, had secured nothing more from the province than a provincially funded institute for the deaf and dumb and a promise that no harvester excursion from other parts of the country would threaten to take harvest work away from Saskatoon's jobless in the fall. Clearly, some change in unemployment relief policy at the federal level was required. That change came when Prime Minister King dissolved Parliament and called a federal election for July 1930.

Historian James Struthers has argued that the 1930 general election "was the first modern federal election in which the issue of unemployment proved decisive."[22] The two main national parties' fundamental disagreement over the nature of the unemployment situation during the election campaign seems to confirm Struthers' observation. On one hand, King's ardent refusal to believe that unemployment had reached national proportions or that appeals for federal aid to municipalities and provinces constituted anything more than blatant and unwarranted cash grabs revealed the prime minister's misunderstanding of the depths to which some parts of the country had fallen. Opposition Conservative leader Richard Bedford Bennett, on the other hand, seemed more in touch with the frustrating intractability of the unemployment problem—at lease on the surface. Either as a simple election ploy designed to differentiate his campaign from that of the federal Liberal Party or without genuine concern for the estimated 13 percent of Canadians without work, Bennett promised a wary electorate that "[t]he Conservative Party is going to find work for all who are willing to work or perish in the attempt." Bennett handily defeated King's Liberals in the election, perhaps as much on the strength of his promise to "end unemployment" as on King's callous dismissal of any unemployment problem at all.

Almost immediately, Bennett introduced two bills designed to lift Canada out of the Depression. The first, and in Bennett's opinion the most important, involved the traditional Conservative Party tactic of raising the tariff. Increasing the tariff would not only protect Canadian manufacturers from the cancerous outside world, but would also create jobs, end unemployment, and "blast a way into the markets of the world." The second, of more immediate importance to municipal authorities in Saskatoon, involved a $20 million unemployment relief package to support urban public works and direct relief schemes. Enacted on 26 September 1930, the *Unemployment Relief Act* provided $16 million to cover the federal government's promised 25 percent share of the cost of public works construction. The remaining 75 percent share, divided between the provincial and municipal governments at 25 and 50 percent respectively, covered the balance.

Set to expire the following spring, the *Unemployment Relief Act* illustrated the prevailing belief that the unemployment problem was temporary and that the nation, with the help of the tariff, would soon be on more stable ground. Bennett introduced the legislation with the determined intention of banishing unemployment; Minister of Labour Gideon D. Robertson optimistically explained that the unemployment problem facing the nation was "serious…but surely not insurmountable."[23] Unfortunately for Canada's jobless, the two unemployment measures essentially constituted the new Conservative government's entire solution to the unemployment problem.

When news of the dominion scheme reached Saskatoon, Mayor Hair presented the provincial government—who retained responsibility for the approval process—an ambitious $700,000 public works proposal which included a subway over 19th Street, storm sewer work, and a new wing on the City Hospital. The province approved the city's $300,000 19th Street subway plan and $150,000 storm sewer work, both of which promised employment to Saskatoon's jobless labourers, but dismissed the $250,000 City Hospital wing. Since the hospital wing would offer employment primarily to tradesmen, and since many of Saskatoon's tradesmen were already employed on other municipal work, including a technical school and the provincial institute for the deaf and dumb, provincial authorities argued that the $250,000 could be better spent on a building in Regina.[24] Rather than forgo the hospital wing's relief potential, city officials opted to finance the project independent of provincial or federal support.

By January 1931, the Engineering Department was employing some 500 married men per week on the 19th Street subway, various storm sewer work through the city, and the wing on City Hospital. Depending on the size of their families, the men who qualified for employment on the projects worked between one and three weeks out of every month for eight hours per day, and earned forty-five cents per hour.[25] While the three relief projects, combined with other local improvements, significantly relieved the unemployment situation, they collectively offered work to less than one-third of the city's estimated 1,700 jobless married men. And because the city offered no relief assistance without some contributory work, surplus unemployed married men sanded streets, cleared snow, or performed shrub and bush work for relief. Through the spring and summer of 1931, Saskatoon's city council tried, generally with limited success, to secure more federally and provincially financed public works. On March 18, 1931, for example, the city appealed to the provincial government for approval of an extension of the sewer and water-main work begun the previous year. The province approved only $15,000—a mere fraction of the $180,000 the city had requested.[26]

With unemployment numbers still climbing by June 1931, Saskatoon's work relief policies grew ever more coercive and restrictive to reduce the number of residents who qualified for relief. For example, relief department officers struck from the relief rolls any unemployed resident refusing to participate in "created work" schemes. This measure caused the unemployed's long simmering frustration with a relief system they neither embraced nor trusted to boil over. On 1 June, a delegation numbering between 700 and 800 marched on City Hall demanding work or wages for the unemployed.[27] But Saskatoon's city council could do little more than look to Regina and Ottawa for financial help. But the provincial government, consumed with worsening conditions in rural Saskatchewan, responded to Saskatoon's appeals by denying that "the situation has reached proportions where it is too large for local urban municipalities."[28] The federal government, on the other hand, dispatched Minister of Labour Gideon Robertson across the nation to assess the effects of the federal unemployment initiatives and discuss possible solutions with provincial and municipal authorities. Robertson reached Saskatchewan on 19 June 1931.

Upon his return to Ottawa, the labour minister described alarming conditions which suggested that neither the tariff nor the $20 million relief scheme had made a significant dent in the unemployment situation. The Bennett government hurriedly pushed new legislation—the *Unemployment and Farm Relief Act*—through Parliament on Dominion Day. Even though this second unemployment relief act offered more financial muscle than its predecessor did—the federal government now offered fifty cents on the dollar for all approved municipal and provincial public works—it differed little in substance. Although the federal government remained vague about the total amount it was willing to expend, it clearly set the Act to expire on 1 May 1932, once again reflecting the assumption that the unemployment problem would disappear by spring.

When word of the new federal relief scheme arrived in early August, Saskatoon applied for approval of another $300,000 storm sewer project. In submitting the proposal, Mayor Hair reminded the provincial minister of Railways, Labour and Industries how badly Saskatoon needed employment, estimating a total of 1,500 unemployed married men in the city, 50 of whom were "very distressing cases."[29] Hair asked the minister if the city could begin work on enough of the sewer project to provide employment for the fifty men. Although the new Act had yet to be officially enacted by Parliament, the minister approved $30,000 of the $300,000 proposal on the understanding that the city abide by the terms of the federal scheme and spend no more than 40 percent of the cost on materials and no less than 60 percent of the cost on labour.[30]

By early September 1931, with the federal *Unemployment and Farm Relief Act* firmly in place, Saskatoon's city council turned its attention to the Broadway Bridge project. Municipal authorities had viewed a bridge as an ideal relief project since at least the summer of 1930, when a Toronto urban planning firm hired by the city recommended construction of a main traffic artery connecting Broadway Avenue on the south side of the Saskatchewan River with 19th Street on the north. Expected to provide enough work to at least maintain the city's jobless population, the bridge seemed at first a viable, constructive solution to Saskatoon's unemployment problem. But as worsening conditions forced the city to increase its summertime estimate that 1,500 men would be unemployed by autumn, it became nothing less than an essential relief measure.[31]

On 18 September 1931, Chief Engineer Archibald grimly revealed to Commissioner Leslie that more than 2,400 married men were registered with the city's Relief Department.[32] Even with Archibald's estimate that 25 percent of this number were physically unfit for manual labour, the Engineering Department still had to find useful employment for nearly 2,000 men. Of course, neither Commissioner Leslie nor the city's unemployed needed Engineering Department statistics to tell them what they already knew. Archibald's count only confirmed what was readily apparent in the city's soup kitchens and along the city's bread lines—Saskatoon's unemployment levels were higher than they had ever been before. To make matters worse, the end of the harvest season was rapidly approaching, and this was sure to push transient farm workers into the city for the winter. Although municipal authorities had long evaded responsibility for transient workers, recent changes to provincial relief policy dictated that

> because the Dominion and province pay at least 65 percent of
> public works costs, the municipality, in all fairness, should be
> expected to take care of all persons resident in the municipality
> and who have no fixed abode.[33]

Now more than ever, Saskatoon's municipal officials and the unemployed alike desperately needed the city's newest public works proposal to come to fruition. But with the city already courting bankruptcy and with no real ability to generate any significant new revenue, the success of any work relief proposal rested entirely on approval from the senior governments.

Saskatoon's city council consequently pursued official approval for the project through the late summer and early autumn of 1931, with a determination and vigour once reserved only for city boosting. But the city council's dogged support for the bridge project was neither strictly altruistic nor entirely benign. Municipal authorities had almost as much to gain from the tripartite-funded Broadway Bridge as did the city's jobless for whom the project was primarily designed. The corollary economic and social benefits the city expected from the bridge project informed and directed Saskatoon's work relief policies at least as much as did the bridge's primary function of relieving the city's unemployed.

The needs of the city's unemployed were fairly simple: Saskatoon's jobless required enough regular employment to sustain themselves and their families through the coming winter and maintain some degree of dignity in the process. The city's needs, on the other hand, were more complicated but no less important in directing relief policy; nor were they fundamentally different from, or necessarily at odds with, the needs of the city's jobless. First, municipal authorities in Saskatoon expected the bridge project to provide as much employment to the city's jobless as possible, at as little cost to the city's ratepayers as possible. Secondly, municipal authorities expected the bridge project to provide the city with a lasting and useful asset at a reasonable cost. A new bridge, spanning the South Saskatchewan River from Broadway Avenue on the south side to Fourth Avenue on the north, would not only offer a much needed conduit between the Nutana residential area and the downtown core, but would also relieve subway traffic on the decrepit and overly narrow 19th Street Bridge. Finally, the bridge project would help counteract the instability and potential civil unrest associated with high levels of urban unemployment. Keeping idle hands occupied on the bridge would prevent a jobless population, angry and frustrated at a system which had failed them, from agitating on street corners and in union halls and from planning mass demonstrations, protests, and riots through city streets and market squares.

The apparent economic benefits the bridge project offered Saskatoon's unemployed are easily identifiable. On the surface, the Broadway Bridge promised thousands of man-hours of regular work and a minimum wage of forty-five cents per hour. If Engineering Department implementation plans were accurate, each man who qualified for work on the bridge could expect sustained employment for at least three weeks out of every month for the duration of the project's construction.[34] This came as no small relief to hundreds of Saskatoon's jobless, many of whom had been without regular employment for months. Less easily identifiable was the dignity inherent in earning an honest wage doing meaningful and useful work. The humiliation of sudden unemployment was difficult to bear for many of the city's residents, particularly for those who prided themselves on their self-sufficiency and thrift. Such humiliation, of course, was not limited to Saskatoon: for unemployed men in urban centres across the country, standing before the relief officer, hat in hand, and declaring complete and utter destitution remained a sign of personal failure—this despite climatic and economic conditions and systems certainly beyond their control. One relief office employee in Edmonton, for example, described the difficulty some unemployed men had in accepting relief: "I've seen tears in men's eyes, as though they were signing away their manhood."[35]

For Saskatoon's nearly two thousand *bona fide* married reliefers, then, the bridge project offered some dignified salvation from their feelings of inadequacy, some sense that they could make a contribution to the city through their labour, that they were not shiftless or lazy or paupers. But dignified salvation during the autumn of 1931 remained an elusive commodity for many of the city's unemployed. Because the city insisted that the unemployed work for relief—even in the absence of meaningful and useful work—a good many unemployed men found themselves employed on various created-work schemes while the city finalized arrangements for the tripartite-funded bridge project.[36] Defined by municipal authorities as works that would not be undertaken under normal economic conditions, Saskatoon's created-work projects merely tested the unemployed's willingness to work, often in degrading and meaningless ways.

On the surface, little distinguished employment on the city's created-work schemes from employment on the bridge project: after all, work was work, especially for those with bills to pay and dependents to support. Below the surface, however, created-work schemes differed from work on the bridge project in two ways. First, created work did not offer a real wage. Men working on snow removal, bush work, or street sanding were generally paid only in shelter and groceries vouchers. While shelter vouchers paid the rent and utilities bills, they also served as monthly reminders of the reliefers' poverty. Similarly, while food vouchers eased a family's hunger, a simple trip to the grocery store turned into a public display of personal failure. Payment in straight goods rather than in cash also suggested that municipal authorities lacked confidence in the unemployed's ability to make responsible consumer decisions. Secondly, the city made no attempt to ensure worker efficiency on created-work projects. This meant that the city did not consider such work as either necessary or useful—hardly the kind of projects which engendered the satisfaction of performing honest and meaningful work.

Among those toiling on one of the city's created-work projects while the city awaited firm federal support for the bridge project during the autumn of 1931 was A. C. MacNeil. Laid off from his job as a salesman at the Massey-Harris Company in December 1930 and without steady employment for nearly ten months, MacNeil was only too familiar with the indignities associated with the city's created-work schemes. While the Engineering Department made surveys and sank test holes on the riverbank in preparation for the bridge project, for example, MacNeil joined other unemployed men performing clean-up work at the city's nuisance grounds as a work test for groceries.[37] The created work at the city dump was degrading—the site offered neither a heated shack for shelter nor a place to eat lunch nor even simple toilet accommodation. The work at the dump was as unpopular as it was degrading—so unpopular that near the end of August 1931, at least five men defied the foreman and refused to do the work allotted to them. Nevertheless, MacNeil preferred his job outside the city at the dump to other created work schemes such as sweeping city streets because, as he explained, "I would not want any of my friends to know or even suspect that I was forced into this corner."[38]

The bridge project also offered the city significant economic benefits. In real terms, partial financing from the senior governments translated into a significant and useful local improvement at a fraction of the cost the city would have had to expend under normal economic conditions. The new *Unemployment and Farm Relief Act* promised that the federal and provincial governments would collectively bear some 65 percent of the bridge project's cost, leaving the city responsible for the balance. The Act also made provision for the federal government to underwrite the issue of bonds necessary for raising the city's share of the project. This meant that Saskatoon could borrow its share of the project's cost at a rate about 20 percent less than if the city was forced to raise the entire municipal share alone.[39]

The bridge project did not merely offer a local improvement at a bargain price. With an alarmingly high number of unemployed men in the city during the autumn of 1931, the bridge project represented a stability which could only come from an occupied working population. American social scientists Frances Fox Piven and Richard Cloward have posited that seemingly progressive and benevolent state intervention into market economies through measures such as public works projects constitute little more than attempts to maintain social control over the working population during times of mass unemployment. In this view, the bridge project replaced the stability of fixed occupational roles once provided by private industry. Saskatoon's explicit policy of aggressively denying relief to those not willing to work, not willing to participate, suggests that municipal authorities perceived public works as a component in bolstering civil order.

Beginning as early as 1930, municipal authorities viewed the city's jobless as paupers requiring relief as well as potentially dangerous elements demanding serious municipal attention. And providing the unemployed with work—some productive exercise designed to occupy otherwise idle time—was rapidly becoming the city's new strategy to disarm potential civil unrest. In fact, municipal authorities had identified the potential problems associated with masses of idle unemployed through their experience with the steadily increasing numbers of the unemployed through most of 1930: "It is very evident that single men are starting to flock into Saskatoon," Mayor Hair confided to all the new candidates for alderman in November 1930, "and it is also very evident that there are agitators of the worst type trying to create trouble amongst the single men."[40]

Mayor Hair's concerns were not entirely unsubstantiated. Local unemployed groups representing the city's jobless had been organizing demonstrations against the city's "unfair" relief policies since at least the summer of 1930, and had been urging single unemployed men not to accept jobs on surrounding farms for their board as early as the winter of 1929. Groups such as the Communist-affiliated Saskatoon Unemployed Association (SUA) attempted to organize Saskatoon's jobless and agitate for better relief policies on their behalf. Members of the SUA were initially dismissed by Saskatoon's municipal authorities as little more than harmless shirkers or small-scale agitators lacking significant influence amongst the city's jobless.[41] In fact, during the spring and summer of 1930, Saskatoon's city council refused to even recognize the SUA as a legitimate representative of labour at all. But the summer of 1930 was long past, and unemployment numbers by the autumn of 1931 had grown exponentially. Nearly two full years of relief expenditures seriously compromised the city's ability to provide meaningful work for the unemployed. The sheer number of jobless by November 1931 compounded the city's inability to secure any real occupational stability, and increased the perceived threat of Communist infiltration and the associated rise of civil disorder. Added to this was the end of the harvest season, the onset of another winter, and the early completion of the $300,000 storm sewer project, expected to throw another two hundred men out of work. Never before had worker dislocation been more widespread in Saskatoon; and, perhaps, never before had the potential threat of civil disorder caused by mass worker dislocation been more palpable.

Although real violence, instigated by local Communists and carried out by the local unemployed, had yet to descend on the city, there were real reasons for municipal authorities to take the Communist threat seriously. Just days before construction on the bridge began, the National Unemployed Workers' Association, parent group of the SUA, warned the city council of potential violence unless the city heeded the unemployed's concerns: "Our condition is very serious regardless of statements made by [Mayor] Hair," NUWA secretary and known Bolshevist Steve Forkin wrote in a 9 December letter to city council. He continued:

> There are hundreds of us penneless [sic] and poorly clad. The city's relief policy is probably the most callous on the continent. Saskatchewan jails however are preferable to present conditions. We assure the city that if the present policy is not changed we will not starve without a struggle and it will be an organized struggle bringing into play our full mass force in organized bitter resistance.[42]

The thinly veiled militant tone of Forkin's letter, combined with the increase in the numbers of unemployed, perhaps offers partial explanation for the city's determination to bring the bridge project to fruition. If there was ever a time when the city needed a large relief project able to provide a significant number of unemployed with work, then the autumn and early winter of 1931 was that time. And although the openly Communist-led SUA had organized non-violent mass demonstrations before, the recent Estevan Riot testified that the Communists, if properly provoked, were capable of violent action. The events of 29 September in Estevan, wherein striking miners under the cooperative leadership of the Communist Workers' Unity League and the Mine Workers' Union of Canada clashed with police, leaving three miners dead and at least twenty-three injured, were still fresh in the minds of municipal authorities through the last three months of 1931. Legitimate or not, fears of a lean and hungry jobless population disrupting the existing economic and social order were present in every Canadian city during the autumn of 1931. Certainly, municipal authorities in Saskatoon felt threatened by potential civil disorder caused by unemployment. And while they did not expect the bridge project to banish civil disorder through occupational stability, they at least hoped it would undermine Communist agitators by robbing them of their primary weapons—namely widespread poverty and dissatisfaction amongst the jobless.

On the morning of 12 December 1931, Mayor Hair returned to Saskatoon after a three-day conference with representatives of the provincial government at Regina. He carried with him a signed agreement authorizing the city to begin construction of the Broadway Bridge under the terms of the *Unemployment and Farm Relief Act*.[43] Within days of the project's approval, the first shift of some fifty jobless men was busily inserting drainage pipes for the south abutment of the bridge while another fifty men hauled stone, gravel, and sand in preparation for the construction of the concrete piers by 17 December 1931. Under the watchful eye of Chief Engineer Archibald, each man worked one of three seven-and-a-half hour shifts. The shifts operated consecutively nearly around the clock. The Engineering Department distributed work based on names drawn entirely from the city's unemployment register and divided into categories according to family size. Designed to ensure that those men with the most dependents received the most work, the Engineering Department's labour distribution system reinforced the city's gender assumptions about the nature of work, unemployment, and relief. "It is quite apparent," Mayor Hair reasoned in September 1931, "that the married man with no children does not require as much as the married man with a family of five or six."

The first month-and-a-half of construction on the bridge project had been a relatively smooth affair. The total wages paid to Saskatoon's jobless between mid-December 1931 and the end of January 1932 amounted to $42,000. The Relief Department had issued 750 work cards, and at least 700 men had actually worked on the bridge contract. R. J. Arrand, general contractor for the project, expressed general satisfaction with most of the workers despite the fact that many of the city's unemployed had little practical experience with bridge work. Finally, the nearly completed piers jutting out of the water and running in steady succession across the river hinted at the majestic structure regarded as an integral feature of the city's skyline today. The coming and going of workers, the rumble of machines, and the clouds of steam rising from the Saskatchewan River into the icy air all gave the work site every bit the appearance of bustling, productive animation.[44]

But the apparent success of the project belied a growing level of worker dissatisfaction amongst the rank and file jobless. In fact, most men preferred storm sewer work to working on the bridge. Representatives of the men working on the bridge brought their constituency's concerns before a special meeting of the city's Committee on Unemployment on 14 February 1932. Secretary Anderson of the Saskatoon Local Unemployed Association (SLUA) and representing the workers, cited thirty-three cases where men reported to work their shift on the bridge only to be dismissed—without pay—for lack of available work.[45] Travel to the worksite with little transportation but their own two feet was no easy task for many of the unemployed, particularly for those who lived as far away from the site as the other side of town. And the icy prairie winter of 1931–32, extraordinarily cold even by Saskatchewan's standards, made the trek even more onerous. During the construction of the piers, for example, the temperature hovered around forty degrees below zero. Further, because all the workers on the bridge were unemployed and on relief, it is unlikely that more than a few men could afford the "luxuries" of warm clothes or a healthy diet. Ill-clad and under-nourished, most men made the formidable journey only with extreme difficulty. The workers' anger and frustration at arriving at the worksite only to be turned away is hardly surprising; nor is it surprising that the workers demanded direct relief as compensation for their time in going to the bridge. The city council, however, denied the workers' demands after Arrand reported that some men "wait twenty to thirty minutes for work to begin and then they disappear when they are called to work."[46]

Saskatoon's jobless also leveled complaints of favouritism against the Engineering Department. On 23 February, City Foreman W. J. Myatt faced an inquiry before a special committee to answer to charges that he had been "employing about a dozen men to do special work more or less continuously when there are other men in need of employment capable of taking their turn at such jobs."[47] The dozen men, employed primarily on drainage work to strengthen the river bank for the south bridge approach, became the focus of SLUA's objections to the city's labour distribution system. Although the charges were serious, SLUA had little direct evidence linking Myatt to any conscious wrongdoing, and the matter subsided. But the frustration amongst the city's jobless, borne out or the dismissals for lack of available work, the safety concerns, and the charges of favouritism, remained.

If the relief workers' patience seemed near breaking point by the spring of 1932, municipal authorities were also rapidly losing patience with the unemployed. On March 23, Relief Officer Rowland declared a war on frauds—those unemployed men and women who applied for relief under false pretenses—and reduced the number of men eligible to work on the bridge. Rowland's evidence of relief abuse included one man who, after receiving work relief for months, admitted to having sent at least two thousand dollars to relatives in Hungary "for safekeeping." In another case, relief officials determined that a married woman claiming estrangement from her husband and receiving relief was actually "in contact" with her husband and that she had money. Relief abuse, of course, was neither a new development nor an entirely unavoidable one; but Rowland's explicit response of "punishing to the full extent of the law…anyone found guilty of deliberate misrepresentation" was different. Saskatoon's crack-down on frauds further reflected the city's increasing difficulty in providing relief to the more than 2,100 unemployed married men.[48]

Saskatoon's difficulty in providing unemployment relief was also reflected in the City Council's adoption of a new, more restrictive relief policy on March 26. Designed to reduce the city's relief expenditures, the new policy affected nearly 1,200 families by denying work relief to all unemployed men with less than two children. Other restrictions outlined in the new relief policy included denying the two meals per day able-bodied single unemployed men had been eligible to receive since 1929, and denying work relief to any unemployed man who married after 31 December 1929. Municipal authorities hoped this latter measure would circumvent unemployed men "who got married merely to get on relief."[49]

The city's relief office was not alone in pointing out relief abuse. One city alderman, for example, characterized the relief gangs on the bridge as nothing more than loafers. "If one man wants a match to light his pipe," he complained, "four or five seem to go into conference on the matter and it takes about five minutes to arrange all the details." Relief Officer Rowland expressed similar frustration when it became apparent that the foremen had no control: "If we only had provincial authority to compel the jobless to work for their relief groceries," Rowland pointed out, "then we could cut them off relief immediately that they refused to put in a decent day's work."[50] Rowland's remarks did little to improve relations between the city and the unemployed. In the early morning hours of Sunday 8 May 1932, attempts were made to burn two separate city relief offices; although fire investigators were unable to lay any charges, specific signs cast considerable suspicion on dissatisfied relief workers. Once hailed as the salvation of dignity amongst the city's jobless, the Broadway Bridge bad become a lightning rod of worker discontent; once regarded as the answer to Saskatoon's unemployment problems, the bridge now seemed to cause more problems than it solved.

Despite the clear deterioration in relations between the city's jobless and Saskatoon's municipal authorities through the spring and summer of 1932, the bridge project had been at least a qualified success. By mid June, the project had provided more than 1,400 unemployed men with work and had paid nearly $200,000 in wages since construction began seven months earlier.[51] Workers had finished pouring concrete into the piers by late July and had laid part of the bridge's surface by August; but the nearly completed bridge made manifest the problems surrounding the presence of unoccupied and unemployed men in the city. On 14 September Commissioner Leslie announced what most of the city's residents had long suspected: Saskatoon could no longer provide work relief to the city's jobless. Although the federal government had extended the *Unemployment and Farm Relief Act* past the March 1932 deadline, allowing works in progress to be completed, no new dominion funds for urban public works projects were forthcoming. In September 1932, even the most stubbornly optimistic residents harboured no doubts as to the longevity and seriousness of the unemployment problem. Gone were the days when better times were said to be just around the corner; and although the city had collectively planned, initiated, and constructed an impressive series of public works, those days were gone too. Work relief costs had simply grown too high too quickly, and rather than embark on a new variation of the old work for wages theme, Prime Minister Bennett withdrew financial support for urban public works in favour of the less expensive direct relief. To compensate Canadian cities suddenly left with legions of unemployed men with nothing to do, Ottawa and the provinces opted for financing relief camps for the unemployed.

But the federal promise to finance relief camps for the urban unemployed did little to ease the fears, uncertainty, and tension amongst Saskatoon's jobless. On 7 November, the city's unemployed clashed with local police over the opening of a federally and provincially sponsored relief camp for the single unemployed. The *Star Phoenix* carried a description of the day's violence:

> Wielding blood-soaked batons and sticks, police and the unemployed clashed in a fierce pitched battle at two o'clock this afternoon. Charging a yelling mob of workless, nearly ninety officers accounted for a dozen or more casualties and half-dozen arrests.[52]

Construction on the Broadway Bridge began during a time of relative uncertainty. In December 1931, neither the federal nor the provincial nor even the municipal governments could foresee the development of events through the following year that led to the first appearance of violence associated with Saskatoon's unemployment problem. But the federal withdrawal from financing urban work after November 1932 exacerbated an increasingly tense relationship between Saskatoon's unemployed and the city's municipal officials. Although the federal withdrawal from financing urban work programs seemed inevitable, it was no mere policy shift: rather, it was a complete reversal of the federal unemployment strategy. During his 1930 election campaign, Prime Minister

Bennett had promised work for wages, the abolishment of the dole, and an end to unemployment. By 1932, unemployment levels were higher than ever, direct relief was Ottawa's new approach to the unemployment problem, and the era of work for wages was over. A federal policy shift of such proportions was not just an admission that work relief was insufficient: it was an admission that the Depression could no longer properly be termed a short-term emergency—it had become a long-term crisis.

The Broadway Bridge stands today much as it did in November 1932. Though Saskatoon's skyline has since grown, the bridge remains one of its more recognizable features; and although other spans have been built across the South Saskatchewan in the years following the Depression, the Broadway Bridge remains a convenient and much used conduit between the popular Broadway district and the city's downtown. But the Broadway Bridge is more than a recognizable feature or a convenient conduit: it is a reminder, a physical manifestation, of the city's attempts to deal with the mass unemployment of the 1930s; it is a reminder of the end of work relief and the beginning of direct relief; and it is a reminder of the short-term emergency that became a long-term crisis.

NOTES

This article was first published in *Prairie Forum* 26, no. 2 (2001): 169–186.

1 Quoted in *Labour Gazette*, December 1929: 1326.
2 City of Saskatoon Archives [hereafter SA], D500 III 895, Chief Engineer Archibald to City Commissioner Leslie, 24 December 1929.
3 In fact, a September 1924 Provincial-Dominion unemployment conference concluded that "all federal, provincial, and municipal work now under construction should be continued with full complement of employees during the winter months."
4 *Star Phoenix* [hereafter SP], 8 September 1929.
5 SA, D500 III 895, Deputy Minister Molloy to Leslie, 16 December 1929.
6 Ibid.
7 *Labour Gazette*, February 1922, pp. 192–93. Termed "local responsibility," both tradition and the order-in-council left responsibility for the urban unemployed clearly in municipal hands.
8 SA, D500 III 893, Saskatoon Unemployment Conference Report, 23 December 1929.
9 SA, D500 III 895, Mayor Webb to Mayor Hair, 1 February 1930.
10 National Archives of Canada [hereafter NA], RG 27, vol. 3133, Conference Minutes, 1 March 1930.
11 Ibid.

12   Quoted in J. H. Thompson and A. Seager, *Canada, 1922–1939: Decades of Discord* (Toronto: McLelland and Stewart, 1985), 197.

13   Contributory, as well as non-contributory unemployment insurance plans were widely discussed solutions to unemployment well before the onset of World War 1. Little progress on the topic had been made by 1930, and certainly no consensus as to their viability or implementation had ever been agreed upon. See James Struthers, *No Fault of Their Own: Unemployment and the Canadian Welfare State, 1914–1941* (Toronto: University of Toronto Press, 1983), 13, 22–23, 44.

14   SA, D500 III 895, Conference between Hair and City Foremen, 27 April 1930.

15   *SP*, 11 April 1930.

16   Ibid.

17   Ibid., 10 July 1930.

18   SA, 1069-1521 (3), Lily Whaley to Hair, 7 July 1930.

19   SA, 1069-1521 (3), Archibald to Hair, 9 July 1930.

20   *SP*, 28 June 1930.

21   SA, D500 III 895, Council Minutes, 7 July 1930.

22   Struthers, *No Fault of Their Own*, 44.

23   *Labour Gazette*, September 1930: 996.

24   SA, D500 III 895, Council Minutes, 13 October 1930 and 26 October 1930.

25   SA, 1069-2055 (8), City Clerk Tomlinson to Calgary City Clerk, 12 January 1931.

26   SA, 1069-2055 (9), Saskatoon to provincial government, 18 March 1931.

27   SA, 1069-1522 (2), Council Minutes, 1 June 1931.

28   SA, 1069-2055 (5), Premier Anderson to Tomlinson, 9 July 1931.

29   The two federal unemployment relief acts required municipal authorities to submit proposals through their respective provincial governments rather than through the federal government directly. This measure reduced federal administrative costs significantly.

30   SA, 1069-1573 (3), Hair to Merkley, 4 August 1931 and 6 August 1931.

31   SA, 1069-1573 (3), Meeting between Hair, Leslie, and Archibald, 15 July 1931.

32   SA, 1069-1573 (3), Archibald to Leslie, 18 September 1931.

33   SA, 1069-1521 (1), Molloy to Tomlinson, 13 October 1931.

34   SA, 1069-219 (l) and (12), Archibald to Leslie, 18 November 1931.

35   B. Broadfoot, *Ten Lost Years: Memories of Canadians Who Survived the Depression* (Toronto: Doubleday Canada, 1973), 70.

36   SA, 1069-2055 (8), Tomlinson to Charlotte Whitton, 6 January 1931.

37   SA, 1069-2055 (1), A. C. MacNeil to Hair, 25 September 1931.

38   SA, 1069-2055 (1), Council Minutes, 31 August 1931.

39   *SP*, 5 September 1931.

40   SA, D500 III 893. Circular letter from Mayor Hair to all new aldermanic candidates, 17 November 1930.

41   SA, D500 III 895, Council Minutes, 10 July 1931. Demonstrations of the unemployed had generally been peaceful. On 1 June 1931, for example, a crowd of some three hundred jobless marched on Mayor Hair's Saskatoon home and demanded immediate relief. Hair assured the crowd that the city was doing all it could and that "none will starve." On the same day, Saskatoon's City Council blamed Saskatoon Local Unemployed

Association President Steve Forkin for the demonstration and branded him an "agitator" and a "parasite."

42 SA, 1069-2055 (1), Steve Forkin to City Council, 9 December 1931.
43 *SP*, 12 December 1931.
44 "Broadway Bridge Construction," reel to reel film (Local History Room, Saskatoon Public Library 1932).
45 SA, 1069-219 (12), Special Committee Minutes, 14 February 1932.
46 Ibid.
47 *SP*, 23 February 1932.
48 Ibid., and ibid., 23 March 1932.
49 *SP*, 26 March 1932.
50 *SP*, 19 April 1932.
51 NA, RG 27 vol. 2247, File Progress Report, December 1932.
52 *SP*, 7 November 1932.

12. Robert Weir: Forgotten Farmer-Minister in R. B. Bennett's Depression-Era Cabinet

Gregory P. Marchildon and Carl Anderson

As federal minister of Agriculture from 1930 to 1935, Robert Weir held an important post during one of the most difficult decades in Canada's history: the Great Depression. Falling prices for wheat and other staple exports, rampant unemployment and a series of major drought-induced crop failures on the prairies are among the more familiar misfortunes experienced in the 1930s. Weir was responsible for developing and administering a number of policies to facilitate recovery, from overseeing the expenditure of millions of dollars worth of federal relief aid to avert mass starvation on the prairies to promoting diversified farming and orderly marketing to improve farm commodity prices. However, his chief legacy was his creation of what would become known as the Prairie Farm Rehabilitation Administration (PFRA)—a federal agency with a mandate to restore and stabilize agricultural production in the drought-prone Palliser Triangle through soil and water conservation initiatives and land use readjustment and resettlement programs. But despite all this, Weir is a forgotten individual both in Canada and in Saskatchewan.

Robert Weir was a reluctant politician. In fact, journalists of his day compared him to the ancient Roman hero Cincinnatus, who was coerced by his countrymen to leave his quiet, simple life on the farm for a time to lead the Roman army in a desperate but successful attempt to rout an enemy invasion.[1] As head of the federal Department of Agriculture during the Great Depression, Weir had to deal with an "enemy" that no one man or government was capable of overcoming. Although world wheat prices and the weather could not be controlled, Weir gradually realized that the application of scientific soil and water conservation methods on Palliser Triangle farms could at least reduce

Robert Weir (Courtesy of the Provincial Archives of Saskatchewan / R-B 11272).

the hazards associated with grain growing during drought. Faced with quickly deteriorating economic, social and political circumstances on the prairies in his final year in office, Weir brought new money and a stronger focus to existing federal drought mitigation activities through the Prairie Farm Rehabilitation Act—the enabling legislation for what would become the Prairie Farm Rehabilitation Administration (PFRA). Although the PFRA would achieve a considerable respect and fame for its efforts in reclaiming the vast tracts of Dust Bowl land, it was William Lyon Mackenzie King's Liberal government in general and his minister of Agriculture, James G. Gardiner, in particular, who took the political credit for its achievements. Dying unexpectedly in a freak accident less than four years after his departure from government, Weir had limited opportunity to defend his legacy or set the record straight about the PFRA. In the end, history is largely written by victors or survivors. Robert Weir was neither.

ROBERT WEIR'S LIFE BEFORE POLITICS

Robert Weir was born in Huron County, Ontario on 5 December 1882.[2] He grew up on the family farm, was educated in a small rural school and later went to high school in the town of Clinton. He attended teachers' college, then known as normal school, in London, Ontario. He then worked briefly as a schoolteacher in his home county before serving a four year stint as a school principal in the town of Marmara near Peterborough. He used his savings from these and other jobs to finance his further education at the University of Toronto where he graduated with a first-class degree in mathematics in 1911. This led to a new career as an actuary with the Confederation Life Insurance Company in Toronto.[3] Weir then spent his spare time studying graduate-level actuarial science but the combined pressures of work and school resulted in a breakdown in his health—the first of many that would plague his short life. In 1912, he moved to Saskatchewan to take a less stressful job as a mathematics teacher at Regina Collegiate Institute, a high school that had just been built in 1909.[4]

Weir stood out as a teacher. According to the reports of school inspectors, his teaching in mathematics was "vigorous and effective" with the lessons "developed logically" and the classes themselves "thoroughly stimulated and controlled."[5] Weir was also popular with his students, and his own highly disciplined nature made him a natural leader in extracurricular activities. He was an outstanding athletic coach in charge of the Collegiate's rugby, hockey and track teams.[6] In 1914, when some 1,200 high school boys from across Saskatchewan attended a provincial track meet at Fort Qu'Appelle, four of Weir's boys captured sixty-one out of a possible sixty-four prizes at the competition; his boys also won first prize for shooting as well as a "large silk Union Jack" flag for the best disciplined team at the event.[7] He also oversaw

Robert Weir with his basketball team at Regina Collegiate Institute in 1915 (Courtesy of the Provincial Archives of Saskatchewan / R-B 2999).

the physical and rifle drills as instructor for the Collegiate's Cadet Corps that had the privilege of serving as Guard of Honour for the Duke of Connaught when he visited Regina in October 1912.[8] Weir himself had joined the local militia earlier that year.[9]

The outbreak of World War 1 cut short Weir's teaching career. Almost immediately after the 1914–15 academic year he enlisted in the 95th Saskatchewan Rifles, a unit that was part of the 195th Overseas Battalion of the Canadian Expeditionary Force.[10] Wanting to fight for King and country, Weir waited impatiently to be sent to the front lines. Weir's Battalion arrived in England in February 1916. His competency as a training officer led to a series of promotions, from Lieutenant to Captain and then to Major by October of 1916. But instead of being shipped to the front, he remained in England training troops. Frustrated, he finally gave up his rank as Major in order to get himself transferred to the 78th Overseas Battalion on the front line in France in February 1917.[11]

During his first months of heavy fighting, Weir was fortunate enough not to suffer any injury or illness more serious than "trench fever"—a common bacterial infection among soldiers. However, his luck would run out at the Battle of Passchendaele at the end of October 1917. Weir was showered with shrapnel from an exploding German artillery shell and incapacitated for the rest of the war.[12] While recovering from his extensive injuries in a hospital bed in London, he came up with the idea of a correspondence course for disabled soldiers, and he set out at once to organize the Correspondence Department as part of Canada's existing Khaki University in England.[13] He was made director of this new department, and by November 1918 it had an enrollment of some five thousand soldiers.[14]

Still, demobilization meant that even the most disabled soldier-students would soon be returning to Canada, and this presented Weir with a dilemma about his own future. Having had the experience of managing a large educational department, Weir was unwilling to return to his life as a teacher. He carried on a lengthy correspondence with the Liberal Premier of Saskatchewan, W. M. Martin, whom he had met when Martin visited the Khaki University in the summer of 1918.[15] Weir lobbied Martin on the idea of the province establishing an immigration office in London, similar to offices then being operated by Ontario, British Columbia and Alberta, suggesting that he was particularly suited to be Saskatchewan's official representative in Britain.[16] Martin was cool to the proposal. In his response, Martin noted that Manitoba had no representative and Alberta had just recalled its representative and concluded that the question of immigration was really one for the Dominion government.[17]

Instead, Martin, who was much more focused on the need for improving the quality of education for non-English-speaking immigrants in rural Saskatchewan, offered Weir the job of school inspector for the Kerrobert School Division, west of Saskatoon.[18] Weir's new job involved constant traveling. Between June and December 1919 alone, he drove exactly 3,281 miles to visit seventy-eight of the ninety-four rural and urban school districts within the Kerrobert School Division, mainly working with new immigrant communities of Ukrainians, Russians and Mennonites.[19] Still, the job was onerous, and Weir's sensitivity to stress combined with his war injuries led to his losing a remarkable fifty-five days to illness in 1919.[20]

Weir continued working as a school inspector for a couple more years until his doctors finally advised him to consider a less stressful occupation, preferably outdoors. In 1922, at forty years of age, he bought a quarter section farm three miles east of the village of Weldon, Saskatchewan, between Melfort and Prince Albert. He selected the land with the help of his brother who farmed in the area.[21] Located in the scenic Carrot River Valley, his land was ideal for the type of mixed farming he was so familiar with in Ontario. The region's sub-humid climate and fertile black soils were well adapted for growing a variety of cereal, hay and forage crops, and its gently rolling topography, abundant bush and plentiful streams and sloughs provided ample shelter and water for livestock.[22] However, Weir's new farm required clearing, and he kept his job as school inspector until 1924 while he prepared it for cultivation and raised enough money to buy livestock. He also got married at this time.[23]

As it turned out, Weir's new career was a perfect fit. He applied to agriculture his mathematical mind, managerial abilities and personal devotion to higher learning with diligence and enthusiasm. He invested strategically in land and purebred livestock when agriculture was in a recession in the years after World War I.[24] Weir had a keen sense of judging livestock—a skill he had likely developed during his university days when he was a regular "rail bird" at livestock shows. He also grew much of his own livestock feed to keep his operating costs low; his fields were cultivated with cereals such as wheat, oats, barley and flax and pasture crops of clover and rye grass. As well, Weir made good use of the best scientific advice and professional guidance available to run his farm as efficiently as possible, and he gradually turned his acres into a farm laboratory. He developed friendships with such agricultural experts as Professors Lawrence Winters and L. E. Kirk of the Saskatchewan College of Agriculture at Saskatoon and John Latham, the dean of the American Hereford Breeders and a respected stock judge in selecting his animals. He even hired trained farm managers to help him develop scientific breeding and feeding procedures to improve the quality of his stock and to grow experimental varieties of oats and alfalfa suited for the Carrot River Valley's relatively short and cool growing season.[25]

Within a decade, Weir's hard work and determination had transformed a modest quarter section of land into one of Canada's most successful farms. By 1930, his farm—officially named "Hereford Park Farm"—occupied seven quarters (1,120 acres compared to the average farm size of 400 acres) and featured many fine buildings and a first-class assortment of purebred livestock including 70 head of Hereford cattle, 20 registered Percheron horses, 75 Shropshire sheep, 12 Berkshire swine and a sizable Flock of registered Plymouth Rocks.[26] He regularly attended major livestock shows across North America and his animals often won blue ribbons and gold medals.[27] Because of this, Weir's farm became a major attraction in its own right; almost every weekend he and his wife would entertain crowds of visitors from near and far wanting to tour the farm and view the livestock. In 1930, he and his wife hosted a picnic at their farm for the Canadian Hereford and Percheron Associations in conjunction with the Canadian National Railways.[28] Little did Weir know that as the 1920s drew to a close he would soon leave his beloved farm in the hands of his manager and his wife to enter the world of politics and government.

ROBERT WEIR'S ENTRY INTO FEDERAL POLITICS

In 1930, Robert Weir—along with millions of his countrymen—could only watch helplessly as the prosperity of the previous decade gave way to a global economic depression with Prairie grain farmers hit particularly hard. Agriculture was Canada's largest single industry at the time, employing roughly one third of the country's workforce. It provided raw materials for many Canadian manufactures, and its products made up three-fifths of Canadian exports.[29] During the 1920s, Canada's economy had become especially dependent on the production and sale of wheat on world markets; by 1929, wheat exports were worth roughly *one third* of the value of all Canadian exports.[30] By this time, however, worldwide overproduction of agricultural products combined with a post-war recovery in Europe led to a sharp fall in international prices, and markets for Canadian agricultural exports all but vanished. A bushel of No. 1 Northern wheat that had sold for $1.23 in 1925 fetched only 49¢ in 1930.[31] Many countries reacted by levying stiff import duties to protect their own economies. In March 1930, for example, the United States, a major market for Canadian beef, dairy and poultry products, enacted the Hawley-Smoot tariff, which erected barriers against the importation of these and other commodities.[32] The resulting decline in farm incomes had grave repercussions for Canada's manufacturing, transportation and service industries, causing further cutbacks in investment, production and staffing. The unemployment rate was 12.5 percent in 1928 and climbing by the winter of 1930.[33]

At the same time, W. L. Mackenzie King, the incumbent Liberal Prime Minister, insisted that the federal government had no obligation to provide relief to the unemployed. In contrast, R. B. Bennett, the Conservative party leader, promised to provide employment "for those of our people who are able to work" and to fix the country's ailing wheat economy.[34] Bennett understood that his party's best hopes of winning a parliamentary majority lay in wooing rural voters, especially in the Prairie Provinces. The first plank in the Conservatives' eight-point election platform promised new tariffs to restore the home market for both manufacturers and farmers. Bennett assumed that higher Canadian tariffs might one day "blast away" into other desirable markets for Canadian farm products by forcing other countries to enter into reciprocal tariff-lowering agreements with Canada.[35] The second plank committed the party to "foster and develop agriculture and the livestock and dairy industries" so that home production would replace imports from other countries.[36]

The Conservatives looked for attractive candidates capable of selling their solution to the Depression. When the election was announced in May 1930, numerous delegations showed up at Hereford Park Farm urging Weir to run for Parliament despite the fact that he had attended only one political meeting in his life and had never held an elected position, except that of rural school trustee. Weir insisted that he was non-partisan and saw politics through the single lens of what would benefit farmers. The Conservative organizers listened to his argument that farmers in his area wanted to be "represented by a person who had been a farmer but had not been tied down to any political party, whether Liberal, Conservative or Progressive."[37] To some extent, Conservative worries about Weir's non-partisan nature were put to rest by Weir's longtime friendship with Saskatchewan's most prominent Conservative, Premier J. T. M. Anderson. Anderson had managed to forge an alliance with provincial Progressives to form a government after the election of 1929, and he encouraged Weir to enter federal politics under the Conservative banner.[38]

Once Weir's name was put forward as one of four Conservative Party nominees, his candidacy immediately gained momentum. He was known as a successful yet generous man, known to lend tractors, farm implements, supplies of livestock feed and even the breeding services of his bulls and stallions to his neighbours.[39] His school inspectorship had brought him into contact with the European-born farmers of northern Saskatchewan, an electoral bloc in the Melfort constituency which, prior to Weir, had not been drawn to the Conservative Party. At the nominating convention in June 1930, Weir obtained a majority vote on the first ballot. After a "great outburst of cheering," he pledged to run "as an independent Conservative" who would always vote "in the interests of the farmers of Canada."[40]

In the general election, Weir faced Malcolm McLean, the Liberal incumbent who had vanquished his Conservative opponent in the 1925 and 1926 federal elections.[41] Perhaps because of the impact of the recession, voter turnout in the Melfort riding on 28 July 1930 was higher than average. Weir received 7,535 votes, a clear margin of victory over McLean's 6,248 votes, and a Farmers' Party candidate who was relegated to a mere 1,187 votes.[42]

Despite his popularity with farmers, Weir still remained a political neophyte surrounded by a number of experienced Conservative candidates from across Canada and should not have expected to enter Bennett's cabinet.[43] However, a number of influential voices would convince the Prime Minister to make him Minister of Agriculture. Two of Premier Anderson's provincial ministers, W. C. Buckle (Agriculture) and J. F. Bryant (Public Works), had written to Bennett immediately after the election urging him to include Weir in his cabinet.[44] In his letter, Bryant was impressed at how Weir's efficient and scientific breeding and feeding techniques were netting him top-quality livestock and fair profits despite falling farm commodity prices. He explained how Weir had

> bought six hundred chicks, culled out the roosters and paid for the chickens and for the feed for them until they grew up by the sale of the roosters. He then had one of the Government officials cull the hens and kept only the good layers so that when they were a year old he had one hundred and fifty Plymouth Rock chickens which averaged twelve dozen…eggs per day, for which he obtained $6.00 per day [about $75 in 2007 dollars] in the month of January. His henhouse was not heated in any way and he got results by a special feed which he had prepared himself, and by putting straw over the top of the hen house with a window at the end of the loft with a screen over it, so that the air would not be too cold on the hens when it came down, and by properly eliminating the foul air. Ordinarily, brooding hens would brood for a week or two but Major Weir got around this by putting the hens in a nest with slats at the bottom so that the breast of the hen would not be kept warm and they quit brooding within a day or so.[45]

Livestock associations in Saskatchewan and Alberta had also flooded the Prime Minister's office with telegrams endorsing Weir as Minister of Agriculture. They pointed to his agricultural successes in their petitions and felt generally that he had the expertise necessary to make Canada's ailing livestock industry profitable once again.[46] But when asked by Bennett to be the minister of Agriculture, Weir hesitated, telling Bennett that he was uneasy because of his political inexperience. Bennett reassured him that he wanted him "not to be a minister of politics but Minister of Agriculture" and Weir accepted.[47]

ROBERT WEIR'S FIRST RESPONSE TO THE GREAT DEPRESSION

Overnight, Robert Weir had been catapulted from his life as a mixed farmer living in relative isolation in north-central Saskatchewan to a federal minister in Ottawa who assumed the role of "a farmer speaking to farmers."[48] He quickly realized, however, that R. B. Bennett was in charge. As historian Larry Glassford has noted, the only outstanding minister permitted in the new Conservative cabinet was Bennett "because the prime minister neither wanted nor would permit anyone else to excel."[49] Bennett insisted on making and announcing the important decisions, and he often introduced legislation in the House of Commons that should have been handled by ministers. Bennett decided how to deal with the crisis of the Great Depression. Just five weeks after the election, Bennett called an emergency session of Parliament. The Unemployment Relief Act was passed to provide $20 million for direct relief and to help the provinces and municipalities finance job-creating public works projects.[50] Bennett then announced a series of tariff increases on manufactured goods such as textiles, iron and steel products and machinery—mainly from outside the British Empire.[51] Beyond relief, nothing addressed the desperate situation of Prairie wheat farmers facing both drought and collapsing wheat prices.

The dramatic fall in wheat prices after 1929 stemmed largely from a glut of wheat on world markets brought on by bountiful grain crops in Australia, Argentina, Russia and Canada. Nowhere in the country was the impact felt more strongly than in Weir's home province. In 1929, about 85 percent of Saskatchewan's workforce was dependent on agriculture, and three-quarters of all agricultural revenues in the province were derived from wheat.[52] Indeed, Saskatchewan had earned a reputation as "Canada's Bread Basket" by this time. In the bumper harvest of 1928, the province produced over three-fifths of all wheat grown in the Prairie Provinces (some 321 million bushels—half of Canada's total wheat crop) and possessed a slightly greater proportion of total prairie wheat acreage, and the falling wheat prices would cause the average per capita income in Saskatchewan to drop by 72 percent between 1929 and 1933.[53] The global wheat glut had also left the prairie wheat pools stuck with vast reserves of unsold grain, and in the fall of 1930 Prime Minister Bennett had been forced to commission his chief grain advisor, John I. MacFarland, to liquidate the pools' assets to save them from bankruptcy.[54]

As Weir saw it, it was time for Canada to become less dependent on King Wheat and the export market. As a mixed farmer with a substantial personal stake in stock breeding, Weir's policy interpretation reflected his own approach to agriculture. "The only difference office will make to me," Weir affirmed in one of his first public addresses as Minister of Agriculture "is that I now consider my farm has had its boundaries extended across the whole of Canada."[55] Indeed, only a portion of Canada's wheat exports were actually No. 1 grade and the cheaper, lower-grade grains were often fed to livestock when they reached their markets. Weir—along with other agricultural analysts at the time—felt that some or all of these grains could, and should, be kept in Canada where they could be fed to Canadian livestock.[56] Not only would they be removed from the competition of other countries' lower quality grain on world markets (thereby raising the price for No. 1 Canadian wheat), they might be sold to Canadian farmers at a cost comparable to or better than the world price and be "manufactured" into finished livestock and livestock products for export.

To be sure, Weir was aware that not all parts of Canada were adapted for mixed farming. As a former resident of Regina, he would have understood that the majority of farmers in the Palliser Triangle of southeastern Alberta, southern Saskatchewan and the southwestern tip of Manitoba had long specialized in the production of cereals, especially wheat. This immense and semi-arid expanse of land not only experienced an annual moisture deficit but was prone to periodic cycles of severe drought.[57] Wheat's deep roots allowed it to survive in a semiarid climate better than other cereals, while the flat, almost treeless landscape in large parts of the region lent itself well to extensive grain growing.[58] Though farmers in the Palliser Triangle depended on wheat for their income, they still kept some cattle, sheep, swine and poultry in addition to their workhorses for subsistence and a little extra income.[59] In the Palliser Triangle's driest and more rugged areas in southeastern Alberta, cattle ranches had supplanted wheat farms.[60] Weir's plan was to encourage a dramatic increase in livestock production that in turn would create a "home market" for feed grains benefiting at least some Prairie farmers.

Part of this plan required that Weir find new markets for Canadian livestock. The Conservatives had long since written off the American market as too volatile. They had instead hoped to win favour in the British market, and Bennett had promised to negotiate a new trading system within the British Empire based on "reciprocal preference" during the election campaign. Weir was particularly enthusiastic about increasing shipments of cattle, Canada's chief live animal export at the time. Even though the country's cattle exports were worth a tiny fraction of the value of its wheat exports, he pursued his goal with his characteristic determination.[61] Within a week of taking office, he announced his plans to secure lower ocean freight rates and outfit ships to carry a trial shipment of cattle from eastern Canada to England to learn how shipping costs might be reduced. Soon thereafter a load of steers from Alberta and Saskatchewan was sent.[62] Weir also advocated lower interprovincial shipping rates to help Canadian stock raisers take advantage of prairie grains, and he had soon arranged a 50 percent freight reduction on feed shipped from Saskatchewan's central and northern grain belts to the southern rangelands.[63]

Weir was determined to run the federal Department of Agriculture with the same emphasis on efficiency and shrewd management that he had used on his own farm. He therefore sought to promote greater cooperation between the provinces and the federal Department of Agriculture to elimi-nate overlapping of administration. He acknowledged that he was a political novice, and he therefore solicited professional advice to help him flesh out his agricultural policy. In early November 1930, Weir invited the provincial Ministers of Agriculture and professors from agricultural colleges across Canada to a conference at Ottawa—the first such meeting of its kind. The conference outlined certain measures—known as the "National Agricultural Policy"—to reduce production costs and to raise the quality of livestock and livestock products at the farm level.[64] On 22 November, Weir announced that his department would begin lending purebred bulls and selling top quality sows to farmers at reduced shipping rates. In March 1931, further steps were taken to help western farmers establish themselves in the breeding of beef and dairy cattle by refunding freight charges on carloads of accredited stock from eastern Canada.[65]

Weir also promoted the scientific use of home-grown feed products for livestock; control of poultry diseases; and careful study of the science of rural marketing. In a letter to one correspondent in late 1930, Weir asserted that "many farmers could be benefited if they were in possession of the ideas of more constructive farmers and of the results of experiments that would prevent waste of time and feed on their part in finding out for themselves."[66] Weir understood that most Canadian farmers did not have the time, money or facilities to refine or disseminate these experiments. He felt this should be the government's responsibility, and one of his main goals as Minister of Agriculture was to bring them in closer contact with the Dominion Experimental Farms Service (DEFS).

Founded in 1886 as a branch of the Department of Agriculture, DEFS was operating twenty-nine Experimental Farms and Stations and eleven substations across Canada as of 1931, amassing an enormous volume of data on plant and animal breeding and field and animal husbandry methods. Traditionally, DEFS had broadcast its research results to the public through pamphlets, bulletins and farm journals, through field days at the farms and stations and through a network of over two hundred Illustration Stations spread across Canada.[67] The final installment in Weir's agricultural policy—first made public in *Maclean's Magazine* in March 1931—was to transform DEFS facilities into "local educational centers" that would actively seek farmers' attention. Seed grain inspection and assistance with soil testing and the application of fertilizers would be given to grain farmers to increase yields and grades. Free disease inspections for poultry were conducted to weed out unproductive birds. As well, more research on feeds and education campaigns was undertaken in order to acquaint farmers with those feeds that gave the best results.[68]

It was not long before Weir's "National Agricultural Policy" caused a stir, and the Liberal opposition was especially vocal. Though the Conservatives had won a majority in 1930, the Liberals were still numerous enough in the House of Commons to put up a spirited resistance. In a letter to one correspondent that December, opposition leader Mackenzie King criticized Weir's "home market doctrine" given the fact that "Canada depends on the sale of her wheat more than all else."[69] King had a point. Assuming that Canadian farmers could rapidly enlarge their livestock herds, they would still only use a mere fraction of the hundreds of millions of bushels of grain prairie farmers grew each year.[70] And while higher tariffs might have helped the manufacturers of central Canada, they did nothing for those Canadians who relied on export markets. In fact, they were a disadvantage, since other countries were not inclined to admit Canadian farm products—no matter what the quality—if Canada refused to accept their products in return. Between 1930 and 1931, the number of live Canadian cattle shipped out of the country had fallen by a staggering 80 percent and the value of exports of dairy and meat products dropped by one third and two thirds, respectively. From 1929 to 1933, the average for all Canadian farm prices had fallen nearly 60 percent.[71] With no major foreign markets for Canadian livestock, whatever "home market" there might have been for prairie grains all but vanished. World wheat prices had meanwhile continued to fall; a bushel of wheat worth $0.49 in 1930 had dropped to $0.35 by 1932.

When Parliament opened in 1931, the Liberal opposition (especially the prairie Liberal MPs) took every opportunity to blast the Conservatives for their handling of the agricultural crisis. On 28 April, Manitoba Liberal MP J. L. Brown opened an extended debate on farming conditions and unemployment, expressing regret that the Bennett government "had failed to implement its definite promises with respect to agriculture."[72] Bennett vehemently denied this allegation, but the Liberals continued to harass the Conservatives about what concrete plans they had to deal with slumping farm prices. Although Parliament had been in session for seven weeks, Weir had still not made an official announcement of his policy to the House. On May 5, W. R. Motherwell—Liberal MP for Melville, Saskatchewan and the Minister of Agriculture in the previous government—suggested before the House that this was because he had been "on the leash and under the gag" of the Prime Minister.[73]

On May 7 Weir finally made his first address to Parliament. Delivered at the brisk rate of two hundred words per minute, Weir delivered what should have been an hour-long speech within the Parliamentary limit of forty minutes. By the time he had finished attacking the Liberal opposition, he only had minutes to explain his policies on encouraging the livestock industry. His partisan speech was followed by "an outbreak of Conservative cheering and desk-thumping" which lasted many minutes.[74] However, he dodged the wheat situation entirely, and Jack Vallance—Liberal MP for Saskatchewan's South Battleford riding—was quick to point out his apparent disregard for the prairie wheat grower. According to Vallance, Weir had

> amply demonstrated beyond a doubt that he had no knowledge of either politics or agriculture. If I were to ask the people of Canada, what is the most outstanding question before the agricultural people of this country to-day, with one voice they would answer: Markets for wheat. Yet the Minister of Agriculture never mentioned that subject. Perhaps his forty minutes was not long enough, but he took seven minutes to deal with matters that were of absolutely no consequence to this country.[75]

Although Weir told the press that he originally intended to address wheat policy in the concluding part of his speech but time had run out, it was more likely that Weir did not know what to say, and prairie Liberal MPs continued to accuse Weir of pandering to Alberta ranchers and Saskatchewan stock farmers who wanted to make "a second Ontario" out of the region.[76] Some

Conservatives even began to doubt Weir's ability to speak for prairie agricultural interests. In March 1931, for example, one party insider from Weyburn, Saskatchewan wrote to Bennett stating that "the North of this Province is vastly different from the South" and he urged him to consider F. W. Turnbull, the Conservative MP for Regina as an ideal spokesman for wheat farmers in the event of a cabinet shuffle.[77]

ROBERT WEIR AND SEVERE DROUGHT IN THE PALLISER TRIANGLE

Unfortunately for Weir, collapsing world markets and low wheat prices were only part of the problem facing western farmers in the early 1930s. A severe drought had struck the Palliser Triangle in the summer of 1929. By autumn, it was clear that Saskatchewan's wheat harvest was only one half of what it had been the year before.[78] At first, the drought was dismissed as a temporary phenomenon but drought would become a permanent guest in the Palliser Triangle for the remainder of the decade. The situation in 1930 was bad enough but 1931 was devastating. In that year, the Saskatchewan wheat harvest was nearly 20 percent smaller than that of 1929.[79] The reduced production combined with the lower grain prices threatened to completely wipe out farm incomes. By 1931, an estimated 150,000 people in Saskatchewan alone were completely destitute due to crop failures, and they were unable to buy such necessities as food, clothing and fuel to make it through the winter.[80]

Successive crop failures also decimated supplies of seed grain, making it impossible for countless farmers to plant a crop without emergency relief to purchase more seed. In addition, oats, barley and other feed crops withered, threatening hundreds of thousands of livestock in the Palliser Triangle with starvation.[81] Speaking to the House in July 1931, Bennett admitted that the prairie drought was perhaps "the greatest national calamity that has ever overtaken this country."[82] He introduced the Unemployment and Farm Relief Act to provide federal relief aid for the drought stricken prairie farmers. Its terms were more generous than those of the 1930 Act: Ottawa now paid 50¢ of every relief dollar spent. But he still refused to commit to a permanent relief policy (the Act was set to expire on March 1, 1932) and he continued to insist that the provinces be responsible for distributing the money.[83] Due to the sheer magnitude of the disaster in Saskatchewan, the Anderson government set up the Saskatchewan Relief Commission (SRC) to distribute provincial and federal relief to its residents. Since so much federal money was now flowing into relief for prairie farmers, Weir kept in close touch with the Conservative chairman of the new relief commission.[84] After a thousand-mile tour of Saskatchewan's drought area in August 1931, he concluded that much of the land in the districts he visited "will be abandoned, so far as farming is concerned, for better land."[85] Indeed, countless Palliser Triangle farmers had suffered their third consecutive crop failure by this point, and many of them pulled up stakes in desperation and were moving into the more humid northern grain belt. In the House and in cabinet, Weir came under increasing pressure from the Liberal opposition and his own party to explain the vast amount of federal relief money pouring into his home province.

By the end of 1931, Weir had suffered yet another breakdown in his health, likely due to the stresses of office.[86] A year later, Weir complained in writing that it was becoming ever more difficult "to keep continuously before the minds of Cabinet, the difference in the Saskatchewan situation."[87] Desperate to reduce the number of western farmers on relief, Weir supported what appeared to be a cheaper and more convenient 'solution' to the prairie drought crisis including helping farmer families move north out of the Palliser Triangle.[88] Beyond this, however, Weir was not sure what to do. Part of his difficulty stemmed from his inability to appreciate the vulnerability of the Palliser Triangle relative to farms in the more northern fertile belt like his own in the Carrot River Valley. While wheat yields in Saskatchewan's four southernmost crop districts averaged just four bushels per acre in 1931, farmers in Weir's home crop district were harvesting twenty-three bushels per acre. In fact, Saskatchewan's central

Typical dust bowl storm in the Palliser Triangle in 1934 (near Lakeheath, Saskatchewan) (Courtesy of the Provincial Archives of Saskatchewan / R-A 4665).

and northern grain belts were receiving above average moisture conditions that year, and water for livestock and vegetable gardens was plentiful.[89] By contrast, streams, sloughs and even wells began drying up throughout the Palliser Triangle, forcing many farmers and ranchers to haul water for their livestock from two or more miles away. They could improve their lot by digging deeper wells or constructing dugouts and stock watering dams to trap whatever moisture fell from the sky. However, such projects were expensive, and with agricultural incomes at their lowest level in decades, few could afford them.[90] Indeed, Weir himself would admit that livestock had to have water within two miles of their pasturage if they were to remain in good condition.[91]

What is more, soils in parts of the Palliser Triangle had become so dry that they blew away in the wind. For decades, governments and corporations with a stake in western agriculture had been exhorting prairie farmers to summerfallow a portion of their land every year to help "store up" moisture for the next year's crop. However, the frequent cultivation required to clear the soil surface of moisture-robbing vegetation pulverized it almost to a powder, making it highly susceptible to wind erosion in drier years. The technique was largely responsible for the infamous "black blizzards" that darkened prairie skies in broad daylight—one of the most pronounced images of the Great Depression. Even pasture grasses withered. The minimum acreage required to provide pasture and feed per head of stock (horse or cow) for one year on the plains ranged from 30 acres in an average year to as much as 120 acres during a drought.[92]

For Weir, the question was no longer how to reduce dependence on wheat, but how to reduce the hazards of grain-growing in the drought prone Palliser Triangle. Fortunately, the Department's experimental stations were in a position to offer solid policy advice.[93] In response to a severe drought from 1917 to 1919, DEFS Stations at Lethbridge, Alberta (established in 1912), and Swift Current, Saskatchewan (established in 1920), had been studying strip farming and trash-covered fallow as a means of controlling soil erosion.[94] The Dominion Forage Crops Laboratory at the University of Saskatchewan had also been experimenting with drought-resistant grasses during the 1920s to reseed areas that had been overgrazed and reclaim inferior cropland, and successful field tests with these grasses had been carried out at the 18,000-acre Range Experimental Station at Manyberries in southeastern Alberta which had also experimented with a series of deep dugouts and earth dams on coulees to collect runoff for permanent stock watering and irrigation water supplies. By the early 1940s, these had raised the station's stock-carrying capacity from less than 100 head of cattle to 300 cattle plus 500 sheep and provided enough water to flood irrigate over 300 acres of land for hay production. In 1931, the

Department of Agriculture had acquired control of two forest nursery stations in Saskatchewan in order to provide suitable trees and shrubs to prairie farmers for shelterbelts to control soil erosion.[95] By May 1932, the Indian Head forest nursery station had provided thousands of tree and caragana seedlings for shelterbelt demonstration plots at the Regina jail, and supplies of clover and grass seed were supplied from elsewhere.[96] Weir also tried to funnel federal money into Saskatchewan to develop dams for water conservation but Bennett refused to pay the $200,000 requested.[97]

Meanwhile, the federal Conservatives were being blamed for the Great Depression. In response, Bennett and his cabinet began to pursue more radical policies. In April 1934, Weir introduced the Natural Products Marketing Act in Parliament, which created marketing boards for producers of primary food products (i.e., fruits, legumes, and dairy products) to protect them from further price deflation. He argued that the new law would give farmers "a parliament of their own in which to decide what would be the best and most efficient means in marketing their own products."[98] Shortly thereafter, Bennett piloted the Farmers' Creditors' Arrangement Act through Parliament. Through the appointment of official receivers as well as a board of review in every province, this law—the object of which was, in Bennett's words, "to keep the farmer on the land"—encouraged farmers and creditors to reach compromise settlements on outstanding debts.[99]

As for rehabilitating the drought-stricken Palliser Triangle, Weir suggested that his Department's existing work on the prairies could be reorganized into a more comprehensive plan of attack on the drought problem. Early in 1934 he had asked the directors of all experimental farms and stations in the Prairie Provinces to coordinate whatever information they had on soil-drifting control and plan further studies.[100] That June, the director of DEFS, E. S. Archibald informed Weir in a letter that his officials were prepared to discuss the results

> in a round table conference with Provincial men in each of the three provinces, where those interested from the colleges and provincial departments may criticize and generally support the work we anticipate doing on Experimental Farms, existing Illustration Stations and if necessary a few additional special Illustration Stations originated for this purpose.[101]

Pursuant to this, Archibald submitted a new set of DEFS initiatives to Weir on 17 July 1934.

The Saskatchewan election result of 19 June 1934 struck fear into the hearts of federal Conservatives. The Anderson Conservatives lost every seat while the Liberals roared back, winning almost every seat in the provincial Legislature.[102] Bennett and Weir now faced an experienced Liberal Premier in Saskatchewan: the pugnacious and highly partisan James G. Gardiner.[103] To make matters worse, drought returned with a vengeance in the summer of 1934. Dust storms and livestock feed shortages were worse than ever. Interestingly, prairie farmers were keeping more livestock than ever before, despite record low cattle prices. Between 1931 and 1935, the number of cattle in the Alberta and Saskatchewan drought areas rose from 1.2 million head to nearly 1.5 million head.[104] That fall, provincial authorities estimated that $7 million in relief feed and fodder was required for the coming winter, let alone basic relief provisions.[105]

To deal with the problem of starving cattle, Weir announced a plan to finance half the cost of shipping the stock to packing plants elsewhere in Canada, the provinces paying the other half.[106] However, the plan seemed too small and indirect a measure to redress the drought problem, and the newspapers joined Gardiner in condemning Weir and Bennett.[107] "It may be," wrote the editor of the Regina *Leader-Post*,

> that Ottawa does not like the present government of Saskatchewan and does not approve the methods for handling relief set up by the Gardiner Administration. It might provide or lend money to Saskatchewan if the Government of Saskatchewan were willing to do things in a different way...By next year it is highly probable that there will be a new Government at Ottawa and it is possible that a new set of men will give real consideration to the problem of Saskatchewan. New federal members from Saskatchewan may have more influence at Ottawa than the present members who have been concerned chiefly with assisting Mr. Bennett to pass legislation that has added little to the welfare of Western Canada...Those from the West who have had to deal with Hon. Robert Weir at Ottawa report his attitude as hopeless on the matter of the western relief situation.[108]

Some federal politicians were even suggesting that large areas of the Palliser Triangle should be *completely* evacuated. In February 1934, for example, British Columbia Senator A. O. Rae argued that the Dry Belt of southeastern

Alberta and southwestern Saskatchewan "should have been left to the cows," and that Ottawa would be stuck supporting the thirty thousand families in the region "for as long as they live" unless they were moved to areas where they could make a living.[109] Whatever Weir may have felt about the merits of depopulating the region, there were both practical and political impediments to pursuing this policy. The logistics of moving thirty thousand farm families out of the Dry Belt—much less the more than one hundred thousand farm families living in the rest of the Palliser Triangle—boggled the mind. More importantly, the northern agricultural frontier could only accommodate the smallest fraction of displaced Palliser Triangle farmers. These tended to be wooded or swampy areas that were difficult or impossible to prepare for cultivation. Northern migrants generally had little capital with which to buy land and equipment, and most still needed relief once they reached their destination, creating a huge burden for the northern RMs.

Northern settlement was also unpopular with corporations that had a stake in the region. For example, E. W. Beatty, president of the Canadian Pacific Railway, subsequently announced to the press that his company had lost an estimated $3 million in emergency freight rate reductions for prairie farm relief between 1930 and 1935.[110] Having toured southern Saskatchewan in August 1934, Beatty insisted that the region's problems could not be solved by moving its residents to other parts of the province. Such a policy, he argued,

> would be unfair to the people involved, unfair to the drouth areas and a great mistake for the province...The solution of the problem lies rather in the governments standing by the farmers with required assistance to bring them through the emergency, coupled with soil conservation on lands adapted to grain growing and the development of grazing land for grazing purposes, and a policy of water development and conservation for use on the farms.[111]

Weir hit back. Rewriting history, he argued in a press statement that he "had never taken the view" that a large number of the families in southern Saskatchewan's drought area should be moved elsewhere and added that "[a]nyone who looks back over the great crops these districts have produced must be convinced that with proper methods they could be made big produc-ers again."[112] He toured southern Saskatchewan to try and reassure farmers and salvage his reputation. Speaking to a Weyburn audience in October, he indicated that "if he were farming in the south he would stay here," and he used horror stories of northern resettlement to explain why. Weir also outlined the various soil and water conservation strategies that his Department had been working on. But because control of all lands and natural resources lay with the provinces, he suggested a cooperative strategy. Still, he added that "the situation is one primarily for the province to deal with as the dominion can only take such action as the provincial government will permit."[113]

It was apparent that the provinces were determined to do something with or without federal help. Gardiner was supported by Premier John Bracken of Manitoba, a dry farming expert in his own right.[114] Crop conditions in southwestern Manitoba were just as bad in as in southern Saskatchewan in the summer of 1934, and Bracken had written to Bennett in several occasions describing the conditions.[115] Although Manitoba's drought area was much smaller than that in Saskatchewan, the drought combined with low grain prices had a major impact on the economy of Winnipeg, the heart of the Canadian grain trade.[116] Bracken gave an important address on prairie drought rehabilitation at the Canadian Club in Winnipeg in October 1934. "The problem has now assumed proportions of national scope," Bracken declared, and he outlined a fourfold program of reclamation for the prairie drought areas. First, more trees should be planted for shelterbelts and more dugouts constructed for water storage purposes where stream water was not available. Second, inferior crop land should be withheld from settlement and instead regrassed for pasture. Third, education programs should be conducted to inform farmers about soil and moisture conservation. Finally, all reclamation activities should be guided by thorough soil, topographical and climatic surveys and economic studies of farms in the Prairie Provinces. Bracken ended with this appeal:

> Our duty is clear. We need a central coordinating body to bring unity and direction to the plan. The Dominion is that authority that should set it up. We need the cooperation of all the prairie provinces. We need the advice of the best technical men of the nation... The program, if it is to be worth while, will require heavy expenditures; the Dominion government is the only government that can provide the necessary additional funds.[117]

For his part, Bennett was facing increasing political pressure to do something more than simply provide relief to farm families in the Palliser Triangle. In one telling letter, an ex-Conservative MLA for Saskatchewan explained the prairie situation to his Conservative colleagues in Ottawa:

We need some propaganda out right now ourselves to put us right with the people. Conservatives have not got their ear close enough to the ground, we are not listening as our Liberals friends are doing. Rooseveldt [*sic*] is sure going over big in the U.S.A. No reason why we cannot do the same."[118]

In January 1935, Bennett presented his own "New Deal" through a series of paid radio broadcasts. Meanwhile, Gardiner—inspired by Bracken's ideas—invited the Alberta and Manitoba Premiers and their respective Ministers of Agriculture to meet at Saskatoon that month. They formed a committee to gather and make available "all scientific information" on climatic and soil conditions and proper farming methods in the drought area.[119] Gardiner then informed Weir of the meeting in a telegram and asked for federal representation on the committee, arguing that "similarity of problems in three provinces and national importance of putting agriculture of drought stricken area on a more sound basis seemed to us to warrant common plans and concerted action."[120] The committee planned to meet again on 7 February, and to cover the expenses of compiling the drought rehabilitation information each province was asked to put up $5,000, and it was hoped that Ottawa would match that total with $15,000.[121]

Weir refused to participate, telling Gardiner that one of the two delegates he had planned to put on the committee was sick, thus making the meeting date impossible.[122] In a private letter to Bennett dated 30 January 1935 he explained his *real* reason for abstaining:

There is no doubt…that the recommendation will be for the Federal Government to supply all finances to the provinces. My own opinion is that Premier Gardiner's move is purely political. The provinces really have no outstanding men for this work, and I believe Premier Gardiner wants to get some credit for setting up machinery, which will only find out what is already known, while the officials of the Federal Department of Agriculture will do the work, assisted by the provinces spending money advanced by the Federal Government.[123]

Instead, Weir focused on getting the Prairie Farm Rehabilitation Act through Parliament by April 1935. Equipped with a $4.75-million budget and a five-year lease on life, activities under the Act included strategies to alleviate severe soil erosion and to develop surface water resources on the southern prairies. In just over a year, twenty-five DEFS Illustration Stations were converted and expanded into forty Dominion Experimental Sub-Stations to serve the varying soil and climatic conditions within the Palliser Triangle. These demonstrated to farmers in the surrounding countryside how wind erosion could best be prevented through strip farming and trash-covered fallowing. In addition, "Agricultural Improvement Associations" were organized and financed within the drought area to foster cooperative community action on soil drifting. Nine soil reclamation projects, one in southwestern Manitoba, two in southern Saskatchewan and six in southeastern Alberta were established on land that had been abandoned due to severe soil drifting. A separate Water Development Committee, comprised of personnel from the federal Department of Agriculture and the water-rights branches of each prairie province was also formed.[124] It provided financial and engineering support to aid in the construction of dugouts and small dams for stock-watering and domestic use, as well as small irrigation projects for the production of forage for livestock feed.[125] By 1945, farmers in the Palliser Triangle were benefitting from 19,000 dugouts, 4,312 stock watering dams and 1,004 irrigation projects initiated and funded by the PFRA.[126]

Vanguard Reclamation Project, 11 May 1939 (Courtesy of the Provincial Archives of Saskatchewan / R-B 7835).

After the Prairie Farm Rehabilitation Act, Weir was unable to initiate any new policies and programs other than securing the funding for a new Experimental Farm near Melfort. Time was running out on a government increasingly under siege. Bennett sent Weir along with fellow cabinet minister, R. J. Manion, to Regina to deal with the On-to-Ottawa trekkers who had been forcibly stopped in Regina. However, Weir and Manion were unable to stop what would become known as the Regina Riot and the resulting loss of life.[127]

On 14 October 1935, the Bennett Conservatives went down to a crushing defeat at the hands of Mackenzie King's Liberals. In western Canada, only three Conservatives managed to hold on to their seats. Weir was not among them despite the fact that the *Melfort Journal* made an impassioned plea on his behalf, spelling out his many contributions:

> He has developed the Department of Agriculture from the minor position it held in past governments to the most important of the branches of the government services. Then again we have to consider what [he] has...done for the Carrot River Valley. He has given more publicity to the area than all the previous members of parliament put together. Day and night he planned so that the Valley will become noted for its fine horses, cattle, swine, etc...He has been the means of a tremendous sum of money being placed in the pockets of farmers in the Carrot River Valley by finding a market for our swine and cattle, stabilization of wheat and by other means.[128]

Despite this, Weir lost to Malcolm McLean—the same Liberal candidate he had beaten five years before—by over 1,500 votes. Less than a hundred votes separated Weir from the third-place Social Credit candidate.[129] It was a humiliating result given how hard he had worked to defend the flow of federal relief to Saskatchewan and to reorganize and redouble the fight against the drought in the Palliser Triangle.[130] In the admittedly biased view of the *Melfort Journal*, it seemed "a tragedy that men of high caliber are cast by the wayside by the whims of fickle opinion."[131]

Weir returned to his farm. He could only watch from afar as the Supreme Court of Canada struck down his Natural Products Marketing Act along with other of Bennett's "New Deal" legislation. It was declared unconstitutional for going beyond the federal government's jurisdiction in creating the single Dominion Marketing Board. He expressed his bitterness in a letter to his old boss and comrade R. B. Bennett, who was now Leader of the Opposition in Ottawa:

> I take it that this means the BNA [British North America] Act as it now stands does not give Canada the right to give effect to the wishes of the majority of the people when agreed to in both the Federal Parliament and the Legislatures.[132]

The activities under the Prairie Farm Rehabilitation Act, by contrast, would not only survive, but thrive under Liberal tutelage. They were now under the direct control of James G. Gardiner, who had left provincial politics in order to become the Minister of Agriculture in the federal government. Gardiner expanded the PFRA's mandate and activities. In February 1937, Gardiner pushed through an amendment to the Prairie Farm Rehabilitation Act to include land use adjustment and resettlement activities.[133] He then set up a separate PFRA office in Regina, ensuring that it had sufficient autonomy from the Department in Ottawa. In 1939, the statutory time limit on activities under the Act was removed altogether.[134]

Still running the Liberal machine in Saskatchewan, Gardiner also used the PFRA to extend his party's political influence throughout the Prairie Provinces during his twenty-two-year stint as Minister of Agriculture.[135] Weir was especially outraged when Gardiner appointed John Vallance (the only Saskatchewan Liberal to be defeated in the 1935 election and Weir's old nemesis in the House of Commons) as the PFRA's first manager. As he told Bennett, such a move showed a "lack of vision" on Gardiner's part. In Weir's eyes, Vallance was a political cipher, a Liberal "bum" who did not have the expertise or experience to take on such an important job. Among many other examples of Liberal patronage, Weir thought that Vallance's appointment was nonetheless "one of the crudest things done."[136] He hated the fact that Gardiner and the Liberals took all the credit for the PFRA, going so far as to drop the PFRA's assistance to farmers to excavate dugouts and then reintroducing the assistance a few months later at a slightly higher rate as if it were a new Liberal program.[137]

Weir would not have to endure such outrages for long. In early March 1939, he was killed in a freak farm accident at fifty-six years of age. While hauling registered seed barley from Weldon to his farm, Weir's sleigh became hung up in a snow drift. When the sleigh slid down, the load tipped, overturning the sleigh and the sacks of grain, crushing him. He died almost instantly from internal injuries.[138] Shortly after his funeral, Weir's wife and children moved to Alberta, leaving Hereford Park Farm forever.[139]

CONCLUSION

Robert Weir is the forgotten man of Canadian politics. Although he occupied a key ministerial position in the midst of the social, political and economic upheaval of the Great Depression, his name would not likely be recognized by historians of the era. This is in part a function of R. B. Bennett and the highly centralized manner in which he ran his cabinet. Although Weir was identified as one of the more talented members of the cabinet, he and his colleagues were limited in what they could say or do by Bennett. More importantly, however, Weir's tenure as a minister during the worst years of the Great Depression, however unfairly, condemned both him and his government by association.

At a minimum, Weir deserves to be known as the originator of the PFRA, the one organization that, at a fraction of the cost for relief, attempted to rehabilitate the most devastated portions of the Palliser Triangle. While he came to this policy late in his tenure—and can easily be criticized for focusing for too long on a misguided policy of expanding and protecting a larger home market for agricultural products—he nonetheless set into motion the initiative that would subsequently be celebrated as one of the very few policy successes of the Great Depression, much less the Bennett New Deal. Unfortunately for Weir, Jimmy Gardiner took both possession and credit for the PFRA.

NOTES

This article was first published in *Prairie Forum* 33, no. 1 (2008): 65–98.

1   See P. M. Abel, "Saskatchewan's Cincinnatus," *Country Guide* (September 1930): 5, 63 and 66; and M. Grattan O'Leary, "Cabinet Portraits," *Maclean's Magazine* (15 November 1930): 19, 59, 60 and 61.

2   Weir's parents, Robert and Jane (née Johnson) had five other children. See J. K. Johnson (ed.), *The Canadian Directory of Parliament, 1867–1967* (Ottawa: Public Archives of Canada, 1968), 595–96; *Saskatoon Star-Phoenix*, 8 March 1939, 1.

3   G. Carlyle Anderson, "'Bob' Weir: Teacher, Soldier, Farmer," *Saskatchewan Farmer*, 15 August 1930, 15.

4   See Abel, "Saskatchewan's Cincinnatus," 5, although the exact nature of Weir's "breakdown" is not explored.

5   Provincial Archives of Saskatchewan, Regina (hereafter PAS), W. M. Martin Fonds, R-7.2, File #49, 17903.

6   PAS, 1912–13 Yearbook for the Regina Collegiate Institute *(The Collegiate Souvenir)*, 44–52, Regina Collegiate Institute Fonds, R-E2106, File #1.

7   *Melfort Journal*, 6 August 1935, 3.

8   PAS, 1912–13 yearbook, 43, Regina Collegiate Institute Fonds, R-E2106.

9   Library and Archives Canada (hereafter LAC), Canadian Expeditionary Force (CEF) service files for Major Robert Weir, RG-150, Accession 1992–93/166, Box 10207-12 (hereafter CEF service files for Weir).

10   Ibid.

11   Anderson, "'Bob' Weir," 15; LAC, CEF service files for Weir.

12   Surgeons were unable to remove all the shrapnel from Weir's right arm, impairing some of his mobility for the rest of his life. LAC, CEF service files for Weir; SAS, letter, Robert Weir to Hon. W. M. Martin, 26 February 1919, 17490, W. M. Martin Fonds, R-7.2, File #49; Abel, "Saskatchewan's Cincinnatus," 5.

13   The Khaki University, first set up in Britain in 1917, was operated by the Canadian Army until 1919 and then re-established in 1945–47. Its mandate was to help demobilized soldiers prepare for their re-entry into society by encouraging them to continue their education in agriculture, business, mechanics, teacher training, legal studies and medical instruction. It functioned in several camps and hospitals in Britain, and some fifty thousand soldiers were enrolled by the end of 1917. See James A. Draper, "Khaki University," The Canadian Encyclopedia (Toronto: McClelland and Stewart, 2000), 1242.

14   Melfort Journal, 6 August 1935, 3; Abel, "Saskatchewan's Cincinnatus," 5.

15   PAS, letter, Robert Weir to W. M. Martin, 5 July 1918, 17423, W. M. Martin Fonds, R-7.2, File #49.

16   Ibid., letter, Robert Weir to W. M. Martin, 26 February 1919, 17491, File #52.

17   Ibid., letter, W. M. Martin to Robert Weir, 18 March 1919, 17494-5.

18   On W. M. Martin's concerns about education, see Ted Regehr, "William M. Martin," in Gordon L. Barnhart (ed.), Saskatchewan Premiers of the Twentieth Century (Regina: Canadian Plains Research Center, 2004), 53–55.

19   Weir would later reflect on the important contributions such communities made to the country's development. Melfort Journal, 6 August 1935, 3.

20   PAS, "Summary of Inspectors' Work, 1919," 16616–17, Department of Education Fonds, R-177.10/2, File #1.

21   Abel, "Saskatchewan's Cincinnatus," 5, 66; Leaves Green and Gold: Weldon, Shannonville, Windermere (Weldon: Weldon and District Historical Society 1980), 440.

22   According to long-term yield records, the Carrot River Valley (also known as the "Melfort Plain") stands as Saskatchewan's most productive agricultural region and one of the most productive farmland areas in Canada. The region has never known a drought or a major crop failure. See D. F. Acton et al., The Ecoregions of Saskatchewan (Regina: Canadian Plains Research Center, 1998), 114–15; Daria Coneghan, "Melfort," in The Encyclopedia of Saskatchewan (Regina: Canadian Plains Research Center, 2005), 594.

23   He married Dorothy Vance. His wife was one of the many nurses hired by the Saskatchewan Department of Education to travel with school inspectors on their rounds. The couple would go on to have a daughter (Dorothy) and a son (Robert). See Abel, "Saskatchewan's Cincinnatus," 5–6; Melfort Journal, 15 July 1930, 1; J. K. Johnson (ed.), The Canadian Directory of Parliament, 1867–1967 (Ottawa: Public Archives of Canada, 1968), 595–96.

24 He acquired his first Percheron mare for $225 and bought the foundation stock for his Hereford herd (consisting of three cows with calves at foot) for $375. See Abel, "Saskatchewan's Cincinnatus," 63.

25 Abel, "Saskatchewan's Cincinnatus," 63, 66; Anderson, "'Bob'Weir," 15.

26 *Melfort Journal*, 15 July 1930, 1; *Melfort Journal*, 26 August 1930, 1; *Melfort Journal*, 6 August 1935, 3; Canada, *Seventh Census of Canada, 1931, Vol. II and IV* (Ottawa: King's Printer, 1933), 600–01.

27 Weir's Hereford bulls and heifers had won first prize at the Toronto Royal Winter Fair and the Chicago International Fair, respectively. In 1929, his Percheron horses had also won a gold medal at the above-mentioned Toronto fair for the best group of Percherons on the continent and won him $3,000 in prize money in the show circuit the next year. In November 1933, one of Weir's yearling purebred Percheron stallions even won first prize, Junior Championship and Reserve Grand Championship at Toronto. *Melfort Journal*, 15 July 1930, 1; *Melfort Journal*, 8 August 1930, 11; *Melfort Journal*, 6 August 1935, 3; *Regina Leader-Post*, 8 August 1930, 11.

28 *Regina Daily Star*, 8 August 1930, 5.

29 In 1929, agricultural products accounted for 59 percent of the value of all Canadian exports. Canada, *Canada Year Book, 1932* (Ottawa: King's Printer, 1932), 175.

30 Ibid., 427.

31 Canada, Statistics Canada Website: http://estat.statcan.ca/cgi-win/CNSMCGI.EXE, Table #001-0017.

32 From 1929 to 1933, Canadian cattle exports to the United States fell from $13.8 million to $400,000 and of milk and cream from $3.8 million to $700,000. Canada, *Report of the Royal Commission on Dominion-Provincial Relations, Vol. I* (Ottawa: King's Printer, 1940), 145.

33 Ibid., 143, 146; John Herd Thompson with Allen Seager, *Canada, 1922–1939: Decades of Discord* (Toronto: McClelland and Stewart, 1985), 195–98; James Struthers, *No Fault of their Own: Unemployment and the Canadian Welfare State, 1914–1941* (Toronto: University of Toronto Press, 1983), 42.

34 R. B. Bennett quoted in J. Castell Hopkins, *Canadian Annual Review of Public Affairs, 1930–31* (Toronto: The Canadian Review Co. Ltd., 1932), 101.

35 Larry Glassford, *Reaction and Reform: The Politics of the Conservative Party under R. B. Bennett, 1927–1938* (Toronto: University of Toronto Press, 1992), 78.

36 Quoted in J. Castell Hopkins, *Canadian Annual Review of Public Affairs, 1929–30* (Toronto: The Canadian Review Co. Ltd., 1930), 96.

37 Robert Weir quoted in Canada, *House of Commons Debates*, 7 May 1931, 1356.

38 Patrick Kyba, "J. T. M. Anderson," in Barnhart (ed.), *Saskatchewan Premiers of the Twentieth Century*, 120–21. See also Peter Russell, "The Co-operative Government in Saskatchewan, 1929–1934" (M.A. thesis, University of Saskatchewan, 1970); *Regina Daily Star*, 26 August 1930, 9.

39 Abel, "Saskatchewan's Cincinnatus," 63; LAC, letter, James Bryant to Hon. R. B. Bennett, 29 July 1930, R. B. Bennett Fonds, Reel #M-967, Vol. 102.

40 *Melfort Journal*, 10 June 1930, 1. Canada, *House of Commons Debates*, 7 May 1931, 1358. In a private letter to Mackenzie King, Weir's Liberal opponent indicated that Weir "went through the campaign talking about his own horses, and cattle, farm and home,

and posing as an independent" with "little or nothing to say about politics" [LAC, letter, Malcolm McLean to W. L. Mackenzie King, 14 August 1930, William Lyon Mackenzie King Fonds, Reel #C-2320, Vol. 177, 151140].

41   In the 1925 election, McLean got 3,638 votes while the Conservative candidate, Herbert Elwood Keown, received 2,646 votes, and the Progressive candidate got 2,178 votes. In the following election, the Progressives did not run a candidate, and McLean got 7,270 votes and Keown a mere 4,306 votes. *Melfort Journal*, 10 June 1930, 1.

42   Federal Election Results by Electoral District, Melfort, 1925, 1926, 1930, SAE, *Saskatchewan Executive and Legislative Directory* (Online) Available: www.saskarchives.com/web/ seld/3.04.pdf (Accessed 28 March 2007).

43   Glassford, *Reaction and Reform*, 105.

44   J. F. Bryant (a Conservative) had spoken for Weir on three occasions at the largest points in his constituency during the 1930 federal election campaign and had visited Hereford Park Farm at least once. W. C. Buckle (also a Conservative) had farmed in the neighbouring Tisdale district since 1905. In his telegram to Bennett, Buckle "personally" recommended Weir as a "suitable appointee" and added that his "qualifications and ability to administer position" were "undoubted" [LAC, telegram, W. C. Buckle to R. B. Bennett, 1 August 1930, R. B. Bennett Fonds, Reel #M-966, Vol. 101; Patrick Kyba, "Walter Clutterbuck Buckle" in Brett Quiring (ed.), *Saskatchewan Politicians: Lives Past and Present* (Regina: Canadian Plains Research Center, 2004), 32–33.

45   LAC, letter, James Bryant to R. B. Bennett, 29 July 1930, R. B. Bennett Fonds, Reel #M-967, Vol. 102.

46   Ibid., telegrams, 66927-28, 66931, 66941, 66964, Reel #M-966, Vol. 101; *Regina Leader-Post*, 1 August 1930, 1.

47   Quoted in Canada, *House of Commons Debates*, 7 May 1931, 1358. As was the custom of the time, Weir had to go through a by-election after he was appointed minister. In the end, however, the Liberals chose not to oppose him—the risk of political embarrassment was too great—and he won by acclamation on 25 August 1930. It was even rumoured that the Liberals considered running a star candidate, Charles Dunning, former premier of Saskatchewan and former federal minister of finance, against Weir in the by-election, but decided against doing so shortly before the election. LAC, letters, E. M. Bigelow to J. R. Graham, 9 August 1930, 151142 and Mackenzie King to Malcolm McLean, 22 August 1930, 151144, Mackenzie King Fonds, Reel #C-2320, Vol. 177; *Regina Daily Star*, 23 August 1930, 1.

48   *Toronto Globe and Mail*, 20 November 1930, 1.

49   Glassford, *Reaction and Reform*, 105.

50   *Statutes of Canada, 1930*, 21 Geo. V, c.1.

51   In 1929, Canada imported nearly 1.4 million bushels of wheat. M. C. Urquhart (ed.), *Historical Statistics of Canada*, 2nd ed. (Ottawa: Statistics Canada, 1983), Series #M301-309.

52   Bill Waiser, *Saskatchewan: A New History* (Calgary: Fifth House, 2005), 278; Saskatchewan, *A Submission by the Government of Saskatchewan to the Royal Commission on Dominion-Provincial Relations* (Canada, 1937), 173.

53   Canada, *Royal Commission on Dominion-Provincial Relations*, 150, Table 50.

54   John H. Archer, *Saskatchewan: A History* (Saskatoon: Western Producer Prairie Books, 1980), 216.

55   Robert Weir quoted in *Regina Daily Star*, 29 August 1930, 4.

56   For example, A. M. Shaw, the dean of the Saskatchewan College of Agriculture at Saskatoon held this view. He claimed to one audience in 1931 that he saw "very large quantities" of Canadian wheat being fed to hogs in Denmark during the winter of 1928–29. A. M. Shaw, "Reasons for Diversification in Canada...," *Saskatchewan Farmer*, 2 February 1931, 7.

57   Throughout much of the Palliser Triangle, precipitation constitutes less than 70 percent of potential evaporation, except for an area on the Alberta-Saskatchewan border known as the Dry Belt where precipitation constitutes less than 60 percent of potential evaporation. Donald Lemmen and Lisa Dale-Burnett, "The Palliser Triangle" in Ka-iu Fung (ed.), *Atlas of Saskatchewan, Second Edition* (Saskatoon: University of Saskatchewan, 1999), 41.

58   Paul Voisey, *Vulcan: The Making of a Prairie Community* (University of Toronto Press, 1988), 89.

59   According to the 1931 federal census, field crops represented 74 percent of the value of agricultural products sold on farms in the seven census districts (Nos. 1, 2, 3, 4, 6, 7 and 8) that lay roughly within Saskatchewan's portion of the Palliser Triangle, and wheat and oats (its support crop) made up 73 percent of this figure. Concerning livestock, four-fifths of all farms in the abovementioned census districts reported horses; over two-thirds reported cattle (a certain percentage of these were on ranches); half reported swine and nearly three-quarters reported poultry. The average farm in the Palliser Triangle in 1931 was 443 acres in size, 162 acres of which were left "unimproved"—mostly natural pasture. Canada, *Seventh Census of Canada, 1931*, 600–01, 604–05, 612, 620–21.

60   Gregory P. Marchildon, "Institutional Adaptation to Drought and the Special Areas of Alberta, 1909–1939," *Prairie Forum* 32, no. 2 (2007): 251–72.

61   In 1929, Canada's live cattle exports were worth just 3 percent of the value of its wheat exports. Canada, *Canada Year Book 1932*, 426–29.

62   *Melfort Journal*, 26 August 1930, 2; *Saskatchewan Farmer*, 2 September 1930, 3.

63   Canada, *House of Commons Debates*, 7 May 1931, 1360.

64   Hopkins, *Canadian Annual Review of Public Affairs, 1930–31*, 475–75; *Toronto Globe and Mail*, 5 November 1930, 10.

65   *Regina Daily Star*, 6 September 1930, 4; *Toronto Globe and Mail*, 20 November 1930, 2; Canada, *House of Commons Debates*, 7 May 1931, 1360; Hopkins, *Canadian Annual Review of Public Affairs, 1930–31*, 479.

66   LAC, letter, Robert Weir to E. C. Gilliat, Managing Secretary of the Winnipeg Board of Trade, 3 November 1930, 54811, R. B. Bennett Fonds, Reel M-954, Vol. 84.

67   The Illustration Stations were located on private farms across Canada and demonstrated approved crop varieties and rotations as well as cultivation methods determined by years of research on the main experimental farms and stations. Canada, *Canada Year Book, 1932*, 179–83.

68   Richard Churchill, "Canada's New Agricultural Policy," *Maclean's Magazine*, 15 March 1931, 12, 64; James H. Gray, *Men Against the Desert* (Saskatoon and Calgary: Fifth House Publishers, 1996), 93–94.

69 LAC, letter, W. L. Mackenzie King to Donald MacGregor, 3 December 1930, 150827, W. L. Mackenzie King Fonds, Reel C-2320, Vol. 177.

70 Canada, *Canada Year Book, 1932*, 426–29.

71 Canada, *Canada Year Book, 1932*, 428–29; 432–33; *Report of the Royal Commission on Dominion-Provincial Relations*, 145.

72 Canada, *House of Commons Debates*, 28 April 1931, 1072.

73 Ibid., 5 May 1931, 1263.

74 *Toronto Globe and Mail*, 8 May 1931, 1.

75 Canada, *House of Commons Debates*, 7 May 1931, 1363.

76 *Toronto Globe and Mail*, 8 May 1931, 1; *Globe and Mail*, 11 May 1931, 1

77 LAC, letter, H. C. Saylor to R. B. Bennett, 31 March 1931, R. B. Bennett Fonds, RG-26K, Reel #M-967, Vol. 102.

78 Saskatchewan, *Agriculture Report*, 1937.

79 Saskatchewan, *Submission to the Royal Commission*, 148.

80 LAC, R. B. Bennett Papers, MG-26K, Reel #1433, Vol. 779, "Report of The Minister of Labour in Connection with Western Enquiry on Unemployment, 1 July 1931," 4–5.

81 The 1931 federal census counted some 1.4 million horses, cattle, sheep and swine and nearly 5 million poultry in the seven census districts that lay roughly within Saskatchewan's portion of the Palliser Triangle. Canada, *Seventh Census of Canada, 1931*, 620–21.

82 Canada, *House of Commons Debates*, 1 July 1931, 3247.

83 *Statutes of Canada*, 21–22, Geo. V (1931), c. 58.

84 E. W. Stapleford, *Report on Rural Relief due to Drought Conditions and Crop Failures in Western Canada, 1930–1937* (Ottawa: King's Printer, 1939), 32.

85 Robert Weir quoted in *Western Producer* (20 August 1931): 1.

86 In a 9 December 1931 letter to Henry Black, Robert Weir expressed regret that he had "not been West sooner" because "My illness in Toronto upset all my plans." Henry Black Fonds, private collection of Don Black, Regina, SK.

87 Robert Weir quoted in Gregory P. Marchildon and Don Black, "Henry Black, the Conservative Party and the Politics of Relief," *Saskatchewan History* 58, no. 1 (2006): 12–13.

88 Gray, *Men Against the Desert*, 202.

89 In the period 1929–1935, average precipitation in Crop District #8 (that portion of Saskatchewan northeast of the intersection of Highways 2 and 5 to the Manitoba border) was 25 percent higher than the provincial average. Saskatchewan, *Annual Report of the Department of Agriculture, 1940* (Regina: King's Printer, 1941), 102; G. E. Britnell, *The Wheat Economy* (Toronto: University of Toronto Press, 1939), 51.

90 "The bright boys who talk glibly of mixed farming" wrote one prairie farmer's wife to the editor of the *Western Producer* in 1931 "know little if anything of the water problem existing on most of the farms in the west. We have eleven horses, fourteen cattle, five of them are milk cows working full steam ahead for us at present, bless 'em, two hogs, 125 pure bred chickens, but our old well, seepage from the slough, could not provide enough water for this bunch during dry spells so we had a well drilled, went to a depth of three hundred and sixty feet to get water and sunk my husband in such a hole of debt he was just crawling out of when this year's troubles

gave him such a crack he flopped right down a[g]ain." Building a stock watering dam was also an expensive proposition, sometimes costing as much as $15,000 each (about $227,000 in 2007 dollars) by one estimate. *Western Producer*, 29 January 1931, 11; Alberta, *A Report on the Rehabilitation of the Dry Areas of Alberta and Crop Insurance* (Edmonton: King's Printer, 1936), 38.

91 *Weyburn Review*, 11 October 1934, 1.

92 Alberta, *Report on the Rehabilitation of the Dry Areas*, 38.

93 In his maiden speech to Parliament, Weir indicated that he had recently asked the DEFS Station at Rosthern, Saskatchewan to carry out some "simple experiments" with feed grains for cattle. Canada, *House of Commons Debates*, 7 May 1931, 1360.

94 At the Swift Current Station, the plow and the disc harrow as summerfallowing instruments were virtually gone by 1932 and were replaced by the one-way plow, the moldboard plow, the duck-foot cultivator and the rod weeder. These implements destroyed weeds while leaving the soil surface in a ridged, lumpy condition with other 'trash' or protective cover intact. At the Lethbridge Station, another anti-soil erosion measure known as 'strip farming' (arranging fields into alternating 50-foot strips of crop and summerfallow at right angles to the prevailing winds) had been studied. Department of Agriculture, Experimental Station, Swift Current, Sask., *Results of Experiments, 1931–1936 Inclusive* (Ottawa: F. A. Acland, King's Printer, 1938), 18–19; SAS, Department of Agriculture Papers, R-261, File #22.15, letter, W. H. Fairfield to F. H. Auld, 27 January 1932.

95 Canada, Dominion Range Experimental Station, Manyberries, *Alberta, Progress Report, 1937–1947* (Ottawa: King's Printer, 1947), 10–13; Gray, *Men Against the Desert*, 102–04, 174–75; Canada, *Canada Year Book, 1932*, 180.

96 PAS, letter, J. F. Bryant to C. J. Mackenzie, 25 May 1932, J. F. Bryant Fonds, M-10, File #61.

97 PAS, Newsclipping, *Regina Leader-Post*, 24 September 1931, File #86; PAS, letter, J. F. Bryant to A. J. H. Bratsberg, 17 November 1931, J. F. Bryant fonds, File #67.

98 Robert Weir quoted in the *Melfort Journal*, 6 August 1935, 3.

99 Glassford, *Reaction and Reform*, 145.

100 LAC, letter, E. S. Archibald to Robert Weir, 8 June 1934, Dominion Department of Agriculture Fonds, RG-17, Vol. 3263, File #435 (2); letter, E. S. Archibald to Deputy Minister of Agriculture, 17 July 1934, Ibid., Vol. 3264, File #435 (8).

101 LAC, letter, E. S. Archibald to Robert Weir, 8 June 1934, Department of Agriculture Fonds, RG-17, Vol. 3263, File #435 (2).

102 Waiser, *Saskatchewan: A New History*, 318.

103 *Regina Leader-Post*, 10 September 1934, 1–2.

104 Gray, *Men Against the Desert*, 156.

105 *Regina Leader-Post*, 10 September 1934, 1–2.

106 *Western Producer*, 13 September 1934, 1.

107 See *Regina Leader-Post*, 13 February 1934, 4; 2 October 1934, 4; *Weyburn Review*, 26 July 1934, 4; *Swift Current Sun*, 14 August 1934, 4.

108 *Regina Leader-Post*, 2 October 1934, 4.

109 Canada, *Debates of the Senate*, 1 February 1934, 46.

110 *Swift Current Sun*, 26 March 1935, 6.

III   E. W. Beatty quoted in *Western Producer*, 30 August 1934, 1.

112   Ibid., 13 September 1934, 3.

113   *Weyburn Review*, 11 October 1934, 1.

114   An agronomist by training, John Bracken had been a professor of Agriculture at the University of Saskatchewan from 1910 to 1920. In the latter year he moved to Winnipeg to become president of the Manitoba Agricultural College. Bracken was an expert on soil science and dry farming and had published two books based on his numerous bulletins and pamphlets written while he had worked in Saskatchewan— *Crop Production in Western Canada* (1920) and *Dry Farming in Western Canada* (1921). See John Kendle, *John Bracken: A Political Biography* (Toronto: University of Toronto Press, 1979), 24, 107–19.

115   See LAC, R. B. Bennett Papers, MG-26K, Reel #M-1282, Vol. 567, John Bracken to R. B. Bennett, 8 June 1934; 18 June 1934; and 3 July 1934.

116   Kendle, *John Bracken: A Political Biography*, 107–19.

117   John Bracken quoted in *Western Producer*, 1 November 1934, 8.

118   LAC, letter, W. O. Fraser to M. A. MacPherson (forwarded by MacPherson to R. B. Bennett), 12 November 1934, R. B. Bennett Fonds, 13 November 1934, MG-26K, Reel #M1282, Vol. 567.

119   Quoted in *Regina Leader-Post*, 14 February 1935, 1.

120   Quoted in Canada, *House of Commons Debates*, 12 February 1937, 820.

121   *Regina Leader-Post*, 14 February 1935, 5.

122   Canada, *House of Commons Debates*, 12 February 1937, 820.

123   LAC, letter, Robert Weir to R. B. Bennett, 30 January 1935, R. B. Bennett Fonds, MG-26K, Reel #M-1280, Vol. 562.

124   Canada, *Prairie Soil, Prairie Water: The pfra Story* (Regina: Centax Printers, 1987), 17.

125   In order to qualify for assistance, dugouts had to be constructed to certain specifications. A typical farm dugout as designed by PFRA had to provide all the water needs of a farm garden, household and twenty-five head of livestock. Particularly, dugouts had to be long, wide and deep, or about 150 feet long, 60 feet wide and 12 to 14 feet deep. This design ensured at least a year's water supply, and was at the same time deep enough to overcome the effect of evaporation during the summer. Gray, *Men Against the Desert*, 105.

126   *Regina Leader-Post*, 25 January 1938, C3; Canada, *Report on Prairie Farm Rehabilitation and Related Activities, 1952–53* (Prairie Farm Rehabilitation Administration Branch, Regina, SK), 65, Appendix IV; Canada, *Prairie Soil, Prairie Water*, 18.

127   W. A. Waiser, *All Hell Can't Stop Us: The On-to-Ottawa Trek and Regina Riot* (Calgary: Fifth House, 2003); V. Howard, *"We Were the Salt of the Earth!": The On-to-Ottawa Trek and the Regina Riot* (Regina: Canadian Plains Research Center, 1985).

128   *Melfort Journal*, 8 October 1935, 2.

129   The final results for the Melfort constituency were: 6,389 for McLean (Liberal); 4,814 for Weir (Conservative); 4,721 for Arthur John Lewis (Social Credit); and 2,977 for Dorothy C. Pope (Co-operative Commonwealth Federation) [PAS, Saskatchewan Executive and Legislative Directory Online, Accessed 28 February 2006: www.saskarchives.com/web/seld/3.04pdf].

130 Malcolm McLean was defeated in the Melfort federal riding in March 1940. He died two years later. Parliament of Canada Website: http://www2.parl.gc.ca (accessed 9 May 2007).

131 *Melfort Journal*, 22 October 1935, 2.

132 LAC, letter, Weir to Bennett, 28 January 1937, 530553, R. B. Bennett Fonds, MG-26K, Reel # M-1484, Vol. 851.

133 *Statutes of Canada*, 1 Geo. VI (1937), c. 14.

134 Ibid,. 3 Geo. VI (1939), c. 7.

135 Historian Norman Ward has noted that the ten thousand dugouts the PFRA had completed by 1940 meant "ten thousand contacts with individual farms." The Liberal Party also used the PFRA in other ways; in 1950, for example, CCF MP Ross Thatcher told the House of Commons: "[i]n my opinion the PFRA is accomplishing much in the prairie provinces, yet I wonder how at every election these PFRA trucks can run around working for Liberal candidates." Norm Ward, "The Politics of Patronage: James Gardiner and Federal Appointments in the West, 1935–57," *Canadian Historical Review* 58, no. 3 (September 1977): 305–06.

136 LAC, letter, Robert Weir to R. B. Bennett, 15 February 1937, 604154-160, R. B. Bennett Fonds, Reel M-3178, Vol. 954.

137 Ibid.

138 Weir's elderly father-in-law, J. E. Bedford, was with him that day. Although not seriously injured in the upheaval, Bedford was unable to move the sacks off Weir. Instead, he ran to get the help of neighbours who then removed the sac and transported Weir to his home, and then called upon some doctors who flew to Weldon from Prince Albert. In the opinion of the doctors, however, Weir had died instantaneously of internal injuries. *Saskatoon StarPhoenix*, 8 March 1938, 1.

139 Weldon and District Historical Society, *Leaves Green and Gold*, 440.

13. Alberta Social Credit Reappraised: The Radical
Character of the Early Social Credit Movement

Alvin Finkel

When Orvis Kennedy resigned in 1982 as president of the collapsing Alberta wing of the Social Credit party, the ancient party warrior reminded Albertans that the party had been founded to "save free enterprise" during the depths of the Great Depression of the 1930s.[1] Such a view of the party's origins was shared by the aged handfuls of party faithful who had remained with the party for five decades, and had watched sadly as the party failed to recruit younger members after World War II[2] and finally fell from power in 1971. Historians, concentrating largely on the implausible monetary theories of the party founders, have also largely accepted the view that Social Credit was, from the beginning, a right-wing populist movement hostile to government economic intervention except with regards to the evil bankers.[3]

In fact, however, Kennedy, the retrospective free-enterpriser, secured a parliamentary seat (Edmonton East) in 1937 with the acknowledged aid of Communist campaign workers.[4] And many early Social Crediters were at best ambivalent on the question of socialism versus free enterprise. An examination of the behaviour of the party in its early years, and of the first Aberhart government, demonstrates considerable openness on the part of early Social Crediters to government interventions of various kinds outside the field of banking. What follows is an analysis of the early Social Credit movement which de-emphasizes the well-documented party discussions regarding the banks, and concentrates on the attitudes and prescriptions of the party and government on broader economic and social issues. It also assesses the views of the opponents of Social Credit and notes that their fears of Aberhart and his colleagues went well beyond concerns for the fate of the bank branches in Alberta—whose safety from Aberhart's clutches had been established by the courts before the end of Aberhart's first term in office.[5]

The Social Credit party, which swept the provincial elections of 1935, had enrolled over thirty thousand members before the election was called.[6] Yet the Alberta Social Credit League had made the decision to enter the electoral arena only six months previously.[7] Before then, the League had spent its time organizing social credit clubs and lobbying the provincial government to implement William Aberhart's schemes. Aberhart, as all historians of Social Credit agree, dominated the Alberta movement despite his inability to comprehend the intricacies of Major C. H. Douglas's social credit theory.[8] Aberhart, a radio evangelist with a loyal following, and a Calgary high school principal, became the symbol of the struggle to secure a more just social order. His correspondence shows him to be what his detractors claimed: a vain, authoritarian, short-tempered man whose oratorical abilities far exceeded his intellectual capacities.[9] Aberhart was, however, also deeply distressed by the poverty and hopelessness which surrounded him and genuinely committed to seeking solutions to Depression conditions.[10] While he remained convinced to his death that public control over the financial system was the key to ending poverty, he proved willing at least to consider other options as it became clear that only the federal government had the constitutional authority to regulate banks and currency.

Aberhart and his followers did not commit themselves to a thorough criticism of the capitalist system such as the Co-operative Commonwealth Federation (CCF) had made in the Regina Manifesto of 1933. But the early party avoided attacks on the manifesto and on the CCF, preferring to paint banks rather than socialists as the enemies of prosperity. In part, this can be explained by the lack of a socialist threat in Alberta. Despite Kennedy's protestations that Social Credit was needed to save free enterprise in Alberta, the political forces of socialism in the province were weak at the time Social Credit decided to transform itself into an electoral party. While the United Farmers of Alberta organization (UFA) had affiliated with the CCF, the provincial UFA government took little notice and governed indistinguishably from a Conservative or Liberal government. Because of the affiliated character of the CCF organization, no attempt was made to establish a new organization composed of UFA members and others who rejected the orthodox economic policies pursued by the provincial government. The provincial Labour party was avowedly socialist, but it lacked organization outside of the two major cities and some of the mining districts; by 1935 it was, in any event, on the decline.[11]

The CCF's weakness was not the sole reason why both that party in particular and socialism in general were not attacked by Social Credit. The Social Credit leaders and members were ambivalent about market-based economics and, before the early forties, did not reject out-of-hand notions of a planned economy or even of public ownership. They did not embrace state planning and public ownership as central doctrines as the CCF did; "funny money"—government-printed-and-distributed "social dividends" meant to boost purchasing power—provided the party's fundamental platform. But Social Crediters also toyed with CCF doctrines.

Aberhart's *Social Credit Manual*, which was widely distributed throughout the province during the 1935 provincial election, reflected his party's confusion about the extent to which the state should be involved in economic life. The manual's opening comments indicated that the party rejected the traditional views of political economists that the marketplace rather than the state must act as the guarantor of economic justice. The party's "basic premise," it claimed, was that

> It is the duty of the State through its Government to organize its economic structure in such a way that no bona fide citizen, man, woman, or child shall be allowed to suffer the lack of the base [*sic*] necessities of food, clothing, and shelter in the midst of plenty or abundance.[12]

The state, it argued, should not confiscate the wealth of the rich and distribute it to the poor. Party doctrine recognized individual enterprise and ownership, but the party also believed the state must outlaw "wildcat exploitation of the consumer through the medium of enormously excessive spreads in price for the purpose of giving exorbitant profits or paying high dividends on pyramids of watered stock."[13] It could prevent such exploitation by systematically controlling prices "for all goods and services used in the province" and fixing minimum and maximum wages for each type of worker.[14] This was hardly a prescription for saving a market-based free enterprise economy, though it substituted state regulation of pricing for the socialist solution of state control of industry.

Aberhart's proposals were riddled with contradictions. Though he proclaimed that Social Credit would not take from the rich to give to the poor, he also promised that a Social Credit government would "limit the income of the citizens to a certain maximum" because "no one should be allowed to have an income that is greater than he himself and his loved ones can possibly enjoy, to the privation of his fellow citizens."[15] While he insisted that Social Credit recognized individual enterprise, he promised to break up the large oil companies' control of the oil industry and to allow new entrants into the field.[16]

On the whole, then, Social Credit anticipated using the state as a lever to restore a smallholders' democracy. It was less interested in free enterprise—indeed it was hostile to the market system—than it was in a wide dispersion of business ownership. While Aberhart's rhetoric against capitalists was relatively moderate, he appropriated the ccf's phrase, "fifty big shots," to describe the country's ruling economic clique.[17] Some of his supporters were more strident. The *Social Credit Chronicle*, the party's official journal, editorialized in September 1934:

> How many of these capitalistic lions will support Social Credit? Not one of them. How many of them will try and obstruct the bringing in of Social Credit principles? Every one of them.... They know that if ever Social Credit is adopted in Alberta it will only be the beginning of a new era, it will be the overthrow of their power...
>
> Let the supporters of Social Credit stand firm on this issue, let Alberta take the lead in showing the country that the people have broken away from the old yoke of the capitalistic system.[18]

The capitalists did indeed try to obstruct Social Credit's progress. Their attack was led by the boards of trade in Calgary and Edmonton. Before the provincial election of 1935, the boards had decided that businessmen should set up an organization whose sole purpose was to oppose Aberhart's social credit movement. As J. H. Hanna, secretary of the Calgary Board of Trade, commented to his counterpart in Drumheller, direct opposition by boards of trade to Social Credit would be regarded with suspicion because "those who take so readily to such schemes as Social Credit look upon our organization as having the capitalistic viewpoint."[19] But the founding of the Economic Safety League by the businessmen was unsubtle and it is unlikely that many were deceived that this was a broadly-based organization.[20] Nor were the businessmen deceived about public feeling towards them. Commenting on the election results, Hanna observed:

> We should keep in mind that the majority of the people who support these new and radical plans blame the so-called capitalist class for their troubles and are prejudiced against Boards of Trade

because they believe they are the servants of the capital class and are not interested in the welfare of the people generally.[21]

From the businessmen's point of view, then, Social Credit was hardly the saviour of free enterprise which Orvis Kennedy retrospectively claimed it was intended to be. Nevertheless, Hanna noted that many small retailers who had kept their opinions to themselves during the election openly applauded the Aberhart victory. To some extent the division of business opinion on Social Credit was between big and small business, between successful operations and those forced to the wall by Depression conditions. But organized business as a whole opposed Social Credit from the beginning and only relented in the 1940s when Aberhart abandoned the reformist plans which his government and party embraced during the Depression. The opposition was not restricted to the boards of trade in the two large cities. The boards in smaller towns such as Drumheller, Stettler, and Medicine Hat went on record in opposition to Aberhart's plans during the election of 1935 despite the professed non-partisanship of boards of trade.[22]

In general, Social Credit attracted the support of the poor and was rejected by the better-off. In Claresholm, for example, the president of a men's club in which businessmen predominated observed:

> We are composed of a membership of about seventy-five, perhaps sixty being businessmen or associated in a business or profession and perhaps fifteen being farmers, retired farmers, etc. I think 75 percent are opposed to Social Credit including myself and all our executive. Among the affiliated legion members, many of whom are in poor condition financially the percentage of those supporting Social Credit would be considerably greater. There are I think four merchants, one lawyer, one dentist and one medical man here supporting Social Credit.[23]

During its first term in office, Social Credit appeared uncertain about how far it wished to go to implement election promises in the face of implacable opposition from most of the provincial economic elite as well as local elites in most rural areas. Aberhart's procrastination with regards to banking legislation and the promised social dividends of twenty-five dollars per adult per month have been well-documented.[24] So have the government's broken promises to treat the unemployed with greater humanity than the United Farmers of Alberta government had demonstrated.[25] Nevertheless, from the start, business found much to be alarmed about in Social Credit actions and their fears seemed to grow throughout Social Credit's first term.

The first session of the legislature under Aberhart opened early in 1936 and passed several pieces of legislation that were denounced as "fascist" as well as "socialist" by the Calgary Board of Trade, which was not known for precision in its use of either term. Among the offending items of legislation were male minimum wages (minimums for women had existed since 1920), compulsory membership of teachers in the Alberta Teachers' Association, motor vehicle licences for all drivers, and legislation restricting various trades to licensed individuals.[26] While male minimum wages and restricted entry into trades offended employers, they won the government considerable support among workers. The unions, we shall see, were largely hostile to the Social Credit administration during its first term; but, unlike the business groups, their objection was that Social Credit was doing too little for the province's workers.

The businessmen feared not only Social Credit's legislation but the government's intentions regarding legislation already passed by the United Farmers of Alberta administration, especially the Department of Trade and Industry Act of 1934. This act allowed businessmen in a particular industry, whether in manufacturing, wholesaling or retailing of a product, to combine to write a "code of fair practice" for the industry, which could include price-fixing and the setting of production quotas; the code regulations would be enforced by the government.[27] While the legislation proved generally attractive to small businessmen, it was greeted with hostility by large retailers and wholesalers who claimed that it would keep small, inefficient firms afloat at the expense of the consumer. While the UFA, which had unsuccessfully attempted to win consensus for codes before imposing them, had implemented few, Social Credit proved more daring. Within a year of taking office, it had established codes for retailers, wholesalers, and a variety of service industries. These codes included price schedules, hours of work for employees, hours of operation for firms, and proscriptions against such practices as offering loss leaders. They were warmly greeted by small business and attacked by large firms who claimed correctly that they made the government, rather than the marketplace, the arbiter of prices and business practices.[28]

The opposition to "codes" was mild in comparison to the opposition to the Licensing of Trades and Industry Act passed in October 1937. The act gave the Minister of Trade and Industry sweeping powers to determine who could operate a business in the province. The minister could "provide for the registration of all persons engaged in or employed in any business or any description or class thereof so designated and prohibit the carrying on of that business or the engagement in that business of any person who is required to be licensed and who is not so licensed."[29] The minister could impose whatever license fees he regarded as appropriate for firms in particular industries and could prohibit licensed firms from engaging in operations other than those which they had been authorized to perform. A license could be cancelled if a firm or individual contravened more than once the Department of Trade and Industry Act, one of the Minimum Wage Acts, the Hours of Work Act, or the Tradesmen's Qualification Act. Stiff fines would be imposed against violators of the Act's provisions.

Predictably, boards of trade, in which the small businessmen who supported Social Credit appear to have lacked influence, unanimously opposed the legislation. So did the provincial branch of the Canadian Manufacturers Association.[30]

A legal challenge to the Licensing Act, launched by a Calgary automobile dealer with financial aid from boards of trade,[31] stalled the government. The Honourable Mr. Justice Howson, who had been leader of the provincial Liberal party during the 1935 provincial election, ruled in favour of the dealer because the Attorney General's department had made technical mistakes in its drafting of the legislation.[32] So the legislation was re-drafted and reintroduced; a second appeal by the car dealer was dismissed by a justice of the Alberta Supreme Court. The federal government had rejected business pleas that the legislation be disallowed.[33]

The government meanwhile had fulfilled the business community's worst fears by giving itself the absolute right to broadly regulate all industries. A Provincial Marketing Board was established in 1939 with the power

> to buy and sell and deal in any goods, wares, merchandise and natural products, or any of them whatsoever, either by wholesale or by retail, or both by wholesale and retail, and to act as a broker, factor or agent for any person in the acquisition or disposition of any goods, wares, merchandise or natural products, and for the purpose to do and transact all acts and things which a natural person engaged in a general mercantile business had the capacity or the power to transact.[34]

The Board was also given the sweeping power "to engage in any or all of the following businesses, namely manufacturing, producing, processing, handling or distributing of any goods, wares, merchandise or natural products," and in the process, "to acquire by purchase or otherwise any land or any other property required by the Provincial Board for the purpose of or incidental to any such business."

The Edmonton Chamber of Commerce warned ominously:

> The full exercise of such powers will transform Alberta into a corporative state: the partial exercise without any safeguards which do not appear in the bill, will endanger democratic freedom and private enterprise, and discourage investment in all lines of industry.[35]

The frustration of the government's efforts to restore prosperity by monetary tinkering had led to a reawakening of its interest in the "just price" and the result was a piece of legislation which would have enabled a socialist government to nationalize and operate any industry it wished. Social Credit preferred to leave businesses under private ownership, but despite its later professions of total opposition to public ownership and regulation, it was prepared in the late thirties to consider a giant leap to the left, as the Marketing Act demonstrates. Government officials had at least toyed with the idea of establishing a complete enough control over industry to yield the funds needed to provide the chimerical social dividends that had proved so alluring to the electorate in 1935.

Alfred W. Farmilo, the secretary-treasurer of the Alberta Federation of Labour, recorded notes of a meeting in July 1937 with the powerful emissaries to Alberta of Major C. H. Douglas, the founder of Social Credit. Both G. F. Powell, and L. D. Byrne were interested in finding ways that the government could secure the funds to begin paying social dividends.

> He [Powell] then said do you not think productive industry could be controlled in a manner similar to the pools and cooperatives.
>
> We then discussed the possibility of the Province of [sic] setting up an institution similar to the Savings Department into which the flow of currency or money might be diverted through the control of industry. Powell looked over to Byrne, and asked if he had considered this phase and the answer was in the affirmative. It would therefore be as well to keep in mind that the treasury department may eventually be used along these lines.[36]

Byrne and Powell and some of the Social Credit MLAs, however, were devotees of Douglas and their views at any given time shifted as the views of the unstable founder of Social Credit shifted.[37] One can over-emphasize the extent to which the Social Credit government leaned towards interventionist solutions in its first term of office. Certainly, however, there were enough statements made and actions taken to justify the anxieties of the business community that an anti-capitalist government was in charge of Alberta's affairs.

Within the party at large, socialist and left-wing reformist views were certainly influential. Historians have over-stated the extent to which devotion to Aberhart and the simplistic lure of the twenty-five dollar social dividends attracted members to Social Credit.[38] An analysis of the resolutions of provincial conventions of the party, and of local Social Credit clubs indicates that party members sought reforms beyond simplistic monetary experiments promised by Aberhart; and municipal alliances with Communists and CCFers demonstrated the rank-and-file feeling that Social Credit's natural allies were the collectivist parties rather than the free-enterprise parties. State medicine, which would be viciously denounced by Social Credit from the mid-forties onwards, was part of the platform approved by the convention of the Social Credit League in 1935 that sanctioned the League's entry into the electoral arena.[39] Every convention from 1937 to 1940 reaffirmed the party's commitment to prepaid coverage of medical and hospital bills for all citizens. The 1938 convention, for example, resolved "that we request the Government to immediately formulate a scheme of state medicine and hospitalization and state insurance to cover time lost while sick."[40]

Provincial Social Credit conventions from 1937 to 1940 also called for free enterprise textbooks in Alberta schools, producers' marketing boards, the eight-hour day in industry, and direct and generous relief for single men on relief (as an alternative to soup kitchens and bed tickets for bunkhouses).[41] The 1940 convention also endorsed a resolution on war profiteering that paralleled CCF resolutions on the issue. The resolution said party members

> are opposed to profiteering out of the sale of armaments and also opposed to profiteering out of the sale of foodstuffs, clothing and the necessities of life. Be it therefore resolved that conscription of capital and finance must precede any other form of conscription that the exigencies of war may make.[42]

Many local constituency groups went beyond the resolutions of the provincial conventions to call for government initiation and operation of manufacturing firms to put the unemployed back to work and for government ownership of the petroleum and hydro-electric industries.[43] Such resolutions usually came from Social Credit clubs in the cities and in the mining areas where Communist influence among Social Credit members was pronounced. Communist influence led to the formation of a number of electoral united fronts at the municipal, provincial and federal levels from 1936 to 1939. The Communists, who had initially denounced the Social Credit movement as "fascist,"[44] were aware that a considerable number of unemployed individuals who had joined Communist-led unemployed groups had also joined the Social Credit party. It feared that strident denunciations of Social Credit would alienate these individuals and ruin the party's long-term chances of exposing Social Credit as a fraud and then recruiting Aberhart's former supporters.[45]

Rank-and-file Social Crediters proved friendly to the Communist embrace, though Aberhart did not. The Lethbridge constituency organization, dominated by the unemployed,[46] declined to nominate a joint federal candidate with the Communists only after pressure from senior party officials.[47] The Crowsnest Pass Social Credit groups, which included many miners, worked closely with the local Communists.[48] It was in the two major cities, however, that close Communist-Social Credit links caused Aberhart the greatest concern. In 1936, the Social Crediters of Edmonton agreed to a Communist plan for a joint nomination of "progressive forces" in a city-wide provincial by-election, and the candidate chosen by a joint Communist-Social Credit meeting was Margaret Crang, a left-wing Labour alderman. Crang was expelled from the Labour party and the CCF for accepting the nomination and the CCF candidate polled enough votes to deprive her of a victory.[49] But a united front of Communists and Social Crediters in the municipal elections of 1936 convinced some Labourites that the progressive vote was being unnecessarily divided between two groups. They cooperated with the Social Credit-Communist alliance in Edmonton and Calgary in municipal elections in 1937, but afterwards returned to their former go-it-alone policy.[50] Communists, however, worked in front groups with Social Crediters for another two years, and a Communist alderman, Patrick Lenihan, was elected in Calgary in 1938 with Social Credit votes.[51] Orvis Kennedy's election in a federal by-election in 1937 on the Social Credit ticket resulted from a joint Social Credit-Communist campaign.[52]

Aberhart made clear to the Calgary Social Crediters that he opposed their political alliances and their municipal platform. He wrote Ethel Baker, secretary-treasurer of the Calgary provincial constituency association (Calgary and Edmonton both formed single constituencies with five seats each), to register his disapproval of the platform which Social Credit had approved in 1938 in conjunction with its Communist friends. The platform pledged, for example, "to help and develop trade unionism in every way in the City of Calgary." Commented Aberhart: "This is a pure labour plank to which Social Credit could not wholly subscribe. The beliefs of trade unions are not altogether in harmony with the program of Social Credit." To the platform call for a "humanizing of relief rates and relief rules; clothing allowance to be increased," Aberhart retorted: "This will give the person who supports it very great difficulty in carrying it out."[53] The Calgary Social Crediters, however, ignored Aberhart's misgivings and stuck to this platform during the municipal election.[54]

The willingness of urban members of Social Credit to support policies that went beyond the official monetary panaceas that were the original *raison d'être* of the party demonstrates the fluid character of radical thought in Alberta. Many individuals had joined the Social Credit League because they regarded Aberhart as a champion of the underdog; but they remained open to influences that suggested monetary reform was insufficient to make the economic system work for the poor. As we saw earlier, some actions of the Aberhart government indicated that its members also recognized the need for other reforms if only because a constitutional straightjacket inhibited them from making monetary adjustments.

Rural members of Social Credit, like their urban counterparts, supported non-monetary reforms and at times made alliances with socialists and Communists. As noted earlier, party conventions had supported producer-controlled marketing boards. Social Crediters were also behind the establishment of the Alberta's Farmers' Union (AFU), a rival to the United Farmers of Alberta. The AFU manifesto adopted by the founding convention in 1939 announced that the organization intended to

> initiate a policy of direct action in the way of non-buying of machinery strike: and the non-delivery of grain strike....In other words to adopt the same methods as the organized labourers, and withhold our production from the industrial set-up the way they withhold their services from the industrial concerns for whom they work, and a definite, direct way of protest against the lowering of their living standards.[55]

Such a stance reflected a far more militant posture than the UFA adopted. Many Social Credit farmers regarded the UFA as too cautious and objected to its leadership's continuous stream of anti-Social Credit rhetoric.[56] The AFU's early leadership included a large contingent of east Europeans and many of the early members were sympathetic to Communism as well as Social Credit.[57] Their views on the efficacy of militancy in obtaining results were reminiscent of the attitudes of the Communist-led Farmers' Unity League in the early thirties.

While Aberhart did not share rank-and-file willingness to unite Social Credit with other reformist elements, some Social Credit leaders viewed positively the possibilities of an alliance with the CCF. E. G. Hansell, the secretary of the federal Social Credit caucus, wrote Aberhart in March 1939, of the caucus's interest in including the CCF within a coalition for the upcoming federal election for which Social Credit had already made an alliance with W. D. Herridge's New Democracy movement.[58] The CCF, however, proved as unwilling as Aberhart to form such an alliance.

Indeed, the philosophical underpinnings of the CCF and Social Credit and even more so of the Communists and Social Credit were so different that alliances between them were, not surprisingly, short-lived. But the rank-and-file of Social Credit were generally unconcerned about philosophical differences between their party and socialist parties; they wanted unity against the "big shots" whom they believed were oppressing them and appeared little concerned about the discrepancies between socialist theory and Douglas's monetary reform ideas.

Party rivalries, in the end, as much as philosophical differences, prevented unity among the anti-establishment parties in Alberta. The Communists largely abandoned united-front politics when they proved unable to win significant support outside their own ranks for Canadian neutrality in World War II (a position they set aside when the Soviet Union was invaded in June 1941).[59] The CCF leadership meanwhile was dominated by provincial labour leaders who regarded Aberhart as hostile to unionism and wished to see him deposed.[60] Labour interestingly was as suspicious of the Social Credit regime as business—though the post-Aberhart period demonstrated that it was only labour that had legitimate long-term fears about Social Credit's aims.[61]

Labour's attack on the Aberhart movement however had always had contradictory threads. On the one hand, the leaders of the Alberta Federation of Labour charged that Aberhart's announced intention to control the banks and currency in the province had scared away investors[62]—a charge also made by organized business.[63] On the other hand, as leading members of the socialist CCF, the same labour leaders denounced Social Credit for not having nationalized the hydro-electric and petroleum industries,[64] hardly moves that would have endeared a government to investors. The labour leaders' main reason for opposing Social Credit, however, was fear that Social Credit's policy of establishing wages by government decree would destroy collective bargaining and trade unionism.[65] Aberhart had ignored the question of the role of trade unions in his discussions of wage-setting and thereby contributed to labour fears.[66]

His government did pass several pieces of legislation which labour had requested, most notably legislation establishing collective bargaining contracts as legal contracts.[67] But the premier, short-tempered with all opponents, proved particularly cantankerous to the labour leaders[68] who had been accustomed to friendly relations with the UFA administration from 1921 to 1935.[69]

Despite the labour leaders' close alliance with the CCF in the provincial election of 1940, Social Credit retained the loyalty of most workers and farmers who had turned against the old-line parties. As *People's Weekly*, the unofficial CCF organ, conceded, "the progressive voters of the province are remaining loyal to the government they elected in 1935."[70] The days when the left-wing parties and even the old-line parties could attack Social Credit as a small-c conservative party were still in the future.

Indeed, the old-line party supporters were sufficiently determined to overthrow Social Credit to unite in so-called "People's Leagues" that nominated a single anti-Social Credit candidate for each constituency. The unity on the right produced a close contest in the popular vote though Social Credit retained a comfortable majority of legislative seats.[71] The losers were not especially gracious. A year later the boards of trade of the two major cities were still condemning the Alberta administration as hostile to the private sector. The secretary of the Calgary Board of Trade wrote: "it is evident that the Government's interpretation of social credit is merely one of an autocratic state socialism."[72] The secretary of the Edmonton Board of Trade added uncharitably:

> You may wonder how such a Government was re-elected but you must take into account that we have a very large foreign population that will believe anything and is responsible for this result. Even a rudimentary knowledge of economics and monetary science will demonstrate the infeasibility of such fatuous policies.[73]

The premier's response was characteristically strident:

> It is unfortunate and yet not surprising that the organizations from whom the attacks originated have been consistently and

bitterly opposed to any movement of social or economic reform. Dependent as they are, however, upon the good will of the banking institutions and subject to the undemocratic control of the present money system, their attitude is not unexpected.[74]

Fifteen years later, these organizations were among the most vocal supporters of the Social Credit government led by Ernest Manning, William Aberhart's protégé and his successor as premier. The Edmonton Chamber of Commerce, for example, praised government policies in a submission to the Board of Industrial Relations in 1956:

> The prosperous condition of the province is, in large measure, due to the fact that the Government and the Boards of Government have supported free enterprise, and have followed the positive policy of the minimum of interference with business.[75]

Clearly, circumstances had changed. Social Credit had become the free enterprise party which Kennedy wrongly claims it had been all along. What had caused the change? Historians who have concentrated on Social Credit's monetary fixations have had little difficulty with this question. From their point of view, once the courts had ruled out the possibility of provincial tinkering with monetary policies, Social Credit was prevented from taking action in the one area where social credit doctrine proposed radical interference in the free market.[76] As we have seen, however, Alberta Social Crediters, including both rank-and-file and some leaders, had an eclectic approach to economic reform that did not limit them to seeking monetary changes. So, some explanation is required of why these people turned from reformers into reactionaries.

In part, the answer lies in a change in the character of the party from 1935 to 1943, the year when Aberhart died and was succeeded by Manning. In 1935, the party was a broadly-based and growing organization of about thirty thousand members. Its membership peaked at almost 41,000 in 1937, but in 1942 it registered only 3,500 members. Membership was so low in 1943 that the Social Credit League decided against holding the annual convention and instead simply held a conference open to all League members.[77] In part, the League's loss of over 90 percent of its 1937 membership can be seen as a reflection of better economic times; just as the majority of the UFA's 38,000 members in 1921 had retreated from politics as prosperity returned,[78] many early Social Credit activists abandoned politics as their individual economic situations improved. But the slide in party membership had begun in 1938, when party membership dropped by half despite a continuation of Depression conditions.[79] That drop was partially the result of the disillusionment that set in when it became clear that the courts would not allow the provincial government to carry out its promised monetary reforms. It was also, no doubt, a reaction to the government's unwillingness to brook criticism from the Social Credit groups. Aberhart's letters in response to criticism from party groups were as tactless as his responses to criticisms from other sources. It is unlikely that members remained after being told by Aberhart:

> I am very surprised at anyone calling himself a social crediter who appears to be so far out of touch with what the government is doing or attempting to do that a letter like the one referred to should be written.[80]

Alberta's Social Credit League, as C. B. Macpherson has noted, gave unusual power to its leader, including the right to choose candidates (constituencies drew up a list of five names, from which Aberhart and a hand-picked board chose a candidate). Although the Social Credit clubs and constituency organizations as well as provincial conventions made constant attempts to influence government policy, Aberhart proved aloof from the organizations whose existence had been spawned by his rhetoric. Increasingly, what had been a broadly-based secular reformist party became the political home of the Douglas dogmatists and of fundamentalist Christians who supported Social Credit less because of specific policies than because of the party's leadership by radio evangelists, that is Aberhart and Manning.[81] With the purge of the evangelical Douglasites in the late forties because of their professed anti-Semitism,[82] Manning's control of the party and government was unchallenged.

When Manning took over the party and government, the party was no longer a mass party and Manning reasoned shrewdly that the government could be re-elected by stressing its good administrative record rather than by embarking on a new anti-establishment course that would rekindle the initial populist spark that had put the party in office. Profoundly conservative himself, Manning was, like his predecessor, a religious man whose entry into politics had not altered his fundamental otherworldliness.[83] He assumed not only Aberhart's premiership but also his weekly Bible hour and continued to do the Bible show for many years after he had resigned as premier. Manning had never been part of the Social Credit alliances with socialist groups, and he took a hard-line stance against socialism, equating all forms of socialism with German "national socialism."[84] The CCF had become the major opposition political force in the province during the war,[85] and Manning was prepared to pull all stops to beat back the socialist challenge.

The business community, once so repelled by Social Credit, embraced the Manning administration as the only alternative to the CCF, and Manning proved willing to welcome successful businessmen into a party which previously had largely been the domain of plebeian elements. The Licensing and Marketing legislation, while it remained on the books, became a dead letter.

Left-wing resolutions still occasionally made it to the floor of provincial Social Credit conventions. So, for example, the 1951 convention debated resolutions in favour of state medicine (which had formed part of party policy at least until 1940), an increase in old-age pensions, state automobile insurance, state ownership of hydroelectric utilities, provincial subsidies to co-operative building associations, and the establishment of old-age homes by the province in each constituency. Significantly, all of these resolutions were defeated, some without even coming to a vote.[86]

Indeed, Social Credit conventions, once the scene of endless speeches denouncing bankers and profiteers, now became the scene of endless speeches extolling the free enterprise system and denouncing socialism of every description. Prosperity, Ernest Manning, and the growing political apathy which had induced most of the early Social Crediters to leave the party even before Manning's accession to power, had produced a spectacular political transformation. Social Credit, a monetary-reform party, which had attracted to its ranks workers and farmers who held a variety of reformist views, had become a party beloved of the financial establishment with which it had once tangled. The determination of the first Aberhart government to establish state control over the cost of living had given way to a solemn rejection of interference in the marketplace so thorough that the party rewrote its history to make it appear that it had always stood for rigid free-enterprise principles.

NOTES

This article first appeared in *Prairie Forum* 11, no. 1 (1986): 69–86.

1   *Edmonton Journal*, 9 June 1982, 1.
2   The lack of young faces became a constant theme of Social Credit conventions after the war. The conventions proposed programmes to stimulate youth interest in the party but in vain. Ernest Manning to Mrs. Marion Krough, 5 December 1947, Premiers' papers, Provincial Archives of Alberta, File 1461; "Resolutions of the Seventeenth

Annual Convention of the Alberta Social Credit League, 1951." Premiers' papers, Files 183 and 1846 B.

3 This view is expressed, for example, in C. B. Macpherson's classic history of the origins of Social Credit in Alberta, *Democracy in Alberta: Social Credit and the Party System* (Toronto: University of Toronto Press, 1962). Macpherson concentrates on the social credit monetary doctrines, the conspiratorial theories of Major Douglas, the Social Credit founder, and the authoritarian aspects of both social credit theory and Aberhart's practice. He ignores Social Credit government interventions in non-monetary fields and fails to analyze party demands for bolder programmes of intervention. Macpherson's analysis is unchallenged in more recent accounts such as Walter Young, *Democracy and Discontent: Progressivism, Socialism and Social Credit in the Canadian West* (Toronto: McGraw-Hill, 1978), 83–108. One recent article that raises the question of Aberhart's vaunted conservatism is David Elliott, "William Aberhart: Right or Left?," in *The Dirty Thirties in Prairie Canada: 11th Western Canada Studies Conference*, eds. D. Francis and H. Ganzevoort (Vancouver: Tantalus Research, 1980), 11–31. But Elliott deals only briefly with the Social Credit administration and not at all with the Social Credit organization. His view that fascism and socialism are similar ideologies (both are allegedly authoritarian) creates some imprecisions in the article.

4 Ben Swankey, "Reflections of a Communist; 1935 Election," *Alberta History* 28, no. 4 (Autumn 1980): 36. Swankey notes with reference to the late thirties:
    "It was in this period that close relationships were established between the Communist Party and sections of the Social Credit movement including its MLAs which included, for example, Communist support for the election of Orvis Kennedy in an Edmonton by-election in March 1938, where the victory parade following the election included Leslie Morris, western director of the Communist Party, in its front ranks."

5 The major account of the constitutional battles regarding the Alberta government's schemes to control finance is J. R. Mallory, *Social Credit and the Federal Power in Canada* (Toronto: University of Toronto Press, 1954).

6 Premiers' papers, File 1124.

7 Macpherson, *Democracy in Alberta*, 147.

8 Young, *Democracy and Discontent*, 88–89: Macpherson, *Democracy in Alberta*, 149–50.

9 Typical of Aberhart's responses to suggestions for changes in government policy is this reply to the provincial secretary of the Alberta Motor Association who forwarded to the premier the organization's resolution that revenues from gasoline taxes and motor licences be earmarked for highway construction and maintenance: "We have answered the type of resolution so many times that it seems to us we are wasting our time and paper in replying further to them. We do not believe that the Calgary Branch of the Alberta Motor Association has any right to direct this Government in what it shall do with its unexpended revenue," Aberhart to S. W. Cameron, 2 March 1942, Premiers' papers, File 1221 B.

10 Elliott, "William Aberhart," 12.

11 Alvin Finkel, "Populism and the Proletariat: Social Credit and the Alberta Working Class," *Studies in Political Economy* 13 (Spring 1984): 118–20.

12   William Aberhart, *Social Credit Manual: Social Credit as Applied to the Province of Alberta*, c. 1935, 5.

13   Ibid., 7.

14   Ibid., 21, 41–43.

15   Ibid., 55.

16   Ibid., 62.

17   Ibid., 13. Aberhart wrote somewhat incoherently: "At the present time this great wealth (machinery and natural resources) is being selfishly manipulated and controlled by one or more men known as the 'Fifty Big Shots of Canada.'"

18   *Social Credit Chronicle*, 21 September 1934, 2.

19   J. H. Hanna to John Mackay, secretary, Drumheller Board of Trade, 27 May 1935, Calgary Board of Trade papers, Glenbow-Alberta Institute (hereafter CBT, GAI), Box 2, File 13.

20   The *Edmonton Bulletin*, which had supported the Liberals in the election, complained afterwards that the Economic Safety League campaign proved counter-productive for the anti-Aberhart forces:
      "Its grotesque campaign methods and lavish expenditures gave credence to this campaign (whispering campaign against the League) as its radio and publicity material was considered of the most reactionary kind, while the fact that its membership was anonymous, as was the source of its funds, gave Mr. Aberhart and his followers a priceless opportunity to point to it as being a glaring example of financial control from the East."
      Edmonton Bulletin, 26 August 1935, 3.

21   J. H. Hanna to E. C. Gilliat, managing secretary, Winnipeg Board of Trade, 12 September 1935, CBT, GAI, Box 2, File 13.

22   John Mackay, secretary, Drumheller Board of Trade, to Hanna, 3 May 1935; Stettler Board of Trade to Calgary Board of Trade, 12 August 1935; Medicine Hat Chamber of Commerce to Calgary Board of Trade, 9 August 1935: CBT, GAI, Box 2, File 13.

23   P. J. Carroll to Hanna, 10 August 1935, CBT, GAI, Box 2, File 13.

24   Young, *Democracy and Discontent*, 98.

25   Alvin Finkel, "Social Credit and the Unemployed," *Alberta History* 31, no. 2 (Spring 1983): 24–32.

26   "Report of Legislative Committee to the Council of the Board of Trade," 15 April 1936, CBT, GAI, Box 1, File 1.

27   "An Act for the Establishment of a Department of Trade and Industry and to Prescribe its Powers and Duties" (Assented to 16 April 1934), *Statutes of Alberta, 1934*, Chapter 33.

28   Among the organizations supporting codes, the Alberta branch of the Retail Merchants' Association was prominent. Premiers' papers, File 921A; the large chain stores opposed the legislation: P. W. Abbott, legal representative of "T. Eaton Company and several others of the larger retail establishments in Edmonton" to Aberhart, Premiers' papers, File 921A.

29   An Act to Amend and Consolidate the Licensing of Trades and Business Act" (Assented to 5 October 1937), *Statutes of Alberta, 1937*, Third Session, Chapter One.

30   Among the boards whose opposition to the bill is recorded in the Premiers' papers are the boards in Edmonton, Calgary, Red Deer, Medicine Hat, High River, and

Lacombe. Premiers' papers, File 922; F. Ashenhurst, secretary, Alberta Branch, Canadian Manufacturers Association, to Aberhart, 29 September 1937, Premiers' papers, File 922.

31 CBT, GAI, Box 1. File 5.

32 H. J. Nolan, lawyer with Bennett, Hannah, Nolan, Chambers and Might to L. A. Cavanaugh (the automobile dealer), 8 November 1938, CBT, GAI, Box 1, File 7.

33 *Calgary Albertan*, 9 September 1939, 1; Hanna to W. L. Mackenzie King, 13 January 1938, CBT, GAI, Box 1, File 7.

34 "An Act Respecting the Marketing of Natural Products and other Commodities and to Provide for the Regulations Thereof Within the Province," *Statutes of Alberta, 1939*, Chapter 3.

35 Ibid.

36 "A meeting with Messrs. Glen L. MacLachlan, Powell, Byrne. 9 July 1937," Alfred Farmilo papers, Provincial Archives of Alberta, Box 1, Item 44.

37 Macpherson, *Democracy in Alberta*, 193.

38 Ibid., 162, for example, claims: "The social credit political theory and the inspirational quality of Aberhart's leadership, which demanded and received the complete submergence of his followers' wills, combined to put any problem of the popular control of the legislature out of sight, or at least in abeyance."

39 *Edmonton Journal*, 5 April 1935, 1.

40 Premiers' papers, File 1105.

41 Ibid., Files 1105, 1106, 1117B.

42 Ibid., File 1117B.

43 Ibid., Files 1068A, 1119, 1128.

44 *Edmonton Journal*, 27 March 1935, 14.

45 The Communist change of heart regarding Social Credit was expressed in various issues of the *Western Clarion*, a Communist party organ, during 1936 and 1937.

46 Herbert Clark, secretary-treasurer of Lethbridge (provincial) constituency organization, to Aberhart, 2 May 1938, Premiers' papers, File 1125B.

47 A. E. Smith, chairman, Lethbridge federal constituency, to William Aberhart, 22 April 1939; Aberhart to Smith, 28 April 1939; Smith to Aberhart, 29 April 1939, Premiers' papers, File 1055.

48 W. B. McDowall, president, Castle River Social Credit zone, to Aberhart, 1 May 1938, Premiers' papers, File 1109. McDowall enclosed a resolution passed at a mass meeting called by Social Credit "in deference to the wishes of a number of our supporters who are not or only a few of them members of the group" and who "have a leaning towards communism ever since they belonged to that party when miners." The meeting was addressed by two Social Credit MLAs and the socialist mayor of Blairmore. The resolution said in part: "The meeting feels very strongly now that our common enemy has been brought out into open view and the battle joined that all progressives should close their ranks in a united front. It would be suicidal at this time to allow differences of opinion to the best final solution to divide them."

49 *People's Weekly*, 13 June 1936, 4; and 27 June 1936, 1.

50 Finkel, "Populism and the Proletariat," 125.

51 *People's Weekly*, 26 November 1938, 1.

52 See footnote 4. The cooperation with the Communists later proved embarrassing to a militantly anti-Communist Manning government. Elmer Roper notes, that as CCF leader in the legislature, he retorted to Manning's charges of Communist sympathies in the CCF by showing the legislature the photograph of Communist leader Leslie Morris on the running board of the Social Credit victory vehicle alongside the victorious Kennedy. Finkel interview with Elmer Roper, Victoria, 21 February 1984.

53 Ethel Baker to Aberhart, 4 October 1938; Aberhart to Baker, 7 October 1938, Premiers' papers, File 1115.

54 *People's Weekly*, 26 November 1938, 1.

55 In H. E. Nichols papers, Glenbow-Alberta Institute, Box 7, File 42.

56 *People's Weekly*, 5 October 1946, 1.

57 Nichols papers, Box 4, File 28.

58 E. G. Hansell to Aberhart, 17 March 1939, Premiers' papers, File 1055.

59 Ivan Avakumovic, *The Communist Party in Canada: A History* (Toronto: McClelland and Stewart, 1975), 139–40.

60 Fred White, president of the Alberta Federation of Labour, had been a Labour MLA from 1921 to 1935, representing Calgary. Defeated by Social Credit in 1935, he ran again unsuccessfully in the 1940 provincial election under the CCF banner. *Canadian Parliamentary Guide*, Aberhart and the union leaders were on poor terms. Responding to a letter from a United Mine Workers' local protesting the premier's dismissive treatment of an Alberta Federation of Labour delegation, Aberhart wrote in part:

> "I was rather surprised to hear that the leaders of the Alberta Federation of Labour have evidently decided to make a political instrument out of the Federation. Ever since the Government came into office it has given the greatest consideration to the resolutions of your Federation, notwithstanding the fact that Mr. White and Mr. Berg have been bitter political opponents of our policies....
>
> Now it would appear that these same leaders, who were treated so courteously by us, are now sending out circular letters to try to stir up the members of the Federation in a political way. Surely it should be understood that no Government can be expected to meet with or discuss its policies with any other political party. I should therefore suggest that since your Federation has not entered the political field and since it can in no way be considered a political party this course of action by your leaders in attempting to infuse political flavor into your Federation should be resented by you."

Aberhart to A. Orlando, secretary, Cambrian Local Union #7330, District 18, United Mine Workers of America, Wayne, Alberta, 3 March 1939, Premiers' papers, File 1227.

61 On Social Credit-labour relations in the post-war period, see Warren Caragata, *Alberta Labour: A Heritage Untold* (Toronto: Lorimer, 1979), 140–42.

62 AFL executive members Carl Berg and Alfred W. Farmilo are quoted to this effect in the *Edmonton Journal*, 31 May 1935, 17.

63 *Calgary Herald*, 8 August 1935, 1; *Edmonton Journal*, 8 August 1935, 1.

64 *People's Weekly*, 10 February 1940, 5.

65 Carl Berg made this charge publicly—*Edmonton Bulletin*, 8 August 1935, 1. Farmilo expressed this view in his outline of a meeting between labour leaders and government

officials. "A meeting with Messrs. Glen L. MacLachlan, Powell, Byrne, 9 July 1937," Alfred Farmilo papers, Provincial Archives of Alberta, Item 44.

66 The *Social Credit Manual* (1935), 41–43, asked "How can just wages be fixed?" and answered:

> "Just wages are fixed today by the Minimum Wage Act. Experts would fix the minimum and maximum wage just as they could fix the price of goods. It is understood, however, that wages must not be reduced on account of the issuance of the basic dividends."

67 Labour's gratitude for this legislation was expressed at the Alberta Federation of Labour annual convention in 1938. "Proceedings of the 22nd Convention of the Alberta Federation of Labour, 28–30 November 1938," Farmilo papers.

68 See footnote 60.

69 A Labour party member, Alexander Ross, was a Cabinet minister in the first UFA administration. On relations between Labour and the UFA, see Finkel, "Populism and the Proletariat," 117–19.

70 *People's Weekly*, 30 March 1940, 7.

71 The best account of the 1940 provincial campaign is Harold J. Schultz, "A Second Term: 1940," *Alberta Historical Relief* 10, no. 1 (Winter 1962): 17–26.

72 T. E. D. McGreen to Auckland Chamber of Commerce (as reported in an unidentified newspaper and sent to Aberhart, 16 July 1941), Premiers' papers, File 1089.

73 J. Blue to Auckland Chamber of Commerce, Premiers' papers, File 1089.

74 No date, Premiers' papers, File 1089.

75 Edmonton Chamber of Commerce submission to the chairman and members of the Board of Industrial Relations for the Province of Alberta," 11 January 1956, Alberta Liberal Association papers, Glenbow-Alberta Institute, Box 35, File 174.

76 Macpherson, *Democracy in Alberta*, 206.

77 Premiers' papers, Files 1117A, 1124, 1129.

78 Macpherson, *Democracy in Alberta*, 64.

79 Premiers' papers, File 1124.

80 Aberhart to William Holowaychuk, secretary-treasurer, Paulus Social Credit group, Chipman, Alberta, 16 December 1938, Premiers' papers, File 1128. Petulant letters of this kind abound in Aberhart's correspondence as premier.

81 For an analysis of the latter-day Social Credit party, see Owen Anderson, "The Alberta Social Credit Party: An Empirical Analysis of Membership, Characteristics, Participation and Opinion" (unpublished Ph.D. dissertation, University of Alberta, 1972).

82 Macpherson, *Democracy in Alberta*, 211–12.

83 As one commentator observed after interviewing Manning, the Alberta premier's strong opposition to socialist philosophy rested on religious doctrine. Socialism to Manning "deemphasizes the individual struggle for salvation" and the attainment of grace by placing responsibility for the individual on the shoulders of the state rather than the individual himself. Social benefits such as medicare and guaranteed incomes breed idleness and permit "the evil tendencies of the individual to come to the fore, thereby causing a breakdown of his relationship with God." Dennis Groh, "The Political Thought of Ernest Manning" (M.A. thesis, University of Calgary, 1970), 65.

84 For example, Manning wrote to one correspondent in 1944:

"...it is an insult to suggest to the Canadian people who are sacrificing their sons to remove the curse which the socialism of Germany has brought on the world that their own social and economic security can be attained only by introducing some form of socialism in Canada. The premise embodied in your proposed resolution, namely, that there is such a thing as democratic Socialism, contradicts itself in that it attempts to associate together two concepts of life which are diametrically opposed and opposite." Manning to J. B. Hayfield, Bittern Lake, Alberta, 3 February 1944, Premiers' papers, File 1242.

85   CCF membership of twelve thousand in 1944 in the province exceeded Social Credit membership by four thousand, Alberta CCF provincial office to Margaret Telford, CCF national office, 4 November 1944, Alberta CCF papers, Glenbow-Alberta Institute, Box 5, File 42. The CCF received 25 percent of the provincial vote in 1944, almost double the vote of the third-place Independents. *Canadian Parliamentary Guide*, 1945, 381–82.

86   Premiers' papers, Files 1843 and 1846B.

14. The Rural Prairie Novel and the Great Depression

Victor Carl Friesen

A significant number of Canadian prairie novels which have a rural background deal with the Great Depression of the 1930s. An examination of these works demands first a brief consideration of the Depression itself. For the prairie dweller, particularly the farmer, the Great Depression was not a wholly new experience. Most farmers by 1930 had already been living under depression conditions for a part of their lives. Many were of the first generation to be born on the prairies, and so belonged to the West's initial baby boom, an attempt by their pioneer parents to populate the vast prairie emptiness. But unlike the parents, the many children could not obtain cheap homestead land when they became adults. Instead, they were forced to buy land—on time—when prices were high, as prices were during World War I, and then to try to pay off their mortgages during the recession that followed the war. And of course, drought and other plagues of the farmer were present in the 1920s as well as in the following decade.

Dr. G. E. Britnell, former head of the Department of Economics and Political Science at the University of Saskatchewan, writing in the *Canadian Forum* during the middle of the Great Depression, makes the point that the depression on the prairies did not stem from any extravagances of the 1920s. In the 1920s, he tells us, only 3 percent of Western farms had electricity, while 95 percent had access to dirt roads only; children seldom saw oranges from one Christmas to another, and most household "linen" was made from flour sacks.[1] What made the 1930s depression unique was the *unrelieved* drought, the accumulation of debts so that "arrears of interest alone often exceeded the...value of the mortgaged property,"[2] and the unemployment. It was three depressions in one, as James Gray notes in his book, *The Winter Years* (1966).

Canadian prairie novelists tend not to dwell on the economic forces underlying the Great Depression in their delineation of that era.[3] Here they are unlike their American counterparts, for a reason that seems obvious. The American Depression novel tended to be published *in* the Depression, culminating with Steinbeck's *The Grapes of Wrath* in 1939. These novels were works of social protest, written in the heat of the moment. Art became a weapon; fiction took on Marxist shadowings as writers forgot their traditional alienation from society and identified themselves with the struggling workers. The Canadian novel dealing with the Depression on the prairies tended to be published *after* the event. Of course, portions of some of these novels may have been, and probably were, written during the Thirties, but by the time of final revisions and publication, the cancer had been cured. Only a few of the works involved enough social and political comment to be called "protest." Instead, the writer's interest became focused upon the individual's every-day reaction to the manifestations of the Depression—the wind, the drought, and the hardships they caused.

In this paper, a number of these rural prairie novels are examined according to three broad, and sometimes overlapping, themes: first, the political or socio-economic background; second, the prairie West as "garden"; and third, the psychological impact of the Depression on the characters. Because the prairies, unlike other regions of Canada, endured three depressions simultaneously, the effect on the area's economy was so great that not only were there

Dust storm on a rural road (Courtesy of the Provincial Archives of Saskatchewan / R-B9063).

traumatic social consequences but also lasting political developments. Both the Social Credit and CCF parties sprang from prairie soil in the Depression. That these two parties should germinate in the West spoke for the self-reliance and grass-roots democracy which Frederick Jackson Turner posited for a frontier or western society.⁴ At the same time, the collective action needed to combat the depression conditions showed that the West could be other than a beneficent garden, an agricultural paradise which served as a safety valve refuge for the despairing poor elsewhere. The West, it turned out, was a place to escape *from* during the Depression, and yet Turner's "safety-valve" hypothesis, with modification, was applicable to the Canadian West during the Thirties. Finally, if, as Barry Broadfoot claims, the decade was "the most debilitating, the most devastating, the most horrendous" of our nation's history,⁵ surely it was most strikingly so on the prairies. The Depression, he says, still affects our everyday life, and for prairie dwellers over forty the "ten lost years" may ever remain as the most significant factor in their lives. The psychic scars created in people then could well serve the novelist as subject for his art, provided that the time lapse before the writing of the novel was not so great that they would be partly forgotten or else gilded by a warm nostalgia.

The earliest of the novels under consideration is Sinclair Ross's *As for Me and My House*, coming out in 1941. Certainly this book retains the flavour of the Depression: always the wind is blowing; always the dust is everywhere—it seems to cover every page as much as it does the open diary which the narrator Mrs. Bentley is keeping. The other works to be considered, in greater or lesser detail, appear over a span of two decades but continue on the whole to present a realistic account. Edward McCourt's *Music at the Close* and W. O. Mitchell's *Who Has Seen the Wind* both were published in 1947, Vera Lysenko's *Westerly Wild* in 1956, Patricia Blondal's *A Candle to Light the Sun* in 1960, Margaret Laurence's *The Stone Angel* in 1964, and Robert Kroetsch's *The Words of My Roaring* in 1966.⁶

The novels by McCourt and Kroetsch, like those of their American counterparts, do treat of the political aspect of the Depression. In McCourt's *Music at the Close*, the central figure, Neil Fraser, fails at farming—his immediate thought was that "with any kind of luck he could clean up in a very short time" (135)—then plays the grain market. When the market crashes in 1929, he finally gets a job as a strikebreaker in the coalfields of Saskatchewan. It is here that McCourt can bring in political comment, for Neil believes that the strike is caused by communist agitators. When he meets the strikers, he discovers that his old friend Gil Reardon is one of the leaders. Gil's explanation of the cause of the strike might have been taken from *The Grapes of*

Wrath: "If a man is a Red because he demands a decent living standard and humane treatment for himself and his fellow men, you're right," he tells Neil (152). The implication seems to be that there was no Red agitation at the time.[7]

In Gil's lengthy analysis of the farmer's relation to this situation, the harangue is so skillfully organized that we must believe Gil to be a very astute politician or else that McCourt is here speaking directly to the reader. The passage is worth quoting in full:

> Neil, the farmer is a great guy. In a lot of ways he's the best guy on earth. But as far as he's concerned, only one thing matters, wheat! As long as there's a market for his wheat he doesn't give a hoot about the industrial worker—doesn't know he exists. But once the bottom drops out of the wheat market, he can be led by the nose by any political racketeer who has a formula for upping the price. It never occurs to him that he and the worker are caught in the same trap. And you're a farmer, Neil. You've got chaff and dust and tractor oil in your blood. There's no market for wheat—and so you swallow a line that wouldn't fool an intelligent six-year-old. Chase all the Reds like me back to Russia—restore the industrial economy—and the price of wheat will go up! And if the miners live on the thin borderline of starvation—if their wives are old at thirty and their kids rickety and half-starved and half-frozen—what's the difference so long as the Bolshies are driven out and the price of wheat goes up! Neil—you make me sick. (154)

Notice how in the first few sentences a tribute is given to the farmer generally and later on to Neil specifically—with the tractor oil in his veins. There is a reference to a common enemy, the political racketeer, and an appeal to sentiment with the mention of wives and children. All this is a preparation for the punch line—an attempt to instill self-disgust and hence an arousal to action: "Neil—you make me sick."

The noted critic Malcolm Cowley has analyzed the many strike novels which appeared in the United States in the 1930s and calls attention to the rigidity of their pattern:

> The hero was usually a young worker, honest, naive and politically undeveloped. Through intolerable mistreatment, he was driven to take part in a strike. Always the strike was ruthlessly

suppressed, and usually its leader was killed. But the young
worker, conscious now of the mission that united him to the
whole working class, marched on toward new battles.[8]

We can see how conventional McCourt is in his portrayal of a Canadian
strike. Neil's political naïveté prompts Gil's tirade, and Neil, having been
mistreated as were the miners themselves, is ready to march with them. He
sees the universal significance of their actions. They are like the "hungry
generations" of Keats's poem,[9] representative of mankind's struggle through
the ages for a better life. However, with the killing of their leader, Neil loses
his sense of mission, and McCourt here departs from the typical format.

Neil is *always* the dreamer and therefore not much given to action; he
has given himself to life on this occasion but then quickly lapses back into
his usual stance, that of an observer. This fact is nowhere as obvious as later
when he listens to "Bible Bill" Aberhart expound his Social Credit policies
at a political meeting in Alberta. Neil is not caught up in the hysteria which
grips the people about him. He is too much preoccupied with the spectacle
of it. He can see that the others, because they will not accept what has happened to them, are putting a desperate trust in the new "prophet," who, it
turns out, does win the election with their help. Their refusal to give up is
their strength, Neil believes, and the author implies that successful political
activism of any kind does demand from its followers something which Neil
unfortunately lacks "the finest faith there is. Faith in mankind" (156).

In Kroetsch's book, *The Words of My Roaring*, the central character, Johnnie
Backstorm, is depicted as a political candidate in the 1935 provincial election
in Alberta which swept Aberhart into power. Backstrom is apparently running on the Social Credit ticket, although the real name of the party and
its leader are not given. However, the phrase "flow of credit" (40) and the
leader's name, "Applecart," make the identification unmistakable. Johnnie,
like his leader, attacks the Eastern big-money interests in his speeches: "Oh,
sure,...they send us a few apples and some salted codfish.... All they want
in return is our farms. Our land and our businesses and our flesh and our
tears and our blood. That's all" (110–111). Then he grins to show he is being
sarcastic, remembering that he has a magnificent set of teeth. For Johnnie
Backstorm is a fake. He too, like Neil, is out to make a killing—but in politics. His actions, though, come to have a redemptive effect on the people he
meets. They need something or someone to believe in when their world has
gone wrong. They are grasping at straws in the wind. Even such a morally
frail person as Johnnie can be something to cling to. He has promised rain for

the election, or so his query of "Mister, how would you like some rain?" (8) is construed. Hopes are renewed, and the rain, surprisingly, comes. As Johnnie drives his team at night through the mud in the downpour, farm couples wait along the road with lanterns to guide his way and with cocoa and sandwiches to serve as refreshment.

The book's forte is in the telling of just such little human kindnesses—and also of little human failings—characteristic of the Depression. The politics in the book, on the other hand, the reader cannot feel sure of. How much is serious? How much is slapstick? And how should we separate the one from the other? The problem occurs because the author's focus is on Johnnie the narrator, who, in an understatement, admits that he "exaggerate[s] a little" (20). When Johnnie describes his leader's radio broadcast as "a voice blasting away into the darkness...one big blabbering mouth" (94), are we learning especially about the platitudinous quality of politicians? of this particular speaker? or about the darkness of Johnnie's own soul and of the self-doubts raised there by the continuous, exhorting voice? Johnnie does recognize his own frailties, and such moral sensitivity should give some credence to any political remarks he makes. These, however, do not go beyond the intensely personal, while the radio comments of the leader remain distant and mechanical. Kroetsch purposely avoids making a political statement, but he is showing us that something more than apples and codfish are needed when a farmer's "one lifetime" is struggle and heartbreak, represented by nothing more than the items on that auction bill which announces his defeat (56).

That both Kroetsch and McCourt choose to deal with the rise of the Social Credit party, however briefly, must stem in part from the authors' being originally Albertans. But one would suspect that this party, more so than the CCF, lends itself well to the designs of these two novelists. First its leader was charismatic and could easily be presented vividly, even caricatured. More importantly, ideology here was not very significant; the authors generally could save themselves the difficult task of trying to dramatize political tenets, because their chief concern remained the portrayal of character in the Depression: the recounting of two ways of coping with harsh conditions, Neil's introspection and Johnnie's lusty bravado.

While socio-economic background is part and parcel of the political references in *Music at the Close* and *The Words of My Roaring*, it is another book, W. O. Mitchell's *Who Has Seen the Wind*, that has become a classic evocation of prairie life during the Thirties. It deals with the broad social and economic theme—and particularly with one aspect of it, the rift between town and country—apart from the considerations of politics. Mitchell does so by seeing the world mainly through the eyes of a child, Brian O'Connall, to whom politics can have no direct meaning. The young Brian, growing up in a small Saskatchewan town, is hardly touched by the Depression and its effect on the farming community—and here he is like many of the adults in the town. But whereas their attitude is often uncaring, his is merely innocent. Several of the incidents that mark his growing up have nothing distinctly "Depressionistic" about them. They are simply incidents common to the lives of most boys growing up at any time, such as experiencing the mysteries of birth and death and becoming aware of the place of these two phenomena in life's pattern.

Where the Depression does enter into Brian's life is in his changing relationship to the prairie circling the town. His attitude in the course of the novel changes noticeably and so becomes a contrast with that of others. At the beginning of the book, the first time that he is alone on the prairie, it is not a depression-scarred view that he beholds—not the bones of a former plenty,[10] not the "skeleton requirements" (3) of Saskatchewan landscape, land and sky, with black topsoil banked against the fences. Brian's prairie is a happy place: a meadowlark sings "deliciously," while the rock on which the boy sits is pleasantly "warm." And the most pervasive element there, the wind, is "warm and living" against the boy's face and in his hair (11).

As Brian becomes older, his moments of empathy with nature become less frequent. Instead, he gains an objective awareness of what the forces of nature can do to the land and its people and in this regard has advanced beyond his indifferent townsmen. Having a farmer uncle helps Brian to be sympathetic to the farming community. For instance, he hears his Uncle Sean describe Saint Sammy, another farmer, who lives out on the prairie in a piano box: "Yearsa gittin' rusted out an' sawflied out an' cutwormed out an' 'hoppered out an' hailed out an' droughted out an' rusted out an' smutted out; he up an' got good an' goddam tired out. Crazier'n a cut calf" (118). When Brian visits Saint Sammy near the end of the story, the prairie is no longer a happy place for the boy. It is "inscrutable and unsmiling,…strung with the black crosses of telephone poles" (265). The wind again is the most pervasive element, as a storm is developing. But now the wind is no longer friendly; the boy feels it "sting his face with dust and snatch at his very breath" (270) as it scours the countryside. At the end of the story Brian seems to feel some responsibility to improve the plight of the land and plans to be a soil scientist when he grows up.

The rift between town and country is also apparent in Laurence's *The Stone Angel*. This book's central character, Hagar Currie, an elegant town girl, begins her personal depression by marrying a poor farmer. When she is reduced to filching some of the eggs laid by their own hens so that she can sell them on the sly in town for pin-money, it is she who is laughed at by the town girls as the "egg woman" (132). She eventually leaves this life, her husband, and the farm, and goes to the West Coast before the Great Depression begins, but comes back in the mid-1930s when her husband is dying. The description that follows, of the farm in the Depression, seems to be told as though by an outsider. Expressions like "the Russian thistle flourished, emblem of want" (168) or "only the grasshoppers grew, leaping and whirring in the bone-dry air" (169) seem too polished and sophisticated to originate with someone who has actually lived through such experiences. This kind of description can be justified, for Hagar after all is telling her own story, and she has been away since before the drought began.

Hagar, unlike Brian O'Connall but like his fellow townsmen, had continually resisted gaining an empathic kinship with the farmland and its people. "I'd read of the drought," she said before returning, "but it didn't mean a thing to me. I couldn't imagine it" (168). When she does see it, her response is imaginative only in a literary sense, not in an emotional one. The reader is not convinced that she really *feels* it. And the rift between town and country, in spite of the levelling effect of the Depression, exists as before. The fact that she had married her husband as an act of rebellion *against* her town's mores was evidence of the rift in the past; now she sees the episode repeated in another town girl out with her farmer son, "flaunting him like a ragged flag" (199).

It appears that novelists may have given us a truer picture of the cultural gap separating the farmer from the small-town dweller in the Thirties than have the social scientists. The latter are apt to lump the small town and the country together as "rural" in their studies,[11] in spite of the basic difference in how the occupants of each make their living and the contrasting attitudes which this difference generates. Mitchell dwells on the antagonism at its worst, accentuated by the Depression. Saint Sammy accusingly points his finger at the town people and declaims that its citizens are the cause of the drought; the town's banker, in turn, opines that "farmers are not a thrifty lot" (44) and blames them for the Depression. Laurence, meanwhile, seems to suggest that a prolonged depression may be something of a leveller, although the rift is not eliminated. If farmers can be reduced to the same footing, as Hagar's husband and his neighbours are, then too dwellers in town *and* country may find a concern in common problems and be, even as two old people, "no longer haggling with one another, but with fate, pitting [their] wits against God's" (212). As for Hagar, she again does not stay on the farm, as one would expect; she returns to the Coast, travelling west to that seeming Garden of Eden, as so many Depression victims had done.

The idea of some part of the West being a garden, a kind of paradise, is worth looking at in itself with regard to the Depression since the notion appears in almost all the works under consideration in this article. The Canadian prairies were settled largely by middle-European immigrants leaving an oppressed homeland (some via a brief stay in the American midwest) and by Eastern Canadians seeing in the western provinces greater opportunities than in their own area. Both groups therefore could visualize the West, even the prairie region, as a garden. But the idea, at least on this continent, is older than the time of prairie settlement. It goes back to the time of the very first colonies on the Eastern seaboard. All development, all opportunity, had to lie to the west, as Frederick Jackson Turner pointed out in his *The Frontier in American History*. The fertile groves and plains were waiting for their Adam, someone to hold dominion over them. And so European man, with the Biblical injunction that nature was his to keep and to subdue, started to march across the continent and came first to the midwest, then to the prairie.

The Adam who came to the Canadian prairie can hardly be thought of as the innocent in the garden of the West, who "falls" and learns disillusionment when the Depression comes along and destroys his Eden. Instead, he has either been disillusioned in his former home and has come west to *gain* his paradise, or learned disillusionment in his pre-Depression days in the West but has doggedly persisted in trying to *make* it an Eden. For the prairie is not paradise, as the diaries and reminiscences of the pioneer settlers attest. These accounts are filled with heartbreak and loneliness.[12] The problem is that many of these "Adams", consciously or otherwise, have interpreted the injunction that one should subdue nature to mean that one should exploit it. Thus they have helped to make their potential Eden infertile, and must seek another elsewhere once the Depression accentuates their misuse of the land.

One of the authors under consideration does describe the early-day southern Canadian prairie in Eden-like terms. The environs of the fictional Mouse Bluffs in Manitoba, in Blondal's *A Candle to Light the Sun*, resemble a garden with a creek spraying "tiny rainbows into the pale air," and with a "green valley where colours glinted more brightly than on the sun'sucked prairie, the oaks catching the sun on flickering oily rich leaves,...a cornucopia of gentle beauty" (p. 69). Such imagery is usually reserved by the chroniclers of the Depression for a promised land elsewhere, either in British Columbia or in the northwestern area of the prairie provinces. Turner's previously mentioned safety-valve refuge, that unoccupied land stretching ahead of the settled area, had merely moved farther north or as far west as it could ultimately go. It still served as a place where a man had a chance to start all over again.

The Peace River country in northern Alberta was conceived to be such an area, and many victims of the drought trekked there in the Thirties. In Lysenko's book, *Westerly Wild*, one of the trekkers writes back to describe the new home in these glowing words:

> You should see our beautiful Peace River plateau.... The grass is green, about a foot high, there are flowers, trees, luxuriant crops, wood for fuel, game for meat, wild berries and good water.... Our garden is a fairyland of flowers.... There are sweet peas, hollyhocks seven feet tall, vegetable marrow, mallows, cosmos, stocks, daisies, Russian pumpkins, pinks, raspberries, poppies, onions and asparagus." (147–148)

The correspondent, apparently overwhelmed herself, is trying to overwhelm us as well. Neil Fraser in McCourt's book also sees the Peace River area as a "promised land" with "purple distances" (183). It is his wife who brings him back to reality—and we wonder how true Lysenko's picture has been. Moira Fraser says that by moving there they would simply be stuck away in the bush country and would eventually starve to death. How can they have an Eden there, she implies, when they have not tended their garden here, such as it is.

The thing to do, it appears, is not to change one's locality but to change one's attitude, from that of exploiter to that of keeper, and make an Eden in the "wasteland." This has been done by characters in two of the novels. They are simply acting out changes which Turner himself had to make in his frontier hypothesis when free land was no longer available. He declared in 1924: "I place my trust in the mind of man seeking solutions by intellectual toil rather than by drift and by habit, bold to find new ways of adjustment, and strong in the leadership that spreads new ideas among the common people."[13] In each of the two novels in question, a character tries to change the attitude of his fellows toward the land. In *Who Has Seen the Wind*, Brian's Uncle Sean irrigates his vegetable garden to show the other farmers what can be done in spite of the drought. He tries, unsuccessfully, to interest them in an irrigation scheme that would dam a river and provide water for the crops, thus anticipating the kind of work that would be done in actuality under the Prairie Farm Rehabilitation Act. But Sean cannot get the farmers to co-operate. In *Westerly Wild* the farmers do co-operate in constructing a water reservoir, but the circumstances described in the book are extreme. The year is 1937, the place is the Dust Bowl of southwestern Saskatchewan. Something simply has to be done now, although the farmers had been antagonistic enough when Marcus Haugen, the chief male figure in the story, had earlier built a dam on his own land to make the farm "an oasis in the middle of a desert" (12).

There are attempts in the other novels to create "oases" too, that is, in the sense of their being pleasant places, miniature refuges, in the midst of a desolate region. Here we think of the arbour, which is compared to the Hanging Gardens of Babylon, created by Johnnie Backstrom's political opponent in *The Words of My Roaring*; or of Mrs. Bentley's efforts to nurture poppies and nasturtiums in a small plot of ground in *As for Me and My House*. Gardens do keep cropping up in Depression fiction, perhaps pointing the way to changing a wasteland into an Eden. But neither of these two books is really concerned with the general theme of the prairie West as garden. Instead Kroetsch and Ross are using the garden image to comment on character or plot: on the sensuality of Johnnie Backstrom (some of his escapades occur in these "Gardens of Babylon") and on the inability of Mrs. Bentley to allay the tension between herself and husband Philip (her flowers curl up against the blistered earth). On the other hand, McCourt and Lysenko show that they understand the philosophical implications of the theme in the context of prairie history. And their books, along with Mitchell's to some degree, dramatize the two alternatives for achieving an Eden: husbanding what one has or starting afresh elsewhere.

Lysenko's book should be considered at some length apart from the "garden" theme. *Westerly Wild* may be the fullest and most balanced account of the Depression that we have in our fiction, if we can overlook the Gothic attributes and machinations of Haugen. Here are described almost all the characteristics of the Depression which we have already seen delineated in the books under discussion. Furthermore, the author is much concerned with the third major theme treated in this article, that of the psychological effect of the drought on the characters. She shows this effect on both minor and major figures. We see farm people whose personalities have become "dust-coloured" (6) by drought, whose laughter "rattle[s] like dry grass" (58). These people are wound up tight like a clock, and they feel they will break down, but they cannot and must not because of their children; "so they suffer, so their faces grow more and more every year like the earth, thirsty, with deep cracks" (105).

Lysenko is particularly skillful in portraying the farm women and children. We see the women standing silently before a store's yard-goods counter, indulging a craving for polka dots and checks, for bright colours and ruffles, merely by looking—there is so much drabness in their lives. While they may have memories of other days in the past to tide them over the present (they can still beam coquettishly at a local dance), the children are for the most part quashed by the Depression. They speak in a kind of Greek chorus:

> I don't remember rain.
> It's wet when it comes down.
> It splashes your face and you stand in it and laugh. (23)

Only one of the children is able to laugh, and she attracts others like a magnet to her simple joyousness.

The plot centers on the love affair of a schoolteacher heroine and the masterful Marcus Haugen, who already has a wife, kept hidden away in an upstairs room! Lysenko sees Haugen as something more than just a Brontë-esque figure, however.[14] The fierce winds have attracted him to the country—they match his restless spirit—and he rides fiercely across the land on horseback, becoming, he tells us, "one with the wind" (89). The nearby farmers think him to be in league with the devil, just as they might regard the scorching westerly wind itself. But even Haugen cannot stand up to its elemental power. At the end of the story, while he is driving his spirited horses in the field, a spring wind starts up and the horses too become wild, trampling Haugen under their hoofs, then dragging his body with them. Swerving before a fence, they pitch the dead man away "with such force…that his body [hangs] transfixed upon the barbed wire like a tumbleweed" (284). On the second page of the story, tumbleweeds have already been described as ending their travels in "crucifixion" on the barbed-wire fences, and Haugen later describes himself as a "tumbleweed" (90). One is led to believe that Haugen's death is a sacrifice and that a new order is forthcoming. A farmer has just spoken of improved moisture conditions and of a project to plant hundreds of tree belts. As in the Christian tradition, Haugen has taken evil upon himself (in identifying himself with the wind) and is killed by the evil: it is the wild westerly which indirectly brings about his sacrifice, and it is the scourge of this very wind for which the farmers seek atonement.

In terms of psychological studies of the Depression, the novel of greatest depth is Ross's *As for Me and My House*. Here also is a suggestion of sacrifice, but its meaning is left somewhat ambiguous. Near the end of this story, fittingly again in spring, Mrs. Bentley, the narrator, stands against the south wall of a grain elevator, "letting the wind nail [her] there." She cowers with a sense of being "abandoned" (159). This token sacrifice, if so it can be called, is of her own volition, and of course there is no death. Mrs. Bentley may be simply dramatizing her situation, and we have only her word to rely on. But a few days later, the woman who had replaced her for a brief time in Philip Bentley's affection does die in giving birth to Philip's child, and hope, apparently, is reborn for the Bentleys and the success of their marriage when they adopt the infant child.

In this novel Ross appears to be touching on a theme that is common in Joseph Conrad.[15] In Conrad's *Heart of Darkness*, for instance, the author places a European in the heart of Africa where the restraints of his former society are replaced by the savagery of the jungle. Can the man in these new circumstances, Conrad asks, retain his civilized values when the environment speaks to a lurking darkness in his own heart? Sinclair Ross does not have to remove his characters to some exotic outpost. The Depression itself has isolated men and women right on the prairies. Can they maintain their normal behaviour in the new circumstances, brought on by drought and wind, in which *they* find themselves? Most of Mrs. Bentley's diary entries begin with a comment on this same drought and wind, and her relationship with her husband during their one-year stay in the small town of Horizon becomes as bleak as the depression world which surrounds the town. Even the town seems a "lost little clutter on the long sweep of the prairie" where the wind is the master too (74). What chance, then, to escape the wind and what it signifies?

The wind and the resulting dry crackle of sand against the windows are always unnerving for Mrs. Bentley: the mere doing of routine domestic chores can be a source of strength in times of trial (Conrad's characters may make a fetish of dress and grooming in the steaming hot jungle), but for her such activities are "rubbed out" by the wind, "so that there's nothing left but Philip and [her] alone [t]here, day after day, night after night, tensely aware of each other through the study door, listening to the whimper in the eaves" (43). At times, in panic, she wishes to thrash out against the wind with her hands, but the real antagonist is within the self, within the heart, whatever its quality of darkness. The capricious winds and the drought which she has described so painstakingly are like an outward manifestation of her insecure and barren life, and that of her husband. She is childless and tries to mother Philip, but her advances result in his retreating white-faced into his study where he draws or pretends to draw. He is frustrated, has only the inclinations and not the perseverance of an artist, and seeks for prestige in his relation with the other woman.

Mrs. Bentley thinks she can escape from the enclosing walls of her morbid thoughts by taking a greater interest in the town's activities, but she chooses to erect a false front between herself and the town in order to keep herself intact. Yet she herself is not distinct from the town. She describes the false fronts of the town's stores as smug-looking and pretentious, but *she* is smug in trying to hold herself apart. There is also a smugness in her attitude towards Philip, at first in her awareness of his inability to do simple mannish chores and later in her secret knowledge of his infidelity. It is perhaps too neat that all these false fronts collapse at the end of the story. As in *Westerly Wild*, the wind which has accentuated an evil now helps to eliminate it; a great dust storm blows down most of the store fronts and, as though taking her cue from the wind, Mrs. Bentley tells Philip that she knows he is the father of the baby. With the barrier down between them, she can show forgiveness at last when she kisses her husband, who is feigning sleep. At least for the present, she has risen above her morbid thoughts, above her own depression.

A character in Blondal's *A Candle to Light the Sun* implies that maintaining the niceties of civilized life is one way of coping with the Depression. Remember, such behaviour is just what we saw Conrad's white traders try to follow in their jungle outposts. In so doing they may look ridiculous, but they stay sane. What Blondal has her character actually say, about life in his little Manitoba town and its environs, seems to have Conrad in mind. "That is what we all do in Mouse Bluffs, dress for dinner in the jungle," he says (116). In a kind of prelude to her book, a prelude which speaks directly about the Depression, Blondal says: "The wind blows the promises thin, the fears in" (10). What she says here has relevance to the effect that the Depression has had on the prairie novel. Before the 1930s man and nature could be seen as equal protagonists. Man's struggle was usually pictured as an external one and often as a romantic one too.[16] But with the Depression, nature overwhelmed man. The prairie novelist, in order to capture the real essence of the Thirties, had to go inside his characters' minds and hearts, like Conrad again, to examine the fears and whatever other reactions might be hidden there.

The psychological reactions might be manifested in practical ways—a concern with politics, economics, social custom, agricultural procedures. These kinds of manifestations pertain to the first two major themes discussed in this paper. Regarding the broad theme of political and socio-economic matters, we saw that politics in the main received but a jocular treatment from one novelist, Kroetsch, and a stereotyped one from a second writer, McCourt.[17] And two novelists, Mitchell and Laurence, expanded upon the social consequences of the town-country rift: Mitchell vehement in his sympathy with the farmer, Laurence dispassionate in her awareness of its continuing nature. Regarding the prairie-as-garden theme, we found the writers simply restating Turner's frontier concept of unspoiled land yet farther west where one might make good; in other words, what was true of the American West was also true of the Canadian Northwest. Some writers, like Mitchell, saw the need, however, for farmers to become "the keeper of the Lord's Vineyard, literally" (18), in their own locale. The proving ground, it was also discovered, was within the self as well. This last idea was effectively dramatized by Lysenko and Ross with their probes into the human psyche.

The writers' treatment of the first two broad themes has documentary value and so is of increasing interest to our own fast-changing society, a society which is prompted to look back in search of its roots the better to understand its needs and motivations. But needs and motivations point to psychological considerations. Canadian prairie novelists of Depression times were sagacious in for the most part not focusing on a fictionalized description of politics, social custom or agricultural practices *per se*. Rather, they examined what is universal in any time: the striving for *emotional* security in an adverse environment. That this world was scoured by gritty winds and bleached by searing sun reduced the total environment, and not just the landscape, to "skeleton requirements": the striving was reduced to elemental terms. In choosing to delineate the struggle, the writers could speak to something basic in all of us. Thus the Depression in its way promoted the growth of the psychological novel in Canadian prairie fiction. On the whole the story elements of plot and setting came to be treated realistically, rather than romantically as in earlier novels; but their major significance was that they served to facilitate real psychological inquiry.

NOTES

This article first appeared in *Prairie Forum* 2, no. 1 (1977): 83–96.

1   See G. E. Britnell, "Economic Conditions in Rural Saskatchewan," *Canadian Forum*, XIV (March, 1934), 209–211.

2   H. Blair Neatby, "The Liberal Way: Fiscal and Monetary Policy in the 1930s," in Victor Hoar, comp., *The Great Depression: Essays and Memoirs from Canada and the United States* (Toronto, 1969), 88.

3   Most Canadian prairie novels written before the Depression are not concerned with economics either. But in them the protagonist is trying to establish a new home in the "wilderness," and the urgency of winning a hand-to-hand combat with nature prevents him from stepping back and thinking of his situation in economic terms. By the 1930s, however, one might have expected him to think in this manner.

4   Turner's first essay on the topic was written in 1893 and entitled "The Significance of the Frontier in American History." It was a seminal work, not only leading to other essays by Turner (collected as *The Frontier in American History* [New York, 1920]) but also to controversy and to replies from other scholars. The gist of Turner's thesis was that a uniquely American civilization arose from the experiences found in its ever-advancing frontier. Individualism and practicality, along with the larger concepts of nationalism and democracy, were some of the characteristics so instilled. With the arrival of the Depression, Turner's theories were discredited, for individualism could not combat hard times. In the past few decades, however, the frontier hypothesis has regained much of its former popularity as *one* interpretation of American history, according to Ray Allen Billington in a foreword to an edition of Turner's book (New York, 1962). There will be further references to Turner in this paper.

5   Barry Broadfoot, *Ten Lost Years 1929–1939* (Don Mills, Ont., 1975), iv.

6   The editions referred to in this essay are the following: *As for Me and My House*, New Canadian Library (Toronto, 1957); *Music at the Close*, New Canadian Library (Toronto, 1966); *Who Has Seen the Wind*, Macmillan paperback (Toronto, 1967); *Westerly Wild* (Toronto, 1956); *A Candle to Light the Sun* (Toronto, 1960); *The Stone Angel*, New Canadian Library (Toronto, 1968); *The Words of My Roaring* (Toronto, 1966). Hereafter, parenthetical page references in the text are to these editions.

7   James Gray, who covered such events in the Thirties as a reporter, says in *The Winter Years* (Toronto, 1966), 28 et passim, that there was Red agitation.

8   Malcolm Cowley "A Farewell to the 1930s," in Henry Dan Piper (ed.), *Think Back on Us…A Contemporary Chronicle of the 1930s* (Carbondale, Ill., 1967), 349.

9   "Ode to a Nightingale," l. 62.

10   Lois Phillips Hudson has written a lengthy novel of the Great Depression entitled *The Bones of Plenty* (Boston, 1962). It is set in North Dakota, and many of the problems faced by the farm family in her book are similar to those just across the border in Canada.

11   In *Westerly Wild*, Lysenko refers to an "absent-minded sociologist" who sees the Depression as "simply an interesting scene for research" and then flees to some "well-watered city haven with his stack of notes" (46).

12   Mary Hiemstra's *Gully Farm* (Toronto, 1955) is an example. It is true that the author's father sees the prairies as a land of the future, "a fair country," with the children being able to have things easier than the parents. But the mother keeps saying, even on the last page of the book: "if I'd known how it would be when I left England wild horses wouldn't have dragged me here" (311).

13   Cited in Henry Nash Smith, *Virgin Land: The American West as Symbol and Myth* (New York, 1957), 302–303.

14   There is a similarity both to Rochester in Charlotte Brontë's *Jane Eyre* and to Heathcliff in Emily Brontë's *Wuthering Heights*.

15   For a treatment of this theme as it relates to Ross's short stories, see my article, "The Short Stories of Sinclair Ross," *Canadian Short Story Magazine* 2 (Fall 1976): 71–73.

16   Examples might be Ralph Connor's *The Foreigner* (Toronto, 1909) or Laura Goodman Salverson's *The Viking Heart* (Toronto, 1923). The novels of Frederick Philip Grove, beginning with *Settlers of the Marsh* (Toronto, 1925) form a notable exception.

17 McCourt, however, is not without his humour too when he portrays candidates at a nomination meeting: "each…concluded with the assurance that if he were chosen to be a party standard-bearer he would represent his constituency to the fullest extent of his ability—if not, he would get behind the successful nominee and work for him to the fullest extent of his ability" (179).

Index

Also in the

HISTORY OF THE PRAIRIE WEST SERIES

The Early Northwest
ISBN: 978–0–88977–207–6

Immigration and Settlement
ISBN: 978–0–88977–230–4

Agricultural History
ISBN: 978–088977–237–3

Business and Industry
ISBN: 978–088977–238–0

Women's History
ISBN: 978–088977–312–7